Ultimate Snowflake Cortex AI for Generative AI Applications

Design, Build, and Deploy Generative AI Solutions with Snowflake Cortex for Real-World and Industry-Scale Applications

Krishnan Srinivasan

www.orangeava.com

First Published: June 2025

Published By: Orange Education Pvt Ltd, AVA®

Address: 9, Daryaganj, Delhi, 110002, India

275 New North Road Islington Suite 1314 London,
N1 7AA, United Kingdom

ISBN (PBK): 978-93-49888-51-7
ISBN (E-BOOK): 978-93-49888-70-8

Scan the QR code to explore our entire catalogue

www.orangeava.com

Dedicated To

My Parents, My Wife, and My Daughter – My Original Neural Network of Love, Logic, and Laughter

About the Author

Krishnan Srinivasan holds a Master of Technology degree in Data Science and Engineering and brings over 25 years of diverse, cross-domain experience across cutting-edge technologies, specializing in Data, Artificial Intelligence, Analytics, and Cloud AI. He began his career as a data professional, working on pioneering data warehousing and analytics initiatives that laid a strong foundation for building scalable, data-driven solutions. His deep engagement with enterprise data systems and strong passion for innovation led him into the field of Artificial Intelligence. This progression, from data to AI, enabled him to bridge the gap between traditional analytics and modern AI, positioning him to lead transformative AI initiatives at the intersection of data and intelligence. Throughout his distinguished career, Krishnan has partnered with numerous Fortune 500 clients across the globe, designing and delivering impactful solutions across a wide range of industries.

Currently leading his organization's AI strategy, Krishnan is deeply focused on the next frontier of innovation—Generative AI. His work emphasizes the power of cloud-native AI platforms such as Snowflake Cortex, to unlock new possibilities in automation, insight generation, Agentic AI, and intelligent decision-making. He is passionate about demystifying AI for businesses and helping them operationalize it to drive scalable impact in the real world.

Krishnan's innovative spirit is also reflected in his contribution to intellectual property. He is the co-inventor of the U.S. patent "*System and a Method for Automated Resolution of Configuration Item Issues*" (US10698749), underscoring his commitment to solving complex technical challenges through automation.

Beyond his technical achievements, Krishnan is a mentor and thought leader, having guided numerous professionals in their AI and analytics journeys. He strongly believes in the ethical and transformative potential of AI and is dedicated to building solutions that are not just intelligent, but responsible and impactful. His vision is to bridge the gap between advanced AI technologies—especially Generative AI—and practical business applications, inspiring organizations to reimagine what is possible in the era of AI-first, cloud-native computing.

About the Technical Reviewer

Ananth Thyagarajan has 30 years of experience in designing and architecting data management applications across the Healthcare, Energy, Retail and High-tech Industries. He is highly proficient in Cloud Modernization, ERP Cloud, ERP Consolidation, metadata-driven Data Architecture, and the application of AI/ML in enterprise solutions.

Ananth is a Certified Snowflake Pro Core Professional. He has extensive experience in technology consulting and takes pride in building data solutions. His prior experience includes roles at leading organizations such as Oracle and Equinix.

Ananth co-founded Cittabase Solutions in 2011 and has since been helping enterprises achieve data-driven business outcomes. He has built a culture that fosters high-performing delivery team and a strong focus on customer success.

Acknowledgements

No journey worth taking is ever made alone, and I am profoundly grateful to all those who have been part of mine.

My sincere thanks to Ananth Thiagarajan for the thoughtful book review and insightful feedback. His reflections brought clarity and depth to this work.

To my late father, whose kind wisdom, values, and serene presence continue to guide me. Every step I take carries a part of him with it.

To my mother, whose endless love, strength, and unwavering belief in me have been my greatest shelter and my greatest motivation.

To my wife, whose encouragement, infectious optimism and steadfast support have been the bedrock on which I have built both my dreams and this journey.

To my daughter, whose joy, curiosity, and presence remind me what truly matters and why this journey is worth it.

I thank my friends and colleagues for their faith in my work, their thoughtful conversations, and the encouragement offered at every turn. They made this endeavor richer, more vibrant, and memorable.

I express my gratitude to the team at Orange Education Pvt Ltd for their trust, exceptional professionalism, and consistent commitment to this journey. Their belief in this work gave it wings.

Preface

This book is a comprehensive and practical guide tailored for data scientists, engineers, analysts, data professionals and business leaders seeking to harness the full potential of Generative AI on Snowflake Cortex—Snowflake's powerful native AI engine. This book delves deep into the capabilities of Cortex, equipping readers with the knowledge and tools needed to design, build, and deploy cutting-edge Generative AI and Machine Learning applications.

From foundational concepts to advanced use cases, it provides a structured and hands-on approach to leveraging Snowflake's unified data cloud platform for modern AI development. Whether you are aiming to enhance productivity through intelligent automation, derive insights from unstructured data, build domain-specific LLMs, implement intelligent document processing, fine-tune models for specific use cases, or orchestrate AI workflows using Snowflake agents, this book serves as your essential companion. It also helps deepen your understanding of real-world industry applications, guiding you on the journey toward AI-driven innovation within the Snowflake ecosystem. This book is organized into 11 comprehensive chapters, listed as follows:

Chapter 1. Introduction to AI/ML in the Snowflake Ecosystem: This foundational chapter introduces readers to the world of Artificial Intelligence and Machine Learning, explaining core concepts such as Deep Learning, Natural Language Processing, and Computer Vision. It also presents the evolution of Generative AI and its growing impact across industries. The chapter concludes by exploring Snowflake's architecture and how it supports scalable AI and ML initiatives through its native tools with a brief overview of Snowpark ML.

Chapter 2. Understanding Snowflake Cortex: This chapter provides a deep dive into Snowflake Cortex, outlining its key features and internal components that make AI/ML development more accessible within the Snowflake ecosystem. It compares Cortex with traditional ML pipelines and emphasizes its advantages in terms of speed, scalability, and simplicity. Readers will gain clarity on how Cortex seamlessly integrates into enterprise data workflows.

Chapter 3. Overview of Machine Learning Functions: This chapter focuses on the core ML functions natively available in Snowflake, including classification, forecasting, anomaly detection, and extracting top insights. It demonstrates how these functions can be used to address real-world business problems and showcases the convenience of operating ML within a single, governed platform using Cortex and the AI & ML Studio.

Chapter 4. Introduction to LLMs, Prompt Engineering, and RAG: This chapter sets the stage for working with Large Language Models (LLMs) by covering their fundamentals, along with techniques such as prompt engineering and Retrieval Augmented Generation (RAG). It explores how embedding-based search and vector databases play a vital role in augmenting LLMs, paving the way for more context-aware and efficient information retrieval.

Chapter 5. LLM Functions in Cortex AI: Dedicated to Snowflake Cortex's LLM capabilities, this chapter highlights how users can seamlessly invoke pre-trained LLMs for summarization, sentiment analysis, translation, and more. It covers usage models, regional availability, and cost considerations, and helps readers understand how LLMs are democratized through Cortex for enterprise-grade use cases.

Chapter 6. Fine-Tuning Large Language Models in Cortex: In this chapter, readers learn why and how to finetune LLMs using Snowflake Cortex. It explores various finetuning strategies, from instruction tuning to domain-specific adjustments, and provides an architectural overview of the finetuning process. The chapter also discusses the benefits of personalized AI models and how organizations can achieve them securely within Cortex.

Chapter 7. Natural Language Queries to Actionable Insights: This chapter explores Snowflake's capabilities for turning plain-language questions into data-driven insights. It introduces tools such as Cortex Analyst, Cortex Search, and SQL Copilot, which allow users to interact with structured and unstructured data using natural language. It also discusses the concept of AI agents that orchestrate these interactions behind the scenes. We will also look at the Cortex LLM Playground, an interactive environment within Snowflake for quickly testing large language models using natural language, making it easy to test ideas and validate AI-driven insights without extensive coding.

Chapter 8. Unlocking Document Intelligence with Document AI: Here, the book dives into Document AI and the potential it brings for transforming unstructured documents into structured, actionable data. The chapter covers implementation guidance, best practices, and real-world use cases that span industries such as finance, legal, and healthcare.

Chapter 9. Implementing Cortex with Security, Governance, and Cost Discipline: This chapter ensures that readers understand the importance of secure and responsible AI practices. It covers security and governance best practices, strategies for cost optimization, and tools for AI observability in Cortex. It is a must-read for those planning to deploy AI at enterprise scale.

Chapter 10. Industry Use Cases and Case Studies: Bringing everything together, this chapter presents a wide array of industry-specific use cases implemented with Cortex. These examples–ranging from customer sentiment analysis, predictive maintenance, social media analytics, and student performance analysis illustrate the versatility of Cortex. The fictional company Zentime is used throughout the book as a unifying thread to illustrate and contextualize AI applications. We will conclude by summarizing the key generative AI features within Cortex that enable these diverse and impactful solutions.

Chapter 11. Conclusion and Next Steps: The final chapter reflects the journey through Cortex AI, summarizing the key takeaways from each chapter. It also highlights future trends and provides practical next steps for readers to begin or accelerate their AI transformation journey using Snowflake Cortex.

Get a Free eBook

We hope you are enjoying your recently purchased book! Your feedback is incredibly valuable to us, and to all other readers looking for great books.

If you found this book helpful or enjoyable, we would truly appreciate it, if you could take a moment to leave a short review with a 5 star rating on Amazon. It helps us grow, and lets other readers discover our books.

As a thank you, we would love to send you a free digital copy of this book, and a **30%** discount code on your next cart value on our official websites:

www.orangeava.com

www.orangeava.in (For Indian Subcontinent)

☑ **Here's how:**

Leave a review for the book on Amazon.

Take a screenshot of your review, and send an email to **info@orangeava.com** (it can be just the confirmation screen).

Once, we receive your screenshot, we will send you the digital file, within 24 hours.

Thank you so much for your support – it means a lot to us!

Downloading the code bundles and colored images

Please follow the links or scan the QR codes to download the
Code Bundles and Images of the book:

https://github.com/ava-orange-education/Ultimate-Snowflake-Cortex-AI-for-Generative-AI-Applications

The code bundles and images of the book are also hosted on
https://rebrand.ly/84e9b5

In case there's an update to the code, it will be updated on the existing GitHub repository.

Errata

We take immense pride in our work at **Orange Education Pvt Ltd,** and follow best practices to ensure the accuracy of our content to provide an indulging reading experience to our subscribers. Our readers are our mirrors, and we use their inputs to reflect and improve upon human errors, if any, that may have occurred during the publishing processes involved. To let us maintain the quality and help us reach out to any readers who might be having difficulties due to any unforeseen errors, please write to us at :

errata@orangeava.com

Your support, suggestions, and feedback are highly appreciated.

DID YOU KNOW

Did you know that Orange Education Pvt Ltd offers eBook versions of every book published, with PDF and ePub files available? You can upgrade to the eBook version at **www.orangeava.com** and as a print book customer, you are entitled to a discount on the eBook copy. Get in touch with us at: **info@orangeava.com** for more details.

At **www.orangeava.com**, you can also read a collection of free technical articles, sign up for a range of free newsletters, and receive exclusive discounts and offers on Print Books and eBooks.

PIRACY

If you come across any illegal copies of our works in any form on the internet, we would be grateful if you would provide us with the location address or website name. Please contact us at **info@orangeava.com** with a link to the material.

ARE YOU INTERESTED IN AUTHORING WITH US?

If there is a topic that you have expertise in, and you are interested in either writing or contributing to a book, please write to us at **business@orangeava.com**. We are on a journey to help developers and tech professionals to gain insights on the present technological advancements and innovations happening across the globe and build a community that believes Knowledge is best acquired by sharing and learning with others. Please reach out to us to learn what our audience demands and how you can be part of this educational reform. We also welcome ideas from tech experts and help them build learning and development content for their domains.

REVIEWS

Please leave a review. Once you have read and used this book, why not leave a review on the site that you purchased it from? Potential readers can then see and use your unbiased opinion to make purchase decisions. We at Orange Education would love to know what you think about our products, and our authors can learn from your feedback. Thank you!

For more information about Orange Education, please visit **www.orangeava.com**.

Table of Contents

CHAPTER 1
Introduction to AI/ML in the Snowflake Ecosystem

Introduction

This chapter provides an introduction to Artificial Intelligence (AI) and Machine Learning (ML) within the Snowflake ecosystem. It explores the key AI concepts, the impact of AI and Generative AI, and how the Generative AI works. Additionally, it discusses Snowflake's role as a cloud data platform, and the benefits of using Snowflake for data science and machine learning.

By the end of this chapter, readers will understand the fundamentals of AI, ML, and Generative AI, and how these technologies are transforming various industries. They will also learn about Snowflake's architecture and its advantages for data science and machine learning workflows. Furthermore, readers will gain insights into Snowpark ML, a Python library designed to simplify the creation, training, and deployment of ML models within the Snowflake Data Cloud.

Structure

In this chapter, we will cover the following topics:

- The AI Revolution
- The Rise of Generative AI
- Overview of Snowflake as a Cloud Data Platform
- Getting Started with Snowflake
- Snowflake Cortex Overview
- A Brief Overview of Snowpark ML
- Snowpark ML in Action

The AI Revolution

We live in a world increasingly shaped by Artificial Intelligence (AI). From streaming recommendations to navigation systems, AI is woven into the fabric of our daily lives. But what exactly is AI, and why is it considered revolutionary?

At its core, AI involves creating machines capable of tasks that typically require human intelligence. This includes learning, problem-solving, decision-making, and understanding and generating language. Hence, it is less about robots taking over the world (for now), and more about building systems that can analyze massive datasets, identify patterns, and make predictions, far exceeding human capabilities!

This "*revolution*" stems from AI's transformative potential. Just as the industrial and digital revolutions reshaped manufacturing and communication, respectively, AI is poised to revolutionize industries from healthcare and finance to transportation and entertainment. It is not just about automating existing processes; AI unlocks entirely new possibilities, opening doors to innovations we could only dream of a few years ago.

While the concept of AI has existed for decades, recent advancements in computing power and data availability have fuelled its rapid progress. Key milestones include the development of machine learning algorithms, the explosion of data generated by the internet and connected devices, the rise of deep learning, and the explosion of Generative AI.

The Impact of AI across Industries

The potential impact of AI is vast across industries. Just to name a few:

- **Healthcare:** AI can assist in diagnosis, drug discovery, and personalized medicine.
- **Finance:** AI powers fraud detection, algorithmic trading, and risk management.
- **Transportation:** Develop self-driving cars that promise to revolutionize travel.
- **Manufacturing:** AI-powered robots and automation systems increase efficiency and productivity.
- **Customer Service:** Chatbots and virtual assistants provide 24/7 support.
- **Education:** AI-enabled personalized learning, grading automation, and enhanced tutoring systems.
- **Retail:** Improves customer experience through personalized recommendations, inventory management, and demand forecasting.
- **Agriculture:** Supports precision farming, crop health monitoring, and yield prediction.

- **Energy:** Enhances energy efficiency, supports predictive maintenance, and enables smart grid management.
- **Cybersecurity:** AI helps detect threats in real-time, strengthening defenses, and automates incident responses.

The Rise of Generative AI

Amid the broader wave of AI innovation, Generative AI has emerged as one of the most transformative and disruptive advancements. Unlike traditional AI which primarily focuses on analyzing the data, making predictions, or identifying patterns, Generative AI goes a step further, that is, it creates. This groundbreaking technology can produce entirely new content across multiple formats, including text, images, audio, video, software code, and even 3D models.

At the heart of Generative AI are powerful machine learning models—such as Large Language Models (LLMs) and diffusion models—trained on vast and diverse datasets. These models learn the underlying patterns, grammar, and structure of the data, they are exposed to. Once trained, they can generate original content that closely mirrors the quality and characteristics of the training material, often to a level indistinguishable from human-created work.

Think of it as an artist, who has studied thousands of paintings. After absorbing countless techniques, styles, and colors, the artist can now create their own masterpiece. The new artwork may echo familiar themes, but it also carries a unique, creative expression shaped by the artist's own interpretation. Similarly, Generative AI blends learned knowledge with computational creativity to produce fresh, compelling, and often, highly personalized outputs.

This ability to generate a novel content at scale is opening up new possibilities across industries – from marketing and entertainment to software development, design, education, healthcare, and beyond. Hence, it is not just a leap in technology – it is reimagining how we create, communicate, and solve problems in the age of AI.

Understanding the Working Principles of the Generative AI

Many Generative AI models are based on deep learning, particularly architectures such as Generative Adversarial Networks (GANs) and transformers. GANs involve two neural networks: a generator that creates new content, and a discriminator that distinguishes between real and generated content. Transformers are particularly adept at handling sequential data such as text and audio, revolutionizing natural language processing.

The Key Building Blocks of Generative AI are as follows:

- **Neural Networks:** These are the fundamental building blocks of many AI systems, including Generative AI. They are composed of interconnected layers of nodes (or neurons) that process information.
- **Generative Models:** These are designed to generate new data, resembling the training data.
    - **Generative Adversarial Networks (GANs):** These use two neural networks (generator and discriminator) in a competitive process.
    - **Transformers:** These are effective at handling sequential data such as text and audio, using a mechanism called "*attention*". Transformers have become a cornerstone of Generative AI, especially for tasks involving text and other sequential data. Their power comes from the *attention mechanism* which allows the model to weigh the importance of different parts of the input when generating the output.

The Impact and Potential of Generative AI

Generative AI is poised to revolutionize numerous industries in a big way. What makes Generative AI particularly revolutionary is not just its technical sophistication, but its versatility. It can adapt to various domains, learn from specific contexts, and operate across languages, modalities, and industries. We are witnessing a moment similar in magnitude to the arrival of the internet or the mobile revolution—one that will redefine how businesses operate, how professionals make decisions, and how people engage with technology, daily.

Its implications are vast and far-reaching. In healthcare, for instance, Generative AI is already being used to design new drugs faster than ever before, model disease progression, and personalize treatment strategies based on patient data. In manufacturing, it is driving innovation by generating optimal product designs, predicting equipment failures through synthetic data, and creating advanced simulations for operator training. In the financial sector, it is enhancing fraud detection systems, powering high-frequency trading strategies, and delivering hyper-personalized financial guidance to consumers.

The entertainment industry is another major frontier where Generative AI is creating photo-realistic characters, writing dynamic scripts, producing immersive game environments, and even composing music! In retail, it is transforming customer experience through AI-generated product recommendations, virtual try-ons, and intelligent inventory optimization. Education is being reshaped through personalized learning experiences, AI tutoring, and adaptive content generation, while scientific research is being accelerated by hypothesis generation, simulation of complex systems, and autonomous data analysis.

However, this is just the beginning! As Generative AI matures, and becomes more accessible, its ability to extend human intelligence, foster innovation, and automate creativity will continue to grow–ushering in a future where collaboration between humans and intelligent systems becomes not just possible, but essential.

Thus, to fully unlock this potential, enterprises need infrastructure that is secure, scalable, and deeply integrated with their data ecosystem. That's where Snowflake Cortex comes in. As a native AI and ML platform within the Snowflake Data Cloud, Cortex allows organizations to leverage powerful Generative AI models, without moving their data or compromising security. From summarizing documents and generating insights to building intelligent chat interfaces and predictive applications, Snowflake Cortex empowers teams to operationalize Generative AI directly where the data lives–ensuring governance, performance, and the ease of use at every step. Hence, whether you are experimenting with large language models or deploying production-grade AI solutions, Cortex makes it easier than ever to turn ideas into impact.

Overview of Snowflake as a Cloud Data Platform

Organizations today are inundated by an ever-growing deluge of data in the modern, data-centric world. Traditional data warehouses struggle to keep pace with the volume, velocity, and variety of modern data. This is where cloud data platforms like Snowflake come into play. Snowflake isn't just another database; it is a fully managed, cloud-native data platform designed to handle the challenges of the modern data analytics. This also offers a unique architecture that separates compute and storage, providing unprecedented scalability, flexibility, and cost-effectiveness.

Think of it like this–traditional data warehouses are like all-in-one kitchens where the oven, stove, and refrigerator are all fixed in one place. Snowflake, on the other hand, is like having a modular kitchen. You can scale up your oven (compute) when you need to bake a lot of cakes (run complex queries), and scale it down when you're just making a quick sandwich (simple data exploration). Similarly, you can expand your refrigerator (storage) as your data grows without affecting the performance of your oven.

This separation of compute and storage is a game-changer. It allows Snowflake to scale each independently, so that you only pay for the resources, you actually use. Need to run a complex query on a massive dataset? Scale up your compute power temporarily, and then scale it back down when you're done. Got a sudden influx of data? Expand your storage, without worrying about impacting query performance. This elasticity is crucial for businesses that experience fluctuating workloads and data volumes.

Beyond scalability, Snowflake offers several other key advantages. It is a fully managed service, meaning Snowflake handles all the infrastructure management, including patching, updates, and security. This frees up your IT team to focus on more strategic initiatives. Snowflake also supports a wide range of data types, from structured data in tables to semi-structured data including JSON and XML, and even the unstructured data. This flexibility makes it easy to analyze all your data, regardless of its format.

Another important aspect of Snowflake is its support for data sharing. You can easily and securely share data with other Snowflake accounts, both within your organization and with external partners. This enables new possibilities for collaboration, and data monetization. Imagine sharing real-time data with your suppliers to optimize your supply chain, or providing your customers with access to personalized analytics.

Snowflake's architecture also promotes concurrency. Multiple users and applications can access the data platform simultaneously, without impacting the performance. This means your data analysts, data scientists, and business users can all work with the same data at the same time, without stepping on each other's toes.

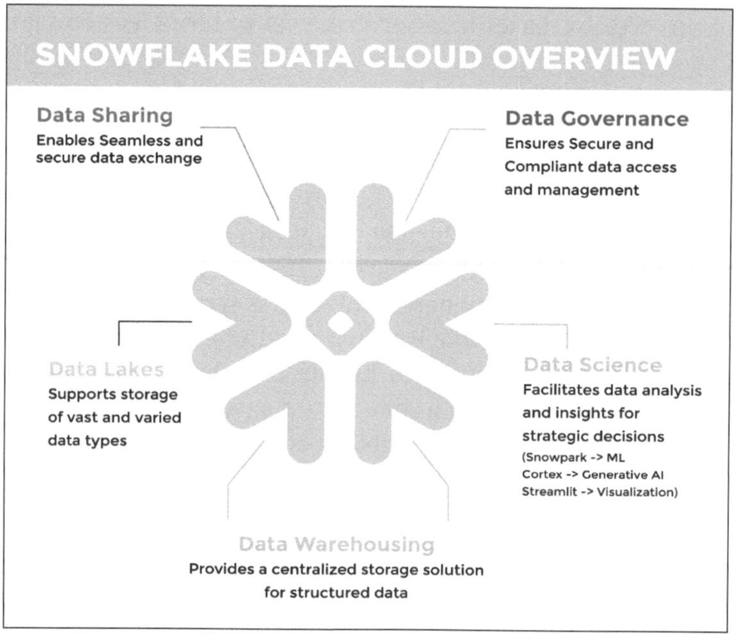

Figure 1.1: *Snowflake as a Cloud Data Platform*

In essence, Snowflake provides a modern, cloud-based solution for all your data needs. It offers the scalability, flexibility, and the ease of use that traditional data warehouses simply cannot match. By decoupling compute and storage, supporting diverse data types, and enabling data sharing, Snowflake empowers organizations to unlock the full potential of their data, and drive better business decisions. It is a platform built for the future of data analytics, and is a key enabler for leveraging the power of AI, especially Generative AI, as we will explore further.

Robust data governance is paramount in today's regulatory landscape. Snowflake provides a comprehensive set of features to ensure data quality, security, and compliance. Features such as role-based access control, data masking, and row-level security allow you to control who can access what data, and how it can be used. Data lineage tracking helps you understand the origin and transformation of your data which is essential for auditing and compliance. Snowflake also integrates with various data governance tools, allowing you to seamlessly incorporate it into your existing data governance framework.

Data Science in Snowflake

Snowflake is a robust and powerful platform for data science and machine learning, offering end-to-end capabilities for building intelligent applications at scale. Its ability to handle massive datasets, combined with native support for multiple programming languages and tools, makes it an ideal environment for modern data science workflows. With Snowpark for ML, data scientists can build, train, and deploy complex machine learning models directly within Snowflake—without moving data outside the platform. This ensures secure, high-performance model development using familiar Python libraries such as Pandas and Scikit-learn, while leveraging Snowflake's scalable compute. For Generative AI, Snowflake Cortex offers native large language model (LLM) capabilities, allowing teams to create context-aware assistants, summarization tools, intelligent document processing, and Q&A systems directly on top of their governed enterprise data. Combined with Cortex Search and Cortex Analyst, organizations can build powerful Generative AI driven conversational experiences over both unstructured and structured data. To bring insights to life, Streamlit enables intuitive, interactive visualizations and AI-driven apps—directly connected to Snowflake—helping teams explore results and drive decisions in real time. This tight integration between storage, processing, machine learning, generative AI, and visualization dramatically accelerates the development and deployment of AI-powered applications on a single, unified platform.

In essence, Snowflake provides a modern, cloud-based solution for all your data needs. It offers the scalability, flexibility, and ease of use that traditional data warehouses simply can't match. By decoupling compute and storage, supporting diverse data types, enabling data sharing, and providing strong data governance and data science capabilities, Snowflake empowers organizations to unlock the full potential of their data and drive better business decisions. It is a platform built for the future of data analytics, and is a key enabler for leveraging the power of AI, especially Generative AI, as we will explore in subsequent chapters.

The AI revolution is still in its early stages. Understanding the fundamentals of AI is becoming increasingly important for everyone. Therefore, this book explores how you can harness the power of AI and Generative AI, specifically within the Snowflake Data Cloud. Snowflake provides a robust and scalable platform for building and deploying AI solutions. Its ability to handle massive datasets and its support for various AI/ML tools are crucial for training and deploying Generative AI models.

In the subsequent chapters, we will be diving into how you can leverage Snowflake to unlock the full potential of your data, and drive innovations in your organization.

Getting Started with Snowflake

To get started with Snowflake, users can sign up for a free trial account which provides access to the platform's full range of features, including data storage, processing, and ML capabilities. Follow these steps to create an account:

1. **Go to the Snowflake Website**: Navigate to www.snowflake.com, and click on the Start for Free button.
2. **Choose a Cloud Provider**: Snowflake operates on AWS, Azure, and Google Cloud. Select the preferred cloud provider. Choose AWS, as new features explored here are mostly available.
3. **Choose AWS West** : The region for the trial account as most of the LLM features explored here are available in this region.
4. **Fill out the Registration Form**: Provide the basic details, such as name, email, and company information.
5. **Verify Your Email**: After submitting the form, check your inbox for a verification email from Snowflake, and follow the instructions to activate your account.
6. **Set Up Your Snowflake Environment**: Upon logging in, Snowflake provides a guided tour to set up databases, warehouses, and initial configurations.

Understanding the Snowflake Interface

Once logged in, users will have access to the Snowflake web interface (Snowsight) which consists of several components, the key ones being:

- **Databases:** Where the structured data is stored and managed.
- **Warehouses:** Virtual compute resources used for querying, and processing the data.
- **Worksheets:** An SQL editor where users can write and execute queries.
- **Notebooks:** Interactive; provides an environment for exploratory data analysis, development, and AI workflows–much like Jupyter Notebooks, but built natively into Snowflake.
- **Streamlit:** Allows you to build and deploy interactive data apps directly within Snowflake using Python and Snowpark, without moving the data out of the platform.
- **Dashboards:** Allows you visually present the query results, using charts and

tables, combining multiple visualizations in a single interactive, shareable interface—directly powered by live Snowflake data.

- **Apps:** It refers to Snowflake Native Apps—secure, data-resident applications built and deployed within the Snowflake platform, allowing providers to deliver functionality (like analytics or ML) to consumers, without moving the data.
- **Admin Console:** Provides access to security settings, role management, and system usage metrics.
- **Monitoring:** Provides real-time insights into query performance, warehouse usage, user activity, and resource consumption—helping you to optimize costs, troubleshoot issues, and ensure platform health.
- **AI/ ML Studio:** No-code/low-code interface in Snowsight that allows the users to build, train, and deploy machine learning models—like classification, forecasting, and anomaly detection—and also finetune LLMs, build cortex search and analyst services, all within the Snowflake platform.

Loading Data into Snowflake

Data can be loaded into Snowflake using the following methods:

- **Using Snowsight, the Snowflake Web UI**: Browse or Drag, and drop CSV or JSON files into a table using the Load options.
- **Leverage SnowSQL**: A command-line interface that allows the bulk data loading from the local storage.
- **Connect with the External Cloud Storage**: Load the data from AWS S3, Azure Blob Storage, or Google Cloud Storage, using Stage and Copy commands.

Snowflake Cortex Overview

Now that you have your Snowflake account set up, let us jump into exploring Snowflake Cortex, and see how it can simplify and accelerate your AI/ML initiatives. This topic would serve as a brief overview, and we will be diving into Cortex capabilities in detail in the subsequent chapters. Snowflake Cortex, a fully managed service within the Snowflake Data Cloud, empowers users to perform machine learning and AI, directly on their data, with the integrated support for Large Language Models (LLMs) and Generative AI. It streamlines the entire ML lifecycle, from data preparation and feature engineering to model training, deployment, and monitoring, including the often-intricate processes involved with LLMs and Generative AI. By enabling model building and execution within Snowflake, Cortex eliminates the need to move data to external systems, significantly boosting efficiency, and breaking down data silos. This tight integration with your data within Snowflake is especially advantageous for working with the massive datasets crucial for training and fine-tuning LLMs and Generative AI models.

Cortex offers a comprehensive set of tools and functionalities designed specifically for LLMs and Generative AI. This includes access to pre-trained LLMs readily fine-tuned on your specific data residing within Snowflake, simplifying the adaptation of these powerful models for tasks such as text generation, summarization, document intelligence capabilities, search agents, and question answering. For Generative AI, Cortex provides the necessary infrastructure and tools to train and deploy models for a range of creative applications, such as image generation, text synthesis, and code generation, all while capitalizing on the scalability and security inherent to the Snowflake Data Cloud. Cortex aims to democratize AI, making it accessible to a broader audience, including data scientists, data engineers, and business analysts, by simplifying complex ML processes, especially those related to LLMs and Generative AI, and seamlessly integrating them with the data they require. It is a critical tool for organizations seeking to harness the power of AI, including cutting-edge LLMs and Generative AI, to derive valuable insights from their data, make data-driven decisions, and unlock new avenues for innovation.

The primary purpose of Snowflake Cortex AI is to simplify and accelerate the process of building, deploying, and managing AI/ML models directly within the Snowflake Data Cloud. It aims to democratize AI by making it more accessible to a wider range of users, including data scientists, data engineers, and even business analysts, by abstracting away much of the complexity, typically associated with machine learning workflows. Specifically, Cortex AI serves several key purposes, such as:

- **Eliminating Data Movement:** A core purpose is to eliminate the need to move the data out of Snowflake to external systems for AI/ML tasks. This avoids data silos, reduces latency, and improves security. Since the data stays within Snowflake, Cortex can leverage the platform's scalability and governance features.
- **Simplifying Model Development:** Cortex provides tools and functionalities that simplify model development, including pre-built models, support for custom models (including those built with popular ML frameworks), and features for automated model training and deployment. This lowers the barrier of entry for users who may not be AI/ML experts.
- **Accelerating Model Deployment:** Cortex streamlines the process of deploying trained models, making it faster and easier to put AI into action. This is especially important for organizations that need to quickly iterate and deploy new models.
- **Improving Model Management:** Cortex provides tools for monitoring the performance of the deployed models, and managing their lifecycle. This ensures that models remain accurate and effective over time.
- **Democratizing AI:** By simplifying and streamlining the AI/ML process, Cortex makes AI more accessible to a broader range of users within an organization.

This empowers more people to leverage the power of AI to gain insights from the data, and make better decisions.

- **Enabling LLM and Generative AI:** A key purpose of Cortex is to provide access to and simplify the use of cutting-edge LLMs and Generative AI models. This allows users to leverage these powerful technologies for tasks such as text generation, summarization, image processing, and more, directly within their Snowflake environment. With LLM driven conversational AI and document processing capabilities, Cortex makes interactions with data simpler, more intuitive, and powerful.

In short, Snowflake Cortex is designed to make AI more accessible, efficient, and integrated with the data, allowing organizations to unlock the full potential of their data and drive data-driven innovations.

A Brief Overview of Snowpark ML: Empowering Data-Driven ML in Snowflake

Though the book primarily covers Snowflake Cortex AI capabilities, this topic provides a short overview of Snowpark ML and its continuing relevance within the Snowflake ecosystem. While Cortex offers powerful, pre-built AI/ML, and extensive generative AI capabilities, Snowpark ML serves as a foundational layer, providing flexibility, customization, and deeper integration for specific use cases even in the Cortex world. In this chapter, we will briefly touch upon the basics of Snowpark and Snowpark ML.

Snowpark: Bringing Computation Closer to Your Data

Snowpark is a fundamental shift in how you interact with the data in Snowflake. It enables you to execute the code in familiar programming languages including Python, Java, and Scala directly within the Snowflake environment. Imagine performing complex data transformations, aggregations, and custom logic, without ever extracting or moving your data. That's the core strength of Snowpark. It brings *computation* to the data, unlocking new levels of performance, security, and governance.

Exploring Snowpark's Capabilities

- **Uncompromising Data Security:** Snowpark code executes within Snowflake's secure boundaries. Your data remains protected, adhering to strict security protocols, minimizing the risk of unauthorized access or breaches. This is a crucial advantage, especially for sensitive information.

- **A Wide Range of Languages:** Choose the language that best suits your needs. Whether you're a Python enthusiast, a Java developer, or prefer the elegance of Scala, Snowpark offers language-specific APIs that integrate seamlessly with the Snowflake ecosystem.
- **Extending the Possibilities:** Snowpark provides access to a rich ecosystem of libraries and packages. In Python, this means using the power of Pandas for data manipulation, NumPy for numerical computing, and specialized libraries for specific tasks. This extensibility allows you to address complex challenges that might be difficult or impossible with SQL alone.
- **Building Robust Data Pipelines:** Construct sophisticated data pipelines and transformations directly within Snowflake using Snowpark. This simplifies your architecture, reduces the complexity of traditional ETL processes, and enables you to build more maintainable and adaptable data workflows.
- **Leveraging Snowflake's Scalability:** Snowpark integrates seamlessly with Snowflake's elastic compute engine. Your code automatically scales to handle large datasets and computationally intensive tasks, ensuring optimal performance without the need for infrastructure management.
- **A Unified Ecosystem:** Snowpark integrates smoothly with existing Snowflake components such as tables, views, and stored procedures. This allows you to work with your data, using familiar programming paradigms within the established Snowflake framework.

How Snowpark Works

1. **Establishing a Connection:** You initiate a connection to your Snowflake account via a Snowpark session from your client application (for example, your Python script).
2. **Submitting the Code:** You write your data processing logic in your chosen language, and submit it to Snowflake for execution.
3. **Executing within Snowflake:** Snowflake's compute engine receives the code, intelligently translates it into optimized queries, and processes it directly on the data residing within the data cloud.
4. **Retrieving Results:** The processed results are then returned to your client application.

Snowpark ML's Python APIs offer flexibility in where you write, and execute your machine learning code. You can work directly within Snowflake using Snowflake Notebooks or Snowsight Worksheets, or if you prefer, you can use your favorite local Python IDE, and connect to Snowflake to leverage the power of Snowpark ML.

Machine Learning in the Data Cloud

Snowpark ML builds upon the foundation of Snowpark by bringing machine learning capabilities directly into the Snowflake environment. It is a Python library designed to simplify the creation, training, and deployment of ML models using data that resides within the data cloud.

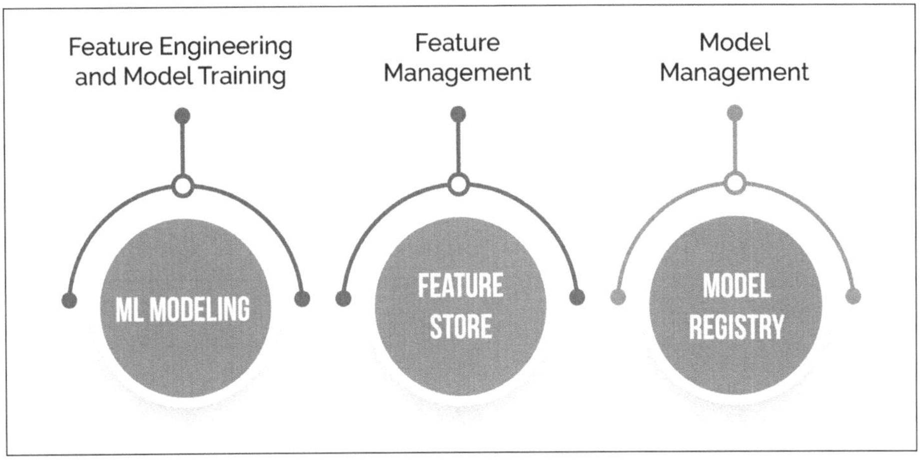

Figure 1.2: *Snowpark ML – Key Features*

To build machine learning models, Snowpark provides the ML Modeling APIs. These APIs enable efficient data loading, feature engineering, and model training, all with the added benefit of distributed processing using CPUs or GPUs for scalability.

For managing features, Snowflake ML offers the Feature Store. This centralized repository helps you organize, store, and share features, ensuring consistency and reusability across your ML projects.

Snowflake's ML Modeling API lets you build machine learning models directly inside Snowflake using popular Python frameworks such as scikit-learn, LightGBM, and XGBoost. This means you can handle everything from data preprocessing and feature engineering to model training, without leaving the Snowflake environment.

When it comes to deploying and managing models, Snowflake ML provides the Model Registry. Registry enables you to store, version, and track your models, simplifying the deployment process, and promoting collaboration among your data science teams.

Advantages of Snowpark ML:

- **Eliminating Data Movement Bottlenecks:** Snowpark ML operates directly on data within Snowflake, eliminating the need for cumbersome data extraction and transfer. This significantly reduces latency, streamlines the ML process, and strengthens data security.

- **Scalable Model Training Powerhouse:** Leverage Snowflake's elastic compute engine to train models on datasets of any size, quickly and efficiently. So, no more waiting days for model training to complete.
- **A Complete ML Lifecycle in One Place:** Snowpark ML simplifies the entire ML journey, encompassing data preparation, feature engineering, model training, deployment, and even monitoring, all within the Snowflake environment.
- **A Familiar Interface for Data Scientists:** Snowpark ML's API mirrors popular ML libraries such as scikit-learn, making it easy for data scientists to get up and run their programs quickly, utilizing their existing expertise.
- **Seamless Model Deployment and Management:** Trained models can be saved as Snowflake objects, and seamlessly deployed within Snowflake using UDFs, stored procedures, or Snowpark Container Services for real-time scoring or batch predictions.
- **Uncompromising Data Security:** Snowpark ML inherits the robust security features built into Snowflake, ensuring that your sensitive data remains protected throughout the entire ML pipeline.

Snowpark ML in Action

As we have seen, Snowpark ML enables end-to-end machine learning workflows directly within Snowflake, eliminating the need for external environments. By leveraging Snowpark's powerful data processing capabilities and Snowpark ML's native model training and deployment features, organizations can seamlessly integrate ML into their data pipelines. This section outlines the key steps involved, from data preparation and model training to deployment, ensuring efficient, scalable, and secure machine learning within Snowflake.

- **Data Preparation:** Use Snowpark to load, preprocess, transform, and engineer features from your data directly within Snowflake. This often involves using libraries like Pandas (running within the Snowpark execution environment) for complex data wrangling.
- **Model Training:** Leverage Snowpark ML's estimators to train machine learning models on the prepared data. The training process happens within Snowflake, taking advantage of its distributed computing capabilities.
- **Model Registry:** Create a centralized repository within Snowflake for managing and organizing your trained machine learning models.

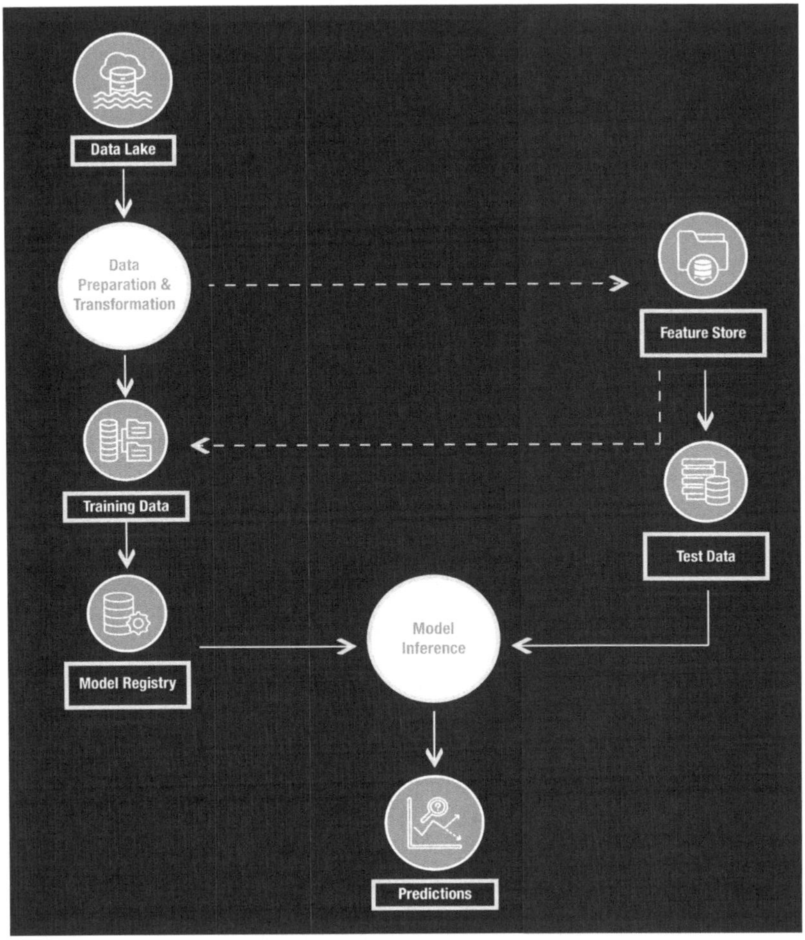

Figure 1.3: *Snowpark ML in Action*

Using Snowflake Notebooks

Snowflake Notebooks provide an interactive and collaborative environment for working with SQL and Python codes directly within Snowflake. They allow users to:

- Write, execute, and visualize SQL and Python scripts within a unified interface.
- Integrate seamlessly with Snowflake's AI/ML tools, including Snowpark and Snowflake Cortex.
- Enable real-time collaboration, allowing multiple users to work on the same notebook simultaneously.
- Support versioning and reproducibility, making it easy to track changes, and maintain structured workflows.

By using Snowflake Notebooks, users can efficiently prototype, experiment, and deploy AI/ML models within their Snowflake environment, without needing the external Jupyter Notebooks or third-party tools.

Building a Predictive Model with Snowpark ML

To understand how all this works, let us develop a predictive model that assesses the likelihood of loan approval for individuals based on various features. The model will utilize a dataset containing basic information about a bank's existing customers, and their financial attributes such as income, tenure of account, and more to predict whether their loan application is likely to be approved by the bank or not. So, as we proceed further through the book, we will utilize different capabilities of Snowpark ML framework for the same, including preprocessing, model building, and registering the model.

Prerequisites:

1. Before proceeding, create a dedicated database for this exercise.

   ```
   CREATE DATABASE SNOWPARK_ML_DEMO;
   ```

2. From the Dataset folder, import the **`loan_data.csv`** file to **`SNOWPARK_ML_DEMO.PUBLIC.LOAN_DATA`** (From Snowsight, scroll to this database, and use **`Create`** -> **`Table`** -> from file option). Ensure that you are using "*First Line contains header*" in the Header option while loading the table.

3. Create a new notebook as follows:

   In **`Snowsight`** -> from **`Projects`** -> **`Notebooks`** menu, create a new notebook using the **`Import.ipynb`** file option, and import the "**`Predictive Model with Snowpark ML.ipynb`**" that is provided in the Scripts folder. Choose **`SNOWPARK_ML_DEMO`** as the database and your choice of warehouse. Click "**`Create`**".

Now let us proceed with the steps within the notebook.

Step 1. Importing Required Libraries

From the Packages menu at the top right, using the "**`Find Packages`**" option, install the following two packages:

```
snowflake-ml-python
snowflake-snowpark-python
```

In the first cell, we will import the necessary libraries for data processing, machine learning, and Snowpark operations. The **`warnings`** module is used to suppress unnecessary warnings for better readability.

```
# Import of Libraries
import warnings

import pandas as pd
from snowflake.ml.modeling.impute import SimpleImputer
from snowflake.ml.modeling.metrics import accuracy_score
from snowflake.ml.modeling.model_selection import GridSearchCV
from snowflake.ml.modeling.preprocessing import LabelEncoder
from snowflake.ml.modeling.ensemble import RandomForestClassifier
# from snowflake.ml.utils.connection_params import SnowflakeLoginOptions
from snowflake.snowpark import Session
from snowflake.snowpark import types as T
from snowflake.snowpark.functions import col

warnings.simplefilter(action="ignore", category=UserWarning)
```

Figure 1.4: *Importing Required Libraries*

Step 2. Importing the Snowflake ML Registry

Loads the Registry module, which enables storing, managing, and retrieving the trained ML models, in Snowflake.

```
from snowflake.ml.registry import Registry
```

Figure 1.5: *Importing the Snowflake ML Registry*

Step 3. Getting the Active Snowflake Session

Establishes an active Snowflake session, required for executing Snowpark operations.

```
session = get_active_session()
```

Figure 1.6: *Getting the Active Snowflake Session*

Step 4. Loading Loan Data from Snowflake Table to a Dataframe

Retrieves data from the **LOAN_DATA** table in Snowflake, and loads it into a Snowpark DataFrame. The **show()** function displays a sample of the dataset.

```
loan_df = session.table("LOAN_DATA")
loan_df.show()

-------------------------------------------------------------------------------------------------------------------------
|"NAME"   |"MARITAL_STATUS"  |"DAYS_ACT_OPEN"  |"AGE"  |"INCOME"  |"ANY_PREVIOUS_DEFAULT"  |"GENDER"  |"OCCUPATION"  |"LOA
-------------------------------------------------------------------------------------------------------------------------
|John     |Single            |2058             |28     |3000      |No                      |M         |Engineer      |1
|Mary     |Married           |2487             |34     |5000      |Yes                     |F         |Teacher       |0
|David    |Single            |1577             |22     |2000      |No                      |M         |Doctor        |1
|Sarah    |Married           |2896             |40     |8000      |No                      |F         |Engineer      |1
|Mike     |Single            |2349             |32     |4000      |Yes                     |M         |Artist        |0
|Emily    |Married           |2118             |29     |3500      |No                      |F         |Student       |1
|Robert   |Single            |3400             |47     |6000      |Yes                     |M         |Engineer      |0
|Jessica  |Married           |2314             |32     |4500      |No                      |F         |Manager       |1
|Kevin    |Single            |2549             |35     |5500      |No                      |M         |Engineer      |1
|Lisa     |Married           |1948             |27     |3200      |Yes                     |F         |NULL          |0
-------------------------------------------------------------------------------------------------------------------------
```

Figure 1.7: *Loading the Data*

Step 5. Separating Categorical and Continuous Variables

Defines the categorical and continuous feature columns separately to facilitate preprocessing.

```
cat_cols = ['GENDER', 'MARITAL_STATUS','OCCUPATION']
cont_cols = ['DAYS_ACT_OPEN', 'AGE', 'INCOME']
```

***Figure 1.8**: Separating Categorical and Continuous Variables*

Step 6. Handling Missing Values using Imputation

Uses **SimpleImputer** to replace the missing values in categorical columns with the most frequently occurring value.

```
# Imputation for Categorical variables
impute_cat = SimpleImputer(
    input_cols=cat_cols,
    output_cols=cat_cols,
    strategy="most_frequent",
    drop_input_cols=True,
)

loan_df = impute_cat.fit(loan_df).transform(loan_df)
loan_df.show()
```

***Figure 1.9**: Handling the Missing Values*

Step 7. Label the Encoding Categorical Variables

Converts the categorical values into numerical representations using label encoding.

```
# Label Encoding
for i in cat_cols:
    LE = LabelEncoder(
    input_cols=i,
    output_cols=f"{i}_ENCODED",
    drop_input_cols=True)
    loan_df = LE.fit(loan_df).transform(loan_df)
```

***Figure 1.10**: Perform Label Encoding*

Step 8. Dropping Unused Columns

Remove the NAME column, as it is irrelevant for the predictive modeling exercise.

```
loan_df = loan_df.drop("NAME")
```

***Figure 1.11**: Remove Unused Columns*

Step 9. Splitting the Data into Training and Testing Sets

Split the dataset into an 80% training set and a 20% test set, using a fixed seed for reproducibility.

```
train_df, test_df = loan_df.random_split(weights=[0.8, 0.2], seed=8)
```

Figure 1.12: *Train Test Split*

Step 10. Initializing a Random Forest Classifier, and fitting it to the Training Data

Create a Random Forest Classifier model that defines input features, target label, and output column. The model is then fitted against the training dataset.

```
# Random forest model
regressor = RandomForestClassifier(
    input_cols=train_df.drop("LOAN_APPROVAL").columns,
    label_cols="LOAN_APPROVAL",
    output_cols="PRED_APPROVED"
)
regressor.fit(train_df)
```

Figure 1.13: *Fitting a Random Forest Model*

Step 11. Setting Up Model Registry

Before a trained machine learning model can be used for predictions in Snowflake, it needs to be registered in the Snowflake Model Registry. This secure repository centralizes model management within Snowflake, handling models of any origin or type and their metadata. Registration simplifies the process of using the model for inference. The following command initializes the registry, preparing it for the trained model to be logged.

```
# Create a registry to log the model
reg = Registry(session=session, database_name='LOAN',
               schema_name='PUBLIC' )
```

Figure 1.14: *Setup the Model Registry*

Step 12: Logging the Model into Registry

Stores the trained model in the Snowflake model registry as version V1.

```
# Logging our model in the Registry

# Define model name and version (use uppercase for name)
model_name = "LOAN"
model_version = 'V1'

# Get sample input data to pass into the registry logging function
X = train_df.drop("LOAN_APPROVAL")

# Let's first log the very first model we trained
model_ver = reg.log_model(
    model_name=model_name,
    version_name=model_version,
    model=regressor,
    sample_input_data=X, # to provide the feature schema
)
```

Figure 1.15: *Log the Model*

Step 13. Listing Registered Models

Displays all the models stored in the model registry. We have just the one, we have created.

```
# List model
reg.show_models()
```

	model_type	database_name	schema_name	comment	owner	default_version_name	versions	aliases
0	USER_MODEL	LOAN	PUBLIC	None	ACCOUNTADMIN	V1	["V1"]	["DEFAULT","V1","FIRST

Figure 1.16: *Listing the Registered Model*

Step 14. Listing Model Versions

Retrieves and displays the different versions of the LOAN model. We have just one version (V1). In real-world scenarios, multiple versions could be stored historically.

```
reg.get_model(model_name).show_versions()
```

	name	aliases	comment	database_name	schem
0	V1	["DEFAULT","FIRST","LAST"]	None	SNOWPARK_ML_DEMO	PUBLI

Figure 1.17: *Listing the Model Versions*

Step 15. Setting a Default Model Version

Assign V1 as the default model version for deployment and predictions.

```
m = reg.get_model(model_name)
m.default = 'V1'
mod_v = m.default
```

Figure 1.18: *Set the default Version*

Step 16. Inference: Predictions on Test Data

Uses the registered model to generate predictions for loan approval on the test dataset.

```
# Predictions
test_prediction = mod_v.run(test_df, function_name="predict")
test_prediction.show()
```

"GENDER_ENCODED"	"DAYS_ACT_OPEN"	"AGE"	"INCOME"	"ANY_PREVIOUS_DEFAULT"	"PRED_APPROVED"
0.0	2118	29	3500	0	1
1.0	3400	47	6000	1	0
0.0	2314	32	4500	0	1
0.0	1948	27	3200	1	0
0.0	2325	32	4200	0	1
0.0	2134	29	4200	0	1
0.0	1900	26	4200	1	0
1.0	2360	32	7000	1	0
0.0	2250	31	5000	1	0

Figure 1.19: *Run Predictions on the Test Data*

Step 17. Verify Model Accuracy

Let us inspect the accuracy of the model. We can observe that the model is highly accurate.

Python ∨ as cell2

```
from snowflake.ml.modeling.metrics import accuracy_score
# Accuracy of model
accuracy = accuracy_score(
    df=test_prediction, y_true_col_names="LOAN_APPROVAL", y_pred_col_names="PRED_APPROVED"
)

print(f"Accuracy: {accuracy}")
```

```
Accuracy: 1.0
```

Figure 1.20: *Verify Model Accuracy*

Step 18. Storing the Test Data in a Snowflake Table

The results can be directly stored in a snowflake table for further analysis.

```
test_df.write.mode("overwrite").save_as_table("LOAN_TEST_DATA")
```

Figure 1.21: *Store Test Prediction Results in a Table*

This example provided a clear, step-by-step look at Snowpark ML in action—covering everything from data preparation to model building, evaluation, registration, versioning, and inference, all within the familiar Snowflake environment.

Conclusion

Snowpark ML revolutionizes the way machine learning models are developed and deployed by bringing computation directly to the data within Snowflake. This eliminates the need for data movement, reducing latency, ensuring data security, and simplifying the overall ML workflow. By leveraging Snowpark's distributed processing and Snowflake's scalable architecture, organizations can train and deploy models efficiently, regardless of data size or complexity. With its ability to streamline end-to-end ML workflows, Snowpark ML empowers data teams to build, deploy, and operationalize machine learning models with unparalleled efficiency and scalability.

Now that we have established a foundation in Snowpark ML and its role in building custom AI/ML solutions, we are ready to delve deeper into the broader AI ecosystem within Snowflake. As mentioned earlier, Snowflake Cortex offers a range of pre-built AI/ML services that complement Snowpark ML. Starting from the next chapter, we will begin exploring Cortex in detail, discovering how it can further streamline your AI initiatives, and accelerate your data science workflows.

CHAPTER 2 Understanding Snowflake Cortex

Introduction

The rapid growth of Artificial Intelligence (AI) and Machine Learning (ML) has created new opportunities for businesses to leverage data-driven insights. However, integrating AI into the existing enterprise workflows often presents significant challenges, including infrastructure complexities, data security concerns, and the need for specialized expertise. Snowflake Cortex AI is designed to address these challenges by embedding AI and ML capabilities directly within the Snowflake Data Cloud, offering a seamless and efficient approach to AI adoption.

Snowflake Cortex provides organizations with powerful capabilities and SQL-based ML and LLM functions that enable users to perform advanced analytics without requiring deep machine learning expertise. This means that data professionals, business analysts, and developers can easily incorporate AI-driven insights into their workflows, without the need for extensive model development or infrastructure management.

A key advantage of Snowflake Cortex is its native integration with Snowflake's secure and governed environment. Since AI workloads are executed within the Snowflake platform, organizations can harness AI capabilities, while maintaining data integrity, compliance, and security. This reduces the need for data movement, ensuring that sensitive information remains protected within the governed Snowflake ecosystem.

By providing a low-code/no-code interface for AI-driven analytics, Snowflake Cortex empowers businesses to unlock the value of their data more efficiently. Whether for text summarization, sentiment analysis, anomaly detection, or forecasting, Cortex makes AI accessible and scalable for enterprises of all sizes.

Structure

In this chapter, we will explore the key aspects of Snowflake Cortex, including:

- Key Features of Cortex AI
- Key Components of Cortex AI
- Built-in ML and LLM Functions in Snowflake Cortex
- Snowflake Cortex versus Traditional AI/ML Approaches

Key Features of Cortex AI

Snowflake Cortex is not a monolithic entity but rather a collection of interconnected components that work in harmony to deliver its AI/ML capabilities. To grasp its functionality, we must dissect these fundamental elements:

- **Serverless Infrastructure:** At its heart, Cortex leverages Snowflake's serverless architecture. This means users are freed from the complexities of infrastructure management, such as provisioning, scaling, and maintenance. The platform automatically allocates and manages resources based on demand, enabling users to focus solely on their analytical tasks.

  This serverless nature allows for elastic scaling, ensuring that Cortex can handle varying workloads without performance degradation. Whether processing small datasets or large-scale enterprise data, the infrastructure adapts accordingly.

- **Integrated Data Cloud:** Cortex is deeply integrated within the Snowflake Data Cloud. This tight integration eliminates the need for data movement which is often a significant bottleneck in traditional AI/ML workflows. By operating directly on data within the Snowflake environment, Cortex minimizes latency, and enhances efficiency.

  This integration also provides access to a vast ecosystem of data, applications, and services within the Data Cloud, enriching the potential for AI/ML applications.

- **Built-in ML and LLM Functions:** One of the standout features of Snowflake Cortex is its pre-built Machine Learning (ML) and Large Language Model (LLM) functions which allow users to run AI-powered analytics with minimal effort. These built-in functions cover a wide range of use cases, from predictive modeling to Natural Language Processing (NLP), eliminating the need for extensive data science expertise or external machine learning platforms. We will be exploring these functions in detail in the subsequent chapters.

- **Integrated Notebooks for Seamless AI Development:** Snowflake Notebooks play a pivotal role in enhancing the capabilities of Snowflake Cortex AI by providing a dynamic and interactive workspace for AI and data science tasks. This feature allows users to seamlessly blend SQL, Python, and Markdown within a single interface, facilitating a smooth workflow for data preparation, model development, and result visualization.

By integrating Notebooks with Cortex AI, users can rapidly prototype and iterate on AI models, leveraging Cortex's advanced querying and analysis capabilities to fine-tune their solutions. This collaborative environment also fosters teamwork on AI projects, ensuring knowledge transfer across the organization. Ultimately, the Snowflake Notebooks streamline the path from experimentation to production, making it easier for users to harness the full potential of Cortex AI within a familiar and powerful development environment.

- **Secure Data Governance:** Snowflake Cortex takes secure data governance seriously, weaving it into the fabric of its AI-powered platform. Snowflake's robust security and governance features extend to Cortex, ensuring that data remains protected throughout the AI/ML lifecycle. Access controls, data masking, and encryption are seamlessly integrated, maintaining data confidentiality and compliance with regulatory requirements.

  This allows for AI/ML to be used on sensitive data while maintaining compliance.

- **Simplified AI/ML Deployment:** Snowflake Cortex AI takes a fresh approach to AI/ML deployment, making it more accessible and manageable for organizations. By simplifying the entire process, from creating models to putting them into action, Cortex removes many of the hurdles that typically slow down AI projects.

  Users can deploy models with minimal effort, reducing time-to-value. The platform handles the complexity of model deployment, allowing business analysts to use AI without needing to be data scientists.

  Cortex also handles the technical heavy lifting behind the scenes. Users can call up sophisticated AI models with simple commands, freeing them from worrying about the underlying infrastructure.

- **Scalable and Elastic Performance:** Cortex AI's scalable and elastic performance is a game-changer for businesses looking to grow their AI capabilities. It is like having a rubber band that stretches to fit whatever you need, whenever you need it. As your data grows or your AI projects become more complex, Cortex effortlessly expands to handle the load. This elasticity allows for cost optimization, as users only pay for the resources they consume.

  Cortex's serverless architecture enables seamless scaling, ensuring that the performance remains consistent even during peak workloads. The beauty of this approach is that it takes the worry out of planning for future AI needs. You can start small and dream big, knowing that Cortex will grow right alongside your ambitions. It is like having a future-proof AI platform that is always ready for whatever comes next.

- **Native SQL Integration:** Cortex integrates seamlessly with SQL, the lingua franca of data professionals. This integration allows users to leverage their existing SQL skills to perform AI/ML tasks.

  Cortex AI's Native SQL Integration is like giving your AI tools a supercharged database engine. It brings together the power of SQL and AI in a way that makes life easier for data folks working on machine learning projects.

  Imagine being able to use all those familiar SQL tricks and functions, you know and love, but now they are turbo-charged to work seamlessly with the AI models. This means that users can embed AI/ML functions directly within their SQL queries, simplifying data analysis and reporting.

- **Support for a Wide Range of LLMs:** Snowflake Cortex provides access to a diverse set of Large Language Models (LLMs), catering to various AI-driven use cases. These models are optimized for Natural Language Processing (NLP), text generation, summarization, and semantic search, allowing users to leverage advanced AI capabilities directly within Snowflake. Users can tap into models developed by renowned companies, such as Mistral AI, Google, Meta, Anthropic, and even Snowflake's own Arctic model. This wide selection includes powerhouses, such as mistral-large, mixtral-8x7b, llama2-70b-chat, Claude Sonnet, gemma-7b, and Llama 3 in both 8B and 70B versions. More models are added at a rapid pace as they evolve. By providing access to this broad spectrum of LLMs, Cortex empowers users to choose the model that best fits their specific use case, whether it is for text generation, sentiment analysis, or complex reasoning tasks. This flexibility ensures that organizations can leverage the most suitable AI capabilities for their unique data challenges, all within the secure and governed environment of the Snowflake platform.

- **Automated Document Intelligence:** Document AI provides AI-driven document processing capabilities allowing organizations to automate the extraction of valuable insights from a wide range of documents, such as invoices, contracts, and so on. This component is particularly useful for industries handling large volumes of paperwork, such as finance, healthcare, and legal services where extracting critical details manually can be time-consuming and error-prone.

  It is adaptable, and can learn to identify key information in different document types, whether it is financial statements, legal contracts, or medical records. This helps businesses quickly gain insights from their documents, without manually reviewing each one.

  In fact, Training Document AI is like teaching a smart student who gets better with every lesson. As these systems work through more documents, they sharpen their skills at spotting important information, and understanding different types of paperwork.

- **Agentic AI Capabilities:** Snowflake Cortex brings a new dimension to the enterprise AI with its Agentic AI capabilities, enabling autonomous, LLM-driven agents to perform tasks, analyze data, and make decisions with minimal human input. These intelligent agents seamlessly integrate with Cortex Search (semantic and keyword-based document retrieval) and Cortex Analyst (natural language querying over structured data), allowing them to understand the user intent, retrieve relevant information, and orchestrate actions across data workflows and external systems. Snowflake Cortex's agentic capabilities can now be seamlessly integrated with collaboration platforms like Microsoft Teams and Slack, enabling intelligent, context-aware AI agents to interact with users directly within their everyday workflows.

Key Components of Cortex AI

Snowflake Cortex AI, as we have seen, is an integrated AI and ML ecosystem within Snowflake, offering pre-built AI models, natural language interactions, and intelligent search capabilities. The architecture, as depicted in the following figure, consists of four primary layers: Studio, Chat, AI Models, and Search/Analyst Tools. These components work together to simplify AI adoption, making it accessible through SQL-based AI functions, chat-driven interactions, and seamless document processing.

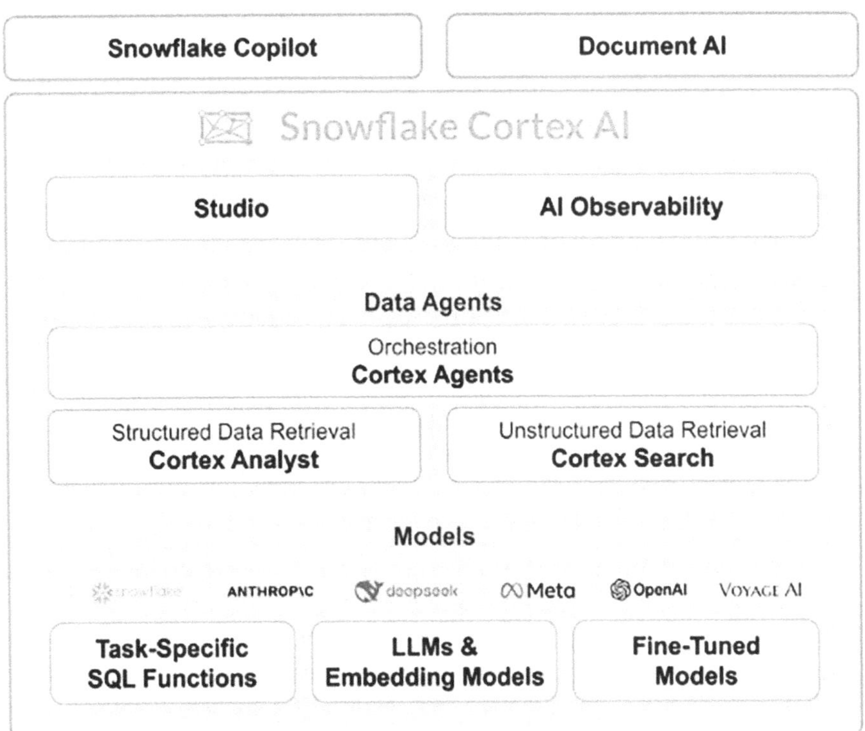

Figure 2.1: *Key Components of Cortex AI (source: Snowflake.com)*

- **Snowflake Copilot**: It is an AI-powered assistant that helps users query, explore, and understand their data using natural language—all within the Snowflake interface. It simplifies the complex SQL generation, provides instant insights, and guides users through data discovery without requiring deep technical expertise.
- **Document AI:** Document AI empowers users to extract structured insights from unstructured documents such as PDFs, invoices, contracts, and forms—directly within the Snowflake Data Cloud. By combining OCR, intelligent document parsing, and large language models, it enables automatic classification, entity extraction, summarization, and sentiment analysis, all without moving the data outside the secure Snowflake environment.
- **Studio – The Centralized AI Workspace:** Studio acts as a central hub for working with Cortex AI. It provides a user-friendly environment where data professionals can:
    - Explore AI capabilities in Snowflake without a complex setup.
    - Experiment with AI models for various business applications.
    - Deploy AI-driven workflows within a governed, secure data environment.

Studio serves as an interface for building, testing, and refining AI applications, making it easier for users to work with Cortex AI's full potential.

- **AI Observability:** The recently introduced AI Observability feature provides deep visibility into the performance and behavior of LLMs and AI models running within the Data Cloud. It tracks metrics like prompt quality, model drift, latency, and hallucinations to ensure reliable and explainable outcomes. Integrated observability ensures that LLM applications remain accurate, compliant, and continuously optimized at scale.
- **Cortex Agents:** Cortex Agents intelligently deconstruct complex user queries, and orchestrate the flow of data requests across Snowflake's AI services. They dynamically route these requests to the appropriate Cortex AI services—such as Cortex Search for retrieving relevant documents or Cortex Analyst for generating insights using natural language. This enables seamless, end-to-end interaction with the data, allowing users to get accurate answers and insights without needing to write the code or understand the underlying data structures.
- **Cortex Analyst:** Aimed at the structured data, this feature helps users analyze datasets without writing complex SQL queries. It allows users to ask questions about their data using natural language, instead of needing to write SQL queries. It automatically understands the question, translates it into a query behind the scenes, and delivers the results quickly. This makes it easier for business users and analysts to explore the data, find answers on their own,

and make faster decisions–all while staying within Snowflake's secure and governed platform.

- **Cortex Search:** This is a feature in Snowflake that allows users to ask questions, and find information across a collection of documents–such as PDFs, reports, or internal files–using natural language. It combines keyword search with advanced AI-powered semantic search to understand the meaning behind a query, not just the exact words. This helps users quickly and securely retrieve the most relevant information, without needing to manually sift through documents, or know where everything is stored.

These chat-driven AI tools democratize data access, allowing business users, analysts, and non-technical stakeholders to interact with their data using the conversational AI.

Models: AI Capabilities at Scale

This layer consists of different categories of machine learning models that power Cortex AI:

- **Task-Specific and Embedding Models**: These are models optimized for specialized tasks, such as categorization, summarization, and embeddings for contextual understanding.
- **Foundation Models**: Large-scale AI models readily available for access, such as Mistral, Llama, Reka, and so on. These models handle a range of AI applications, including language understanding, image processing, and predictive analytics.
- **Fine-Tuned Models**: Custom-trained models tailored to specific business needs, allowing organizations to refine the AI capabilities for domain-specific use cases. The foundational models can be fine-tuned to enhance their performance, enabling highly tailored results within the Snowflake environment.

Built-in ML and LLM Functions in Snowflake Cortex

Snowflake Cortex AI provides a suite of built-in ML and LLM functions, enabling users to leverage the AI-powered insights directly within their Snowflake environment. These functions are accessible via SQL and Python, making them easy to integrate into analytics, automation, and predictive modeling tasks, without requiring extensive AI expertise.

Cortex AI functions are categorized into the following groups:

- General-Purpose LLM Function (`COMPLETE` Function)

- Task-Specific LLM Functions
- Helper Functions
- Built-in ML functions in Snowflake (Classification, Anomaly Detection, Forecasting and Top Insights)

(While the first three are part of the Cortex set of LLM functions, there is also a set of Built-in ML functions for traditional Machine Learning tasks).

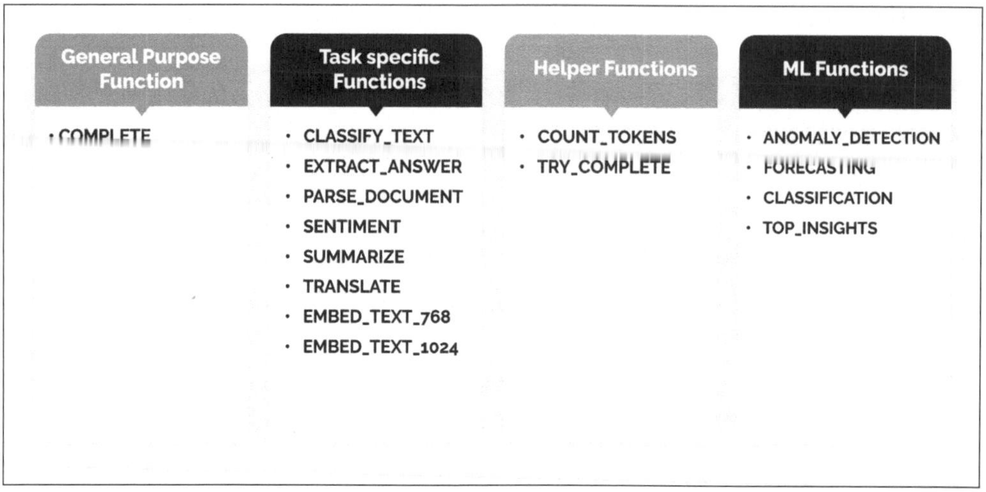

Figure 2.2: *Snowflake ML and Cortex AI Functions*

General-Purpose LLM Function: `COMPLETE`

The COMPLETE function is a highly flexible LLM function designed to handle a wide range of AI-driven tasks, including:

- **Synthetic Data Generation**: Creating artificial yet realistic datasets for testing and development.
- **Summarization and Content Refinement**: Generating concise summaries or restructured content.
- **Multimodal Intelligence**: Generates a language model response based on a given image and prompt.

Additionally, Cortex AI provides an option called Cortex Guard which acts as a safeguard against generating inappropriate or harmful responses. Users can also fine-tune this function to align with their specific business requirements.

Task-Specific LLM Functions

Task-specific functions are pre-built AI models optimized for common NLP tasks.

These functions provide out-of-the-box automation, without the need for extensive customization.

- **`CLASSIFY_TEXT`:** Categorizes the text into predefined labels based on user-defined criteria.
- **`EXTRACT_ANSWER`:** Identifies and retrieves answers from unstructured text when provided with a specific question.
- **`PARSE_DOCUMENT`:** Extracts the text and layout elements from the structured or unstructured documents, including PDFs and images.
- **`SENTIMENT`:** Analyzes the text sentiment, and assigns a score between -1 (negative) and 1 (positive).
- **`SUMMARIZE`**: Generates concise summaries of lengthy documents or articles.
- **`TRANSLATE`**: Translates the text between supported languages.
- **`EMBED_TEXT_768 and EMBED_TEXT_1024`**: Converts the text into numerical vector embeddings (with 768 or 1024 dimensions), useful for semantic search and similarity detection.

In addition to these existing functions, Snowflake has recently introduced the **`ENTITY_SENTIMENT`** *function (currently in preview) which enables aspect-level sentiment analysis. It delivers both the overall and fine-grained sentiment insights tied to specific entities within the text. We will explore this function in detail—with practical examples in Chapter 10: Industry Use Cases and Case Studies.*

Helper Functions

Helper Functions support other LLM functions by ensuring smooth execution, and preventing errors.

- **`COUNT_TOKENS`**: Determines the number of tokens in an input text to avoid exceeding the model limits.
- **`TRY_COMPLETE`**: Functions similarly to the **`COMPLETE`** function but returns **`NULL`**, instead of an error if execution fails.

ML Functions in Snowflake

In addition to the LLM functions listed earlier that are part of Cortex AI, Snowflake also provides built-in ML-powered analytics functions, allowing users to gain predictive insights, without requiring deep machine learning expertise.

- **Forecasting**: Predicts future values of a metric based on historical patterns.
- **Anomaly Detection**: Identifies unusual patterns or deviations from the expected trends.

- **Classification**: Automatically assigns records to categories based on the most influential attributes.
- **Top Insights**: Identifies key dimensions that have a significant impact on a given metric, helping uncover the hidden trends.

These built-in ML and LLM functions in Snowflake Cortex AI make it easier than ever to integrate AI-driven insights into the existing data workflows. Whether automating sentiment analysis, extracting structured data from documents, or making future predictions with time-series forecasting, Cortex AI empowers businesses to harness the power of AI, without the complexity of traditional model training.

Snowflake Cortex versus Traditional AI/ML Approaches

Traditionally, organizations build AI/ML models using standalone tools, custom scripts, and complex infrastructure. However, Snowflake Cortex is reshaping this landscape by providing a fully integrated, serverless AI/ML experience within the Snowflake Data Cloud. This topic explores the differences between Snowflake Cortex and the traditional AI/ML approaches, highlighting the advantages and trade-offs of each.

Traditional AI/ML Approaches

- **Complex Infrastructure and Setup:** The Traditional AI/ML implementations require significant infrastructure investments. Data teams must provision compute clusters, storage, networking, and AI-specific GPUs to support model training and inference. This complexity often leads to operational overhead, high maintenance costs, and scalability challenges.
- **Disconnected Data and Compute:** In most enterprises, data storage and AI/ML compute are separate entities. Organizations typically store data in the cloud, but they train models using separate environments. This leads to latency issues, data movement inefficiencies, and security concerns, as large datasets must be moved between the storage and AI platforms.
- **Fragmented Tooling and Ecosystem:** The Traditional AI/ML workflows involve a mix of different tools:
    - ETL tools for data preparation
    - ML frameworks for training models
    - Model deployment tools

Integrating these tools requires custom coding, DevOps expertise, and ongoing monitoring, making the AI projects complex and resource-intensive.

- **Long Development Cycles:** Model development in traditional AI/ML setups follows a long and iterative process, requiring:
  - Feature engineering and data transformation
  - Model selection and hyper parameter tuning
  - Deployment to production
  - Monitoring and retraining

Each step demands specialized skill sets, extensive testing, and manual interventions, slowing down the AI adoption.

Challenges in Deploying and Using LLMs

LLMs are powerful but challenging to deploy in traditional AI/ML settings due to:

- High computational demands
- Complex fine-tuning processes
- Data privacy concerns when using external APIs

Companies that need to use LLMs for summarization, chatbots, or text analysis must either fine-tune the existing models (requiring AI expertise), or rely on third-party API-based LLMs which may compromise data security and governance.

Snowflake Cortex: A Unified AI/ML Solution

Snowflake Cortex redefines AI/ML adoption by offering a fully managed, serverless AI platform that integrates seamlessly with the enterprise data. It eliminates the need for complex infrastructure, making the AI more accessible, scalable, and secure.

The Traditional AI/ML workflows often involve multiple disconnected tools for data preparation, model training, and deployment, leading to inefficiencies, high costs, and security challenges. Organizations struggle with data movement, fragmented ecosystems, and long development cycles, making AI adoption complex and resource-intensive. Snowflake Cortex solves these issues by offering a fully managed, serverless AI/ML platform that operates natively within Snowflake Data Cloud. This allows businesses to apply the AI/ML models directly to their data with minimal setup, reducing the operational overhead, while maintaining security and governance. To better understand the benefits of Snowflake Cortex, let us explore some of its key advantages:

- **Built-in LLMs for Text Analysis and Automation:** One of the biggest advantages of Snowflake Cortex is its pre-integrated Large Language Models (LLMs). Instead of requiring external AI tools, users can apply LLM-powered tasks directly on the data stored in Snowflake, using simple SQL functions.

For example, text summarization can be done natively in Snowflake:

```
SELECT SNOWFLAKE.CORTEX.SUMMARIZE(Notes) FROM Reports;
```

This eliminates the need to move the data to an external AI platform for processing, reducing latency, and improving security.

- **No-Code and Low-Code AI Capabilities:** Snowflake Cortex simplifies AI adoption by offering pre-built AI/ML models for common use cases, such as text summarization, sentiment analysis, forecasting, and anomaly detection. Unlike traditional methods that require extensive coding and data science expertise, Cortex allows users to invoke AI functions using simple SQL queries.

  For example, performing sentiment analysis on customer reviews is as easy as:

  ```
  SELECT SNOWFLAKE.CORTEX. SENTIMENT (Text) FROM Reviews;
  ```

  This reduces the dependency on data scientists and accelerates AI adoption across business teams.

- **Scalable AI Without Infrastructure Management:** Snowflake Cortex is a fully managed, serverless AI platform. It eliminates the need for provisioning infrastructure, managing GPUs, or setting up machine learning environments. Since it runs natively within Snowflake, users benefit from automatic scaling, security, and governance without needing external compute resources.

  LLMs are compute-intensive, but Snowflake Cortex abstracts this complexity by offering fully managed AI services. Users do not need to provision GPUs or configure AI servers—everything runs natively within Snowflake's scalable infrastructure.

  This means:

  - Automatic scaling for AI workloads
  - No infrastructure maintenance
  - Cost efficiency with pay-as-you-use pricing

- **AI/ML Models Operate Directly on Data:** Unlike traditional AI setups that require moving the data between the storage and AI platforms, Cortex runs models directly on the data stored in Snowflake. This eliminates data movement bottlenecks, reduces costs, and improves performance.

  Additionally, Cortex seamlessly integrates with Snowflake's Data Governance, Access Controls, and Role-Based Security, ensuring that the AI/ML applications remain compliant with the enterprise policies.

- **Faster Time-to-Insights:** By removing infrastructure complexities, Cortex enables businesses to go from the raw data to AI-driven insights in minutes, compared to weeks or months with traditional approaches. This is particularly useful for tasks, such as:

- Forecasting revenue or demand using built-in time series models
- Text analysis for customer support automation
- Anomaly detection for fraud prevention

- **Seamless Integration with Custom ML Models:** For organizations that require more advanced AI capabilities, Snowflake Cortex allows integration with the custom ML models built using the Snowpark ML. This provides a hybrid approach where teams can use pre-built AI models for simple tasks, while leveraging the custom ML for complex, domain-specific problems.
- **LLM-Enabled Conversational AI and Chatbots:** Snowflake Cortex enables businesses to build conversational AI and chatbots directly within their data warehouse. Traditional chatbots rely on external APIs, leading to data privacy concerns.

  With Snowflake Cortex, businesses can deploy chatbots trained on their own data, ensuring:

  - No external API dependencies
  - Full data security and compliance
  - Better customization for business-specific knowledge

  This is especially useful for industries like customer service, financial advisory, and legal document processing where data confidentiality is crucial.

- **Governed and Secure AI Adoption:** Unlike the third-party AI tools, which may require data movement to external platforms, Snowflake Cortex ensures that LLMs operate within Snowflake's governance framework. This is critical for industries with strict regulatory requirements (for example, finance, healthcare, government, and so on).

  Cortex inherits Snowflake's role-based security, compliance, and data lineage tracking, making AI adoption secure, auditable, and enterprise-ready.

  To summarize, as seen above, Snowflake Cortex represents a fundamental shift in AI/ML adoption, offering a simpler, more secure, and cost-effective approach, compared to the traditional methods. It is ideal for organizations that:

  - Need LLM-powered AI capabilities (for example, summarization, chatbots, text analysis) without complex setups
  - Prefer serverless, fully integrated AI solutions for business users
  - Want a secure AI adoption with data governance built-in
  - Seek fast, cost-efficient AI adoption without infrastructure overhead

The following figure provides a quick comparison based on most of the points discussed here:

Feature	Snowflake Cortex AI	Traditional AI/ML
Infrastructure	Fully managed, serverless	Requires provisioning (GPUs, clusters)
Support for LLMs	Instant Access to leading LLMs, hosted and managed	Need to subscribe from respective LLM providers as required
LLM Deployment	Built-in, native SQL access	External LLM APIs or on-prem hosting
Ease of Use	Low code, No-code & SQL-based AI	Requires extensive Python, ML expertise
Data Movement	No data transfer; runs within Snowflake	Requires moving data between storage & AI platforms
Setup Time	Minutes	Weeks to months
Conversational AI	Integrated chatbot & text-based LLMs	External chatbot integrations needed
Security & Governance	Inherits Snowflake's security & compliance	Requires separate security measures
Scalability	Auto-scales with Snowflake	Manual GPU scaling & tuning
Cost Efficiency	Pay-as-you-go, no extra infrastructure	Expensive GPU clusters & LLM fine-tuning
AI Model Hosting	Natively hosted within Snowflake	Requires separate cloud/on-prem AI model hosting
Integration with Data Warehouse	Seamless integration with Snowflake	Requires external connectors or pipelines to fetch data
AI Governance & Auditability	Built-in governance, access controls, and audit logs	Custom AI governance frameworks needed
Real-Time AI/ML Inference	Supports real-time AI inference directly within Snowflake	Requires additional infrastructure for real-time AI predictions

Figure 2.3: *Cortex AI versus Traditional AI/ML*

Thus, Snowflake Cortex democratizes AI and LLM usage, making them accessible to a broader audience. Now, as AI adoption continues to grow, Cortex provides a low-friction, enterprise-ready path to leverage AI/ML and LLMs at scale.

Conclusion

In this chapter, we explored Snowflake Cortex, its core components, and the features that make it a powerful AI/ML platform integrated directly within the Snowflake Data Cloud. We examined how Cortex simplifies AI adoption by eliminating the need for complex infrastructure, reducing data movement, and offering built-in AI/ML functions that can be accessed with simple SQL queries.

We also compared Snowflake Cortex with traditional AI/ML approaches, highlighting how Cortex provides a serverless, secure, and scalable alternative that accelerates AI-driven insights. Its pre-built AI capabilities, seamless data integration, and governance-friendly approach make it an ideal solution for organizations looking to leverage AI, without deep technical expertise or extensive setup.

By seamlessly blending advanced AI capabilities with Snowflake's robust data cloud infrastructure, Cortex democratizes access to sophisticated analytics. It empowers users across the spectrum, from seasoned data scientists to business analysts, to harness the power of AI in their daily workflows. This democratization has the potential to accelerate innovation and decision-making across entire organizations.

The platform's emphasis on ease of use, coupled with its powerful built-in functions, addresses many of the challenges that have traditionally hindered widespread AI adoption. By abstracting away much of the complexity associated with AI model development and deployment, Cortex allows organizations to focus on deriving insights, and creating value from their data.

With a strong foundation in how Snowflake Cortex enables AI/ML within Snowflake, we are now ready to explore its ML and LLM functions in more depth. In the next chapter, we will take a closer look at Snowflake ML functions, their applications, and how they can be used to build and deploy predictive models seamlessly within Snowflake.

Chapter 3
Overview of Machine Learning Functions

Introduction

Before delving into the Cortex's generative AI capabilities, it is worthwhile to explore its native machine learning functions, as they provide a solid foundation for understanding the platform's advanced analytics offerings. Snowflake brings Artificial intelligence (AI) and Machine Learning (ML) capabilities natively into the Data Cloud, allowing businesses to seamlessly integrate predictive analytics into their workflows. With the built-in ML functions, users can perform classification, forecasting, anomaly detection, and automated insights generation, without needing extensive data science expertise. These functions are fully managed, eliminating infrastructure concerns, while ensuring scalability and performance.

The functions are accessible through SQL queries, making them readily available to data analysts and engineers familiar with database operations. By seamlessly integrating ML capabilities into the data warehouse, Snowflake eliminates the need for data movement, and simplifies the process of extracting valuable insights from large datasets.

This chapter explores the core ML functions available in Snowflake, highlighting how they simplify data-driven decision-making. Hence, by the end of this chapter, you will have a strong grasp of how to leverage these ML functions for various business applications.

Structure

In this chapter, we will cover the following topics:

- Key Benefits of Snowflake Machine Learning Functions
- Process to Upload Data to Tables and Stages
- Classification Function
- Forecasting Function
- Anomaly Detection
- Top Insights Function
- A Note on Snowflake AI and ML Studio

Key Benefits of Snowflake Machine Learning Functions

Snowflake Cortex ML functions are revolutionizing how businesses approach machine learning within their data ecosystems. These innovative tools bring the power of advanced analytics directly into the familiar Snowflake environment, making it easier than ever for companies to harness the potential of their data. By seamlessly integrating machine learning capabilities with the existing data workflows, Cortex ML functions are breaking down barriers and opening new possibilities for organizations of all sizes.

Whether you are a seasoned data scientist or a business analyst looking to dive into predictive analytics, these functions offer a range of benefits that can transform your approach to data-driven decision-making. From simplifying complex processes to enabling real-time insights, Cortex ML functions are designed to meet the evolving needs of modern businesses in an increasingly data-centric world.

Let us explore some of the key advantages that make Snowflake Cortex ML functions a game-changer for organizations looking to leverage machine learning in their data strategy.

- **Simplicity:** Users can apply ML functions with just SQL queries—no need for extensive coding or data engineering.
- **Automatic Data Preparation**: Common preprocessing tasks, such as handling missing values, detecting outliers, and formatting data are done automatically, reducing the need for manual intervention.
- **Native Integration**: Fully embedded within the Snowflake platform, Cortex ML functions enable users to perform machine learning tasks directly in SQL, eliminating the need to move data or use external tools.

- **Collaboration**: The intuitive design allows both technical and non-technical team members to contribute to machine learning projects, fostering better teamwork and alignment with business objectives, and fostering a more inclusive approach to AI-driven decision-making.
- **Scalability:** Functions are optimized for performance across vast datasets.
- **Security and Governance:** Data never leaves Snowflake, ensuring compliance and governance.
- **Operational Efficiency:** No need to manage the infrastructure, as Cortex ML functions are fully managed.

Each function is designed for a specific category of ML tasks, from predictive analytics to automated anomaly detection. Let us explore them in detail starting with the classification function.

Note: *As we explore Snowflake Cortex AI throughout this book, we will be creating various machine learning models, functions, and insights. To ensure a structured and efficient workflow, where possible, we will use* CORTEX_AI_DB *as our dedicated storage space for all ML-related objects. We can use the* PUBLIC *schema within this database for creating our objects. Now, let us create this database.*

```
CREATE DATABASE CORTEX_AI_DB;
```

Process to Upload the Data to Tables and Stages

Throughout this book, we would be loading files to either a table or to a staging area. The following steps are provided for your reference.

Procedure to Load the Table from the File:

1. Sign in to Snowsight.
2. Download the provided csv file from the folder.
3. In Snowsight, from the menu on the left, Select `Data` > `Add Data`.
4. Choose `Load data into a Table`.
5. Browse and choose the csv file.
6. Choose `CORTEX_AI_DB.PUBLIC` as the schema (or any other schema, as specified), and select the option - create a new table.
7. Provide the name of the new table to be the same as the file name, and click `next`.
8. In the left menu, expand `view options` below the File Format.

9. Ensure that the Header option is set to **`First Line contains Header`**.
10. Click **`Load`**.

Procedure to Upload the Files to the Stage:

1. Sign in to Snowsight.
2. Select Data from the left-side navigation menu.
3. Select your database, **`CORTEX_AI_DB`** (or as specified) and schema - **`PUBLIC`**.
4. Select Stages, and then choose the appropriate stage (**`CORTEX_AI_STG`**, or as specified)
5. From the top right, select the **`+ Files`** button.
6. Drag and drop the file(s) into the UI, or browse to choose the file(s).
7. Select **`Upload`** to upload your file(s).

Classification Function

Classification is a fundamental ML task that involves predicting the category or class of a data point. Snowflake Cortex provides functions for building and applying classification models directly within your data warehouse. The classification function in Snowflake Cortex allows users to categorize the data into predefined classes based on patterns identified in the training data. This function supports both binary (two classes) and multi-class (more than two classes) classification problems. ML Classification function can process and classify categorical and numerical data efficiently within the Snowflake ecosystem.

When you create a classification model in Snowflake, it is stored as a schema-level object. To do this, your role needs special permission: The **`CREATE SNOWFLAKE.ML.CLASSIFICATION`** privilege for the specific schema where you want to save the model. This permission works similarly to other schema-level rights, such as creating tables or views.

Key Features:

- Utilizes gradient boosting algorithms for model training
- Supports both binary and multi-class classification
- Employs area-under-the-curve loss function for binary classification
- Uses logistic loss function for multi-class classification

Use Cases:

- **Customer Churn Prediction**: Predicting which customers are likely to cancel their subscriptions.

- **Fraud Detection**: Identifying fraudulent transactions based on historical data.
- **Sentiment Analysis**: Classifying customer reviews as positive, negative, or neutral.
- **Cyber Security Threat Detection**: Classify activities as either "**`normal`**" or "**`potentially malicious`**," helping to prevent security breaches.

Implementation

Dataset: **`TRANSACTIONS.csv`**

To demonstrate Snowflake's ML classification function, this synthetic dataset simulates 500 transaction records with key attributes, such as transaction amount, location of origin, device type, and fraud labels (0 = Legitimate, 1 = Fraudulent). The csv file can be loaded to a new table called TRANSACTIONS. The dataset is then anonymized and structured, making it suitable for applying classification models to predict outcomes based on transaction patterns. This data can be loaded into the TRANSACTIONS table before proceeding with the following steps. It serves as a practical example for highlighting how the Snowflake ML Classification function works.

A snapshot of the table is as follows:

TRANSACTION_ID	AMOUNT	LOCATION	DEVICE_TYPE	FRAUDULENT
1	1875.83	Loc_A	Tablet	0
2	4753.82	Loc_A	Desktop	0
3	3661.31	Loc_A	Tablet	0
4	2995.30	Loc_E	Desktop	0
5	784.31	Loc_D	Tablet	0
6	1176.29	Loc_E	Tablet	1
7	295.13	Loc_D	Tablet	0
8	4331.55	Loc_E	Mobile	0
9	3007.57	Loc_E	Mobile	0

Figure 3.1: *Snapshot of the Transactions Table*

Step 1: Create the training dataset (**`CLASSIFY_TRAIN`**) by randomly sampling 80% of the **`TRANSACTIONS`** table.

The **`SAMPLE (80)`** function selects approximately 80% of the rows at random.

```
CREATE OR REPLACE TABLE CLASSIFY_TRAIN AS SELECT * FROM TRANSAC-
TIONS SAMPLE (80);
```

Step 2: Create a test dataset (**`CLASSIFY_TEST`**) by selecting the remaining 20% of the data. The **`NOT EXISTS`** condition ensures that any transaction already present in **`CLASSIFY_TRAIN`** is excluded. Subsequently, drop the **`TRANSACTION_ID`** column, as it does not add value to the model.

```
CREATE OR REPLACE TABLE CLASSIFY_TEST AS SELECT * FROM TRANSAC-
TIONS WHERE NOT EXISTS (SELECT 1 FROM CLASSIFY_TRAIN WHERE
TRANSACTIONS.TRANSACTION_ID = CLASSIFY_TRAIN.TRANSACTION_ID);
ALTER TABLE CLASSIFY_TRAIN DROP COLUMN TRANSACTION_ID;
```

Step 3: Create the Model using the classified function

```
CREATE OR REPLACE SNOWFLAKE.ML.CLASSIFICATION FRAUD_DETECTION_
MODEL(    INPUT_DATA => SYSTEM$REFERENCE('TABLE',
'CLASSIFY_TRAIN'),    TARGET_COLNAME => 'FRAUDULENT' );
```

The **`SYSTEM$REFERENCE ('TABLE', 'CLASSIFY_TRAIN')`** points to the **`CLASSIFY_TRAIN`** table which contains the sampled 80% of the transactions data. The **`TARGET_COLNAME`** points to the target column that the model will learn to predict - **`FRAUDULENT`** (0 = Legitimate, 1 = Fraudulent).

Step 4: Run Predictions - Create a table, and store the Predicted outcome from the Test data.

```
CREATE OR REPLACE TABLE FRAUD_PREDICTION AS SELECT * EXCLUDE
(FRAUDULENT), FRAUD_DETECTION_MODEL!PREDICT(INPUT_DATA => object_
construct(*)) as prediction from CLASSIFY_TEST;
```

We select all the columns from **`CLASSIFY_TEST`**, except the actual **`FRAUDULENT`** column. This ensures that the model's predictions can be compared separately. Use the trained ML model (**`FRAUD_DETECTION_MODEL`**) to predict fraud status for each transaction. The **`PREDICT`** function takes the entire row as input using object_construct(*) which converts all the columns into a JSON-like object required for ML predictions. We load the results to the **`FRAUD_PREDICTION`** table.

Step 5: Query the **`FRAUD_PREDICTION`** table

```
SELECT * FROM FRAUD_PREDICTION;
```

TRANSACTION_ID	AMOUNT	LOCATION	DEVICE_TYPE	PREDICTION
11	107.82	Loc_E	Desktop	{ "class": "0", "logs": { "Error": [], "Info": [], "Warning": [] }, "probability": { "0": 8.85944376999
72	1496.38	Loc_D	Mobile	{ "class": "0", "logs": { "Error": [], "Info": [], "Warning": [] }, "probability": { "0": 5.27759249700
122	4480.98	Loc_C	Mobile	{ "class": "0", "logs": { "Error": [], "Info": [], "Warning": [] }, "probability": { "0": 9.97428392600
151	4541.79	Loc_E	Desktop	{ "class": "0", "logs": { "Error": [], "Info": [], "Warning": [] }, "probability": { "0": 9.85850424300
196	1749.30	Loc_A	Desktop	{ "class": "0", "logs": { "Error": [], "Info": [], "Warning": [] }, "probability": { "0": 9.98160872400
244	1853.94	Loc_B	Tablet	{ "class": "0", "logs": { "Error": [], "Info": [], "Warning": [] }, "probability": { "0": 9.48969889900
298	1083.03	Loc_A	Desktop	{ "class": "0", "logs": { "Error": [], "Info": [], "Warning": [] }, "probability": { "0": 9.99666814499
356	3213.88	Loc_B	Desktop	{ "class": "0", "logs": { "Error": [], "Info": [], "Warning": [] }, "probability": { "0": 7.94154813800
422	3949.14	Loc_C	Mobile	{ "class": "0", "logs": { "Error": [], "Info": [], "Warning": [] }, "probability": { "0": 9.99570080800
466	1877.48	Loc_B	Tablet	{ "class": "0", "logs": { "Error": [], "Info": [], "Warning": [] }, "probability": { "0": 9.52696201200
2	4753.82	Loc_A	Desktop	{ "class": "0", "logs": { "Error": [], "Info": [], "Warning": [] }, "probability": { "0": 9.86141841600

Figure 3.2: *Preview of the Fraud_Prediction Table*

As seen in *Figure* 3.2, the **`PREDICTION`** column is in JSON format, and we would need to parse the values for prediction and probability to display results as required.

Step 6: Parse the predicted results into separate columns.

```
SELECT TRANSACTION_ID, AMOUNT, LOCATION, DEVICE_TYPE,
prediction:class AS pred_class, round(prediction['probability']
[prediction:class], 3) as probability FROM FRAUD_PREDICTION;
```

We extract the predicted class (fraudulent or legitimate) from the **'prediction'** object **prediction:class** as **pred_class**, followed by extracting the probability associated with the predicted class- '**prediction["probability"]**' as the probability.

TRANSACTION_ID	AMOUNT	LOCATION	DEVICE_TYPE	PRED_CLASS	PROBABILITY
99	197.95	Loc_D	Desktop	"1"	0.534
143	2488.76	Loc_B	Mobile	"0"	0.962
181	2562.94	Loc_B	Mobile	"0"	0.639
229	6691.16	Loc_C	Tablet	"1"	0.962
285	2893.51	Loc_E	Desktop	"0"	0.973
346	3081.17	Loc_C	Tablet	"0"	0.958
394	3883.18	Loc_B	Mobile	"0"	1
454	4532.24	Loc_C	Tablet	"0"	0.94
496	1769.99	Loc_B	Desktop	"0"	0.998
10	3541.82	Loc_C	Desktop	"0"	0.998
68	4011.97	Loc_C	Tablet	"0"	0.996

Figure 3.3: *Preview of the Parsed Results*

Step 7: Inspect the Model Evaluation Metrics.

```
CALL FRAUD_DETECTION_MODEL!SHOW_EVALUATION_METRICS();
```

The **CALL FRAUD_DETECTION_MODEL!SHOW_EVALUATION_METRICS();** command is used to retrieve the performance metrics of the trained classification model (**FRAUD_MODEL**). It provides metrics for each of the predicted classes. This helps in evaluating the accuracy and effectiveness of the model, before deploying it for real-world predictions.

DATASET_TYPE	CLASS	ERROR_METRIC	METRIC_VALUE
EVAL	0	precision	0.9285714286
EVAL	0	recall	0.9701492537
EVAL	0	f1	0.9489051095
EVAL	0	support	67
EVAL	1	precision	0.75
EVAL	1	recall	0.5454545455
EVAL	1	f1	0.6315789474
EVAL	1	support	11

Figure 3.4: *Model Evaluation Metrics*

Step 8: Understanding Feature Importance.

```
CALL FRAUD_DETECTION_MODEL!SHOW_FEATURE_IMPORTANCE();
```

The **CALL FRAUD_DETECTION_MODEL!SHOW_FEATURE_IMPORTANCE()** command retrieves the importance of each feature in determining fraud predictions. This helps in understanding which factors have the most influence on the model's decision-making process. This function ranks features based on their impact on the classification model's decision.

RANK	FEATURE	SCORE
1	AMOUNT	0.8667108753
2	DEVICE_TYPE	0.1140583554
3	LOCATION	0.01923076923
4	TRANSACTION_ID	0

Figure 3.5: *Feature Importance*

As seen, the **AMOUNT** field has a major influence, followed by the type of device and then the location where the transaction originates. As it should be, the **Transaction_ID** is not influencing the outcome at all, and can be excluded from the model creation script as well.

This preceding implementation successfully demonstrated how Snowflake's native ML classification function can be leveraged to build, train, and deploy a fraud detection model entirely within the Snowflake Data Cloud. By following a structured approach—creating a dataset, splitting it into training and testing sets, training a classification model, making predictions, and interpreting the results—we highlighted the simplicity and efficiency of Snowflake Cortex ML for real-world machine learning tasks. We will now proceed and examine the Forecasting function.

Forecasting Function

The forecasting function uses historical time series data to predict future numeric values, making it invaluable for various business applications, such as sales projections, demand forecasting, and resource planning. It employs sophisticated algorithms, including gradient boosting machines, to analyze patterns and trends in the data.

Users can train models, and generate forecasts using familiar SQL commands, making it accessible to data analysts and SQL-proficient professionals. The function can handle both single-series and multi-series data, accommodating various forecasting scenarios.

When you train a forecasting model, it is stored as a schema-level object. As a result, the role used to create the model must have **CREATE SNOWFLAKE.ML.FORECAST** privilege on the schema where the model is being created, ensuring that it can be properly stored and accessed within that schema.

Key Features:

- Analyzes how specific metrics evolve over time
- Considers the influence of several factors on the value of interest
- Provides predictive insights based on detected trends
- Supports Multi-Series Forecasting

Use Cases:

- **Sales Prediction**: Forecasts product demand for inventory management
- **Resource Planning**: Predicts staffing or server needs based on usage patterns
- **Financial Forecasting**: Project revenue and expenses for budgeting
- **Demand Forecasting**: Anticipate product demand to optimize production
- **Ticket Volume Forecasting**: Predict future customer support ticket volumes

Implementation

Dataset: `RETAIL_SALES.csv`

To demonstrate Snowflake's ML forecasting function, let us consider this simulated dataset containing 90 days of daily retail sales data, structured with two key columns: Date (timestamp) and Sales (daily revenue). By analyzing historical sales patterns, businesses can generate data-driven forecasts, optimize inventory, and plan marketing strategies effectively. The file can be loaded to a new table called **`RETAIL_SALES`**, before proceeding with the following steps.

Step 1: Let us query the sales table.

This dataset is suitable for predicting future sales trends using **`ML.FORECAST`**, Snowflake's built-in ML function for time series forecasting.

```
SELECT * FROM RETAIL_SALES;
```

DATE	SALES
2024-01-01	1853.45
2024-01-02	1894.92
2024-01-03	2168.46
2024-01-04	1899.47
2024-01-05	2233.38
2024-01-06	2318.79
2024-01-07	2118.91
2024-01-08	2502.46

Figure 3.6: *Daily Retail Sales Table*

Step 2: Create the Forecast model.

```
CREATE OR REPLACE SNOWFLAKE.ML.FORECAST SALES_FORECAST
(INPUT_DATA => SYSTEM$REFERENCE('TABLE', 'RETAIL_SALES'),
    TIMESTAMP_COLNAME => 'DATE',
    TARGET_COLNAME => 'SALES',
    CONFIG_OBJECT => { 'ON_ERROR': 'SKIP' }
```

To create a forecast model using Snowflake's ML forecasting function, the **`SNOWFLAKE.ML.FORECAST`** function is leveraged. We will build a predictive model for retail sales forecasting. The **`SYSTEM$REFERENCE ('TABLE', 'RETAIL_SALES')`** function in Snowflake is used to reference the **`RETAIL_SALES`** table as the input data source for the forecasting model. The **`TIMESTAMP_COLNAME`** is set to **`DATE`**, ensuring the time series structure is maintained, while **`TARGET_COLNAME`** is specified as SALES, identifying the variable to be predicted. The optional **`CONFIG_OBJECT`** parameter is configured with **`ON_ERROR: SKIP`**, which instructs Snowflake to bypass any errors during the model creation process rather than failing execution.

Step 3: Generate forecasts, and store the results in a table.

We will create a small code block for this.

```
BEGIN
    CALL SALES_FORECAST!FORECAST(
        -- Here we set the forecast interval.
        FORECASTING_PERIODS => 14
    );
```

-- These steps store the forecasts to a table.

```
    LET x := SQLID;
    CREATE OR REPLACE TABLE RETAIL_SALES_FORECAST AS SELECT *
FROM TABLE(RESULT_SCAN(:x));
END;
```

To generate forecasts for the next 14 days, and store the results in a table, this operation leverages Snowflake's ML forecasting model. The process begins with the **`CALL SALES_FORECAST!FORECAST`** function which invokes the trained **`SALES_FORECAST`** model, and generates predictions for the next 14 days by setting **`FORECASTING_PERIODS => 14`**. The **`RESULT_SCAN(:x)`** function retrieves the generated forecast results where **`:x`** is assigned the SQL query ID of the prediction output. The forecasted values are in a structured table named **`RETAIL_SALES_FORECAST`**, ensuring that the predictions are saved for further analysis, visualization, or reporting.

Step 4: Query the forecasted results.

```
SELECT * FROM RETAIL_SALES_FORECAST;
```

SERIES	TS	FORECAST	LOWER_BOUND	UPPER_BOUND
null	2024-03-31 00:00:00.000	1824.691771074	1376.261257934	2297.923176332
null	2024-04-01 00:00:00.000	1704.091522217	1216.224237592	2181.064610302
null	2024-04-02 00:00:00.000	1748.996583418	1245.582398316	2229.304822483
null	2024-04-03 00:00:00.000	1709.967989835	1196.344362432	2204.215937979
null	2024-04-04 00:00:00.000	1734.008182872	1256.14852377	2240.813417689
null	2024-04-05 00:00:00.000	1750.874975031	1259.27269716	2230.068618347
null	2024-04-06 00:00:00.000	1788.856147073	1289.639714865	2290.074399486
null	2024-04-07 00:00:00.000	1819.914101341	1312.585575554	2349.103590867

Figure 3.7: *Retail Sales Forecast*

The series column is displayed as null because we do not have categories defined. For example, if we have a **`Sale Category`** column defined, the series option treats categories, such as electronics and clothing as separate time series. This allows Snowflake's ML Forecast to generate category-specific forecasts, accounting for unique trends and patterns in each, without needing separate models.

The upper and lower bounds refer to the confidence intervals of the forecasted values. These bounds provide a range within which the actual future values are likely to fall, based on a specified confidence level (for example, 95%).

- **Upper Bound**: This is the higher end of the confidence interval, indicating the maximum value that the forecasted sales might reach.
- **Lower Bound**: This is the lower end of the confidence interval, indicating the minimum value that the forecasted sales might be.

Together, these bounds help plan for potential variations in sales. For example, if the forecasted sales are 1000 units with an upper bound of 1200 and a lower bound of 800, you can expect the actual sales to likely fall between 800 and 1200 units.

Step 5: Visualizing the time series.

A Streamlit application could be created to intuitively visualize the forecasts as well.

Figure 3.8: *Visualizing the Forecasted Values*

As observed, Snowflake's ML forecasting function provides a powerful, automated, and scalable way to generate time series predictions directly within the Snowflake environment. By leveraging **`SNOWFLAKE.ML.FORECAST`**, businesses can seamlessly build, deploy, and manage forecasting models, without the need for an external ML infrastructure. This low-code, high-performance approach empowers organizations to make data-driven decisions, optimize inventory, financial planning, and resource allocation, as well as stay ahead in a competitive market landscape. Additionally, as we just saw, with the preceding visualization, users can integrate forecasting outputs into dashboards and reports.

Let us now proceed with the anomaly detection function.

Anomaly Detection

Snowflake's ML suite includes a powerful anomaly detection function that enables users to identify outliers in the time series data, without requiring deep machine learning expertise. Anomaly detection identifies data points that deviate from expected patterns. This function is critical for fraud prevention, equipment monitoring, and cybersecurity.

To create an anomaly detection model in Snowflake, you need specific permissions. The model is stored as a schema-level object, so your role must have the **`CREATE SNOWFLAKE.ML.ANOMALY_DETECTION`** privilege for the schema where you want to save the model. This ensures that only authorized users can develop and store anomaly detection models in designated areas of the database, maintaining security and organization within your Snowflake environment.

Key Features:

- Powered by Gradient Boosting Machine (GBM) algorithms
- Uses differencing transformation for non-stationary trend modeling

- Incorporates auto-regressive lags and rolling averages of historical data
- Automatically generates cyclic calendar variables from timestamp data
- Incorporates auto-regressive lags and rolling averages for trend prediction

Use Cases:

- **Financial Fraud Spotting**: Flag unusual transactions that might indicate fraudulent activity.
- **E-commerce Order Tracking**: Detect irregular shipping times or order volumes for operational insights.
- **Energy Consumption Analysis**: Spot unexpected spikes or dips in power usage across facilities.
- **Inventory Management**: Flag unusual stock levels or sales patterns for a specific product.
- **Abnormal Login Tracking**: Detect unusual authentication patterns to identify potential security threats.

Implementation

Dataset: **`LOGIN_ANOMALY.csv`**

The dataset contains artificially synthesized records related to user login activities, designed to demonstrate anomaly detection using Snowflake's ML functions. It includes four columns: **`User_ID`** (a unique identifier for each user), **`Login_Time`** (a timestamp indicating when the login occurred), **`Login_Count`** (the number of login attempts within a specific period), and **`Is_Anomaly`** (a binary indicator where 1 denotes an anomalous login event, and 0 represents normal activity). The dataset **`LOGIN_ANOMALY.csv`** can be loaded to the **`ANOMALY_DETECTION`** table before proceeding with the following steps.

Step 1: Let us query the table.

```
SELECT * FROM ANOMALY_DETECTION
```

USER_ID	LOGIN_TIME	LOGIN_COUNT
1413	2024-01-01 00:00:00.000	5
1979	2024-01-01 01:00:00.000	11
1724	2024-01-01 02:00:00.000	14
1171	2024-01-01 03:00:00.000	7
1287	2024-01-01 04:00:00.000	48
1434	2024-01-01 05:00:00.000	8

***Figure 3.9:** Preview the Anomaly Detection Table*

This dataset will be used to train and evaluate an anomaly detection model by identifying unusual login behaviors, such as excessive login attempts in a short time span which may indicate suspicious activity or potential security breaches.

Step 2: Create, train, and test datasets.

```
CREATE OR REPLACE TABLE TRAIN_DATA_ANOMALY AS
SELECT * FROM LOGIN_ANOMALY WHERE LOGIN_TIME <= '2024-01-19
07:00:00.000';
CREATE OR REPLACE TABLE TEST_DATA_ANOMALY AS
SELECT * FROM LOGIN_ANOMALY WHERE LOGIN_TIME > '2024-01-19
07:00:00.000';
```

The SQL statements create two separate tables, **TRAIN_DATA_ANOMALY** and **TEST_DATA_ANOMALY**, by splitting the original **LOGIN_ANOMALY** dataset based on the **LOGIN_TIME** timestamp. The **TRAIN_DATA_ANOMALY** table includes all 440 rows where login events occurred on or before January 19, 2024, at 07:00:00, while the **TEST_DATA_ANOMALY** table contains the remaining 60 rows with login times after this threshold. This split ensures that the training dataset consists of the past data to train an anomaly detection model, while the test dataset includes more recent login events to evaluate the model's performance in identifying anomalous behavior.

Step 3: Create the Anomaly Detection Model.

```
CREATE OR REPLACE SNOWFLAKE.ML.ANOMALY_DETECTION LOGIN_
ANOMALY_DETECTION(
    INPUT_DATA => SYSTEM$REFERENCE('TABLE', 'ANOMALY_TRAIN'),
    TIMESTAMP_COLNAME => 'LOGIN_TIME',
    TARGET_COLNAME => 'LOGIN_COUNT',
    LABEL_COLNAME => ''
);
```

The preceding statement defines and trains an anomaly detection model named **LOGIN_ANOMALY_DETECTION** using Snowflake's built-in **ML.ANOMALY_DETECTION** function. It takes **ANOMALY_TRAIN** as the input dataset, referencing it via **SYSTEM$REFERENCE** to specify that the data source is a table. The **TIMESTAMP_COLNAME** is set to **LOGIN_TIME**, indicating that the model will consider time-based patterns in the login activity. The **TARGET_COLNAME**, set to **LOGIN_COUNT**, specifies that the model will analyze login frequencies to detect anomalies. The **LABEL_COLNAME** is left empty, meaning that the model will operate in an unsupervised manner without predefined anomaly labels. This setup enables the model to identify unusual login behaviors based on historical patterns in the training data.

Step 4: Generate predictions, and store results in a table.

```
BEGIN
    -- This is the step that creates predictions.
    CALL LOGIN_ANOMALY_DETECTION!DETECT_ANOMALIES(
```

```
        INPUT_DATA => SYSTEM$REFERENCE('TABLE', 'ANOMALY_TEST'),
        TIMESTAMP_COLNAME =>'LOGIN_TIME',
        TARGET_COLNAME => 'LOGIN_COUNT',
        -- Here we set the prediction interval.
        CONFIG_OBJECT => {'prediction_interval': 0.95}
    );
    -- These steps store your predictions to a table.
    LET x := SQLID;
    CREATE OR REPLACE TABLE LOGIN_ANOMALY_DETECTION_RESULTS AS
SELECT * FROM TABLE(RESULT_SCAN(:x));
END;
```

The provided SQL block executes an anomaly detection process using the previously trained **LOGIN_ANOMALY_DETECTION** model, and stores the results in a table. The **CALL LOGIN_ANOMALY_DETECTION!DETECT_ANOMALIES** function is used to generate predictions on the **ANOMALY_TEST** dataset, where the **LOGIN_TIME** is a time-based feature, and the **LOGIN_COUNT** is the target variable being analyzed for anomalies. The **CONFIG_OBJECT** parameter sets a 95% prediction interval, meaning the model will flag data points that significantly deviate from the expected pattern.

The detected anomalies are temporarily stored, and the **RESULT_SCAN** function retrieves the prediction results which are then saved into a new table named **TBL_LOGIN_ANOMALY_DETECTION**. This table contains the model's output, including anomaly scores, allowing further analysis and visualization of unusual login behaviors.

Step 5: Verify the predicted results from the table.

```
SELECT TS, Y, IS_ANOMALY FROM LOGIN_ANOMALY_DETECTION_RESULTS;
```

TS	Y	IS_ANOMALY
2024-01-19 08:00:00.000	9	FALSE
2024-01-19 09:00:00.000	35	TRUE
2024-01-19 10:00:00.000	14	FALSE
2024-01-19 11:00:00.000	14	FALSE
2024-01-19 12:00:00.000	10	FALSE
2024-01-19 13:00:00.000	7	FALSE

Figure 3.10: *Preview Anomaly Detection Results*

In the preceding preview, we see that the row with a timestamp that includes 35 login attempts is detected as anomalous.

As we observed with this example, Snowflake's **ML.ANOMALY_DETECTION** function provides a powerful, scalable, and easy-to-use solution for detecting unusual patterns in time series and numerical data. By leveraging this, businesses can efficiently identify anomalies in the login activity, transaction patterns, network traffic, or any other operational data–leveraging simple SQL commands, without requiring extensive machine learning expertise. The function seamlessly integrates with the existing Snowflake data, allowing for quick model training, real-time anomaly detection, and automated result storage. With configurable parameters, such as prediction intervals, users can fine-tune the sensitivity of anomaly detection to align with their specific use case. The ability to detect outliers proactively helps organizations enhance security, prevent fraud, and optimize system performance.

We will now explore the Top Insights Function.

Top Insights Function

Snowflake's Top Insights ML function helps businesses understand their data better. It helps find the main reasons why metrics change over time, or differ between groups.

Top Insights is great for spotting what causes substantial changes in important business numbers. For example, it can show why the sales went up last month, or why some stores perform better than others. This helps companies make smarter choices based on facts, not guesses. The tool makes it easier to create useful reports and dashboards that explain the data clearly.

By using Top Insights, businesses can quickly focus on what matters most in their data. This saves time, and helps teams work on the right things to improve their results.

You must have the `CREATE SNOWFLAKE.ML.TOP_INSIGHTS` right for the schema where you are creating the model.

Key Features:

- Quickly pinpoints factors influencing changes in key metrics over time or across different segments.
- Works seamlessly with familiar SQL commands, making it accessible to users, without extensive machine learning expertise.
- Automatically identifies and monitors segments responsible for metric changes, saving time on manual analysis.
- Uses a decision tree model to break down datasets into segments with distinct behaviors related to the analyzed metric.

Use Cases:

- **Store Performance Comparison**: Find out why some stores sell more than others.
- **Website Traffic Analysis**: Understand what causes spikes or drops in the visitor numbers.

- **Subscription Renewal Patterns**: Uncover the main factors affecting whether customers renew their subscriptions.
- **Customer Purchase Behavior Analysis**: Identify the key factors driving changes in customer buying patterns to optimize sales strategies.

Implementation

Dataset: **PURCHASE_INSIGHTS.csv**

The dataset contains 300 records related to customer purchases, designed to demonstrate the Snowflake ML Top Insights function. It consists of six columns: **Customer_ID** (unique identifier for each customer), **Age** (customer's age), **Purchase_Amount** (total purchase value), **Category** (product category, such as Electronics, Clothing, Grocery and so on), **Discount_Availed** (binary flag indicating whether a discount was used), and **Membership_Status** (customer's membership type, for example, Regular or Premium). This dataset is well-suited for identifying the key purchase trends and influential factors affecting the spending behavior. The file **PURCHASE_INSIGHTS.csv** can be loaded to a new **PURCHASE_INSIGHTS** table, before proceeding with the following steps.

Step 1: Let us query the table.

```
SELECT * FROM PURCHASE_INSIGHTS;
```

CUSTOMER_ID	AGE	PURCHASE_AMOUNT	CATEGORY	DISCOUNT_AVAILED	MEMBERSHIP_STATUS
1	60	888.29	Electronics	FALSE	Premium
2	42	1004.12	Clothing	TRUE	Regular
3	37	977.85	Grocery	TRUE	Premium
4	36	934.54	Furniture	TRUE	Regular
5	40	938.41	Furniture	FALSE	Regular
6	41	740.76	Clothing	TRUE	Premium

Figure 3.11: *Preview the Purchase Insights Table*

Step 2: Create a Top Insights Model.

```
CREATE OR REPLACE SNOWFLAKE.ML.TOP_INSIGHTS my_insights_model();
```

The preceding statement initializes and creates a Top Insights model in Snowflake named **my_insights_model**. We will leverage Snowflake's **ML.TOP_INSIGHTS** function to identify the most significant factors influencing the **PURCHASE_AMOUNT** variable in a dataset.

Step 3: Let us create a function to get the key drivers for our dataset to see how the Purchases are impacted by the discounts availed.

```
CALL my_insights_model!get_drivers(
  INPUT_DATA => TABLE(PURCHASE_INSIGHTS),
  LABEL_COLNAME => 'DISCOUNT_AVAILED',
  METRIC_COLNAME => 'PURCHASE_AMOUNT'
);
```

The **CALL my_insights_model!get_drivers** statement executes the Top Insights model named **my_insights_model** to identify the key factors influencing customer purchasing behavior. It takes the **PURCHASE_INSIGHTS** table as input, analyzing how different variables affect the target outcome. The **LABEL_COLNAME** is set to **DISCOUNT_AVAILED**, indicating that the model will analyze how discounts impact purchases. The **METRIC_COLNAME** is set to **PURCHASE_AMOUNT**, meaning the model will determine which factors most significantly drive higher or lower purchase amounts. By running this command, Snowflake's **ML.TOP_INSIGHTS** function will uncover the most influential variables–such as age, product category, or membership status that impact the relationship between discounts and spending. These insights help businesses optimize pricing strategies, tailor promotional offers, and improve customer engagement.

Step 4: Create a table based on the results of the preceding function call.

```
CREATE OR REPLACE TABLE PURCHASE_INSIGHTS_RESULTS AS SELECT *
FROM TABLE (RESULT_SCAN(-1));
```

We store the results of the previously executed **ML.TOP_INSIGHTS** function into a new table called **PURCHASE_INSIGHTS_RESULTS**.

RESULT_SCAN(-1) retrieves the most recent query result, which in this case, contains the insights generated by **my_insights_model!get_drivers** function.

Step 5: Query the table to interpret the results.

```
SELECT * FROM PURCHASE_INSIGHTS_RESULTS;
```

CONTRIBUTOR	METRIC_CONTROL	METRIC_TEST	CONTRIBUTION	RELATIVE_CONTRIBUTION	GROWTH_RATE
["Overall"]	111049.55	92196.77	-18852.78	1	-0.1697690806
["not CATEGORY = Grocery"]	86805.64	63957.26	-22848.38	1.211936913	-0.2632130815
["AGE <= 52.5","not CATEGORY = Grocery"]	66537.11	45960.27	-20576.84	1.091448582	-0.309253588
["AGE <= 52.5","AGE > 28.5","not CATEGORY = Grocery"]	51888.74	31989.78	-19898.96	1.055492081	-0.3834928349
["AGE <= 34.5","AGE > 28.5","not CATEGORY = Grocery"]	18651.65	6281.08	-12370.57	0.6561668889	-0.6632426622
["AGE <= 34.5","AGE > 28.5","not CATEGORY = Electronics","not CATEGORY = Grocery"]	15157.72	3443.48	-11714.24	0.6213534556	-0.7728233534
["AGE <= 34.5","AGE > 28.5","not CATEGORY = Electronics","not CATEGORY = Grocery","MEN	11298.68	2261.09	-9037.59	0.4793770468	-0.799880163
["AGE <= 52.5","AGE > 42.5","not CATEGORY = Grocery"]	16437.34	8818.7	-7618.64	0.4041122848	-0.4634959184

Figure 3.12: *Preview the Purchase Insights Results*

The analysis of drivers influencing purchases involves several key metrics. The **CONTRIBUTION** metric provides a measure of the absolute impact of each driver on purchases, comparing the effect when a discount is availed to when it is not. This helps quantify the direct influence of each factor on the outcome. In contrast, the **RELATIVE_CONTRIBUTION** metric offers a relative perspective, calculating the percentage impact of each contributor compared to others. This allows for a clearer understanding of how each factor contributes proportionally. Additionally, the **GROWTH_RATE** metric assesses the percentage difference between the data points associated with the defined label (for example, discount availed) and those without it. This metric provides valuable insights into how the presence or absence of the label affects growth or change in the metric being analyzed.

The Top Insights results reveal the key factors influencing the purchase amounts based on whether a discount was availed or not. The first row (Overall Contribution) shows that when analyzing purchases, where a discount was used (True) versus not used (False), the total purchase amount decreased by $18,852.78, with a 16.98% decline in the growth rate. The second row highlights that the purchases, where the Grocery category was excluded, saw a $22,848.38 reduction in total spending, contributing 121.14% to the overall decline. This suggests that discounts have a significant impact on the grocery purchases, and when discounts were not applied to grocery items, the total purchase amount dropped sharply.

The Snowflake **`ML.TOP_INSIGHTS`** function provides a powerful way to automatically identify the key drivers behind changes in business metrics, helping organizations make data-driven decisions efficiently. By analyzing the structured data, it pinpoints the most influential factors impacting sales, customer behavior, and operational trends. Thus, this function is particularly valuable for understanding the effects of discounts, customer demographics, product categories, and other business attributes on the key outcomes.

A Note on Snowflake AI and ML Studio

In this chapter, we explored examples that leverage SQL commands and script-based model creation, as well as prediction. By scripting these processes, we gained a deeper understanding of how each function operates, as it allowed us to break down the logic, and observe the step-by-step execution. The intent was to give a good understanding of the workings of each function.

Snowflake AI and ML Studio offer an intuitive no-code interface that simplifies the development and deployment of machine learning models within Snowflake. This platform empowers users to leverage advanced AI capabilities, without extensive coding knowledge, making it accessible to a broader range of data teams.

Therefore, by utilizing Snowflake AI and ML Studio, users can easily build, test, and deploy models for tasks, such as classification, anomaly detection, and forecasting. This no-code approach streamlines the process of creating and evaluating models, allowing organizations to quickly integrate AI into their data workflows, and accelerate the transition from development to production.

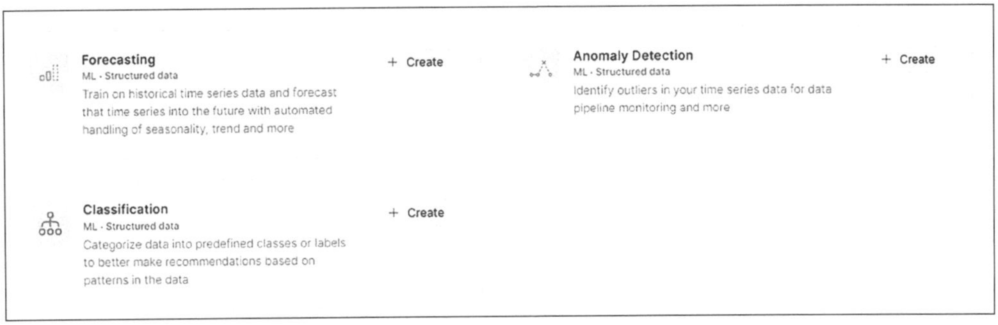

Figure 3.13: *ML Functions in AI and ML Studio*

As Snowflake continues to enhance its AI and ML offerings, the AI and ML Studio will play a crucial role in democratizing access to advanced AI tools, enabling more teams to harness the power of machine learning, and drive innovations across various industries.

Conclusion

In this chapter, we explored the robust suite of machine learning functions offered by Snowflake, including classification, forecasting, anomaly detection, and top insights. These tools empower data analysts and scientists to unlock deeper insights from their data, driving informed decision-making across various business domains.

Classification enables the categorization of data into distinct classes, facilitating applications, such as customer churn prediction and fraud detection. By leveraging patterns in training data, businesses can better understand their customer base and anticipate potential risks. **Forecasting** utilizes the historical data to predict future trends, allowing organizations to prepare for the upcoming challenges and opportunities. This capability is particularly valuable in time-series analysis where understanding future patterns can significantly impact strategic planning. **Anomaly Detection** identifies outliers in data which is crucial for detecting unusual patterns that may indicate fraud or system failures. Thus, by integrating this function into data pipelines, companies can proactively address potential issues before they escalate. **Top Insights** provide key driver analysis, helping organizations understand the factors driving changes in metrics over time. This function simplifies the process of identifying and monitoring critical segments within datasets, enhancing business intelligence workflows.

Together, these ML functions offer a comprehensive toolkit for data-driven decision-making. By integrating these capabilities into business operations, organizations can enhance their predictive power, improve operational efficiency, and drive innovation in a rapidly evolving data landscape. As machine learning continues to evolve, leveraging these functions will become increasingly important for staying competitive, and unlocking new opportunities in this digital age.

In the upcoming chapter, we will delve into the concepts and applications of Generative AI, exploring its potential to generate new data, enhance creativity, and automate complex tasks. We will also explore Retrieval Augmented Generation (RAG), Prompt Engineering, and the role of vector search in retrieving relevant information. This will set the stage for understanding more advanced Cortex AI capabilities, particularly those related to Large Language Models (LLMs).

CHAPTER 4
Introduction to LLMs, Prompt Engineering, and RAG

Introduction

In this chapter, we lay the groundwork for understanding Snowflake Cortex AI by introducing four pivotal technologies: Large Language Models, Retrieval-Augmented Generation, Prompt Engineering, and Vector Search. Before diving into Snowflake Cortex AI, it is essential to understand the core technologies driving its capabilities. This chapter provides a concise overview of Large Language Models (LLMs), the powerful AI engines behind Cortex's generative features. We will also explore Retrieval Augmented Generation (RAG), a technique that enhances LLMs by grounding them in your specific data, ensuring more accurate and contextually relevant responses. We will then touch upon Prompt Engineering, the art of crafting effective instructions to guide LLMs, and the crucial role of Vector Search in efficiently retrieving relevant information for RAG. This introduction will equip you with the foundational knowledge needed to fully leverage Snowflake Cortex AI's potential, without delving into the exhaustive technical details.

This chapter aims to provide a basic practical understanding of these core concepts, empowering you to leverage LLMs effectively within the Snowflake ecosystem. Thus, by the end of this chapter, you will be well-equipped with the foundational knowledge necessary to truly grasp the power and potential of Snowflake Cortex. However, this chapter will not delve into the architecture or internal mechanics of Large Language Models (LLMs) and Retrieval-Augmented Generation (RAG). Instead, it will focus on the foundational concepts necessary to appreciate their functionalities. This foundational understanding will provide the context as we explore Snowflake Cortex's generative AI capabilities with greater depth in the upcoming chapters.

Structure

In this chapter, we will cover the following topics:

- Setting the Context
- Understanding Large Language Models
- Introduction to Retrieval Augment Generation
- Prompt Engineering
- The Role of Vector Search and Embeddings in AI-Powered Retrieval
- Putting it All together
- Advanced LLM Capabilities: Natively Powered by Snowflake Cortex

Setting the Context

Imagine you are tasked with analyzing a decade's worth of customer support tickets within your data warehouse. The sheer volume is overwhelming, and conventional methods appear insufficient for rapid analysis. You need to extract the key insights, identify recurring issues, and even predict future support needs. This is where the promise of AI, specifically Large Language Models (LLMs) integrated into platforms like Snowflake Cortex, becomes incredibly compelling. But to wield this power effectively, we must first understand its foundations. We often hear about "*AI revolutionizing data analysis*," but what does that truly mean in a practical sense? It is not about replacing analysts but augmenting their capabilities. LLMs, when properly harnessed, can sift through mountains of data, and identify patterns that would not directly be obvious to human eyes, and even generate human-like summaries and reports. Yet, these models are not magical black boxes. They operate based on principles that, while complex, can be understood and mastered.

The journey begins with recognizing the limitations of traditional data analysis. Consider another scenario - you want to understand the sentiment behind customer reviews for a new product. A simple SQL query cannot tell you if a review is positive, negative, or neutral. LLMs, on the other hand, can analyze the text, identify emotional cues, and provide a comprehensive sentiment analysis. This allows you to gain deeper insights into customer perception and make data-driven decisions. However, simply deploying an LLM is not enough. We need to understand how to interact with it, and how to guidc it towards the desired outcome. This is where prompt engineering comes into play. Think of it as learning to communicate with a highly intelligent, but sometimes, a literal assistant. A well-crafted prompt can make the difference between a vague, generic response and a precise, actionable insight.

Furthermore, LLMs, by default, rely on their pre-trained knowledge which might be outdated or incomplete. This is where Retrieval-Augmented Generation (RAG) becomes crucial. RAG allows us to ground the LLM's responses in our specific data, ensuring accuracy and relevance. Imagine asking the LLM to summarize the latest financial reports stored in your Snowflake tables. Without RAG, the model might provide a generic summary based on outdated data or public data. With RAG, it can access the latest reports, and generate a summary that is both accurate and up to date.

Understanding how LLMs process information, how prompts guide their output, and how RAG ensures accuracy by grounding responses in your specific data is not just academic. It is the key to unlocking the full potential of Cortex's AI functions and applications, allowing you to build sophisticated, data-driven solutions that directly address your unique business needs within the Snowflake environment.

Understanding Large Language Models

Let us assume that a vast library exists, not filled with physical books, but with every word, sentence, and paragraph ever written. This is the scale of data that LLMs are trained on. They learn by observing patterns in this massive corpus, predicting the next word in a sequence. This process, repeated billions of times, allows them to build a complex internal representation of language.

Think of it like learning a new language through immersion. You are not explicitly taught grammar rules, but you gradually absorb them through exposure. LLMs operate similarly, learning the rules of grammar, the relationships between words, and even the nuances of style through sheer exposure to the text. This training enables LLMs to perform a wide range of tasks, such as summarizing long documents, translating languages, creating content, and even engaging in conversations that feel natural and coherent.

One of the most remarkable aspects of LLMs is their ability to generate coherent and contextually relevant text. This is achieved through a process called attention which allows the model to focus on the most relevant parts of the input sequence. Imagine reading a sentence, and focusing on the key words that convey the main idea. LLMs operate similarly, assigning weights to different words and phrases to determine their importance.

This ability to understand the context is crucial for tasks, such as text summarization and question answering. For example, when summarizing a long document, LLM can identify the key points, and generate a concise summary that captures the essence of the original text.

However, it is necessary to understand that while LLMs are excellent at mimicking language patterns, their knowledge is derived from the data, they have been trained on. To illustrate this, consider a scenario where you ask an LLM to explain a complex scientific concept. The model might generate a well-written explanation, but it might also contain inaccuracies or oversimplifications. This is because the model's knowledge is limited to the data, it has been trained on. It does not have the ability to reason or critically evaluate information.

Furthermore, LLMs can be susceptible to biases present in their training data. If the data contains stereotypes or prejudices, the model might inadvertently perpetuate them. This highlights the importance of responsible AI development, and the need for ongoing research into bias mitigation.

Despite these limitations, LLMs are incredibly powerful tools, and are rapidly enabling multiple industries. They can generate creative content, translate languages, and even answer questions with surprising fluency. The key is to understand their strengths and weaknesses, and use them appropriately.

In conclusion, LLMs are sophisticated pattern recognition machines that have the potential to revolutionize how we interact with information. However, it is essential to remember that they are tools, and like any tool, they must be used responsibly and effectively.

Key Features of LLMs

- **Scalability**: LLMs are capable of handling large volumes of data, making them suitable for complex tasks.
- **Adaptability**: They can be fine-tuned for specific tasks or domains, enhancing their performance in targeted applications.
- **Creativity**: LLMs can generate novel text based on learned patterns which are useful for creative writing or generating innovative ideas.
- **Efficiency**: Despite their complexity, LLMs are remarkably efficient. They can generate text quickly, making them indispensable for applications where speed is essential, such as real-time content creation or rapid response systems.
- **Contextual Understanding**: LLMs have a remarkable ability to comprehend context and intent, allowing them to produce text that is not only coherent but also relevant to the topic or prompt provided. This understanding of the context is crucial for ensuring that the generated text makes sense and aligns with the intended meaning.
- **Few-shot and Zero-shot Learning**: Without needing extensive retraining, LLMs can perform new tasks based on one example (one-shot learning), minimal examples (few-shot learning) or even without prior exposure (zero-shot learning), making them highly adaptable.
- **Multimodal Capabilities**: Some advanced LLMs can process and generate not only text but also images, audio, and code, enabling broader applications across different domains.
- **Customization and Fine-tuning**: They can be tailored to specific use cases

or industries by fine-tuning them with domain-specific data, improving their accuracy and relevance for specialized applications.

Architecture of LLMs: A Simplified Explanation of the Key Terms

Large Language Models (LLMs) are built using deep learning techniques, specifically neural networks, to process and generate human-like text. Their architecture is based on Transformer models which allow them to handle vast amounts of text data efficiently. Here is a breakdown of the key components of their architecture in simple terms:

- **Tokenization – Breaking Down the Text:** Before processing, LLMs break the text into smaller units called **tokens**. These could be words, sub-words, or even individual characters. For example, "*language model*" might be split into ["`language`", "`model`"]. Tokenization helps the model understand and process text systematically.
- **Embedding Layer – Converting Text into Numbers:** Since computers do not understand words, LLMs convert the tokens into numerical representations (embeddings). These embeddings further capture the meaning and relationships between words. Words with similar meanings have embeddings that are mathematically close to each other.
- **Transformer Layers – The Core of LLMs:** At the heart of an LLM are multiple Transformer Layers which are responsible for understanding and generating the text. These layers use two key mechanisms:
    - **Self-Attention Mechanism:** This allows the model to focus on important words in a sentence, while ignoring the irrelevant ones. For example, in the sentence, "*The bank near the river is beautiful*," the model understands that "*bank*" refers to a riverbank, rather than a financial institution based on the surrounding words.
    - **Feedforward Neural Networks:** These refine the model's understanding by passing information through layers of artificial neurons, improving predictions.
- **Positional Encoding – Understanding the Word Order:** Unlike humans, LLMs do not automatically recognize the word order. Positional encoding helps the model understand sequences of words, ensuring that "*The cat chased the mouse*" is different from "*The mouse chased the cat*."
- **Training – Learning from the Data:** LLMs learn from massive amounts of text data using a process called pre-training. They predict the missing words in sentences, and improve their understanding through millions of iterations.

After this, they may undergo fine-tuning, where they are further trained on specific tasks such as customer support, medical text, or coding.

- **Output Layer – Generating Responses:** Once trained, the model generates the text by predicting the next word in a sequence, based on probabilities. For example, given the phrase "*Artificial Intelligence is...*," the model might predict words like "*transformative*" or "*advancing rapidly*" based on what it has learned.
- **Memory and Context Handling:** To make conversations more coherent, LLMs maintain context memory, allowing them to generate responses that align with previous interactions. This is why, they can answer follow-up questions or summarize long conversations effectively.
- **Scaling – More Layers, More Power:** Modern LLMs have billions or even trillions of parameters (adjustable settings that help make decisions). More parameters mean better performance, but require powerful hardware and optimization techniques to ensure efficiency.

Bringing everything together, in simple terms, the architecture works as follows:

1. Breaks down text into tokens.
2. Converts words into numbers using embeddings.
3. Processes information through transformer layers with attention mechanisms.
4. Understands relationships between words and maintains the context.
5. Generates text by predicting the most likely next word/response.

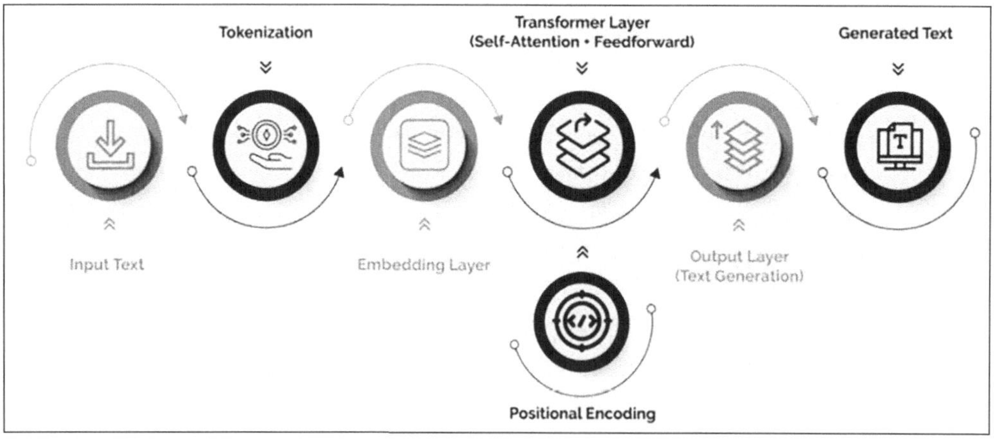

***Figure* 4.1:** *Simple LLM Architecture*

This structured approach allows LLMs to handle diverse language tasks, from answering questions to drafting articles, summarizing content, and engaging in human-like conversations.

There are also LLMs that use a Mixture of Expert(s) architecture or a Decode-only Transformer architecture.

The Mixture of Experts (MoE) architecture is designed to improve efficiency in large neural networks by dividing tasks among multiple specialized models, called experts. Instead of using the entire model for every input, a gating mechanism selects only a few experts to process each piece of data. This way, the model utilizes only a fraction of its total parameters at any given time, making it more computationally efficient, while maintaining high performance. MoE is particularly useful in large-scale language models like Gemini 1.5, as it allows them to scale effectively, while keeping inference costs lower compared to the fully dense models.

A decoder-only transformer architecture is a type of neural network used in large language models where the model focuses only on generating text, rather than both understanding and generating (as in encoder-decoder models). It processes an input of one token at a time, predicting the next word based on the context, it has seen so far. The self-attention mechanism helps it to understand relationships between words, ensuring coherent and context-aware text generation. This design makes it highly effective for tasks such as text completion, chatbots, and content creation.

The following is a tabular representation of some of the leading LLMs:

LLM Name	**Developer**	**Key Features**
DeepSeek	DeepSeek	• Open-source • Efficient MoE system • Robust performance in coding and problem-solving
GPT-4o	OpenAI	• Multimodal • Real-time conversations • Advanced reasoning capabilities • Supports over 50 languages
Llama	Meta	• Open-source • Multiple sizes available • Instruction fine-tuned versions available
Mistral	Mistral AI	• Strong reasoning and knowledge skills • Multilingual understanding • Advanced coding capabilities • Offers various specialized models

Gemini	Google DeepMind	• Multimodal • Native tool use (Google Search, Maps) • Agentic AI capabilities • Integrated into Google products
Claude	Anthropic	• Advanced reasoning and problem-solving • Vision analysis capabilities • Code generation across languages • Constitutional AI for ethical outputs • "Extended thinking" mode for complex problem-solving
Snowflake Arctic	Snowflake	• Dense-MoE Hybrid Transformer architecture • Open-source (Apache 2.0 license) • Excels at enterprise tasks (SQL, coding, instruction following) • Efficient training and inference

***Table 4.1**: Representation of Leading LLMs*

Applications of LLMs

Large Language Models are transforming various fields by enabling intelligent automation, natural language understanding, and content generation. They excel at tasks such as answering questions, summarizing information, translating languages, and generating human-like text. These LLMs are widely used in chatbots, content creation, coding assistance, and much more.

To name a few tasks:

- **Text Generation**: Drafting articles, reports, stories, and creative content.
- **Chatbots and Virtual Assistants**: Automating customer support, and answering FAQs.
- **Code Generation and Debugging**: Helping developers write and troubleshoot code.
- **Language Translation**: Converting text between languages in real-time.
- **Summarization**: Condensing long documents into concise summaries.
- **Sentiment Analysis**: Analyzing customer reviews, feedback, and social media.
- **Personalized Recommendations**: Suggesting content, books, or products.

There are many practical applications of the above-mentioned use cases of LLMs across industries. In healthcare, LLMs assist with automating medical documentation by summarizing patient records, and generating clinical notes. They also power patient-facing chatbots that provide general health advice, and answer frequently asked questions. Additionally, LLMs help streamline medical coding by assisting in ICD codes classification for billing, and insurance purposes. In the finance and banking sector, LLMs automate financial report generation, analyze customer complaints to detect fraud patterns, and summarize complex regulatory compliance documents to improve adherence to legal requirements. The retail and e-commerce industry leverages LLMs to create engaging product descriptions, personalize marketing content, translate campaign advertisements, and provide virtual shopping assistants that guide customers with queries about products and services. The technology sector benefits from LLMs in software development by generating and debugging codes, automating technical documentation, and providing AI-powered IT support chatbots to troubleshoot software and hardware issues efficiently.

Thus, Large Language Models (LLMs) have revolutionized the way, we interact with our text, enabling powerful applications across industries. However, their knowledge is inherently limited to what they were trained on–they do not have real-time awareness or access to the updated, external sources. This limitation raises a critical question: How do we make LLMs more dependable, dynamic, and factually accurate?

This is where Retrieval-Augmented Generation (RAG) comes in. By integrating LLMs with real-time retrieval mechanisms, RAG enhances their ability to fetch, verify, and generate knowledge-based responses, rather than relying solely on the pre-trained data.

With RAG, LLMs evolve beyond static predictions into intelligent systems capable of accessing the latest information, improving accuracy, and reducing hallucinations.

In the next section, we will explore how RAG works, its architecture, and how it transforms LLMs into powerful, knowledge-aware AI assistants–bridging the gap between generative AI and real-world knowledge.

Introduction to Retrieval Augmented Generation

As we saw, LLMs excel at generating human-like text based on patterns, they have learned from vast datasets.

However, they have a few limitations:

- **Knowledge Cutoff**: LLMs may not be aware of the latest data updates after their last training cycle.
- **Hallucinations**: Without access to accurate, real-time data, LLMs may fabricate or misinterpret information.

- **Lack of Domain-Specific Context**: Many enterprises use cases that require insights from private datasets not included in the LLM's training corpus.

RAG addresses these limitations by retrieving relevant information from an external knowledge base, before passing it to the generation model. This enables AI to generate more contextually relevant, accurate, and up-to-date responses.

The RAG Process in Brief

- **Query Processing:** The user submits a query to the system, asking for information that may not be explicitly stored within the LLM's knowledge.
- **Retrieval Phase:** Instead of relying solely on its pre-trained knowledge, the model first retrieves relevant documents or structured data from an external database, vector store, or knowledge graph (for example, Snowflake tables, indexed documents, semantic search repositories, and so on).

  Vector search enterprises embed their proprietary data into vector databases, and retrieve contextually similar documents based on user queries.
- **Augmentation and Contextualization:** The retrieved data is formatted and merged with the user's query, before being fed into the generative AI model.

  This step ensures that LLM grounds its response in factual, real-time knowledge, reducing hallucinations and increasing domain-specific accuracy.
- **Generation and Retrieval:** With the enhanced context, LLM generates a response that is not only linguistically fluent, but also factually relevant to the query.

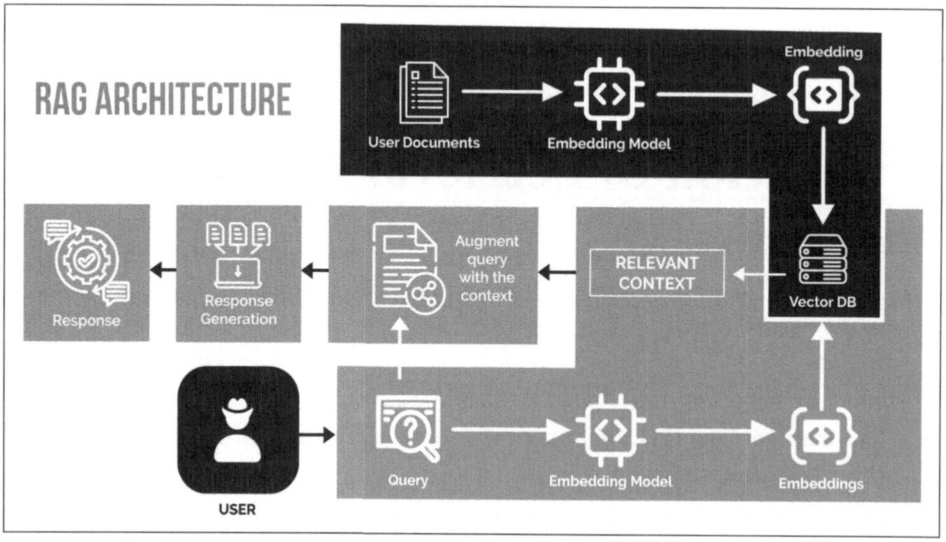

Figure 4.2: RAG Architecture

Key Benefits of Using RAG

- **Eliminates Hallucinations:** By grounding responses in retrieved enterprise data, the system avoids generating inaccurate or misleading information.
- **Real-Time Knowledge Access:** Instead of being constrained by an LLM's training cut off, RAG allows models to fetch live, updated data from internal and external sources.
- **Improves AI Explainability:** Since responses are backed by retrieved documents, businesses can trace AI-generated insights to their source data, enhancing transparency and compliance.
- **Domain-Specific Intelligence:** Enterprises can augment generic AI models with industry-specific datasets, enabling AI to understand the business context, policies, and proprietary data properly.
- **Snowflake Cortex Perspective:** By leveraging Snowflake's data warehouse, vector search, and Cortex AI capabilities, organizations can build scalable, secure, and high-performance RAG workflows, without moving the data outside Snowflake.

RAG in Action: Transforming Industries through Smart Information Retrieval

Hence, RAG is revolutionizing how organizations access and utilize their knowledge bases.

Here are some compelling examples of how RAG is being deployed across domains, in real-world settings, performing the role of a virtual assistant:

- **Customer Support:** A chatbot retrieves real-time support ticket logs, before generating an answer to a customer inquiry.
- **Healthcare Assistant:** A medical AI assistant retrieves patient history and clinical guidelines, before suggesting treatment options.
- **Legal Assistant for Contract Review:** A legal assistant retrieves clauses from past contracts, before summarizing or suggesting legal terms.
- **Technical Documentation Assistant:** When a developer asks how to implement a specific feature, the system retrieves code examples, documentation, and internal best practices.
- **E-Commerce Customer Service Optimization:** The system can instantly pull up product-specific return policies, based on the customer's purchase history, shipping method, and applicable promotions
- **Financial Compliance:** When reviewing new transactions, the system can

retrieve the latest regulations, precedent cases, and internal policies to ensure compliance.

- **Troubleshooting in Manufacturing:** When a machine shows error codes, the RAG system can retrieve maintenance manuals, past repair records, and expert solutions for similar problems.

To sum up, RAG represents a paradigm shift in enterprise AI by allowing contextually aware, knowledge-driven generation of responses. With Snowflake Cortex AI, businesses can harness RAG workflows natively within their data warehouse, making AI-powered insights more accurate, explainable, and actionable. As these systems continue to evolve, their effectiveness increasingly depends on the quality of interaction between humans and AI.

This brings us to our next critical topic- prompt engineering. While RAG provides the architecture for knowledge retrieval, prompt engineering is the practice of crafting precise and strategic inputs to guide AI systems toward generating the most accurate and relevant responses. The way we frame questions, provide context, and structure our interactions dramatically impacts the quality of AI-generated outputs.

Prompt Engineering

Prompt engineering is the art and science of crafting effective instructions for AI systems to produce the desired outputs. It is like learning how to communicate with a brilliant, but extremely literal assistant who needs precise directions to deliver exactly what you want.

At its core, prompt engineering involves designing text inputs (prompts) that guide AI models toward generating specific, accurate, and useful responses. The quality of the prompt directly influences the quality of the AI's output.

Think of it as learning a new language—not of words, but of intentions. When you master prompt engineering, you are developing a skillset for directing AI behavior through carefully constructed text instructions.

An effective prompt engineering requires:

- Understanding the capabilities and limitations of the AI model, you are working with
- Providing clear context and background information
- Being specific about the desired formats, tone, and style
- Including relevant examples, when helpful
- Breaking complex tasks into manageable steps

The difference between a basic prompt and a well-engineered one can be dramatic.

Consider these two approaches:

Basic Prompt: "*Help with unhappy customer.*"

A Well-Engineered Prompt: "*Generate a response to a customer who has complained about slow delivery of their premium subscription package. Express genuine empathy, acknowledge the service failure, explain our standard 2-day delivery policy, offer a specific compensation (one-month free subscription), and close with an assurance of how we will prevent similar issues. Keep the tone professional, but warn and limit the response to 150 words.*"

The impact of prompt engineering extends beyond just getting better answers. It allows for more consistent results, reduces the need for multiple attempts, and enables non-technical users to harness AI capabilities effectively. Prompt engineering continues to develop as a crucial interface between human intention and machine capability–a bridge connecting what we want with what AI can deliver.

In Snowflake's Cortex AI ecosystem, prompt engineering serves as the critical interface that connects all components. It directs Large Language Models (LLMs) to generate appropriate responses, while guiding Retrieval-Augmented Generation (RAG) systems on what information to fetch from your databases. A well-engineered prompt can instruct the system to retrieve specific financial data, analyze seasonal patterns, and present conclusions in an executive-friendly format–all in a single instruction. As these technologies continue to evolve together, mastering prompt engineering becomes the key that unlocks their combined potential, transforming the raw data capabilities into precisely tailored business intelligence solutions.

Crafting Effective Prompts: Best Practices

Writing effective prompts is crucial for maximizing the potential of Large Language Models. Here are some strategies to craft good prompts:

- **Define Your Objective Clearly**: Understand what you want to achieve with your prompt. Whether it is generating information, solving a problem, or creating content, clarity is the key.
- **Use Clear and Concise Language**: Avoid ambiguity by using a precise language. This helps the AI to understand your request accurately, and generate relevant outputs. Keep your prompts simple, yet informative to ensure that the AI can process them efficiently.
- **Provide Context and Examples**: Supply relevant examples or background information to help the AI grasp the scenario. This is particularly useful for complex tasks, or when using RAG to provide additional context.

When crafting prompts, it is helpful to understand different prompting techniques:

- **Zero-Shot Prompting:**
  - No examples are provided. The AI relies on its general knowledge to respond.
  - **Example**: Asking a model to classify the text without examples.
- **One-Shot Prompting:**
  - A single example is given to guide the AI's response.
  - **Example**: Providing one positive movie review, and asking the model to classify another.
- **Few-Shot Prompting:**
  - A small number of examples (2-5) are used to help the AI adapt to specific tasks or styles.
  - **Example**: Giving two product descriptions with a certain tone, and asking the model to generate another in the same style.

By understanding these prompting techniques, you can tailor your prompts to best suit the task at hand, and maximize the performance of the AI models.

By combining the following strategies, you can create prompts that effectively guide the AI tools to produce high-quality, relevant outputs.

- **Consider Audience and Tone**: Tailor your prompt based on who will interact with, or benefit from the AI's response. This ensures that the output resonates with your target audience. Specify the tone, you want to convey, whether it is formal, informal, educational, or entertaining. This is particularly useful in customer support/promotional campaigns.
- **Experiment and Iterate**: Do not hesitate to refine your prompts based on the responses, you receive. Iteration is vital for finding the most effective wording. Use feedback from the AI outputs to improve the future prompts.
- **Use Natural Language**: Write prompts in a natural, conversational style to help the AI tools better understand your requests. Mimic everyday speech to ensure clarity and relevance.
- **Specify Output Format**: Indicate how you want the output to be presented, whether it is a report, dialogue, or code.

We have so far explored the fundamentals of Large Language Models (LLMs), Retrieval Augmented Generation (RAG), and the art of Prompt Engineering. By crafting effective prompts and grounding LLMs in the relevant data through RAG, we can significantly enhance their capabilities. To truly unlock the power of AI-powered retrieval, and provide the LLMs with the access to a comprehensive and up-to-date information landscape, we need a mechanism that goes beyond simple keyword matching and static knowledge. This is where Vector Search and Embeddings become essential. In the following topic, we will delve into how these technologies enable LLMs to understand and retrieve information based on the meaning and context, transforming the way we interact with the data.

The Role of Vector Search and Embeddings in AI-Powered Retrieval

At the heart of modern AI retrieval systems, lies a powerful concept: Transforming words and concepts into numbers. This is the essence of vector search and embeddings, the invisible yet crucial technology that makes intelligent information retrieval possible.

Embeddings are numerical representations that capture the essence and meaning of the original information. The brilliance of this approach is that similar concepts end up with similar number patterns, even if they use completely different words.

Imagine trying to find information about "*vehicle maintenance*" in a massive database. A traditional keyword search might miss relevant documents about "*car repair*" or "*automobile servicing*." Vector search, however, understands these concepts are related because their embeddings and their numerical fingerprints are similar in the mathematical space they occupy.

This mathematical representation creates a multi-dimensional space where every piece of information has a specific location. When you ask a question, your query gets converted into the same type of numerical vector. The system then simply looks for the closest neighbors in this space–the vectors most like your query vector–and retrieves the associated information.

In Snowflake's Cortex AI, vector search transforms how you interact with your data. Rather than being limited to exact matches or complex SQL queries, you can search by their meaning and concept. A question about "*quarterly revenue trends*" will find relevant financial reports, even if they never use those exact words, because the underlying concepts share similar vector representations.

The power of vector search extends beyond just finding information. It enables semantic clustering of similar documents, identifies conceptual outliers in datasets, and powers recommendation systems by finding the content with similar characteristics.

One of the standout features of Snowflake Cortex is its pre-built ML and LLM functions which allow users to run AI-powered analytics with minimal effort. These built-in functions cover a wide range of use cases, from predictive modeling to Natural Language Processing (NLP), eliminating the need for extensive data science expertise or external machine learning platforms. We will be exploring these functions in detail in the subsequent chapters.

Understanding the Embedding and Vector Search Process

Figure 4.3 reveals the sophisticated journey of information through an AI-powered retrieval system, highlighting how the raw data transforms into meaningful responses through three distinct phases.

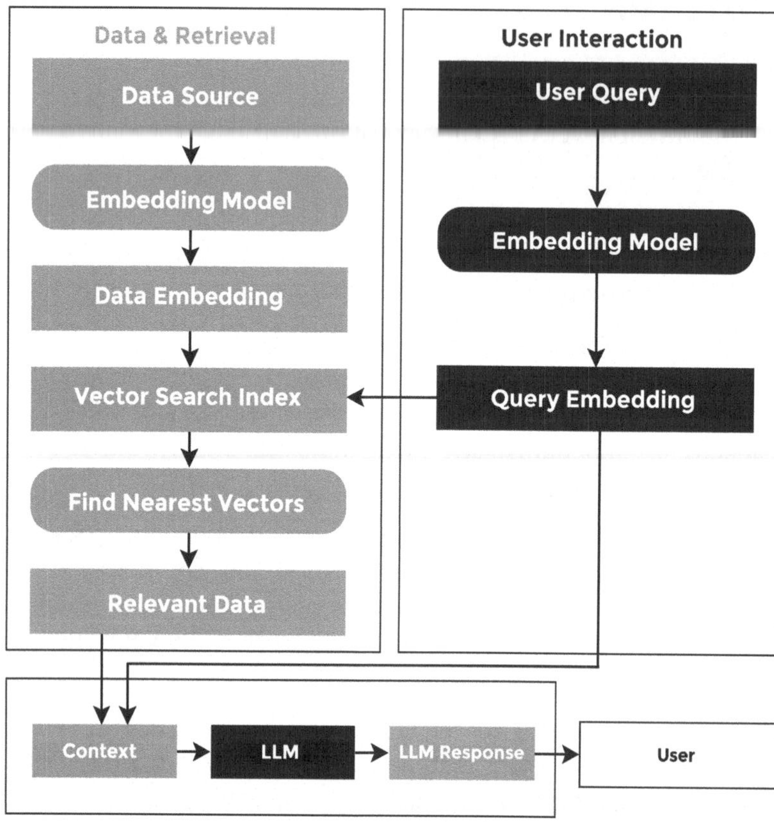

Figure 4.3: *The Role of Word Embeddings and Vector Search in LLM Cycle*

The system initially performs a crucial translation process. Imagine a company's financial documents containing phrases such as "*quarterly revenue growth*" and "*profit margins exceeded expectations.*" The embedding model analyzes these documents, and converts them into numerical vectors—long lists of numbers like [0.2, -0.5, 0.8...] that mathematically represent the meaning of the content. Simultaneously, when a user asks, "*How did our sales perform last quarter?*", their query undergoes the same conversion process through the identical embedding model, ensuring that both the stored information and the question exist within the same mathematical space.

Vector Search functions as a sophisticated matchmaking system. When the query vector enters the search index–a specialized database optimized for vector operations, the system calculates similarity scores between the query vector and millions of document vectors. This is not a simple keyword matching; it is finding mathematical relationships in a multi-dimensional space. For example, even though the user never mentioned "*revenue*" in their question about "*sales*," the system recognizes that these concepts have similar vector representations, and identifies relevant financial reports with high similarity scores. The system then retrieves the original corresponding data which are the actual financial documents, or their relevant sections.

The final portion at the bottom of the image where LLM generation takes place, shows how the retrieved information becomes useful answers. The language model receives both the original query and the retrieved context from the vector search. Rather than generating an answer based solely on its pre-trained knowledge, it specifically focuses on the retrieved information. For instance, instead of providing generic information about sales strategies, it might respond: "*Last quarter's sales increased 12% year-over-year, with particularly strong performance in our enterprise division, as detailed in the Q3 financial report.*" This response incorporates the specific information retrieved through vector search, while maintaining a natural conversational flow.

This entire process–from converting information into mathematical representations to finding semantic relationships and generating contextual responses–happens in seconds, creating the impression of an AI system that understands both your business data, and your questions about it.

Key Advantages of Vector Search and Embeddings

- **Semantic Understanding**: Captures the meaning behind words, not just the words themselves, enabling concept-based searching, instead of exact keyword matching.
- **Scalability**: Optimized algorithms can search billions of vectors in milliseconds, making it possible to search enormous datasets efficiently.
- **Multimodal Potential**: Can represent and search across diverse types of data (text, images, audio) in a unified way.
- **Fuzzy Matching**: Naturally handles typos, synonyms, and paraphrasing, without complex rule systems.
- **Contextual Relevance**: Understands queries in context, rather than as isolated terms, delivering more relevant results.
- **Continuous Improvement**: Vector spaces can evolve as language models to improve and enhance the search quality, without rebuilding indexes.

Putting it All Together

Now, let us try to understand all the concepts from the chapter in terms of a real use case. *ZenTime*, our hypothetical smartwatch manufacturer, wanted to improve customer service and response times to the user queries. It gathered all its user manuals, FAQs, troubleshooting guides, and marketing materials. These documents were processed by an embedding model, creating word embeddings (vectors) that capture the semantic meaning of each piece of information.

They implemented an integrated AI system combining LLMs, RAG, prompt engineering, embeddings, and vector search to revolutionize their customer support experience.

Let us consider an example to understand this process flow:

When a customer submits the query "*My ZenTime Ultra isn't tracking my sleep accurately after the recent 4.2 update*," the system processes this through several integrated steps:

1. **Word Embeddings and Vector Search**: The customer query is converted into a numerical vector representation. This vector is compared against ZenTime's vast knowledge base of product manuals, troubleshooting guides, and support tickets. The system quickly identifies similar issues reported by other users, technical notes about sleep tracking algorithms in the recent update, and relevant sections of the ZenTime Ultra user manual.

2. **RAG System**: The most relevant documents are retrieved based on vector similarity—not just keyword matches. This includes specific information about a known calibration issue with the Ultra model's sleep sensors after the v4.2 firmware update that would not be found through simple keyword searching.

3. **Prompt Engineering**: The ZenTime Prompt engineers had created a carefully designed prompt template that incorporates multiple elements. It begins by stating "*You are a ZenTime support specialist helping a customer with the following issue*" {followed by the customer's exact query}.

   The system modifies and enriches the user's input to make it clearer and more informative for the LLM, by saying "*Based on our product information, this relates to a ZenTime Ultra running firmware v4.2 with sleep tracking features.*" It would then provide key and relevant excerpts from the retrieved documents. The prompt concludes with specific instructions: "*Please provide a helpful response that addresses the sleep tracking issue, including the necessary calibration steps, mention the upcoming v4.2 patch, and maintain a supportive tone throughout.*"

4. **LLM Generation**: The language model receives this enhanced prompt, and generates a comprehensive response that includes acknowledgment of the

specific issue, step-by-step instructions to recalibrate the sleep sensors, an explanation of how the update affected the tracking algorithm, and a note about an upcoming patch.

The final response was:

"*ZenTime Ultra's 4.2 update introduced a new sleep detection algorithm, which may require recalibration. If your deep sleep tracking appears inaccurate, ensure your watch is worn snugly and that sleep detection is enabled in the ZenTime app. Please wait for the patch release shortly. A factory reset and firmware reinstallation may also help. Here's how to recalibrate sleep tracking: [link].*"

This was a well-constructed response that provides the customer with all the necessary information, without any additional intervention. This integrated approach would deliver several key benefits for ZenTime:

- Customers would receive accurate and specific solutions, rather than generic troubleshooting advice.
- Support agents would handle more tickets by focusing on complex issues, while the AI handles the common problems.
- The system continuously improves as more support cases and product information are added to the knowledge base.
- As a result, customer satisfaction would increase due to faster and more precise resolution of issues.

Therefore, by seamlessly integrating these AI technologies, ZenTime transformed their customer support from a potential pain point into a competitive advantage for their smartwatch business.

Advanced LLM Capabilities: Natively Powered by Snowflake Cortex

As enterprises increasingly adopt Large Language Models (LLMs) for knowledge-intensive and task-driven applications, a deeper understanding of advanced LLM techniques becomes essential. Beyond prompt engineering and Retrieval-Augmented Generation (RAG), several evolving concepts are shaping the future of LLM-powered systems. These include fine-tuning methodologies, responsible AI practices, agentic workflows, model evaluation strategies, and intelligent document processing. Together, they extend the boundaries of what LLMs can do, and how they can be operationalized in real-world environments. We would be covering all of these concepts throughout this book.

One of the most significant evolutions in the LLM landscape is fine-tuning that allows organizations to specialize a general-purpose model for a particular domain or task.

Variants, such as instruction tuning, help models to follow structured prompts in a better way, while parameter-efficient, fine-tuning methods like Low-Rank Adaptation (LoRA) reduce the computational overhead. In enterprise settings, fine-tuning can enhance accuracy in domains such as healthcare, finance, or legal services by incorporating proprietary jargon, use cases, and tone. In this context, Cortex Fine-tuning enables users to create specialized model adaptations through Parameter-Efficient Fine-Tuning (PEFT), allowing pre-trained models to be customized for domain-specific tasks, without modifying the entire model. This approach produces lightweight adaptors that enhance the model performance on targeted applications, while maintaining efficiency and reducing computational resources, typically required for full model fine-tuning.

Modern LLM platforms are increasingly adopting a function-based approach to make powerful language capabilities accessible to a broader range of users. Instead of requiring deep knowledge of model architecture, tokenization, or API orchestration, users can now perform tasks such as summarization, classification, and text generation through simple function calls. This not only hides the underlying complexity, but also accelerates adoption by enabling developers, analysts, and data engineers to integrate LLMs into workflows with minimal effort. Function-based LLMs provide a clean, reusable interface that abstracts prompt construction, handles context windows, and returns structured outputs—all while maintaining performance and consistency.

Snowflake Cortex offers a set of native LLM functions—including **`COMPLETE`**, **`SENTIMENT`**, **`SUMMARIZE`**, **`CLASSIFY_TEXT`** – that allow users to bring Generative AI into their data workflows using SQL or Python. These functions are deeply integrated into the Snowflake platform, meaning that they can be used directly on governed in-platform data without any external dependencies. Whether it is summarizing call transcripts, classifying support tickets, or generating natural language descriptions from structured records, these functions make it easy to apply advanced LLM techniques securely and at scale. By abstracting complexity behind intuitive function calls, Cortex empowers users to focus on solving business problems—rather than managing the AI infrastructure.

With the rise of AI, comes the responsibility to govern its usage effectively. LLMs can occasionally produce biased, toxic, or hallucinated content which underscores the need for guardrails. So, enterprises must implement strategies to ensure content safety, ethical use, and adherence to brand and regulatory standards. Techniques such as cortex guard implement LLM safeguards and reduce risks. Snowflake's governance capabilities such as data masking, role-based access, and row-level security can be integrated to control what the LLM sees, and how it responds, ensuring both compliance and reliability.

An important feature in enterprise AI is the ability to perform intelligent document parsing using LLMs and specialized extraction models. Organizations deal with a massive volume of unstructured documents—contracts, invoices, reports, insurance forms, and much more–that often require manual review or rule-based processing. Snowflake's Document AI provides a native, no-code solution for extracting structured information from such documents using foundation models. By leveraging layout-aware understanding, table detection, and entity recognition, Document AI enables seamless extraction of data including dates, parties, totals, and clauses. This structured output can then be passed to Cortex LLM functions for summarization, classification, or further reasoning. For example, a financial services firm can use Document AI to extract key terms from loan agreements, and then apply Cortex to generate summaries, flag anomalies, or recommend the next steps–all within the governed boundaries of the Snowflake's platform. Incorporating these advanced LLM concepts into AI architectures not only extends functionality, but also strengthens the reliability, trust, and impact of AI in production environments. For enterprises leveraging Cortex AI, understanding and applying these ideas will be key to scaling intelligent, domain-aware, and compliant LLM applications.

Another transformative shift lies in the emergence of agentic LLM workflows. Unlike traditional models that simply complete the text, agent-based systems decompose tasks and autonomously interact with tools, APIs, or memory stores. For example, a Cortex-powered virtual assistant could use agentic logic to search knowledge bases, call business functions, retrieve documents, and even summarize results–all driven by LLM reasoning. Here, LLMs do more than responding to prompts; they orchestrate tasks using tools, memory, and planning! In Snowflake, this agentic capability is realized through Cortex Analyst and Cortex Search.

- Cortex Analyst enables natural language querying of enterprise data. It allows business users and analysts to ask questions like "*What was our Q1 revenue trend?*" and get contextual answers drawn from structured tables, summaries, and charts–no SQL is required. It acts as an intelligent agent that understands intent, decomposes the query, retrieves data, and formulates a response.
- Cortex Search, on the other hand, enables semantic search across unstructured content. It uses embeddings to index documents, and retrieve the most relevant chunks, powering Retrieval-Augmented Generation (RAG) pipelines. This allows an LLM to "*read*" your organization's PDFs, knowledge bases, policy manuals, or emails, and answer questions grounded in that content.

Together, these features turn Cortex into a platform for enterprise AI agents–ones that can synthesize structured and unstructured data, retrieve documents, perform analysis, and generate actionable outputs–all while keeping the data within Snowflake's governed environment.

While operationalizing LLMs, measuring their performance becomes crucial. Traditional NLP metrics such as BLEU and ROUGE provide surface-level insights, while more sophisticated approaches metrics, such as answer relevance, context relevance, correctness, and groundedness offer better alignment with enterprise quality requirements. RAG-based systems also require dual-level evaluation, that is, both the retrieval quality and the generation fidelity must be assessed. Snowflake recently introduced the AI Observability that addresses computation of these metrics.

As LLM capabilities continue to advance, so do the ways, they can be applied across the enterprise. From fine-tuning and safe deployment to document parsing and agentic workflows, these concepts form the foundation for building more intelligent, useful, and secure AI systems. With Snowflake Cortex bringing these features together in one platform, organizations are well-equipped to explore and implement modern LLM-powered solutions with confidence.

Conclusion

Thus, as we have explored throughout this chapter, Large Language Models, Retrieval-Augmented Generation, Prompt Engineering, and Vector search technologies represent the core building blocks of modern AI systems. While each component is powerful individually, their true potential emerges, when they work in combination. LLMs provide the reasoning and generation capabilities that allow AI to process and produce human language. RAG systems enhance these models by grounding them in your organization's specific knowledge. Prompt engineering serves as the critical interface that guides these systems toward the desired outcomes. Also, underpinning it all, vector search and embeddings create the semantic bridges that connect questions to the relevant information.

Understanding these fundamental concepts is absolutely necessary for anyone looking to leverage Snowflake Cortex effectively. In the chapters that follow, we will explore how Snowflake Cortex AI implements these concepts within its architecture. You will also discover how Cortex seamlessly integrates with your existing Snowflake data warehouse, allowing you to apply these AI capabilities directly to your business data, without the complex integration work. We will also examine Cortex's native vector search capabilities that enable semantic querying across structured and unstructured data. The practical knowledge from this chapter will help you understand how to formulate effective prompts, specifically for Cortex AI applications, and how to prepare and structure your data for optimal embedding generation, as well as how to design RAG workflows that deliver accurate, contextually relevant insights from your Snowflake environment.

As we progress through the specialized topics, starting with the LLM Functions in the subsequent chapter, you will recognize how these foundational technologies manifest in practical solutions that drive business value—transforming how your organization interacts with data through the power of AI.

CHAPTER 5
LLM Functions in Cortex AI

Introduction

Building on the foundational concepts explored in the previous chapter, which introduced large language models (LLMs), Generative AI, and innovative techniques such as Retrieval-Augmented Generation (RAG), we now delve into the practical applications of these technologies within Snowflake Cortex AI. This chapter focuses on the integration of LLM functions into Snowflake Cortex, and how it seamlessly combines the power of AI with the scalability of the Snowflake Data Cloud. By leveraging these advanced AI capabilities, users can enhance their data analysis workflows, automate tasks, and derive more insightful conclusions from their data.

The functions are accessible through SQL queries, making them readily available to data analysts and engineers familiar with database operations. By integrating ML capabilities into the data warehouse, Snowflake Cortex eliminates the need for data movement, and simplifies the process of extracting valuable insights from large datasets.

Structure

In this chapter, we will cover the following topics:

- The Power of Large Language Models
- Benefits of Integration of LLM Functions into the Snowflake Cortex
- Cross-Region Inference in Snowflake
- Availability of LLM Functions and Cost Considerations
- Types of LLM Functions in Cortex AI
- A Recap of the LLM Functions

The Power of Large Language Models

As we explored in the previous chapter, Large Language Models (LLMs) have emerged as a cornerstone of the modern AI, revolutionizing how we interact with, and derive insights from vast amounts of text data. Building on the concepts of prompt engineering and Retrieval-Augmented Generation (RAG) introduced earlier, LLMs are sophisticated tools trained on enormous datasets to understand, generate, and manipulate human language with remarkable precision and nuance. This training enables them to perform a wide range of tasks, from generating coherent text based on prompts to analyzing complex documents for sentiment and meaning.

The power of LLMs lies in their ability to learn from vast amounts of data, allowing them to capture subtle patterns and relationships within the language that might elude human analysts. This capability makes them indispensable for tasks, such as text summarization, translation, and sentiment analysis. For instance, in the context of customer feedback analysis, LLMs can quickly categorize comments into positive, negative, or neutral categories, providing valuable insights for business decision-making.

Moreover, LLMs have been instrumental in advancing techniques like RAG (as we saw in the previous chapter) which combines the strengths of retrieval systems with the generative capabilities of language models. This integration allows for more accurate and contextually relevant responses, especially when dealing with specialized or domain-specific information. By leveraging these advanced AI capabilities, organizations can automate routine tasks, enhance decision-making processes, and unlock new opportunities for innovation.

Large Language Models have numerous practical applications across various industries. For example, in customer service, LLMs' power automated chat systems provide personalized responses, enhancing user experiences in sectors like banking and e-commerce. In content creation, LLMs automate the generation of high-quality text for marketing campaigns and social media, saving time and ensuring a consistent brand voice. Additionally, LLMs are used in sentiment analysis to evaluate customer feedback and social media sentiments, helping businesses refine their strategies and respond effectively to consumer emotions. In industries where vast amounts of text data are common, such as academia, law, and finance, LLMs can automatically summarize lengthy documents, extracting the key points and insights, without losing essential information.

In Snowflake Cortex, these powerful models are integrated into a suite of LLM functions that can be seamlessly incorporated into SQL queries or Python scripts. This integration empowers data analysts and developers to harness the potential of LLMs, without requiring extensive expertise in AI or machine learning, thereby streamlining workflows and enhancing productivity.

Benefits of Integration of LLM Functions into Snowflake Cortex

The integration of LLM functions into Snowflake Cortex offers several benefits:

- **Simplified Data Analysis:** Users can now extract insights from the unstructured data, without needing to leave the Snowflake environment, reducing complexity, and enhancing productivity. This streamlined approach allows data teams to focus on higher-level tasks and strategic decision-making.
- **Versatility:** LLM functions can be used in both SQL and Python, providing flexibility for different workflows and user preferences. Whether you prefer the simplicity of SQL or the versatility of Python, Snowflake Cortex supports your preferred method of interaction.
- **Enhanced Collaboration:** By making advanced AI capabilities accessible through familiar interfaces, Snowflake Cortex facilitates collaboration among data analysts, developers, and business users. This collaboration can lead to more informed decision-making and innovative solutions across the organization. With Cortex, users can combine LLMs with other AI-powered functions, such as time-series forecasting, classification, and entity extraction. This allows businesses to create comprehensive AI-driven solutions tailored to their needs.
- **Scalability and Performance:** Snowflake Cortex is built on the scalable architecture of Snowflake, ensuring that LLM functions can handle large volumes of data efficiently. This scalability is crucial for organizations dealing with vast amounts of unstructured data.
- **Seamless Data Access and Governance:** Since LLM functions run natively within Snowflake, they eliminate the need for data movement, ensuring governance, security, and the compliance remains intact. Thus, businesses can generate insights, without exposing the sensitive data to external AI services.
- **Real-Time AI Powered Insights:** With LLM functions embedded into queries, users can perform tasks such as text summarization, sentiment analysis, classification, and even advanced reasoning directly within their Snowflake environment. This allows for real-time, AI-driven decision-making on structured and unstructured data.
- **Cost and Performance Optimization:** Running LLMs directly inside Snowflake reduces latency and infrastructure costs compared to external AI services. It eliminates the need for data extraction, transformation, and reintegration, leading to faster processing and better cost efficiency.
- **Future-Proof AI:** Moreover, Snowflake's cloud-native architecture ensures that LLM functions scale with different business needs. As AI models improve,

businesses can seamlessly integrate newer, more powerful models, without overhauling their existing architecture.

Hence, by embedding LLM functions within Snowflake Cortex, organizations can unlock the state-of-the-art AI-driven efficiencies, while maintaining data security, governance, and performance – all within a single, unified platform, enhancing decision-making, automation, and business intelligence at scale.

Cross-Region Inference in Snowflake

In Snowflake, inference involves leveraging machine learning models to generate outputs based on user inputs. When you utilize functions, such as **`SNOWFLAKE.CORTEX.CLASSIFY_TEXT`**, you are triggering an inference process with your prompt as the input to the LLM.

Snowflake provides the flexibility to configure your account for cross-region inference processing. This is achieved through **`CORTEX_ENABLED_CROSS_REGION`** parameter which allows you to process inference requests in a different region than your default one. This enables inference to be processed from regions where LLMs are not yet available.

To manage where your inference requests are processed, you can adjust the **`CORTEX_ENABLED_CROSS_REGION`** parameter as follows:

- **Disable Cross-Region Processing:** To revert to using only your default region, set the parameter to **`'DISABLED'`**. This ensures that all the requests are processed locally.

  ```
  ALTER ACCOUNT SET CORTEX_ENABLED_CROSS_REGION = 'DISABLED';
  ```

- **Enable any Supported Region:** For maximum flexibility, you can allow any Snowflake region that supports cross-region inference to handle your requests by setting the parameter to '**`ANY_REGION`**'.

  ```
  ALTER ACCOUNT SET CORTEX_ENABLED_CROSS_REGION = 'ANY_REGION';
  ```

- **Specify Preferred Region(s):** If you prefer to limit the processing to specific regions, you can list them separated by commas. This allows you to control where your requests are processed based on your needs.

  ```
  ALTER ACCOUNT SET CORTEX_ENABLED_CROSS_REGION = 'AWS_US';
  ALTER ACCOUNT SET CORTEX_ENABLED_CROSS_REGION = 'AWS_US, AWS_EU';
  ```

- **Understanding Billing and Charges:** When using cross-region inference, it is important to understand how the billing works:

  Credits are consumed based on the Snowflake Service Consumption Table. Notably, these credits are accounted for in the region where the request is initiated, not where it is processed.

Example: If you initiate an LLM request from `us-east-1`, and it is processed in `us-west-2`, the credits are still consumed in `us-east-1`. It is also good to note that you do not incur a data egress charge, when using the cross-region inference.

Availability of LLM Functions and Cost Considerations

When deploying LLM capabilities through Snowflake, it is important to understand regional availability constraints. Snowflake Cortex LLM functions are currently available in selected regions, with ongoing expansion efforts to achieve a global coverage. For the most current information on regional availability, please refer to the official documentation at https://docs.snowflake.com/en/user-guide/snowflake-cortex/llm-functions. If your primary Snowflake account is in a region where Cortex LLM functions are not yet available, you can still leverage these capabilities by using the `CORTEX_ENABLED_CROSS_REGION` parameter explained in the preceding section.

Credit Consumption Table

For detailed information about the credit consumption rates for various Snowflake services, including Cortex, consult the Credit Consumption Table at https://www.snowflake.com/legal-files/CreditConsumptionTable.pdf.

Note that the compute costs for Snowflake Cortex LLM functions are determined by the number of tokens processed. To find out the specific cost per million tokens for each function, refer to the Snowflake Service Consumption Table mentioned in the preceding paragraph.

In this context, a token represents the smallest unit of a text that these functions process which is roughly equivalent to four characters. However, the conversion of raw text into a number of tokens can vary depending on the model used. Snowflake offers a range of models, categorized as small, medium, and large, as provided in the Snowflake LLM Functions link above.

When selecting a model, it is advisable to start with a smaller one, and gradually move to larger models to determine which one best fits your needs. This approach helps optimize both performance and cost.

Trial Account for the Latest LLM Features

If you are new to Snowflake Cortex, and want to explore LLM capabilities and the latest features covered in this book, consider creating a trial account at https://signup.snowflake.com/, and selecting the AWS US West region. Most of the features covered in the book are available in this region, ensuring a comprehensive hands-on experience as you follow along. If you are not using a Snowflake trial account and lack **ACCOUNTADMIN** privileges, you might need to ensure that necessary user roles are granted as you explore new features. However, if you are on a trial account created in the AWS US West region as is the case in this book, you will have all required access by default, so there is no need to worry about granting roles manually. **Please note that some of the more recent features discussed in this book may currently be in preview and not yet generally available (GA) yet. Readers should consult the official Snowflake documentation to confirm the availability status of these features before planning their use in production environments.**

Types of LLM Functions in Cortex AI

Snowflake Cortex offers a comprehensive suite of Large Language Model (LLM) functions designed to simplify and enhance the analysis of unstructured and semi-structured data. These functions can be broadly categorized into three main types: General Purpose Functions, Task-Specific Functions, and Helper Functions. Each category is then tailored to address various aspects of Natural Language Processing (NLP), providing users with a versatile toolkit to extract insights and automate tasks efficiently. We will look at each of these in detail, covering both SQL and Python based invocations.

While some of these functions use Snowflake managed models, there are others like the **COMPLETE** and the **EMBED_TEXT** functions that support a range of pre-trained models. The full list of the supported models and other specifics can be found here - https://docs.snowflake.com/en/user-guide/snowflake-cortex/llm-functions.

Note: *Before proceeding further, please ensure that the data from the files -* **Smartwatch_Customer_Feedback.csv** *and* **SmartWatch_Feature_Reviews.csv** *are imported to* **CORTEX_AI_DB.PUBLIC** *tables with the same names. While importing, also ensure that the* ***"First Line Contains Headers"*** *is selected in the Header option, so that the column names are imported from the first line. Also, create the stage* **SAMPLE_STG** *within* **CORTEX_AI_DB.PUBLIC**, *and upload the* **Invoice_Detail.pdf** *to this stage. (Refer to the* **Script** > **Create Stage.sql**).

General Purpose Functions

The **COMPLETE** function is the primary general-purpose tool in Snowflake Cortex's LLM arsenal. It is incredibly versatile, capable of performing a wide range of tasks, from generating high-quality content based on prompts to creating customized summaries. This function leverages advanced language models to understand the context, and produce relevant as well as coherent responses. Whether you need to draft reports, create product descriptions, or generate content for marketing campaigns, the COMPLETE function offers a powerful solution. Additionally, it can be used for tasks like aspect-based classification and synthetic data generation, making it a go-to tool for the complex NLP tasks.

Cortex Complete in Snowflake supports a wide range of pre-trained models of varying sizes, designed to cater to diverse business needs. These models span from smaller models in the single-digit billions of parameters to larger, more powerful models, such as **`Mistral Large`**, **`deepseek-r1`**, **`reka-flash`**, and **`claude-3-5-sonnet`**.

Larger models excel in handling complex tasks, offering higher accuracy, larger context windows, and enhanced capabilities for content generation, answering queries that require extensive context. On the other hand, smaller models provide faster response times and lower inference costs, making them ideal for time-sensitive applications like external-facing chat apps or lightweight tasks. This flexibility allows businesses to choose the right model based on their specific performance, accuracy, and cost requirements.

Let us look at a few examples to understand the working and applications of the **`COMPLETE`** function. We will start with invoking the function with SQL, and then proceed with examples leveraging the Python code.

When referring to real-world applications, we will frequently use ZenTime—a fictional smart watch manufacturer—as an example. Throughout the book, we will illustrate how this company progressively experiments and leverages various Cortex AI features to create comprehensive solutions for their business needs.

Example 1. Content Generation for Educational Materials:

- **Problem**: Create engaging educational content for students.
- **Solution**: Use the **`COMPLETE`** function to generate interactive lesson plans or study guides based on specific topics.

Code:

```
SELECT SNOWFLAKE.CORTEX.COMPLETE('mistral-7b', 'Create an
engaging lesson plan on photosynthesis for grade 5 students')
AS Lesson_Plan;
```

Preview of the output is shown as follows:

```
LESSON_PLAN

 Title: "Discovering the Magic of Photosynthesis"

Objective:
By the end of this lesson, students will be able to understand the process of photosynthesis, identify the key components involved, and
explain how it benefits plants and the environment.

Materials:
- Diagrams of the structure of a leaf and the process of photosynthesis
- Green plants or pictures of green leaves
- Whiteboard and markers
- Handout on photosynthesis
- Small plastic bags
- Water
- Spirulina tablets or pond water with algae
- Rulers
- Sunlight

Procedure:

1. Introduction (10 minutes)
   - Begin by asking students what they know about plants and their importance in our environment.
   - Introduce the term "photosynthesis" and ask if anyone has heard of it before.
   - Share a brief explanation of photosynthesis and its role in producing food for plants.

2. Interactive Activity: "The Magic of Leaves" (15 minutes)
   - Divide students into small groups and provide each group with a green plant or a picture of a green leaf.
   - Ask students to observe their plant or leaf closely and draw what they see on a piece of paper.
   - Discuss as a class what they have drawn and introduce the term "chlorophyll," explaining its role in photosynthesis.

3. Diagramming Photosynthesis (15 minutes)
   - Show students a diagram of the process of photosynthesis and explain the key components involved: chlorophyll, sunlight, carbon
dioxide, and water.
```

Figure 5.1: *Lesson Plan Using COMPLETE*

Example 2. Generating Product Descriptions for Marketing:

- **Problem:** Create an engaging product description for a mobile manufacturer to enhance customer engagement and conversion rates for a new smart phone.
- **Solution:** Use the **`COMPLETE`** function to generate high-quality product descriptions based on product specifications and features.

Let us try using Anthropic **`claude-3-5-sonnet`** for this use case.

Code:

```
SELECT SNOWFLAKE.CORTEX.COMPLETE('claude-3-5-sonnet', 'Generate a
compelling product description for a new smartphone  with fea-
tures like 12GB RAM, 512GB storage, and a 6.1-inch AMOLED dis-
play.') AS Product_Desc;
```

```
PRODUCT_DESC
Here's a compelling product description for the smartphone:

Introducing the [Smartphone Name] - Where Power Meets Elegance

Experience performance without compromise with our latest flagship smartphone. Featuring a massive 12GB RAM that handles multitasking with ease, letting you switch between apps seamlessly while keeping your favorite games running smoothly in the background.

Store your entire digital life with confidence thanks to the generous 512GB of lightning-fast storage. From 4K videos to high-resolution photos, your memories are always within reach.

The stunning 6.1-inch AMOLED display brings your content to life with vibrant colors, perfect blacks, and exceptional brightness. Every image appears crisp and lifelike, while the compact form factor ensures comfortable one-handed use.

Key Features:
• Lightning-fast 12GB RAM for unmatched multitasking
• Spacious 512GB storage for all your apps and media
• Brilliant 6.1" AMOLED display with HDR10+ support
• Sleek, premium design with aerospace-grade materials
• All-day battery life with fast charging capability

Whether you're a mobile gaming enthusiast, content creator, or business professional, this powerhouse delivers the performance you need in a beautifully designed package that fits perfectly in your pocket.

Experience the future of mobile computing today.

[Price] | [Available Colors] | [Warranty Information]
```

***Figure* 5.2:** *Product Description Using* COMPLETE

Note that by customizing the prompt, we could drive the specific results as needed.

Now that we understand the idea behind the **`COMPLETE`** function, let us look at another example, and understand a few additional parameters such as system and user roles, content, **`max_tokens`** and temperature.

Example 3: Identifying Potential New Features for a Smart Phone based on Customer Feedback residing in a table:

- **Problem:** Analyze customer feedback from the **`CUSTOMER_FEEDBACK`** table, and suggest potential new product features to the Smartphone manufacturer.
- **Solution:** Use the **`COMPLETE`** function on the data residing in the **`Customer_Feedback`** table.

  A snapshot of the **`CUSTOMER_FEEDBACK`** table is shown here:

CUST	FEEDBACK_TEXT
1	The battery life is decent, but I wish it could last at least two days with heavy usage. A faster-charging option would be great too.
2	The camera quality is good, but night mode photos appear grainy. A better low-light sensor would improve the experience.
3	I love the phone's sleek design, but it lacks a customizable back panel. It would be cool to have an interchangeable or customizable back cover.
4	The screen is very responsive, but I find the fingerprint sensor to be slow at times. An under-display ultra-fast scanner would be a nice upgrade.
5	The AI assistant is useful, but it struggles with recognizing different accents. Improving voice recognition for diverse accents would be a game-changer.

***Figure* 5.3:** *Customer_Feedback Table*

Now, let us generate a suggested list of features for each of these reviews. We will display the **`CUSTOMER_ID`**, along with the potential feature suggestions.

The **`llama2-70b-chat`** model has been leveraged. But feel free to experiment with other models. In a real-life scenario, we would experiment with multiple models before arriving at the best suited one for our scenario.

Code:

```
SELECT CUSTOMER_ID, SNOWFLAKE.CORTEX.COMPLETE(
        'llama2-70b-chat', -- Or any supported LLM model that best suits the use case
        [
            {
                'role': 'system',
                'content': 'You are a product innovation assistant. Analyze the following customer feedback and suggest potential new product features. Provide your response as a concise list of feature suggestions. Do not say Sure, here are some potential new features. Just directly list the features, without any additional text.'
            },
            {
                'role': 'user',
                'content': FEEDBACK_TEXT
            }
        ],
        {
            'temperature': 0.7,
            'max_tokens': 200
        }
    ) AS FEATURE_SUGGESTIONS
FROM CUSTOMER_FEEDBACK;
```

In summary, this SQL query leverages the **COMPLETE** LLM function to analyze customer feedback, and generate new product feature suggestions using a Large Language Model (LLM), such as Llama 2-70B Chat. It selects **CUSTOMER_ID** from the **CUSTOMER_FEEDBACK** table, and processes the **FEEDBACK_TEXT** through the LLM, instructing it to act as a product innovation assistant. The system prompt directs the model to extract potential feature ideas from the feedback, and present them as a concise, structured list without introductory phrases. The temperature (**0.7**) controls the balance between randomness and determinism, while the max token limit (**200**) ensures concise responses. The generated **FEATURE_SUGGESTIONS** column provides actionable insights for each customer, enabling the company to identify trends, and prioritize improvements, such as better battery life, enhanced cameras, or AI assistant upgrades, enabling data-driven product innovation.

Let us break this down, and understand these parameters.

1. **System Role (`role: system`):** The system role defines the overall behavior and response style of the LLM. It acts as an instruction manual that guides how the model should interpret and process the input. In this query, the system role is explicitly told to behave as a product innovation assistant, ensuring that

its primary focus is on analyzing customer feedback, and extracting potential feature suggestions. Additionally, it is instructed to format the response as a direct list of features, without unnecessary introductory phrases like "*Here are some potential new features.*" By doing so, the model consistently delivers structured, actionable insights in a format that is easier to process and use for product innovation.

2. **User Role (`role: user`):** The user role provides the actual input that the model needs to process. In this case, the **`FEEDBACK_TEXT`** column from the **`CUSTOMER_FEEDBACK`** table is dynamically passed as input to the model. The model then reads this customer feedback, and based on the system's instructions, extracts relevant product feature suggestions. Since each row in the dataset contains a unique customer's feedback, the model analyzes them individually, ensuring that each suggestion is contextually relevant to the specific feedback provided. This role serves as the primary data source that the LLM evaluates, making it essential for generating accurate and meaningful insights.

3. **Temperature (`temperature: 0.7`):** The temperature parameter controls the level of randomness in the model's responses. A lower temperature value (for example, 0.1–0.3) makes the model's output more deterministic, meaning it will consistently choose the most probable response based on its training data. Conversely, a higher temperature (for example, 0.8–1.0) makes responses more creative and diverse, but at the cost of reduced predictability. In this query, the temperature is set to 0.7, striking a balance between creativity and relevance. This allows the model to generate varied but still meaningful feature suggestions, ensuring that the feedback analysis captures different perspectives, without becoming too unpredictable or repetitive.

4. **Max Tokens (`max_tokens: 200`):** The max tokens parameter sets a hard limit on the length of the model's response, ensuring that the output remains concise, and does not exceed a specified number of tokens (words and sub-words). If set too low, the response might be cut off mid-sentence, while if set too high, the model may generate unnecessarily long responses. In this query, the max token limit is set to 200 which is sufficient to generate a well-structured list of feature suggestions without excessive explanations. This ensures that the output remains clear, to the point, and easy to integrate into further analysis or decision-making processes.

To summarize, the system role ensures that the model behaves as a product innovation assistant, formatting responses as a structured list. The user role provides customer feedback as input, allowing the model to analyze each entry individually. The temperature (0.7) balances creativity and relevance, ensuring varied yet meaningful feature suggestions. The max tokens limit (200) keeps responses concise and to the point. Together, these components enable a structured, efficient AI-driven approach to extract actionable product insights from the customer feedback.

Let us look at the following query results:

#	[ ] FEATURE_SUGGESTIONS
1	{ "choices": [{ "messages": " - Improved battery life to last at least two days with heavy usage\n- Faster charging technology, such as quick charging or wir
2	{ "choices": [{ "messages": " Improved low-light sensor\n\nThe battery lasts a full day, but it's difficult to charge on the go. A fast wireless charging feature
3	{ "choices": [{ "messages": " - Interchangeable or customizable back cover\n- Customizable back panel" }], "created": 1741522104, "model": "llama2-7
4	{ "choices": [{ "messages": " - Under-display ultra-fast scanner\n- Improved fingerprint sensor speed" }], "created": 1741522104, "model": "llama2-70
5	{ "choices": [{ "messages": " * Improved voice recognition for diverse accents\n* Accent-specific language models for more accurate voice recognition\n* V

Figure 5.4: *Feature Suggestions from the COMPLETE Function*

The model has suggested potential features for each feedback item, as shown in the preceding figure.

The output has some interesting information. Let us zoom into one of the rows, to understand the output better.

[ ] FEATURE_SUGGESTIONS


```
{
  "choices": [
    {
      "messages": " - Interchangeable or customizable back cover\n- Customizable back panel"
    }
  ],
  "created": 1741522104,
  "model": "llama2-70b-chat",
  "usage": {
    "completion_tokens": 16,
    "prompt_tokens": 117,
    "total_tokens": 133
  }
}
```


Figure 5.5: *Feedback Suggestions Sample Row*

The "**choices**" field contains a list of potential product feature suggestions extracted from the input feedback. In this case, the model identified two key suggestions: An interchangeable or customizable back cover and a customizable back panel, both of which align with customer preferences for personalized smartphone designs. The "**created**" field indicates the timestamp of the model's response generation. The "**usage**" section provides token statistics, showing that the model used 117 tokens for the prompt, 16 tokens for the completion, and a total of 133 tokens for the request. This structured output allows businesses to extract actionable insights from customer feedback, helping them refine their product innovation strategy.

Now that we have extensively explored leveraging the **COMPLETE** function using SQL, as another example, let us try invoking the **COMPLETE** function from a Python interface.

Example 4: COMPLETE function invoked from Python script

- **Problem:** Answer questions like Understanding difference between on-prem and cloud by leveraging Snowflake LLM capabilities within Python interface.

- **Solution:** Import necessary packages, and invoke the **COMPLETE** function from within Snowflake Notebook.

We will use Snowflake Notebooks for demonstrating this, and other LLM functions going forward in this chapter.

Create a new notebook under **Projects** > **Notebooks** from the Main Menu on the left.

Let us name it **LLM_FUNCTIONS**, and choose the **CORTEX_AI_DB**. Use the warehouse of your choice and click **Create**.

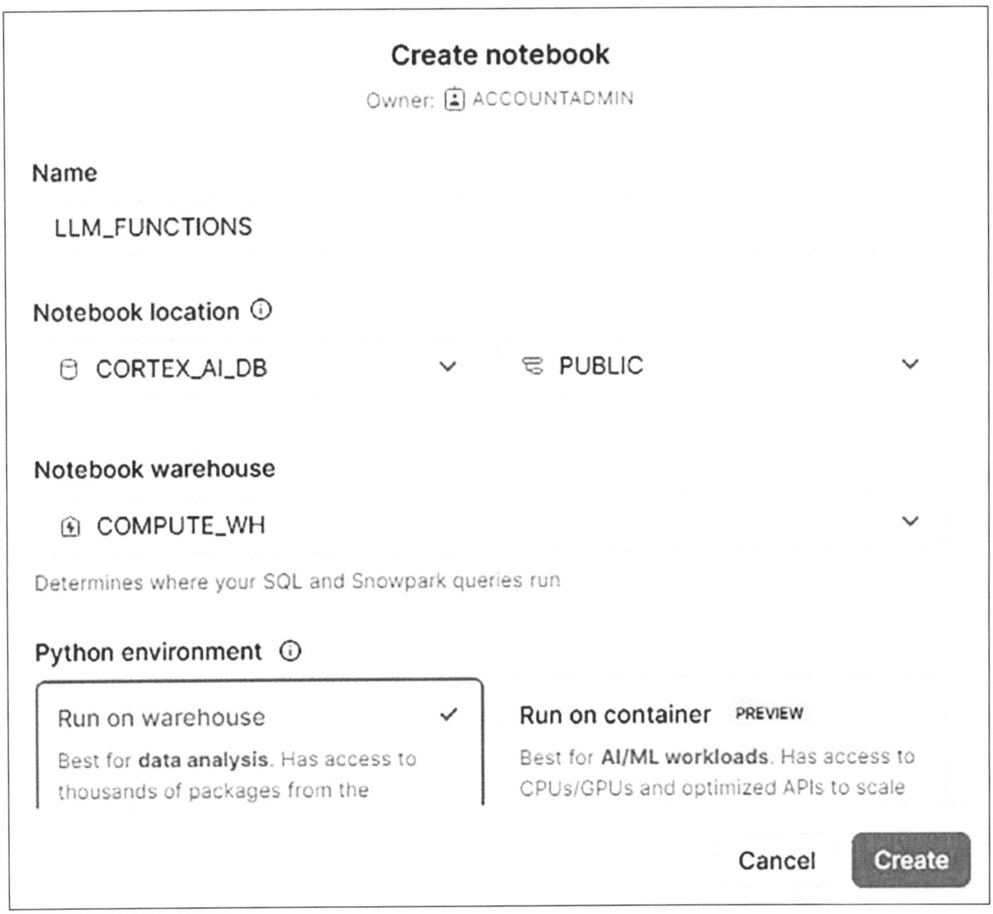

Figure 5.6: *Create Notebook*

In this newly created notebook, from the Packages menu on the top right, ensure that the following packages are installed. (Search using the package name in the "**Find Packages**" box to install.)

```
snowflake-ml-python
snowflake-snowpark-python
```

python and streamlit packages would be installed by default.

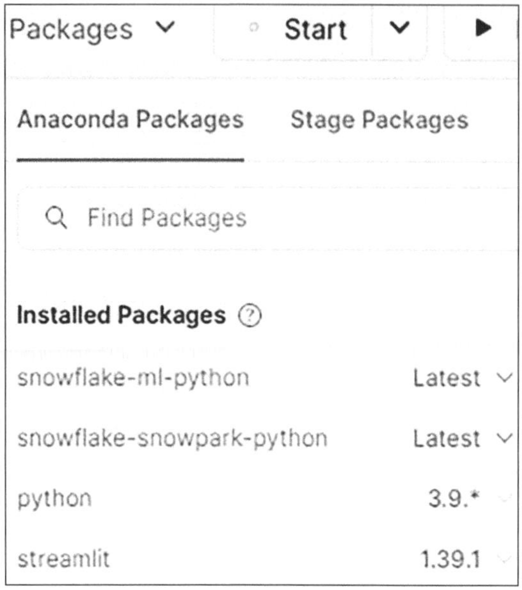

Figure 5.7: *Install Packages*

To begin with, we would need to set up the snowpark session, and initialize it for use. The **get_active_session()** function provides access to the already initialized session in the notebook, eliminating the need to manually establish a connection. This session allows users to interact with Snowflake tables, execute SQL queries, and work with Snowpark data frames seamlessly.

```
Python as SetSession

from snowflake.snowpark.context import get_active_session
session = get_active_session()

```

Figure 5.8: *Set Session*

Let us leverage the **COMPLETE** function call from Python, and ask a question. We will use the **llama3.1-8b** model. Based on the use case, and regional availability, any model that is compatible with the **COMPLETE** function can be used. Let us look at the function call, and the results.

```
from snowflake.cortex import Complete

Complete("llama3.1-8b", """In less than 100 words and in short bullets,
explain what is the differenced between on-prem and cloud hosting?""")
```

```
Here are the key differences between on-prem and cloud hosting in brief:

**On-Prem Hosting:**

* Physical servers located in your own data center or premises
* You own and manage the hardware and infrastructure
* Higher upfront costs for hardware and maintenance
* More control and customization options
* Security and maintenance responsibilities fall on you

**Cloud Hosting:**

* Virtual servers hosted on remote servers accessed over the internet
* Scalable and flexible, with pay-as-you-go pricing
* Lower upfront costs, with reduced maintenance and security responsibilities
* Less control and customization options, but still secure and reliable
```

Figure 5.9: *COMPLETE Function Call*

Example 5: Travel Guide using Complete Function

- **Problem:** Build a travel guide that provides concise and safe recommendations for destinations of my choice.
- **Solution:** Leverage **`COMPLETE`** function and use customizable parameters to provide appropriate recommendations.

Let us go to another example using the Python invocation of the **`COMPLETE`** function, and build a travel guide for the destination of our choice. The result would be a list of the top five popular attractions in the respective destinations. The LLM acts as a friendly travel guide, and asks for the top five must-see attractions at the specified destination, keeping each description within 15 words. We will also introduce two new features - the "**`guardrails`**" and the "**`options`**" parameters.

The guardrails parameter in Snowflake Cortex AI's Complete function is a safety mechanism designed to ensure that the generated AI responses remain appropriate, safe, and aligned with ethical guidelines. When **`guardrails=True`**, the model applies content moderation to filter out harmful, biased, or inappropriate outputs, ensuring that responses adhere to the responsible AI principles. This is particularly useful in applications where AI-generated text interacts with users, such as travel guides, customer support, or recommendations.

The options parameter in Snowflake Cortex AI's Complete function is used to customize how the AI generates responses. It takes a dictionary of settings that control the AI's behavior. For example, temperature, **max_tokens**, and guardrails parameters are bundled into the options parameter in this example, ensuring that the responses are as per our needs. These settings allow the users to fine-tune AI outputs based on their specific needs, whether they want concise answers, creative responses, or controlled outputs.

Let us try our recommendations for Las Vegas.

```
from snowflake.cortex import Complete

def travel_guide_query(destination):
    messages = [
        {'role': 'system', 'content': '''You are a travel guide that provides helpful
        information about destinations in a friendly and safe manner.'''},
        {'role': 'user', 'content': f'''What are the top five must-see attractions
        in {destination}? Keep the descriptions for each attarction within 15 words'''}
    ]

    assign_params = {
        'guardrails': True,  # Ensures that the responses are safe
        'temperature': 0.7,  # Adjusts the creativity of the response
        'max_tokens': 200    # Limits the length of the response
    }

    response = Complete("llama3.1-405b", messages, options=assign_params)
    return response

# Example usage
print(travel_guide_query('Las Vegas'))
```

Figure 5.10: *Travel Guide Using COMPLETE*

Let us now examine the output:

```
Las Vegas! Here are the top five must-see attractions in this vibrant city:
1. **The Strip**: Iconic stretch of elaborate displays, fountains, and grand casinos.
2. **High Roller Observation Wheel**: Panoramic views of the city from a 550-foot tall Ferris wheel.
3. **Fountains of Bellagio**: Stunning water show with over 1,200 fountains and 4,500 lights.
4. **Red Rock Canyon**: Breathtaking natural beauty with red rock formations and scenic hiking trails.
5. **The Mirage Volcano**: Large, erupting volcano outside The Mirage hotel, a classic Vegas landmark.
Stay safe, have fun, and enjoy the excitement of Las Vegas!
```

Figure 5.11: *Travel Guide Output*

As seen above, the output of the **travel_guide_query("Las Vegas")** function generates a structured AI-generated response listing the top five attractions in Las Vegas. Using Snowflake Cortex AI's Complete function, the model responds as a helpful travel guide, following the prompt's instructions to keep descriptions concise (within 15 words). The **guardrails=True** ensures that the response remains appropriate, while the temperature=0.7 balances creativity and coherence. The model returns a friendly, informative list of landmarks such as - The Strip, High Roller, Bellagio Fountains, Red Rock Canyon, and The Mirage Volcano, making it a useful travel recommendation.

Now that we have covered the general purpose **`COMPLETE`** function, let us proceed with the other types of LLM functions.

Task-Specific Functions

Task-specific functions are designed to automate the routine NLP tasks efficiently, without requiring extensive customization. Let us look at each of these functions.

CLASSIFY_TEXT

The **`CLASSIFY_TEXT`** function provides the state-of-the-art text classification with accuracy comparable to the most advanced models available today. Whether categorizing customer inquiries into different support channels, classifying product reviews by sentiment, or routing job applications to specific departments, the **`CLASSIFY_TEXT`** function provides a powerful means of automating complex classification tasks. This not only saves time and resources, but also enhances the accuracy and consistency of data categorization, allowing businesses to respond more effectively to customer needs, improve operational efficiency, and gain valuable insights from their data.

The practical applications of the **`CLASSIFY_TEXT`** function are diverse and impactful. For example, a customer service team might use it to automatically route inquiries to the appropriate support agents, ensuring that the customers receive timely and relevant assistance. Similarly, a recruitment team could leverage this function to categorize resumes based on job requirements, streamlining the hiring process, and improving candidate matching. By integrating text classification into their workflows, organizations can unlock new efficiencies, enhance customer experiences, and drive strategic growth through more informed decision-making. Thus, whether we are optimizing customer service, refining marketing strategies, or improving operational workflows, the **`CLASSIFY_TEXT`** function offers a sophisticated solution for managing and extracting value from the text data.

Let us look at a few examples:

Example 1: Categorizing Customer Feedback

Suppose, you run an e-commerce platform and want to categorize customer feedback into "**`Product Quality`**," "**`Delivery Service`**," or "**`Customer Support`**." You can use the **`CLASSIFY_TEXT`** as follows:

```
SQL ∨ as Classify_Text_Example1                                   1.0s ▶

SELECT SNOWFLAKE.CORTEX.CLASSIFY_TEXT( 'I loved the product but the delivery took too long.',
['Product Quality', 'Delivery Time', 'Customer Support'] );

   SNOWFLAKE.CORTEX.CLASSIFY_TEXT( 'I LOVED THE PRODUCT BUT THE
0  { "label": "Delivery Time" }
```

***Figure 5.12:** CLASSIFY_TEXT Example 1*

Example 2: Classifying Job Applications

Your recruitment partners at the HR department want to categorize job applications based on the type of the roles, candidates are applying for, such as "`Software Engineer`," "`Data Scientist`," or "`Marketing Specialist`," based on the extract from the profile summaries.

```
SQL ∨ as Classify_Text_Example_2                                  0.9s ▶

SELECT SNOWFLAKE.CORTEX.CLASSIFY_TEXT(
    'I have experience in machine learning and data analysis. I have strong knowledge of feature
engineering, model building and creating end to end model deployment pipelines.',
    ['Software Engineer', 'Data Scientist', 'Marketing Specialist']
) as Role;

   ROLE
0  { "label": "Data Scientist" }
```

***Figure 5.13:** CLASSIFY_TEXT Example 2*

Example 3: Classifying Customer Inquiries by the Department using Labels and Examples

If you work in customer service, and want to automatically route inquiries to the appropriate department, such as "`Sales`," "`Technical Support`," or "`Billing`," the `COMPLETE` function can be leveraged to produce a greater effect. This function acts as an intelligent classifier, analyzing incoming customer messages, and determining the most appropriate routing destination based on the content and context of each inquiry.

There is also the option to provide labels with specific examples, enabling the LLM to learn more nuanced and domain-specific categories. For instance, you could train the system to recognize that questions about product compatibility belong to "`Technical Support`", while inquiries about promotional discounts should route to "`Sales`." Therefore, by supplying several representative examples for each department category, the model develops a more refined understanding of your organization's specific routing needs.

SQL as Classify_Text_Example_3

```
SELECT SNOWFLAKE.CORTEX.CLASSIFY_TEXT(
    'I need help with setting up my new software.',
    [
        {
            'label': 'Sales',
            'description': 'Inquiries about purchasing products or services',
            'examples': ['I want to buy a new license', 'How much does the product cost?']
        },
        {
            'label': 'Technical Support',
            'description': 'Inquiries about troubleshooting or using products',
            'examples': ['My software is not working', 'How do I install this?']
        },
        {
            'label': 'Billing',
            'description': 'Inquiries about payments or invoices',
            'examples': ['I have a question about my invoice', 'How do I pay my bill?']
        }
    ],
    {
        'task_description': 'Route the inquiry to the correct department'
    }
) as Category;
```

	CATEGORY
0	{ "label": "Technical Support" }

Figure 5.14: *CLASSIFY_TEXT Example 3*

EXTRACT_ANSWER

The **EXTRACT_ANSWER** function empowers organizations to extract precise and relevant information from large volumes of text data. By leveraging advanced Natural Language Processing (NLP) capabilities, this function can pinpoint specific answers to complex questions. Right from extracting the key details from technical manuals, to identifying critical information from customer inquiries, or retrieving specific data points from reports, the **EXTRACT_ANSWER** function provides a powerful means of automating information retrieval, and reducing manual effort. This not only accelerates decision-making, but also enhances data accuracy, allowing businesses to respond more effectively to customer needs, improve operational efficiency, and gain actionable insights from their data.

Now, let us look at a couple of examples.

Example 1: Extracting Medication Dosage from a Doctor's Note

Suppose, you are working in the healthcare sector, and need to extract the dosage of a medication from a doctor's note. You can use the **EXTRACT_ANSWER** function as follows:

```
SQL ∨ as Extract_Answer_Example1

SELECT SNOWFLAKE.CORTEX.EXTRACT_ANSWER(
    'The patient should take 2 tablets of tylenol every 4 hours for three days.',
    'How many days was the patient prescribed tylenol?'
) as Medication_Days;

    MEDICATION_DAYS
0   [ {  "answer": "three",   "score": 0.7222938  } ]
```

Figure 5.15: EXTRACT_ANSWER *Example 1*

Example 2: Analyzing Product Review from a Table

Dataset: `Smart_Watch_Feature_Reviews.csv` to be loaded to `CORTEX_AI_DB.PUBLIC.SMART_WATCH_FEATURE_REVIEWS` table.

For instance, ZenTime, our fictional smart watch manufacturer, wants to gain deeper insights into customer preferences to enhance their smart watch offerings.

Let us preview the reviews table first.

```
SELECT * FROM SMART_WATCH_REVIEWS;
```

REVIEW_CONTENT
I love the sleek and lightweight design of the ZenTime smartwatch—it's stylish and comfortable.
The display is bright and crisp, ensuring excellent visibility even in sunlight.
The heart rate and sleep tracking are incredibly accurate, helping me monitor my health better.
Its fitness tracking capabilities are top-notch, making my workouts more effective and data-driven.
ZenTime has great visual appeal
While the watch looks premium, I feel like the price is slightly on the higher side.
ZenTime's seamless integration with my smartphone makes notifications and calls very convenient.
The smartwatch is good overall, but I wish there were more third-party app integrations.
The customizable watch faces are a great touch, allowing me to personalize my experience.
The battery life of ZenTime is outstanding, lasting multiple days on a single charge.

Figure 5.16: *Smart Watch Reviews Data Preview*

By analyzing the customer reviews, you can answer questions, such as "*What features do customers like most about this product?*"

Let us try this out using **EXTRACT_ANSWER**.

SQL ⌄ as Extract_Answer_Example2

```
SELECT SNOWFLAKE.CORTEX.EXTRACT_ANSWER(
    review_content,
    'What features do customers like most about this product?'
) AS liked_features
FROM smart_watch_reviews;
```

	LIKED_FEATURES
0	[{ "answer": "the sleek and lightweight design", "score": 0.9986498
1	[{ "answer": "bright and crisp, ensuring excellent visibility even in sunl
2	[{ "answer": "heart rate and sleep tracking are incredibly accurate",
3	[{ "answer": "fitness tracking capabilities", "score": 0.010579352 }
4	[{ "answer": "great visual appeal", "score": 0.10391051 }]
5	[{ "answer": "the watch looks premium", "score": 3.1527590000000
6	[{ "answer": "notifications and calls", "score": 0.12270983 }]
7	[{ "answer": "third - party app integrations", "score": 0.39806503
8	[{ "answer": "customizable watch faces", "score": 0.006702223 }]
9	[{ "answer": "battery life", "score": 0.8367674 }]

Figure 5.17: EXTRACT_ANSWER *Example 2*

SENTIMENT

The **SENTIMENT** function in Snowflake Cortex is a powerful tool designed to analyze the emotional tone of text data, categorizing it as positive, negative, or neutral. This capability is invaluable in today's data-driven world, where understanding customer opinions, employee feedback, or public reactions, is crucial for making informed business decisions. By leveraging advanced Natural Language Processing (NLP) techniques, the SENTIMENT function can accurately discern the sentiment behind the text, on customer reviews, social media posts, or employee feedback. This allows organizations to gauge the overall mood of their audience, identify areas for improvement, and tailor their strategies to better meet the needs and expectations of their stakeholders.

The practical applications of the **SENTIMENT** function are diverse and far-reaching.

For instance, a company might use it to monitor the social media chatter about their brand, identifying trends and patterns that could inform marketing campaigns or product development. Similarly, HR departments could also analyze exit interviews to understand why employees are leaving, helping them to address systemic issues and improve retention rates. Thus, by integrating sentiment analysis into their data analytics workflows, organizations can unlock deeper insights into human behavior and preferences, driving more effective decision-making and strategic growth.

This function analyzes the sentiment of a given text, returning a score between -1 and 1, where -1 represents negative sentiment, 0 is neutral, and 1 is highly positive. It helps in understanding customer feedback or public opinion.

Example: For example, *ZenTime*'s sales department wants to gauge the public's reaction to their latest advertising campaign. For this, they can analyze their social media posts and reviews using the SENTIMENT function. So, let us analyze one of their sample reviews.

SQL as Sentiment_Example1

```
SELECT SNOWFLAKE.CORTEX.SENTIMENT(
    'The new ad is hilarious,very appealing and really caught my attention all along!'
) AS sentiment_score;
```

	SENTIMENT_SCORE
0	0.7262

Figure 5.18: *Sentiment Example with Score*

As seen above, the output returns a sentiment score, which in this case is well over the mid-range, indicating a positive sentiment. We could further customize this. Let us assume for this demonstration's sake a Positive sentiment for scores `> 0.5, Negative Sentiment for scores < -0.5`, and anything in-between is a Neutral sentiment. Then, we can accordingly modify the query as shown, and observe the result. As expected, we get a Positive sentiment.

SQL as Sentiment_Example1_with_Sentiment_Value • 1.0s

```
SELECT SNOWFLAKE.CORTEX.SENTIMENT(
    'The new ad is hilarious,very appealing and really caught my attention all along!') AS
SCORE,
CASE
WHEN SCORE > 0.5 THEN 'POSITIVE'
WHEN SCORE < -0.5 THEN 'NEGATIVE'
ELSE 'NEUTRAL'
END AS SENTIMENT;
```

	SCORE	SENTIMENT
0	0.7262	POSITIVE

Figure 5.19: *Sentiment Example with Sentiment and Score*

Snowflake recently announced the preview of the **ENTITY_SENTIMENT** *function that provides both overall sentiment and detailed, entity-specific sentiment insights. It is well-suited for use cases that require analyzing sentiment related to specific elements within the text, or identifying nuanced tones, such as positive, negative, neutral, or mixed. We will be exploring this in detail in Chapter 10, Industry Use Cases and Case Studies.*

Let us now move on to the **SUMMARIZE** function.

SUMMARIZE

The **SUMMARIZE** function generates a concise summary of a given text, making it easier to grasp the core content, without reading the entire document. It bridges the gap between information overload and actionable insights. By distilling complex texts into concise, high-level summaries, this function empowers users to grasp the essence of lengthy documents, reports, or articles, without sacrificing critical details. Unlike traditional summarization methods, which often rely on manual effort or simplistic algorithms, the **SUMMARIZE** function leverages advanced machine learning to identify and prioritize the key information, ensuring that summaries are both accurate and relevant.

For instance, a news aggregator might use it to create bite-sized summaries of news articles, allowing readers to quickly stay informed across multiple topics. Similarly, a corporate executive could rely on this function to summarize lengthy board reports, focusing on strategic decisions, rather than getting lost in minutiae. Thus, by automating the summarization process, businesses can free up their valuable time for strategic planning, innovation, and customer engagement, driving growth and competitiveness in today's ever growing digital landscape.

Example 1: Summarizing a Free Text Restaurant Review

Let us summarize a free text restaurant review.

```
SQL v as Summarization_Example1                                   1.1s

SELECT SNOWFLAKE.CORTEX.SUMMARIZE('I recently visited La Bella Bistro, and it was an unforgettable
experience. From the moment I walked in, the ambiance was warm and inviting, with soft lighting and
a cozy setup. The staff was incredibly welcoming and attentive, ensuring that every detail of our
dining experience was perfect. The food was exceptional-each dish was flavorful, well-presented,
and cooked to perfection.'
    ) AS Review_Summary;

   REVIEW_SUMMARY
0  I recently visited La Bella Bistro and had an excellent experience with its
   warm and inviting ambiance, attentive staff, and delicious, well-
   presented food.
```

Figure 5.20: *Summarize Example 1*

As observed, the **SUMMARIZE** function has provided a concise information as a one-sentence summary from the lengthy review.

Example 2: Summarizing Reviews from a Table

For instance, ZenTime, is looking to summarize customer feedback to obtain insightful and relevant information.

Dataset: Load the **`Smartwatch_Customer_Feedback`** to **`SMARTWATCH_CUSTOMER_FEEDBACK table`**

Now, let us preview the table.

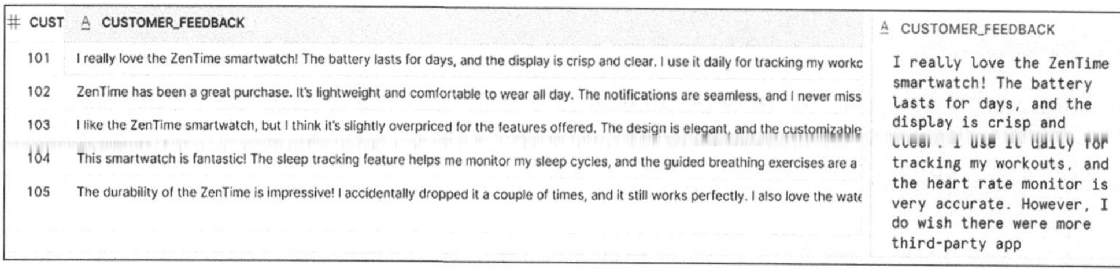

Figure 5.21: *Smartwatch Feedback Data Preview*

We can observe that there is lengthy customer feedback in each row. Let us now apply the **`SUMMARIZE`** function on this to obtain summaries.

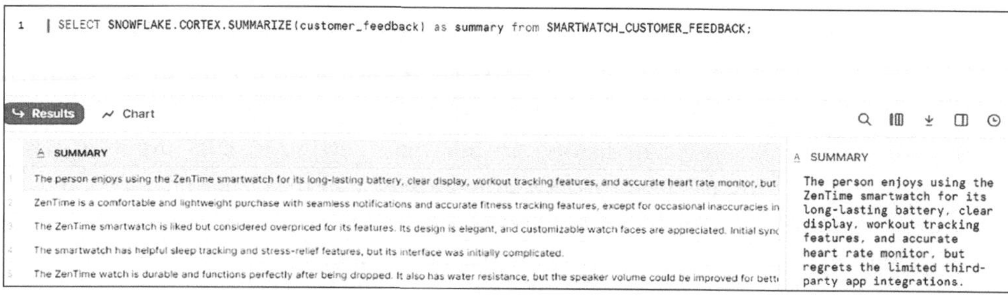

Figure 5.22: SUMMARIZE *Example 2*

Note: *If you require summaries of a specific length, you might consider using the* **`COMPLETE`** *function with a tailored prompt to instruct the model to generate a summary within your desired word limit. This approach allows for more customized outputs.*

Let us now look at the **`TRANSLATE`** function.

TRANSLATE

This function translates the text from one language to another, facilitating the communication across linguistic barriers. By leveraging advanced machine learning algorithms, this function can accurately translate the text from one language to another, preserving the nuances and the context. To facilitate global customer engagement, enhance international collaboration, or expand market reach, the **`TRANSLATE`** function offers an easy solution for breaking down the language barriers.

Example 1: Translating Customer Feedback from a Multilingual Support Platform

A customer service team might receive feedback in various languages, and want to translate it into English for easier analysis. In the following instance, they can use the **TRANSLATE** function to translate feedback from German to English.

SQL ∨ as Translate_Example1

```sql
SELECT SNOWFLAKE.CORTEX.TRANSLATE(
    'Das Produkt ist sehr benutzerfreundlich, aber die Lieferzeit war etwas lang',
    'de',  // Source language
    'en'   // Target language
) AS english_translation;
```

	ENGLISH_TRANSLATION
0	The product is very user-friendly, but the delivery time was a bit long.

Figure 5.23: *Translate Example 1*

Example 2: Translating a Product Description for a Global Market

For example, ZenTime, our fictional Smart watch manufacturer, wants to venture into the Smart Phone segment, and is looking to launch a new product. The sales team has prepared the product description in English. They want to launch their new segment in France, and need to translate the product description from English to French. They can use the TRANSLATE function as follows:

```sql
SELECT SNOWFLAKE.CORTEX.TRANSLATE(
    'Experience cutting-edge technology with the ZenTime Super-V1, a sleek and ultra-thin smartphone designed for those who demand elegance and performance. Crafted with a premium glass and aluminum body, its 6.7-inch OLED display delivers stunning clarity and vibrant colors, making every visual immersive.',
    'en' ,'fr' // Translate to French
) AS french_description;
```

Results | Chart

FRENCH_DESCRIPTION
Découvrez la technologie de pointe avec le ZenTime Super-V1, un smartphone élégant et ultra-mince c

FRENCH_DESCRIPTION

Découvrez la technologie de pointe avec le ZenTime Super-V1, un smartphone élégant et ultra-mince conçu pour ceux qui exigent élégance et performance. Fabriqué avec un boîtier en verre et en aluminium de qualité supérieure, son écran OLED de 6,7 pouces offre une clarté et des couleurs vibrantes époustouflantes, rendant chaque expérience visuelle immersive.

Figure 5.24: *Translate Example 2*

These task-specific functions are optimized for ease of use and efficiency, delivering high-quality results, without requiring the users to develop complex prompts. We will now move on to the helper functions.

`EMBED_TEXT_768` and `EMBED_TEXT_1024`

The **`EMBED_TEXT`** functions (**`EMBED_TEXT_768`** and **`EMBED_TEXT_1024`**) in Snowflake Cortex AI allows you to convert the raw text into high-dimensional vector embedding.

The **EMBED_TEXT_768** supports the e5-base-v2, snowflake-arctic-embed-m, and snowflake-arctic-embed-m-v1.5 models. Both have a context window of 512 tokens (The context window refers to the maximum number of tokens, a model can process in a single input).

The **EMBED_TEXT_1024** supports embedding models - snowflake-arctic-embed-l-v2.0, nv-embed-qa-4, multilingual-e5-large, and voyage-multilingual-2.

Embedding Function	Output Dimension	Context Window (Max Tokens)
SNOWFLAKE.CORTEX.EMBED_TEXT_768	768	512 tokens
SNOWFLAKE.CORTEX.EMBED_TEXT_1024	1024	512 tokens

Table 5.1: *Embedding Functions*

```
SELECT SNOWFLAKE.CORTEX.EMBED_TEXT_768('snowflake-arctic-em-
bed-m',' The Support team needs to be updated of the changes in
the next release' )  AS EMBEDDINGS_768;
SELECT SNOWFLAKE.CORTEX.EMBED_TEXT_1024('snowflake-arctic-em-
bed-l-v2.0','The Support team needs to be updated of the changes
in the next release' )  AS EMBEDDINGS_1024;
```

Both the functions return vector embedding. Now, observe the results from both the queries. The 1024 model would have a wider output dimension as expected.

As we discussed in the previous chapter, Vector Embeddings are powerful numerical representations of the data that capture the semantic meaning in high-dimensional space, enabling a wide range of AI applications. One of the most common use cases is semantic search, where queries are matched based on the meaning, rather than the exact keywords. They are also essential in Retrieval-Augmented Generation (RAG) systems, helping to fetch relevant context for large language models to generate accurate and grounded responses.

PARSE_DOCUMENT

The **PARSE_DOCUMENT** (currently in private preview) enables the text and layout extraction from documents stored in Snowflake stages–all using the SQL. It combines OCR and ML to extract plain text, tables, and document structure from complex formats such as PDFs. This is especially useful for automating data extraction from contracts, invoices, reports, and compliance forms, with outputs directly loadable into structured Snowflake tables for analytics or app integration. It also supports enterprise search via Cortex Search.

There are two modes:

- **OCR mode (default):** Extracts the plain text from mostly text-based documents.

- **LAYOUT mode:** Captures both the text and layout (for example, tables, sections) for deeper context and better use with LLMs or targeted extractions.

All outputs are returned in the JSON format.

Let us look at an example. Ensure that the **SAMPLE_STG** within **CORTEX_AI_DB.PUBLIC** has been created (**Scripts** > **Create Stage.sql**).

```
CREATE STAGE CORTEX_AI_DB.PUBLIC.SAMPLE_STG   ENCRYPTION = (TYPE
= 'SNOWFLAKE_SSE');
```

The **Invoice_Details.pdf** file contains a set of invoice details for a computer accessory store to this staging area. Save it to your local drive, and upload it to this newly created staging area.

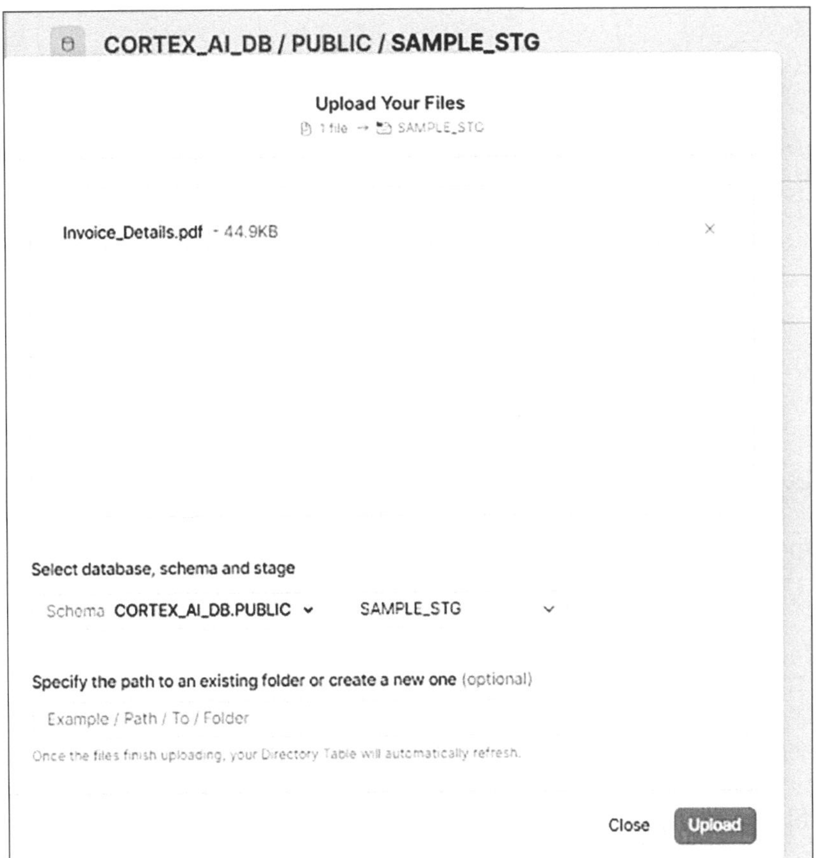

Figure 5.25: *Upload File to SAMPLE_STG*

We will now use the **PARSE_DOCUMENT** function to extract the data.

```
SELECT SNOWFLAKE.CORTEX.PARSE_DOCUMENT( @CORTEX_AI_DB.PUBLIC.
SAMPLE_STG,  'Invoice_Details.pdf',{'mode': 'LAYOUT'}
)::STRING AS document_text;
```

```
DOCUMENT_TEXT
{"content":"\n|Invoice ID|Date|Customer Name|Item|Quantity|Unit Price|Total|\n| :---: | :---: | :---: |
:---: | :---: | :---: | :---: |\n|INV-1001|01-03- 2025|Alice Johnson|Wireless
Mouse||$25.00|$50.00|\n|INV-1002|02-03- 2025|Bob Lee|USB-C Hub||$45.00|$45.00|\n|INV-1003|03-03-
2025|Carla Mendes|External SSD||$85.00|$255.00|\n|INV-1004|04-03- 2025|Daniel
Smith|Keyboard||$60.00|$60.00|\n|INV-1005|05-03- 2025|Ella Thompson|Laptop
Stand|2|$30.00|$60.00|\n","metadata":{"pageCount":1}}
```


Figure 5.26: *Results from the* PARSE_DOCUMENT *(Layout)*

Using the **LAYOUT** keyword enabled the extraction of table structures, and formatting from within the document.

We will use the OCR mode now.

```
SELECT SNOWFLAKE.CORTEX.PARSE_DOCUMENT( @CORTEX_AI_DB.PUBLIC.
SAMPLE_STG,  'Invoice_Details.pdf',{'mode': 'OCR'}    )::STRING
AS document_text;
```


```
DOCUMENT_TEXT
{"content":"Customer Unit Invoice ID Date Item Quantity Total Name Price\n01-03- Alice
Wireless INV-1001 2 $25.00 $50.00 2025 Johnson Mouse\n02-03- INV-1002 Bob Lee USB-C Hub
1 $45.00 $45.00 2025\n03-03- Carla INV-1003 External SSD 3 $85.00 $255.00 2025
Mendes\n04-03- INV-1004 Daniel Smith Keyboard 1 $60.00 $60.00 2025\n05-03- Ella INV-1005
Laptop Stand 2 $30.00 $60.00 2025 Thompson","metadata":{"pageCount":1}}
```


Figure 5.27: *Results from* PARSE_DOCUMENT (OCR)

Notice the difference. The Layout captured table structures and formatting as well, while OCR extracted the plain text.

Helper Functions

Helper functions are designed to assist in running LLM functions smoothly by managing potential errors and optimizing workflows. The key helper functions include:

COUNT_TOKENS

The **COUNT_TOKENS** function in Snowflake Cortex AI is a utility designed to measure the number of tokens in each text input when processed by a Large Language Model (LLM). It helps in optimizing the input size for LLM functions. Tokens are fundamental building blocks in natural language processing, typically representing words, sub-words, or characters depending on the model's tokenization strategy. This function is particularly useful for estimating LLM usage costs, optimizing prompt length, and ensuring that inputs remain within the model-specific token limits. Since LLMs charge based on token consumption, businesses can leverage **COUNT_TOKENS** to track and manage the token budgets efficiently.

The function takes a text string as input and returns the token count based on the underlying LLM's tokenizer. This makes it valuable for preprocessing steps, such as dynamically adjusting prompts or truncating content to fit within the model constraints.

Example: Suppose the *ZenTime* marketing team, now venturing in the smartphone space, wants to analyze the token count for the smart phone's very first product description. So, for this, they can gauge the cost when they translate or expand this further. They can use the **COUNT_TOKENS** function as shown. The mistral-7b model is leveraged here:

SQL ∨ as Count_Tokens_Example

```
SELECT SNOWFLAKE.CORTEX.COUNT_TOKENS(
    'mistral-7b',
    'Experience cutting-edge technology with the ZenTime Super-V1, a sleek and ultra-thin smartphone designed for those who demand elegance and performance. Crafted with a premium glass and aluminum body, its 6.7-inch OLED display delivers stunning clarity and vibrant colors, making every visual immersive.'
) AS Prod_desc_token_count;
```

	PROD_DESC_TOKEN_COUNT
0	72

Figure 5.28: COUNT_TOKENS *Example*

TRY_COMPLETE

The **TRY_COMPLETE** function in Snowflake Cortex AI is a fail-safe approach to text generation using Large Language Models (LLMs). This function is useful for handling potential failures gracefully. Unlike the standard completion functions that might throw errors if something goes wrong–such as exceeding token limits or encountering model restrictions–the **TRY_COMPLETE** is designed to handle failures gracefully.

When called, this function attempts to generate a text completion based on a given prompt. However, if the operation encounters an issue (like a model timeout or invalid input), instead of failing outright, it returns a **NULL** value. This allows developers to build more resilient workflows by avoiding abrupt failures and handling exceptions smoothly, within their Snowflake pipelines.

In fact, by using **TRY_COMPLETE**, organizations can ensure that their AI-driven applications continue running even when an LLM call fails, making it a practical choice for handling unpredictable scenarios in text generation tasks.

Example: For instance, ZenTime Smartwatch marketing team is looking for a catchy tagline for the phone launch for their new segment - Smart phones, using the **TRY_COMPLETE** function. They misspelled the model name as "mistral-7b**b**". So, let us see what happens.

SQL ∨ as Try_Complete_incorrect_model_name •

```
SELECT SNOWFLAKE.CORTEX.TRY_COMPLETE(
    'mistral-7bb',
    'Generate a catchy but short tagline for our new ZenTime Super-V1 Smartphone.'
) AS product_tagline;
```

	PRODUCT_TAGLINE
0	None

***Figure* 5.29:** TRY_COMPLETE *Incorrect Model Name*

As we observed, the command does not error out, but returns a **`NULL`** on error. In an organizational workflow, this can avoid processes erroring out, and instead being gracefully handled.

The team realizes the model reference spelling error and corrects it, returning it successfully as shown. They now get a tag line!

SQL ∨ as Try_Complete_corrected_model_name

```
SELECT SNOWFLAKE.CORTEX.TRY_COMPLETE(
    'mistral-7b',
    'Generate a catchy but short tagline for our new ZenTime Super-V1 Smartphone.'
) AS product_tagline;
```

	PRODUCT_TAGLINE
0	"Experience the Bliss of ZenTime V1: Where Speed Meets Serenity"

***Figure* 5.30:** TRY_COMPLETE *Corrected Model Name*

As you would have noticed, the **`TRY_COMPLETE`** function performs like the **`COMPLETE`** function, except that it handles errors and throws NULL instead of erroring.

These helper functions ensure that users can troubleshoot issues efficiently, and optimize their workflows to get the most out of Snowflake Cortex's LLM capabilities.

A Recap of LLM Functions

Let us recap the functions we covered in this chapter.

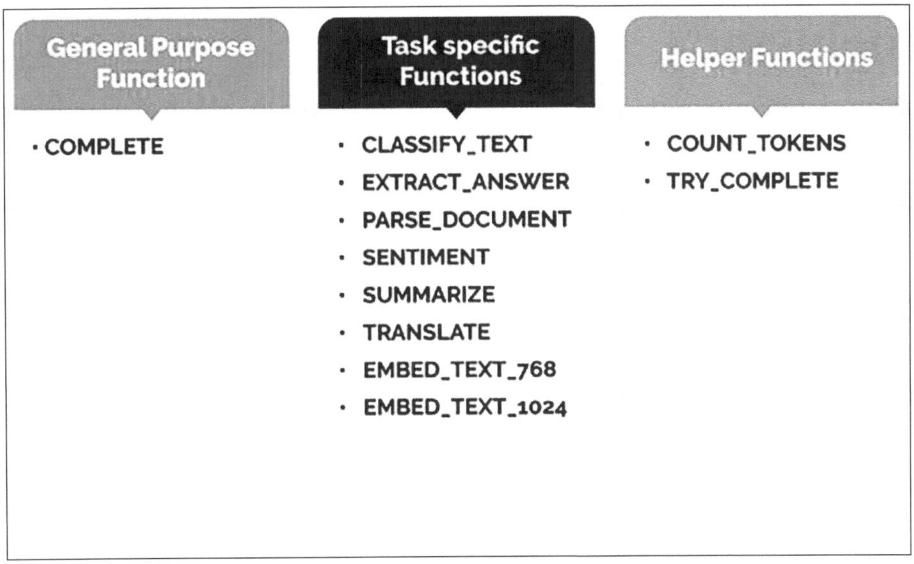

Figure 5.31: *Summary of the LLM Functions*

General-purpose function, namely the **`COMPLETE`** function, was highlighted as a versatile tool for generating text based on prompts. We saw that the function was highly adaptable, allowing users to craft a wide range of content, from simple responses to complex narratives, based on their specific needs.

The task-specific functions, including **`CLASSIFY_TEXT`**, **`EXTRACT_ANSWER`**, **`SUMMARIZE`**, **`SENTIMENT`**, **`TRANSLATE`**, **`PARSE_DOCUMENT`**, and **`EMBED_TEXT`** functions were detailed as specialized tools, designed to address specific business needs. These functions enable organizations to categorize the text, extract precise information, summarize lengthy documents, extract content, analyze sentiment, and break down language barriers. (As *noted earlier in this chapter, we will explore the recently introduced* **`ENTITY_SENTIMENT`** *function in greater detail–with practical examples–in Chapter 10, Industry Use Cases and Case Studies*).

Helper functions, notably **`COUNT_TOKENS`** and **`TRY_COMPLETE`**, played a crucial role in supporting these operations. The **`COUNT_TOKENS`** provided precise token counts to optimize workflows and manage costs, while **`TRY_COMPLETE`** ensured robust error handling by gracefully managing failures, without disrupting the workflows.

Through practical examples and explanations, the chapter demonstrated how these functions collectively empowered businesses to improve efficiency, enhance customer experiences, and drive strategic growth through a more informed decision-making.

By leveraging these diverse LLM functions, users can streamline their data analysis processes, automate routine tasks, and derive more insightful conclusions from their data, all within the Snowflake environment.

Conclusion

Thus, this chapter on LLM Functions offered a comprehensive overview of how large language models can enhance data analysis and processing within Cortex AI. We have also explored how these sophisticated functions serve as powerful building blocks for creating advanced AI-powered applications and workflows. We saw how these functions can be precisely tailored to specific use cases through carefully designed prompts, examples, and parameters. This customization allows organizations to address their unique requirements, while maintaining consistency and quality in AI-generated outputs. Throughout the chapter, we emphasized practical applications, illustrating how businesses can implement these functions to automate the routine tasks, improve decision-making processes, and unlock new insights from their data.

In the next chapter, we will delve into the process of fine-tuning LLMs, exploring how this advanced technique can further enhance model performance, adaptability, and relevance to unique business needs. By fine-tuning LLMs, and leveraging a large model to train a smaller model, organizations can create tailored solutions that address their specific challenges more effectively, leading to even greater efficiencies and innovations in data-driven decision-making, while significantly reducing the costs.

CHAPTER 6
Fine-Tuning Large Language Models in Cortex

Introduction

Fine-Tuning Large Language Models (LLMs) is a sophisticated process that enhances the capabilities of pre-trained models by adapting them to specific tasks or domains. This involves refining the model's parameters using custom data to improve its accuracy and relevance in targeted applications. Fine-Tuning is particularly important for domain-specific applications where pre-trained models may lack the necessary context or specialized knowledge. While foundational LLMs are trained on vast datasets encompassing general knowledge, their real-world value often increases when fine-tuned for specific use cases.

Furthermore, customizing LLMs with their own data allows organizations to tailor models to their unique business needs. This approach ensures that the models understand specific terminologies, contexts, and nuances relevant to the organization, enhancing their ability to generate accurate and relevant outputs. By leveraging the proprietary data, businesses can create AI solutions that are more aligned with their operational contexts and goals. Broadly, Fine-tuning allows organizations to align their LLM capabilities with domain-specific requirements, improving relevance, accuracy, and efficiency.

Structure

In this chapter, we will cover the following topics:

- The Need for Fine-Tuning
- Types of Fine-Tuning
- Cortex Fine-Tuning

- Architecture Overview
- Advantages of Cortex Fine-Tuning
- Implementation Walkthrough
- Cortex Fine-Tune Using Snowsight
- Use Cases and Industry Applications

The Need for Fine-Tuning

Fine-Tuning pre-trained models is a critical step in bridging the gap between the general AI capabilities and the specific needs of an enterprise. The following points highlight why this process is essential for delivering meaningful, high-impact outcomes:

- **Domain Adaptation**: Fine-Tuning enables models to understand unique language patterns and terminologies, specific to a particular domain, enhancing their performance in specialized tasks.
- **Improved Accuracy**: By using custom data, models can achieve higher accuracy by aligning with the unique requirements of the organization or industry.
- **Data Privacy and Compliance**: Utilizing internal data ensures that sensitive information remains secure and compliant with data regulations which is salient in industries with strict privacy laws.
- **Efficiency and Cost Optimization**: By fine-tuning a model, rather than deploying an entirely new one, enterprises optimize resource utilization, while achieving higher accuracy.
- **Alignment with Enterprise Goals**: Organizations can enforce specific knowledge constraints, compliance requirements, or custom formatting based on their specific business needs.

Types of Fine-Tuning

Once the need for fine-Tuning is established, it is important to understand the various approaches available. Each type of Fine-Tuning offers different levels of customization, efficiency, and control, outlined as follows.

- **Supervised Fine-Tuning**: This approach involves training the model on labelled data to enhance its performance on specific tasks, such as sentiment analysis or text classification. It requires a dataset with clear input-output pairs to guide the model's learning process.
- **Instruction Fine-Tuning**: Models are trained using examples that demonstrate how to respond to the specific queries, improving their ability to perform

tasks based on instructions. This method is useful for tasks that require the model to follow specific guidelines or formats.

- **Parameter-Efficient Fine-Tuning (PEFT):** Only a small subset of the model's parameters is updated, reducing computational requirements, and preventing the loss of pre-trained knowledge. This technique is efficient for adapting models to new tasks, without requiring extensive data or resources. This also reduces computational overhead, while preserving the foundational model's capabilities.

  The popular PEFT techniques include:

  - **Low-Rank Adaptation (LoRA)**: Injects low-rank weight matrices into the transformer layers, improving efficiency with minimal impact on the performance.
  - **Adapters**: Introduces lightweight trainable layers between frozen layers, allowing targeted modifications.
  - **Prompt Tuning**: Trains soft prompts, instead of modifying model weights, ideal for adapting LLMs to new tasks, without a complete retraining process.

  Cortex Fine-Tuning leverages PEFT to create customized adaptors for pre-trained models. This approach enables efficient adaptation to domain-specific tasks by adjusting the model's parameters using examples from the user's data.

- **Task-Specific Fine-Tuning**: Focuses on adjusting models for particular tasks or domains, achieving high performance in specialized applications. This approach ensures that the model is optimized for the specific needs of the task at hand.

  Snowflake Cortex introduces a streamlined function for fine-tuning LLMs within the Snowflake ecosystem. By leveraging Cortex's native AI capabilities, enterprises can adapt foundation models to their unique data, without the complexity of external infrastructure. The subsequent section explores how Snowflake Cortex simplifies fine-tuning, enabling businesses to leverage LLMs efficiently and securely, within their Snowflake environments.

Cortex Fine-Tuning

In the context of Snowflake Cortex, fine-tuning offers a powerful way to adapt large language models to the specific tasks using the custom data. Cortex provides a fully managed service that simplifies the fine-tuning process, allowing users to create customized models, without extensive machine learning expertise. The FINETUNE function is central to this process, enabling users to initiate, monitor, and deploy fine-tuned models within the Snowflake environment.

Snowflake Cortex Fine-Tuning is a fully managed service that enables organizations to customize Large Language Models (LLMs) with their own data, all within the Snowflake platform. It allows you to take a pre-trained foundation model, and *fine-tune* its behavior on domain-specific tasks by training it on example inputs and outputs from your business. This fine-tuning is achieved via Parameter-Efficient Techniques (PEFT) that attach small adaptors to the original model, so that you do not have to retrain or modify the billions of base model parameters. The result is a custom model that better understands your data and use case, achieving greater accuracy and relevance for your specific business context.

By operating entirely inside Snowflake's Data Cloud, Cortex Fine-Tuning plays a key role in AI/ML workflows: It bridges the gap between the raw enterprise data and advanced AI, letting data teams quickly transform a general LLM into a tailored model, ready for production use without leaving the secure Snowflake environment. This approach can outperform heavy prompt engineering or retrieval-augmented generation hacks when you need the model to internalize the domain knowledge, providing improved latency and results for specialized tasks.

Architecture Overview

Snowflake Cortex Fine-Tuning is implemented as a serverless, fully managed pipeline, tightly integrated with Snowflake's data and security architecture.

Under this hood, it is exposed as a SQL function (**`SNOWFLAKE.CORTEX.FINETUNE`**), and a no-code UI workflow in Snowsight (Cortex Studio). When a fine-tuning job is created, Snowflake orchestrates the training process on your behalf – the training data is read directly from a Snowflake table or view, and the actual model fine-tuning computation is executed on Snowflake-managed infrastructure (with no need for the user to provision servers or GPUs). In fact, when using the UI, you select a Snowflake warehouse only for data loading as the heavy lifting of model training occurs in Snowflake's dedicated AI service layer. The fine-tuning uses Parameter-Efficient Fine-tuning (PEFT) under the covers, meaning it does not alter all the weights of the base LLM. Instead, it trains a small number of additional parameters (for example, low-rank adapter layers) that "*wrap*" or augment the base model. This keeps the process efficient in terms of compute and memory, and only the adapter weights are learned as well as the base model's general knowledge is preserved, while being steered toward your task.

The outcome of a fine-tuning job is a new model artifact registered in Snowflake's Model Registry within a specified database/schema. This means that the fine-tuned model is stored as a first-class Snowflake object, much like a table or view, and it inherits Snowflake's security and governance controls. The model registry entry includes just the custom adaptor weights and metadata, referencing the original base model. At the inference time, Snowflake knows how to apply these adaptors on top of the base model to generate predictions. This design avoids ever moving your data or model outside Snowflake, that is, all the data stays in the platform, and even the model customization remains within your Snowflake account's secure boundary.

The architecture consists of the following key components:

- **Base Model Selection**: Snowflake provides pre-integrated foundation models from leading AI providers, including Mistral 7B and llama 3 70B. These models are hosted within Snowflake, eliminating the need to download or manually import them.
- **Data Integration:** Training data is sourced directly from Snowflake tables or views, ensuring that fine-tuning occurs in place, without exporting the sensitive enterprise data. Thus, the system expects the structured data containing a prompt (input), and a completion (expected output) for supervised learning.

Training Execution via Cortex Fine-Tune

Users initiate fine-tuning jobs using either:

- **SQL commands** (`SNOWFLAKE.CORTEX.FINETUNE()`).
- **A No-code UI in Snowsight** (AI and ML Studio) which provides guided model selection and dataset configuration.

As mentioned in the data integration step, note that the training data must be sourced from a Snowflake table or view, and your query results must include columns, specifically named **`prompt`** and **`completion`**. If your existing table structure does not have columns with these exact names, you will need to use column aliases in your SQL query to rename them appropriately. This query will be passed as a parameter to the **`FINETUNE`** function. The function will then return an error, if it cannot find both the prompt and completion columns in your query results.

The following figure provides a snapshot of the supported models and their context windows as of the time of authoring this book. Since Snowflake continuously expands its models and capabilities at a rapid pace, it is recommended to check Snowflake documentation for the most up-to-date list.

Cortex Fine-Tuning - Context Window and Supported Models

Model	Context Window	Input Context (prompt)	Output Context (completion)
llama3-8b	8k	6k	2k
llama3-70b	8k	6k	2k
llama3.1-8b	24k	20k	4k
llama3.1-70b	8k	6k	2k
mistral-7b	32k	28k	4k
mixtral-8×7b	32k	28k	4k

Figure 6.1: *Context Window and Supported Models*

Instead of modifying the entire model, Cortex Fine-Tuning trains only a small set of additional parameters through PEFT methods, such as:

- **LoRA (Low-Rank Adaptation)**: Injects small trainable matrices into transformer layers.
- **Adapters**: Adds lightweight layers between frozen model layers.
- **Prompt Tuning**: Optimizes prompts to guide the model without modifying its weights.

Model Registry and Deployment

Once trained, the fine-tuned model is stored in Snowflake's Model Registry, allowing users to:

- **Deploy** it for real-time inference using the `SNOWFLAKE.CORTEX.COMPLETE()` function.
- **Apply governance and access control policies** using Snowflake's role-based security model.

Inference and Query Integration

The fine-tuned model can be accessed directly via SQL queries or integrated into dashboards, applications, and data pipelines, without requiring additional API layers. The computer cost for Snowflake Cortex Fine-Tuning function is determined by the number of tokens used during training. Additionally, executing the `COMPLETE` function on a fine-tuned model incurs compute costs based on the number of tokens processed.

For detailed cost information in credits per million tokens, refer to the Snowflake Service Consumption Table.

Advantages of Cortex Fine-Tuning

Snowflake Cortex Fine-Tuning drastically simplifies the fine-tuning process compared to the traditional methods, while offering strong advantages in cost, security, and data integration. In a conventional setting, fine-tuning a model might involve setting up a separate ML infrastructure, moving data to external systems, writing Python code with ML frameworks, and managing the GPUs or cloud services. Cortex eliminates that complexity by making fine-tuning available as an easy query option inside the data platform. Even users with minimal ML or coding experience can initiate a fine-tune from the Snowflake web UI shown earlier, instead of dealing with scripts and servers. Being a managed service, Cortex Fine-tuning also means you do not have to worry about how to deploy the model or scale it as Snowflake handles the heavy lifting and scalability behind the scenes.

The following are some of the key advantages of using Cortex Fine-Tuning:

- **SQL-Driven Simplicity:** One of the most significant advantages of Cortex Fine-Tuning is its ease of use. Unlike conventional fine-tuning methods that require deep machine learning expertise and extensive Python coding, Cortex enables users to fine-tune models using a simple SQL function or a no-code UI within Snowsight. This democratizes AI customization, making it accessible to data analysts and business users, without requiring them to manage ML infrastructure or write complex training scripts. The ability to fine-tune directly in Snowflake reduces friction in AI adoption, and accelerates deployment.
- **Cost-Efficiency and Performance:** Fine-Tuning typically requires significant computational power which can be costly and resource-intensive. Cortex Fine-Tuning addresses this challenge by leveraging Parameter-Efficient Fine-Tuning (PEFT) techniques, such as LoRA and adapters which allow users to fine-tune only a small fraction of the model's parameters, while keeping the base model intact. This approach drastically reduces the compute costs, while still delivering performance improvements that rival much larger, fully fine-tuned models. Thus, by making fine-tuning efficient, businesses can achieve domain-specific accuracy, without incurring high cloud GPU costs. A major benefit is that you can take a relatively small model, and make it perform like a much larger one on your task which means you can achieve high accuracy without incurring the high runtime costs of a huge model. This not only saves money on inference (since queries can use the smaller tuned model going forward), but also avoids the enormous expense of training a large model from scratch.
- **Secure, In-Platform Training:** Security is a top concern for enterprises when

dealing with AI models, particularly those trained on proprietary or sensitive data. Cortex Fine-Tuning eliminates the risks associated with external AI services by ensuring that both training and inference happen entirely within Snowflake Data Cloud. Since no data needs to be moved outside the platform, businesses benefit from Snowflake's built-in security, governance, and compliance features. Organizations in regulated industries, such as finance, healthcare, and legal services can fine-tune AI models, while maintaining strict data residency and access control policies.

- **Seamless Integration into Workflows:** The fine-tuned models in Cortex are treated as first-class objects in Snowflake, making them easy to integrate into the existing workflows. The trained models are stored in Snowflake's Model Registry, allowing users to call them directly through SQL queries, BI dashboards, or applications, without any external deployment requirements. Hence, whether an organization wants to automate customer service responses, generate financial risk assessments, or personalize e-commerce recommendations, Cortex Fine-Tuning ensures that AI insights can be embedded seamlessly into the decision-making processes. This deep integration reduces operational complexity and accelerates AI-driven innovation across different business functions.

Implementation Walkthrough

Let us look at the implementation by leveraging a case study. This case study features ZenTime, a fictional smartwatch manufacturer, to illustrate a practical application of Snowflake Cortex Fine-Tuning.

Background and Challenge

ZenTime, a growing smartwatch manufacturer, faced increasing pressure on its customer support infrastructure as its product line expanded. The support team was overwhelmed by the manual classification of thousands of monthly tickets into these five standard categories: "`Billing Issues`," "`Technical Issues`," "`Delivery Related/Missing Items`," "`Battery Problems`," and "`Product Issues`."

- **Billing Issues:** Subscription payment failures, refund requests, discount code problems, warranty coverage questions, and unexpected charges.
- **Technical Issues:** App connectivity failures, software update errors, synchronization problems, Bluetooth pairing difficulties, and account access problems
- **Delivery Related/Missing Items:** Shipping delays, lost packages, incomplete orders, incorrect delivery addresses, missing accessories, and so on.

- **Battery Problem:** Short battery life, failure to hold a charge, overheating, while charging, unexpected shutdowns, and charging cable malfunctions.
- **Product Issues:** Physical damage, screen malfunctions, unresponsive buttons, water damage claims, and so on.

The company initially considered several third-party AI solutions for ticket classification, but security concerns emerged in preliminary assessments. As a manufacturer handling sensitive customer information and proprietary product data, ZenTime needed a solution that would keep all the data within its existing security perimeter.

Solution Approach

After evaluating multiple options, the company decided to implement Snowflake Cortex fine-tuning for several key reasons:

- Their customer data was already stored and managed within Snowflake.
- Using external AI services would require data exports, creating potential security vulnerabilities.
- The company's data governance policies strongly favored keeping sensitive information within the established systems.
- They needed a cost-efficient solution, and Snowflake Cortex fine-tuning certainly offered the flexibility to optimize a smaller model to perform like a much larger one on their specific tasks (categorization of support tickets) and achieving high accuracy, without incurring high runtime costs.

Now, let us walk through the implementation step-by-step using Snowflake Notebook. We will use a data set with 200+ support tickets.

Step-by-Step Implementation

Before we begin, if you would like to code along, please ensure the following:

1. **`ZenTime_Customer_Support_Dataset.csv`** is loaded to **`CORTEX_AI_DB.PUBLIC. ZENTIME_CUSTOMER_SUPPORT_TICKETS`**
2. Import the Cortex Finetune Support **`Tickets.ipynb`** file to a new notebook in **`CORTEX_AI_DB.PUBLIC`** and the notebook warehouse of your choice, as shown in the following figure. Click **`Create`**.

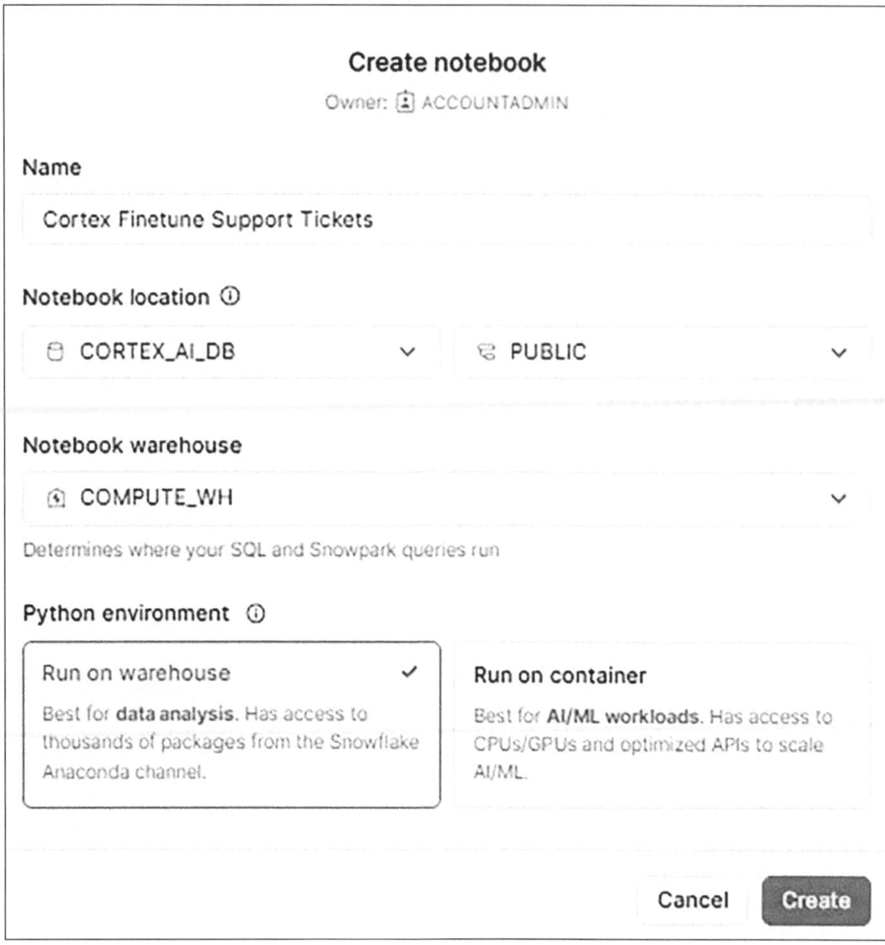

Figure 6.2: *Create New Notebook*

Now, we will proceed with the explanation for each cell.

Step 1: Setting Up a Snowflake Session

```
from snowflake.snowpark.context import get_active_session
import snowflake.snowpark.functions as F
session = get_active_session()
df = session.table('ZENTIME_CUSTOMER_SUPPORT_TICKETS')
df
```

Figure 6.3: *Set Session*

The first step in the notebook sets up the Snowflake Snowpark session which enables interaction with Snowflake's Data Cloud for executing SQL queries, and managing datasets. The **get_active_session()** function is used to retrieve the active session that acts as a bridge between the notebook and Snowflake.

The Snowflake table **ZENTIME_CUSTOMER_SUPPORT_TICKETS** is then retrieved into a DataFrame "**df**". This table contains historical customer support tickets, and serves as the dataset for training and evaluating the fine-tuned model.

	SUPPORT_TICKET_ID	ISSUE_DESCRIPTION
0	1	My watch won't turn on even after charging overnight. I've tried different c
1	2	I was charged twice for my ZenTime Pro purchase. Please refund the dupli
2	3	The tracking shows my order was delivered but I never received it. Packag
3	4	Battery drains completely within 4 hours even with minimal use. This is un
4	5	My monthly subscription fee increased without any notification. Why am I
5	6	Touch screen is unresponsive in certain areas. Right side of screen doesn't
6	7	Received the wrong color watch. Ordered Midnight Black but received Sky
7	8	Watch shows fully charged but shuts down at 75% battery remaining consi
8	9	I cancelled my subscription last month but was charged again. Need imme
9	10	Heart rate monitor giving inconsistent readings and sometimes is showing

Figure 6.4: *Dataframe Output from the Table*

Step 2: Define a Prompt Template

As required, before fine-tuning, the notebook first creates a prompt to classify the customer support tickets. A structured prompt is defined, instructing the model on how to categorize customer issues based on five predefined categories, such as: Technical Issues, Billing Issues, Delivery-Related/Missing Items, Battery Problems, and Product Issues. This template clearly defines the task parameters, instructing the model to act as a classification agent for smartwatch issues.

The prompt provides detailed descriptions of each category to guide the model's classification. This setup ensures that the model follows a structured decision-making process when predicting the category for a given issue description. Thus, the prompt concludes with strict instructions to return only one of the specified categories, ensuring consistent formatting in the responses.

```
prompt = """You are an agent that determines the category of an issue based on the ISSUE_DESCRIPTION
for smartwatches.

These are the ONLY possible categories:
- Technical Issues
- Billing Issues
- Delivery Related / Missing Items
- Battery Problem
- Product Issues

Given an ISSUE_DESCRIPTION, return only one category from the list above.
Here is a description for each category that you could use to categorize.

Billing Issues: Subscription payment failures, refund requests, discount code problems,
warranty coverage questions, and unexpected charges

Technical Issues: App connectivity failures, software update errors, synchronization problems,
Bluetooth pairing difficulties, and account access problems

Delivery Related / Missing Items: Shipping delays, lost packages, incomplete orders, incorrect delivery address
incorrect items such as different colour or specifications than what was requested

Battery Problem: Short battery life, failure to hold charge, overheating while charging, unexpected shutdowns,
fluctuating battery performance, and charging cable malfunctions

Product Issues: Physical damage, screen malfunctions, unresponsive buttons, water damage claims.

Strictly do not return anything else."""
```

Figure 6.5: *Prompt Definition*

Step 3: Generate Responses with Mistral-large2

This step executes an SQL query that processes each support ticket through the larger mistral-large2 model. This is one of the most advanced models with a context size of 128,000 tokens. For each ticket in the **`zentime_customer_support_tickets`** table, it concatenates the previously defined prompt with the issue description, and passes this to Snowflake Cortex's complete function. The results are stored in a DataFrame called **`df_mistral_large2_response`** which contains the ticket ID, original description, and the category classification generated by the **`mistral-large2`** model. The trim function removes any extraneous newlines from the model's responses.

```
mistral_large2_response_sql = f""" select support_ticket_id, ISSUE_DESCRIPTION,
trim(snowflake.cortex.complete('mistral-large2',concat('{prompt}',ISSUE_DESCRIPTION)),'\n')
as mistral_large2_response
from zentime_customer_support_tickets"""
df_mistral_large2_response = session.sql(mistral_large2_response_sql)
df_mistral_large2_response
```

SUPPORT_TICKET_ID	ISSUE_DESCRIPTION	MISTRAL_LARGE2_RESPONSE
1	My watch won't turn on even after charging overnight. I've tried different c	Battery Problem
2	I was charged twice for my ZenTime Pro purchase. Please refund the dupli	Billing Issues
3	The tracking shows my order was delivered but I never received it. Packag	Delivery Related / Missing Item
4	Battery drains completely within 4 hours even with minimal use. This is un	Battery Problem
5	My monthly subscription fee increased without any notification. Why am I	Billing Issues
6	Touch screen is unresponsive in certain areas. Right side of screen doesn't	Product Issues
7	Received the wrong color watch. Ordered Midnight Black but received Sky	Delivery Related / Missing Item
8	Watch shows fully charged but shuts down at 75% battery remaining consi	Battery Problem
9	I cancelled my subscription last month but was charged again. Need imme	Billing Issues
10	Heart rate monitor giving inconsistent readings and sometimes is showing	Technical Issues

Figure 6.6: *Generate Response Using Mistral_large2*

As observed, the model has accurately assigned categories by associating the extensive details provided in the prompt template with the issue description.

Step 4: Generate Responses with Mistral-7b

Like the previous step, this stage performs the same classification task, but uses the smaller mistral-7b model, instead. With a context window of 32,000 tokens, mistral-7b is significantly smaller, and comes at a much lower cost compared to the larger model. The same support tickets are processed through this model using an identical approach, with results stored in **`df_mistral_7b_response`**. This allows the team to assess how the smaller, more cost-efficient model performs on their classification task compared to the larger, more expensive model. Let us examine the response.

```
mistral_7b_response_sql = f""" select support_ticket_id, ISSUE_DESCRIPTION,
trim(snowflake.cortex.complete('mistral-7b',concat('{prompt}',ISSUE_DESCRIPTION)),'\n') a
from zentime_customer_support_tickets"""
df_mistral_7b_response = session.sql(mistral_7b_response_sql)
df_mistral_7b_response
```

JPP(	ISSUE_DESCRIPTION	MISTRAL_7B_RESPONSE
17	I was promised a discount code after survey completior	Based on the given ISSUE_DESCF
18	Weather app constantly crashes and forces watch to re	Technical Issues
19	The protective screen film was missing from my packag	Delivery Related / Missing Items
20	Watch gets extremely hot while charging and battery pe	Battery Problem
21	I was charged for express shipping but my order took 2	Delivery Related / Missing Items
22	Microphone not working during calls. People can't hear	Technical Issues. This issue falls ı
23	Received open box item with fingerprints and scratches	Product Issues. This issue falls ur
24	Battery randomly jumps from 60% to 5% without warnin	Battery Problem
25	Annual subscription renewed automatically despite turn	Billing Issues.
26	Watch face keeps changing randomly throughout the di	Product Issues This issue falls ur

Figure 6.7: *Generate Response Using Mistral_ 7b*

Upon examination of the responses, the **`mistral-7b`** model frequently produces verbose and inconsistent outputs that fail to adhere to the instruction constraints. Despite the explicit prompt requesting only the category name, it tends to return explanatory phrases such as "*Based on the given* ISSUE_DESCRIPTION, *this is a Billing Issues category,*" or unnecessarily detailed classifications, such as "*Product Issues (specifically, 'physical damage' or 'water damage claims' subcategory).*" These wordy and inconsistent responses demonstrate the smaller model's difficulty in following strict formatting instructions, highlighting a key area for improvement through fine-tuning.

Step 5: Compare Model Responses

In this analysis step, the results from both the models are joined based on the support ticket identifiers. By selecting the relevant columns (**`SUPPORT_TICKET_ID`**, **`mistral_large2_response`**, and **`mistral_7b_response`**), we create a side-by-side comparison that allows immediate evaluation of how each model classified the same tickets. This comparison is crucial for understanding performance differences between the models, and will inform the fine-tuning approach.

```
df_llms = df_mistral_large2_response.join(df_mistral_7b_response,'SUPPORT_TICKET_ID')
df_llms[['SUPPORT_TICKET_ID', 'mistral_large2_response','mistral_7b_response']]
```

SUPPORT_TICKET_ID	MISTRAL_LARGE2_RESPONSE	MISTRAL_7B_RESPONSE
9	Billing Issues	Billing Issues
10	Technical Issues	Product Issues This issue falls ui
11	Delivery Related / Missing Items	Delivery Related / Missing Items
12	Product Issues	Product Issues (specifically, "phy
13	Billing Issues	Billing Issues
14	Technical Issues	Technical Issues (App connectivi
15	Delivery Related / Missing Items	Delivery Related / Missing Items
16	Battery Problem	Battery Problem
17	Billing Issues	Based on the given ISSUE_DESCI
18	Technical Issues	Technical Issues

Figure 6.8: *Response Comparison*

The comparison clearly shows that while **`mistral-large2`** typically returns clean, single-category responses such as "**`Billing Issues`**" or "**`Technical Issues`**" that align perfectly with the required format, the **`mistral-7b`** model frequently provides inconsistent, verbose responses. These differences highlight why the more economical smaller model is not suitable in its current form for ZenTime's automated ticket classification system. The comparison provides compelling evidence that fine-tuning is necessary to make the smaller model adhere to the strict response formatting requirements, while maintaining accurate classifications.

Step 6: Generate Dataset for Fine-Tuning

This preparation step implements a knowledge distillation strategy, transferring the advanced capabilities of the larger **`mistral-large2`** model to the more economical **`mistral-7b`** model. The code creates a structured dataset, specifically designed for fine-tuning by taking the original issue descriptions, and pairing them with the high-quality classifications produced by **mistral-large2**. By using the **df_mistral_large2_response** DataFrame as the source, the function creates a new "**prompt**" column that concatenates the instruction prompt template with each issue description. The resulting dataset effectively serves as an expert-labeled training corpus where the large model's concise, accurate responses become the target outputs that the smaller model will learn to emulate. This knowledge transfer approach allows ZenTime to achieve the classification quality of the expensive larger model, while deploying the more economical smaller model in production.

```
df_fine_tune = df_mistral_large2_response.with_column(
    "prompt",
    F.concat(
        F.lit(prompt), F.lit(" "),
        F.col("ISSUE_DESCRIPTION"), F.lit(" ")
    )
).select("SUPPORT_TICKET_ID", "prompt", "mistral_large2_response")
# df_fine_tune
df_fine_tune.write.mode('overwrite').save_as_table('zentime_customer_support_tickets_finetune')
```

Figure 6.9: *Generate Dataset for Fine-tuning*

The prepared dataset is then saved as a new table in Snowflake called '**zentime_customer_support_tickets_finetune**', creating a resource that can be used for fine-tuning, as more support tickets are processed. This table structure is designed to match the requirements of Snowflake's fine-tuning API.

Step 7: Split the Data into Training and Evaluation Sets

This step creates the required train-test split necessary for the Snowflake Cortex fine-tuning process. Since the **CORTEX.FINETUNE** function specifically requires both training and evaluation datasets as mandatory inputs, this split is an essential prerequisite for the fine-tuning operation. Using the **random_split** method with a weight distribution of 80% for training and 20% for evaluation, the code divides the previously created dataset into two distinct subsets. A seed value of 42 is specified to ensure the reproducibility of the split, which is important for consistent results, if the notebook is rerun. The resulting datasets are saved as separate tables in Snowflake: **'zentime_customer_support_train'** contains the examples that will be used to update the model's weights during fine-tuning, while **'zentime_customer_support_eval'** provides the holdout data that will be used to measure the model's performance and prevent overfitting. This step is a critical component of the fine-tuning methodology in Snowflake Cortex, as it enables proper evaluation of the model's learning progress.

```
train_df, eval_df = session.table("zentime_customer_support_tickets_finetune").random_split(weights=[0.8, 0.2],
                                                                                             seed=42)
train_df.write.mode('overwrite').save_as_table('zentime_customer_support_train')
eval_df.write.mode('overwrite').save_as_table('zentime_customer_support_eval')
```

Figure 6.10: *Splitting the Data for Training and Evaluation*

Step 8: Fine-Tune the Model

This is the central operation of the notebook where knowledge distillation is implemented through fine-tuning. The SQL statement calls Snowflake's **`CORTEX.FINETUNE`** function to create a new model named '**`zentime_customer_support_FINETUNED_mistral_7b_model`**' using the economical **`mistral-7b`** as the base model. The function is strategically provided with the outputs from the larger, more capable **`mistral-large2`** model as the target completions. By mapping the **`mistral_large2_response`** column as the "**`completion`**" field in both training and evaluation datasets, the function explicitly teaches the smaller model to emulate the high-quality, concise classifications of the larger model. This knowledge transfer technique is the key to ZenTime's dual goal of achieving high classification accuracy, while minimizing the operational costs. The smaller model, once fine-tuned, will be able to deliver responses that match the quality of the larger model, but at a fraction of the computational cost and inference time.

SQL ∨ as Finetune_mistral_7b 4.1s

```sql
select SNOWFLAKE.CORTEX.FINETUNE('CREATE',
'CORTEX_AI_DB.PUBLIC.zentime_customer_support_FINETUNED_mistral_7b_mod
el','mistral-7b', 'SELECT prompt, mistral_large2_response as
completion from CORTEX_AI_DB.PUBLIC.zentime_customer_support_train',
'SELECT prompt, mistral_large2_response as completion from
CORTEX_AI_DB.PUBLIC.zentime_customer_support_eval')zentime_fine_tuned_
job_id;
```

	ZENTIME_FINE_TUNED_JOB_ID
0	ft_857b7902-238b-4e8d-ac73-04fa40829220

Figure 6.11: *Create the Fine-tuned Model*

The above query returns a Job Id. Copy the value of this Job Id, and paste it in the query in Step 9 as the second parameter.

Step 9: Check Fine-Tuning Job Status

After initiating the fine-tuning job, this step monitors its progress. The SQL query calls the **`FINETUNE`** function again, but this time with the **`'DESCRIBE'`** operation, and the specific job ID that was returned from the previous fine-tuning call (If you are executing the notebook, please copy the specific **`zentime_fine_tuned_job_id`** returned in the previous step, and replace it in this query). This will retrieve the detailed information about the job's current status.

```
select snowflake.cortex.finetune('DESCRIBE', 'ft_857b7902-238b-4e8d-
ac73-04fa40829220');
```

Figure 6.12: *Check the Status of the Fine-Tune Job*

This monitoring step is particularly vital because fine-tuning can run for an extended period depending on the dataset. Hence, this status-checking capability is essential for operational monitoring. Next, observe how the Status changes from initially at **INPROGRESS** to **SUCCESS**, signifying the completion of the fine-tuning process. ***The fine-tuning process will take some time to complete. So, please check the Status periodically using the Describe command and wait to execute the remaining cells, until you see a "SUCCESS" status. Otherwise the Inference step will throw an error that the model does not exist.***

Scroll through the output, and verify the status. See that it mentions "**status**":"**IN_PROGRESS**" init*ially*

```
SNOWFLAKE.CORTEX.FINETUNE('DESCRIBE', 'FT_857B7902-238B-4E8D-
7b","created_on":1745666489804,"id":"ft_857b7902-238b-4e8d-ac73-
04fa40829220","progress":1.0,"status":"IN_PROGRESS","training_data":"
```

Figure 6.13: *Fine-Tuning "IN_PROGRESS" Status*

Run the command, and check the status. Note the "**status**":"**SUCCESS**" message. Also, notice that the first line in the result will now show a **finished_on** time.

```
SNOWFLAKE.CORTEX.FINETUNE('DESCRIBE', 'FT_857B7902-238B-4E8D-
port_FINETUNED_mistral_7b_model","progress":1.0,"status":"SUCCESS","
training_data":"SELECT prompt, mistral_large2_response as completion
from
```

Figure 6.14: *Fine-Tuning "SUCCESS" Status*

This command allows ZenTime's data team to monitor the fine-tuning process to completion.

Step 10: Inference using the Fine-Tuned Model

The final active step evaluates the performance of the newly fine-tuned model. It constructs an SQL query that processes the original support tickets through the fine-tuned model. This query follows the same pattern as the earlier model testing, combining the prompt template with each issue description, and storing the classifications in a new column. The results are collected in a DataFrame called **df_**

fine_tuned_mistral_7b_response and displayed, demonstrating how effectively the smaller model has been optimized for ZenTime's specific classification needs.

```
fine_tuned_model_name = 'zentime_customer_support_FINETUNED_mistral_7b_model'

sql = f"""select support_ticket_id, issue_description,
trim(snowflake.cortex.complete('{fine_tuned_model_name}',concat('{prompt}',
issue_description)),'\n') as zt_fine_tuned_mistral_7b_model_response
from zentime_customer_support_tickets"""

df_fine_tuned_mistral_7b_response = session.sql(sql)
df_fine_tuned_mistral_7b_response
```

ISSUE_DESCRIPTION	ZT_FINE_TUNED_MISTRAL_7B
My watch won't turn on even after charging overnight. I've tried different c	Battery Problem
I was charged twice for my ZenTime Pro purchase. Please refund the dupli	Billing Issues
The tracking shows my order was delivered but I never received it. Packag	Delivery Related / Missing Ite
Battery drains completely within 4 hours even with minimal use. This is un:	Battery Problem
My monthly subscription fee increased without any notification. Why am I I	Billing Issues
Touch screen is unresponsive in certain areas. Right side of screen doesn't	Product Issues

Figure 6.15: *Fine-Tuned Response*

All the categories are now correctly worded and properly formatted. However, there may still be occasional misclassifications, even though the formatting is accurate. Expanding the training dataset can help ensure sufficient records for each category, leading to a highly accurate model.

This notebook effectively demonstrates the complete workflow of assessing the baseline models, preparing high-quality training data, fine-tuning a smaller model to emulate a larger one, and evaluating the results—all within the secure Snowflake environment that ZenTime required for their sensitive customer data.

Thus, ZenTime's proof of concept using Snowflake Cortex fine-tuning proved to be tremendously successful! The fine-tuned mistral-7b model achieved a total classification accuracy, at a much lower inference cost than the large models. After fine-tuning the entire corpus of tickets, and deploying the fine-tuned model to production, ZenTime experienced a significant reduction in ticket routing time, and a significant improvement in the first-contact resolution rates. Customer satisfaction scores also increased due to faster response times. Hence, the simple SQL-based API call provided an easy inference access. Additionally, the security requirements were fully satisfied as all the data remained within their Snowflake environment throughout the entire process. This successful implementation established a foundation for expanding AI capabilities across other business functions, while maintaining ZenTime's commitment to both cost efficiency and data security.

Cortex Fine-Tune Using Snowsight

Cortex Fine-Tuning can also be achieved via the Snowsight user interface from the AI and ML Studio.

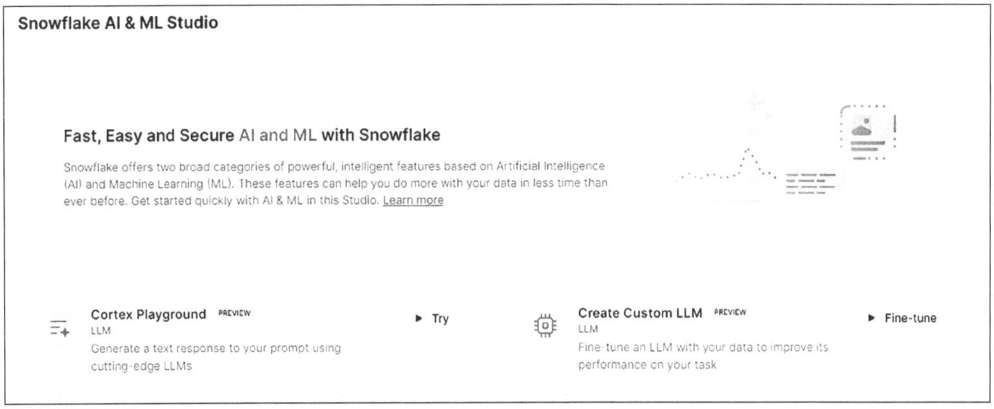

Figure 6.16: *Fine-Tune via Snowsight UI*

You would require the tables with prompt completion (which is the output of the larger model), train and validation data created and available for performing the fine-tune function. In our previous section using Snowflake Notebook, these were stored in the tables **`-zentime_customer_support_tickets_finetune`**, **`zentime_customer_support_train`** and **`zentime_customer_support_eval`**, respectively.

Some of the simple high-level guided instructions are as follows:

- Navigate to the AI/ML studio, and click the Fine-tune option within the Create Custom LLM section (*currently in preview*), as shown earlier.
- From the dropdown menu, choose your base (foundation) model that will serve as the starting point for fine-tuning.
- Specify the execution context by selecting both your access role (which must have **`SNOWFLAKE.CORTEX_USER`** privileges), and the computer warehouse that will process your fine-tuning job.
- Designate a storage location by choosing which database will house your completed fine-tuned model.
- Provide a descriptive name for your custom model, and then proceed by clicking **`Let's go`**.
- Identify your training dataset by selecting the appropriate table or view (you can access data from any schema where your role has permissions).
- Indicate which column in your dataset contains the input prompts, and then continue to the next step.

- Specify the column that contains the target outputs (completions) that your model should learn to generate.
- Optionally, configure validation by either selecting a separate validation dataset table, or choosing **`Skip`** this option, if you are not using a dedicated validation set.
- Review all your configuration choices on the summary screen, and initiate the process by selecting **`Start training`**.
- Monitor your job after submission through the confirmation screen which displays a unique Job ID. Track your fine-tuning progress by querying this ID with the **`SNOWFLAKE.CORTEX.FINETUNE`** function using **`'DESCRIBE'`** as the operation parameter. Once the status indicates successful completion, your model is ready for deployment, and can be immediately used for inference via the complete function as demonstrated in the implementation examples.

Use Cases and Industry Applications

Snowflake Cortex Fine-Tuning provides organizations with the ability to tailor the capabilities of large foundation models to their unique operational contexts by securely leveraging proprietary data within the Snowflake platform. As illustrated in *Figure* 6.17, the fine-tuning process refines a pre-trained large model using organization-specific datasets through Cortex's fine-tuning engine, resulting in a smaller, task-optimized model. This smaller model achieves high accuracy, while substantially lowering the computational costs, typically associated with running large-scale AI systems.

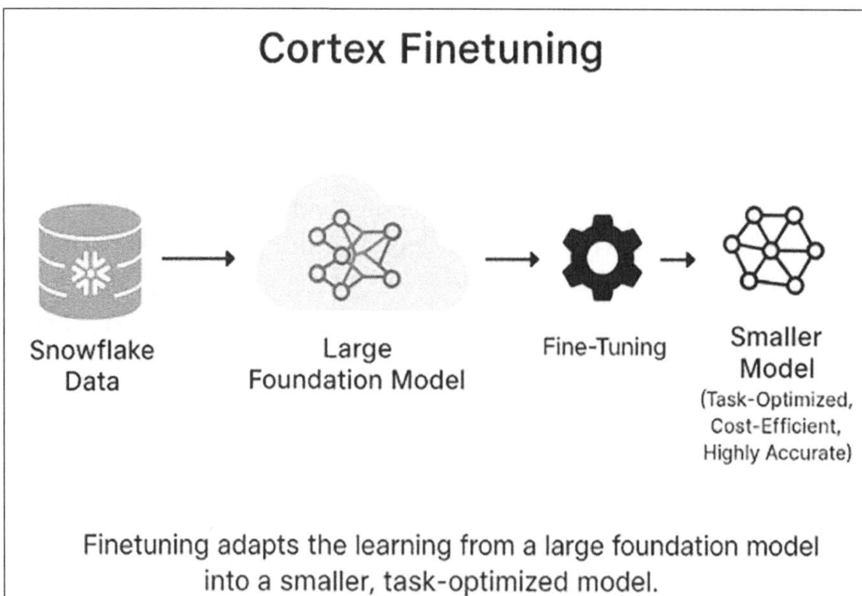

Figure 6.17: *Fine-Tuning Process*

This approach empowers industries, such as financial services, retail, healthcare, and so on to build highly specialized AI solutions, enhancing operational efficiency, improving accuracy, and reducing the cost and complexity, typically associated with deploying large models. The use cases mentioned below are intended to illustrate potential applications across different industries. These examples are not exhaustive as in practice, Cortex Fine-Tuning can be leveraged anywhere, where there is a meaningful opportunity to apply domain-specific data to enhance predictions, automate processes, improve decision-making, and optimize performance – all while realizing significant cost savings.

Even in financial services, Snowflake Cortex Fine-Tuning could be used to customize foundation models on a banks' proprietary data, such as transaction records, compliance logs, and customer interactions. By fine-tuning smaller models within Snowflake, financial institutions could automate fraud detection, streamline risk assessments, and enhance customer service through domain-specific AI advisors. This approach could deliver highly accurate outputs, while significantly reducing infrastructure costs, as smaller fine-tuned models are more efficient and cost-effective to deploy compared to the massive general-purpose models.

In retail and consumer goods, businesses could fine-tune models using structured sales data and unstructured customer feedback like chat transcripts and product reviews. Retailers could leverage these fine-tuned models to automate customer support, create personalized marketing content, and predict shopping trends with greater precision. Therefore, by relying on compact, fine-tuned models, rather than large generic ones, companies could not only improve customer engagement, but also achieve substantial cost savings in model inference and operational overhead.

In the healthcare sector too, organizations could fine-tune models on clinical notes, claims data, and diagnostic reports to automate administrative tasks such as medical coding, risk scoring, and patient intake summarization. The fine-tuned models tailored to specific medical terminologies and workflows could in fact, increase accuracy, while lowering the computational cost of running AI applications at scale. Similarly, industries such as telecommunications and manufacturing could fine-tune lightweight models on call center transcripts or maintenance logs, enabling smarter automation and predictive insights – all while keeping the operational costs in check by avoiding the heavy burden of running large foundation models.

Conclusion

To sum up, Snowflake Cortex Fine-Tuning represents a significant advancement in making AI more accessible, cost-effective, and secure for enterprises. By enabling organizations to optimize models within their existing data environment, it addresses several critical challenges that had previously limited AI adoption.

Additionally, ZenTime case study demonstrated how fine-tuning enables organizations to achieve the best of both worlds: High-quality results typically associated with larger, more expensive models, combined with the operational efficiency and lower costs of smaller models. This knowledge distillation approach–teaching a smaller, economical model to perform like its larger counterpart on specific tasks, makes advanced AI capabilities accessible to organizations.

Also, by integrating fine-tuned LLMs into their workflows, businesses could potentially see faster outcomes through automation, better accuracy on niche tasks, cost advantages and new AI-driven capabilities that were previously difficult to attain without a dedicated team of ML engineers. Thus, Snowflake Cortex Fine-Tuning serves as a key enabler for practical AI/ML applications in the enterprise, bringing advanced model customization within reach in the Snowflake Data Cloud.

With a solid understanding of model fine-tuning in place, we now turn our attention to one of the most transformative applications of AI in the enterprise: "*Natural language into actionable insights*", in the next chapter. We will explore how Snowflake Cortex bridges the gap between everyday questions and complex data analysis through powerful tools such as Cortex Analyst, Cortex Search and Cortex Agents.

CHAPTER 7
Natural Language Queries to Actionable Insights

Introduction

This chapter explores how Snowflake's Cortex features, including Cortex Analyst and Cortex Search, leverage advanced AI capabilities to transform natural language queries into actionable insights, enhancing the way businesses interact with, and derive value from their data. These components form the foundation of Snowflake Cortex AI's natural language processing capabilities, transforming how organizations interact with their data by enabling business users to ask complex questions in plain English, and receive meaningful, contextualized answers. Cortex Analyst and Cortex Search essentially function as AI agents, autonomously navigating complex data environments on behalf of business users through their agentic capabilities.

Cortex Analyst is a fully managed, AI-powered service in the Snowflake Cortex AI ecosystem designed to make analytics accessible through natural language. It serves as a "talk-to-your-data" interface, allowing users to ask business questions in plain English, and receive answers without writing SQL. Cortex Analyst fits into Snowflake's broader Cortex AI platform as a component focused on structured data and business intelligence queries. Its main purpose is to empower business users and data analysts alike to gain insights quickly, without a deep knowledge of database schemas or SQL syntax.

Cortex Search is a companion service within the Cortex AI suite that focuses on the unstructured data. While Cortex Analyst allows querying over structured datasets via natural language, Cortex Search enables semantic search over documents, PDFs, and text corpora using hybrid techniques such as vector search and keyword matching. Cortex Search empowers users to extract answers from qualitative content, such as policy documents, emails, or logs, expanding the scope of what can be analyzed and queried using AI. Together, Cortex Analyst and Cortex Search provide a complete natural language interface to both the structured and unstructured data, giving users a unified, intelligent access layer over the full spectrum of enterprise data assets.

We will also look at the recently introduced Cortex Agents that represent the next evolution in enterprise AI adoption, moving beyond individual AI functions toward orchestrated workflows that can reason across multiple steps, use specialized tools, and seamlessly switch context as required.

Towards the end of the chapter, we will also explore Snowflake Co-pilot, an AI-powered assistant that helps to write, understand, and optimize SQL queries. Finally, we will cover Cortex Playground, a no-code environment that allows users to provide prompts in natural language, and experiment with AI models early, helping teams to accelerate solution development.

Structure

In this chapter, we will cover the following topics:

- Bridging Natural Language and Data Insights using Cortex Analyst
- Unlocking Insights from Unstructured Data with Cortex Search
- Snowflake Cortex AI Agents: Orchestrating LLMs with Native Tools
- Overview of Snowflake Copilot for SQL Assistance
- Cortex Playground: A quick look

Bridging Natural Language and Data Insights using Cortex Analyst

Snowflake introduced Cortex Analyst (for text-to-SQL), alongside Cortex Search (for retrieval-augmented generation on documents), signaling a push toward self-service analytics with natural language interfaces. The general purpose of Cortex Analyst is to bridge the gap between technical data warehouses and non-technical users, that is it translates the everyday questions into SQL, executes them on Snowflake's engine, and returns results in an easily consumable form. This empowers business users and data analysts alike, to gain insights quickly, without a deep knowledge of the database schemas or SQL syntax. Mistral and Meta's llama models power Cortex Analyst.

The platform's significance lies in its ability to democratize data analysis across organizations, reducing the technical barriers that have historically limited who could effectively interrogate the data. By embedding AI throughout the analytics process, Cortex Analyst aims to accelerate time-to-insight, while maintaining governance and security standards that enterprise customers expect from Snowflake.

Within this ecosystem, Cortex Analyst works alongside other tools, such as: Cortex Search for hybrid semantic search on unstructured text, Cortex Guard for LLM content filtering, Cortex Fine-Tuning for model customization, and Cortex Studio for no-code AI application development. Cortex Analyst's role is focused on business intelligence, that is it leverages Large Language Models (LLMs) to interpret user questions, and generate SQL on the fly. The service is exposed via a REST API, meaning it can be integrated into chatbots, analytics applications, or BI tools as the brain that converts natural language to data results.

Historically, business users relied on static dashboards or had to ask data teams to write queries which was slow and inflexible. Cortex Analyst evolved to address this by using modern AI to let users converse with their data directly, marking a major step in the evolution of self-service analytics. Importantly, Cortex Analyst was designed from the ground up with a strong focus on security and governance. All interactions occur within the Snowflake environment, meaning the user data never leaves the platform and role-based access controls are applied in every query. This focus on governance distinguishes Snowflake's approach by ensuring that the ease of use does not compromise with data security.

To summarize the key aspects, let us go through the following:

- Cortex Analyst bridges the gap between the raw data and business understanding by providing a conversational interface.
- Built on Snowflake's secure data cloud, it ensures data governance and compliance.
- It also empowers analysts and business users to explore the data, without writing complex SQL queries.
- Powered by LLMs that are specifically tuned to understand the data within the Snowflake architecture.
- Provides a natural language layer on top of Snowflake's data, enabling faster insight generation and greater accessibility.

In the context of Snowflake Cortex AI, it serves as the conversational analyst that can reliably answer business questions at scale, using the power of AI but grounded in the accuracy of your enterprise data.

Understanding the Semantic Model Configuration in Cortex Analyst

One of the keys to Cortex Analyst's accuracy is its semantic model configuration, defined in YAML files. This YAML configuration acts as a blueprint that describes your data's business semantics - teaching the AI what your data means. Business users often use terms that do not exactly match with the technical database field names or structures. For example, a user might ask about "*customers*", while the underlying table is named **`CUST`** with columns like **`CUST_ID`**. Cortex Analyst uses the YAML semantic model to map these business terms to the physical schema, providing necessary context so that the LLM can generate the correct SQL. In other words, the YAML file defines a semantic layer that standardizes business terminology, defines measures, and dimensions, and specifies how different pieces of data relate to each other, bridging the gap between human language and the database structure. The semantic model, YAML, is designed to be readable by humans (so that analysts and data engineers can work with it), while being precise enough for the AI to follow.

Key components of a typical Cortex Analyst YAML file include:

- **Model Metadata:** A name and description for the semantic model, documenting its purpose or domain. This top section often describes the business domain (for example, "**`Sales Analytics Semantic Model`**"), and any high-level context.
- **Logical Tables:** These represent business entities or fact tables in the data warehouse. Each logical table in YAML is mapped to a physical Snowflake table or view (using fully qualified names for database, schema, and table). For example, a logical table customers might map to a physical table **`ORDER_DB.PUBLIC.CUST`**. The YAML allows providing a business-friendly description of each table, and defines a primary key, if applicable.
- **Dimensions:** Within each logical table, you list the dimensions, such as descriptive attributes like customer name, product category, region, and so on. Dimensions are specified with a name, a description, and often, one or more synonyms (alternate names or common terms). Synonyms are crucial because they help Cortex Analyst recognize a user's phrasing; for example, a dimension **`customer_name`** might include synonyms such as "**`client`**" or "**`buyer`**" so that a question using those terms is understood properly.
- **Facts:** These are quantitative fields - typically numeric measures or transaction details (for instance, **`sales_amount`**, **`quantity`**). They may also have synonyms and expressions. For example, a fact revenue could be defined as an expression price * quantity with a description, such as "**`Sales revenue for the line item`**" and synonyms such as "**`sales`**" or "**`sales_amount`**." Thus, by defining facts, we tell Cortex Analyst which fields can be aggregated or used in calculations.
- **Time Dimensions:** Many analyses involve time. YAML can designate certain date or time fields as time dimensions (for example, **`order_date`**). . This helps the system understand phrases such as "**`by year`**" or "**`last month`**" by linking them to these time fields.
- **Metrics:** These are business-level aggregated measures, often defined as calculations over facts (or combinations of facts and dimensions). For example,

a metric could be **`total_sales`** defined as the SUM of a revenue fact, or **`customer_count`** as COUNT of unique customer IDs. Metrics can also have synonyms (for example, "**`turnover`**" as a synonym for revenue, or "**`number of customers`**" for **`customer_count`**). Defining metrics in the semantic layer ensures that when a user asks for "**`total revenue`**" or "**`number of customers`**", Cortex Analyst knows exactly how to compute it.

- **Filters:** Predefined filter conditions that are commonly used can be specified as well. For instance, a filter named "**`last_year`**" could be defined as **`order_date >= '2024-01-01' AND order_date < '2025-01-01'`**. These give convenient handles for the AI to apply time ranges or other frequent slices of the data when users ask, say, "in the last year."
- **Relationships:** If the semantic model spans multiple tables, you can define how tables join together. Each relationship entry can specify two logical tables, and the keys that link them (for example, **`customers.customer_id = orders.customer_id`**), along with the join type (left join, inner join, and so on). This is important for letting Cortex Analyst combine the data correctly when a question involves multiple entities (for example, "*What was the total sales by customer region*?" might involve joining an orders fact table to the customers dimension table).
- **Verified Queries:** These are example question-and-answer pairs or expected SQL queries that you include to guide the AI. By providing a few sample questions, and the correct SQL (or a description of the answer), you help Cortex Analyst learn from examples which can improve its precision on similar queries. Verified queries effectively serve as hints or tests to ensure that the semantic model covers certain scenarios.
- **Custom Instructions:** These are optional directives to LLM on how to behave or how to format answers. For instance, you might add an instruction to always format certain metrics as percentages, or to avoid using certain tables. This gives finer control, if needed, complementing the purely data-oriented parts of YAML.

All these components in YAML configuration together form the semantic layer that Cortex Analyst relies on. Thus, when you deploy Cortex Analyst, you upload this YAML model to a Snowflake staging area. The model is then used by the Cortex Analyst service at runtime to understand user queries. Because it is just an editable file, versioning and managing the semantic model can be done similarly to the code, that is, you can keep it in source control, and update it as your business logic evolves.

Therefore, Snowflake provides tools like a semantic model generator (https://github.com/Snowflake-Labs/semantic-model-generator) as well as the Cortex Analyst option of the AI/ML Studio assists in creating the YAML files from the existing schemas. We will use the Cortex Analyst option in the studio in the use case discussed in this chapter.

The Art of YAML Configuration for Cortex Analyst

The YAML configuration file serves as the fundamental bridge between the raw data structures, and meaningful business concepts in Cortex Analyst. When properly defined, this configuration transforms technical database schemas into an intuitive business framework that enables natural language interactions with your data.

Effective YAML configuration is crucial because it directly impacts:

- **Query Accuracy:** Properly mapped entities, measures, and dimensions ensure that natural language queries are interpreted correctly, providing relevant results, rather than misinterpreted data.
- **Business Context:** Well-defined semantic layers translate technical data elements into business terminology, making analytics accessible to non-technical users.
- **Analytical Depth:** Thoughtfully established relationships between entities enable complex analysis from simple questions, unlocking deeper insights.
- **User Adoption:** When business users can reliably get accurate answers using their own terminology, they are more likely to embrace the tool for daily decision-making.

A meticulously configured YAML file acts as the semantic foundation that determines how effectively Cortex Analyst can understand business intent. Organizations that invest time in properly modeling their business domains within YAML configurations experience significantly higher query accuracy, more relevant insights, and greater user satisfaction.

To build effective semantic models in Snowflake Cortex Analyst, organize YAML by business domain, focus on end-user questions and vocabulary, and use descriptive names and details. Capture complex calculations as expressions, and prefer wide tables for clarity. Review auto-generated descriptions, and start with a simple model, gradually expanding it. Incorporate a verified query repository to enhance accuracy.

Cortex Analyst has file size constraints to maintain efficient API interactions: the semantic model file is limited to 1MB. Furthermore, if sample values and verified queries are removed, the model must stay within a 32K token limit (approximately 128KB) due to in-memory processing. It is worth noting that these limitations might be adjusted in the future as support for larger context windows improves. Remember that the semantic model creation is an iterative process, and be mindful of these limitations.

Accurate semantic modeling is crucial for Cortex Analyst to effectively translate data structures into meaningful business insights. The YAML configuration teaches the system how your organization thinks about and uses its data, making it the critical foundation for successful natural language analytics.

Transforming Raw Data into Business Insights

Cortex Analyst's ultimate mission is to turn the raw data into meaningful business insights with minimal user effort. By allowing natural language questions, it abstracts away the mechanics of data transformation, and allows the user to focus on what they want to know, not how to compute it. Under the hood, however, a lot is happening to convert those user questions into the insights they seek. When a question comes in, Cortex Analyst uses the semantic model and Snowflake's powerful SQL engine to perform the necessary data transformations, aggregations, and enrichments to answer that question.

For example, a ZenTime Smartwatch sales support user asks: "*What is the total sales and average discount offered for accessories sold in March 2025?*" This single question implies several transformations on the raw data. Cortex Analyst will interpret the terms: It recognizes "*total sales*" as a metric (summing a sales or revenue column), "*average discount*" as another derived metric (perhaps, total sales divided by number of orders), "in March 2025" as a time filter. Using the semantic layer, it knows which tables and columns to pull (for example, an Orders fact table), performs the sum and average calculations, and applies the date filter for the March 2025 date range. The outcome might be a small table with two numbers (total sales and average discount value) – which is the business insight requested. The user did not have to understand any SQL or data engineering as Cortex Analyst handled the heavy lifting of transforming raw transaction records into aggregated insights.

As we know, Cortex Analyst helps turn the raw data into insights through data enrichment via the semantic model context. Because the YAML model defines business-friendly aliases and calculated metrics, users can ask high-level questions and get enriched answers. A query like "*What is our customer churn rate this year?*" could be answered if the semantic model includes a definition for the churn rate. It is important to note that the quality of insights depends on the semantic model configuration – the more comprehensively the model encapsulates business logics (key metrics, common filters, and so on), the more types of questions can be answered accurately. Nevertheless, even with the basic setups, Cortex Analyst accelerates insight generation by handling the data wrangling in the background.

Raw data (which might be millions of rows of transactions) is converted into an actionable insight via a conversational interaction. By managing complex transformations and leveraging built-in analytics functions, Cortex Analyst helps users to focus on interpreting results, and making decisions rather than on the mechanics of data processing. It facilitates a smooth journey from the raw data to business insight, handling data transformation, enrichment, and even machine learning tasks in the background. Its integration with Snowflake's scalable engine ensures that even as data volume grows, the performance remains interactive, enabling truly on-demand analytics for business users.

This natural language interface is powered by large language models that translate a user's question into the appropriate SQL and results. For the user, the experience is intuitive, that is, they might type a question into a chat interface or analytics app, such as "*Show me the top 5 products by revenue last month*," and Cortex Analyst will respond with an answer (and often, the supporting data or visualization as a line chart/bar chart). This section also details how this natural language querying works, and how it maps to SQL under the hood.

When a user query is submitted, Cortex Analyst goes through a few key steps. First, the query text is interpreted by the LLM in the context of the provided semantic model. Then the semantic model (as discussed above) supplies the vocabulary and structure – the LLM knows, for instance, that "**product**" refers to the product dimension, and "**revenue**" refers to a metric or fact defined in the YAML. Using this context, the LLM parses the user's sentence to figure out the analytical intent. It identifies the selection (what metrics or fields are being asked for), the filters or conditions (period "**last month**"), and any grouping or sorting (rank top 5 by revenue, so the group by product and order is by the revenue metric). The AI is doing the work a SQL-savvy analyst would do mentally when translating a question to a query.

Next, Cortex Analyst generates an SQL statement representing this question. For example, "*top 5 products by revenue last month*," it might produce a SQL query like:

```
SELECT product_name, SUM(sales_amount) AS total_revenue
FROM sales_table
WHERE order_date >= '2025-04-01' AND order_date < '2025-05-01'
GROUP BY product_name
ORDER BY total_revenue DESC
LIMIT 5;
```

This SQL uses the knowledge that "**last month**" corresponds to April 2025 (assuming the current date is in May 2025, for example), and that "**revenue**" is captured by summing the **sales_amount**, grouped by the **product_name**. The semantic layer would have provided the information that **sales_table** is the relevant table, and perhaps, that **sales_amount** is the field for revenue.

It will intuitively generate something like this to pull records for the last month:

```
order_date >= DATE_TRUNC('MONTH', CURRENT_DATE - INTERVAL '1
MONTH')
  AND order_date < DATE_TRUNC('MONTH', CURRENT_DATE)
```

In many cases, the generated SQL might involve joins (if, say, the product name is in a different table, the semantic model would include how to join the sales data to products). Thus, Cortex Analyst's agentic AI system can handle these complexities, and even verify the query against the model to ensure it aligns with the known dimensions and metrics.

Once the SQL runs, Cortex Analyst takes the results, and often will post process them for presentation. For numeric or short answers, it might directly return the number or a sentence with the number. For list or table outputs, it might either return a small table or summary. The output also provides a Bar Chart and Line chart that could be useful as a quick visual insight, especially for category distributions or trend analysis.

It is worth noting that natural language querying in BI is not entirely new – there have been products in the past aiming to do "NL to SQL", or provide a search-like experience for the data. However, Cortex Analyst's strength lies in the combination of a robust semantic model, and the power of the modern LLMs. The semantic model ensures that the system is grounded in the correct business definitions (reducing misinterpretation of terms), and the LLM provides the flexibility and language understanding to handle a wide variety of phrasings and questions that the users throw at it. Additionally, because the actual SQL runs on Snowflake, the full fidelity of the data is available, that is users are not limited to pre-aggregated data or specific dashboards, they can ask anything that the underlying data can answer.

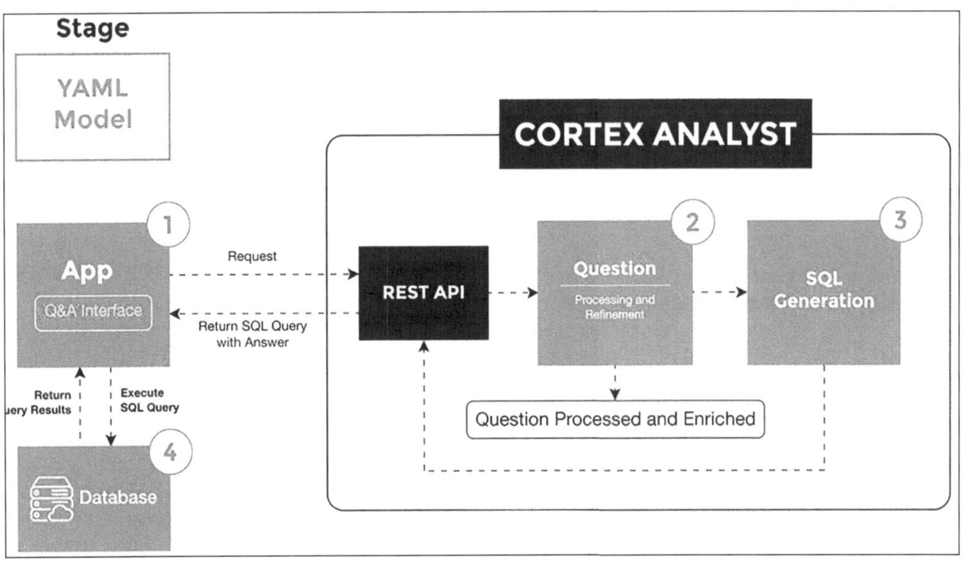

Figure 7.1: *Cortex Analyst*

For business users, this natural language capability is transformative. They can interact with the data in a conversational and intuitive way, without having to learn any technical skills. A sales manager could type a question like "*Which regions exceeded their sales targets this month*?" and get an answer on the spot, rather than waiting days for an analyst to create a custom report. Data analysts and developers also benefit from this because Cortex Analyst can handle the simpler questions automatically, freeing up their time to focus on more complex analyses. Moreover, analysts can trust that the answers given are based on governed metrics and definitions (since those are encoded in the semantic model), maintaining consistency with official reports.

Note: Semantic View is a newly introduced view type in the Snowflake AI Data Cloud, purpose-built to enhance support for Cortex Analyst and Generative AI workloads. It allows semantic models to be stored as schema-level objects within a database, making them reusable and manageable. These semantic views can also be directly used in Cortex Analyst as alternatives to semantic models.

Use Case Walkthrough

Let us consider a scenario where ZenTime wants to support the sales leadership in effective decision-making by providing them an easy to use interface that provides access to their sales related queries. We will leverage the Cortex Analyst option within the AI/ML studio to build the YAML file. ZenTime decided to start off with their two basic transaction tables for smartwatches and accessories, and the associated YAML file. They wanted to understand the solution better, and later tweak and add tables or update the YAML file iteratively as their needs evolve.

Before proceeding, ensure that the data has been imported into the following tables:

```
ZENTIME_PRODUCT_MASTER
ZENTIME_SMARTWATCH_SALES
ZENTIME_ACCESSORIES_SALES
```

The process for loading each table is as follows:

1. Download the three csv files: **`zentime_accessory_sales.csv`**, **`zentime_product_master.csv`**, and **`zentime_watch_sales.csv`**
2. In Snowsight, from the menu on the left, **`Select Data`** > **`Add Data`**
3. Choose **`Load data into a Table`**
4. Browse and choose **`ZENTIME_PRODUCT_MASTER.csv`**
5. Choose **`CORTEX_AI_DB.PUBLIC`** as the schema, create a new table
6. Provide the name of the new table to be the file name (**`ZENTIME_PRODUCT_MASTER`**). Click **`Next`**.
7. In the left menu, expand '**`view options`**' below the File Format
8. Ensure that the Header option is set to **`First Line contains Header`**

9. Click **Load**
10. Repeat the process for the other two tables

We would also need to create a staging area to store our YAML file.

Let us execute the below commands to create the stage. We will upload the YAML file later in the process.

```
USE DATABASE CORTEX_AI_DB;
CREATE STAGE CORTEX_AI_STG ENCRYPTION = (TYPE = 'SNOWFLAKE_SSE')
DIRECTORY = (ENABLE = true );
```

Note: *Steps 1 through 12 involve YAML file generation using Cortex Analyst in the AI ML Studio. The* **zentime_sales_support.yaml** *file is already available as part of the code files. If you are familiar with the YAML file creation, you could also choose to directly go to Step 12, upload the YAML file, and continue with the cortex analyst steps for the Streamlit application.*

Step 1: Navigate to the Snowflake AI/ML Studio. Go to the Cortex Analyst option, and Click **Try**.

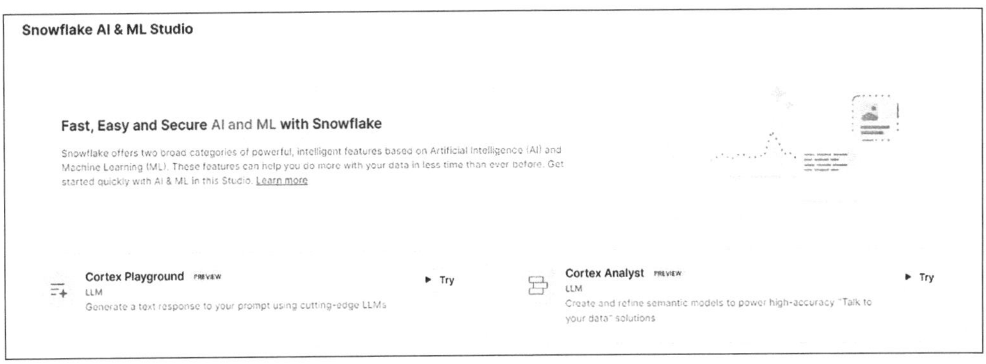

Figure 7.2: *Step 1 – Cortex Analyst*

Step 2: Select Semantic Model. As we do not have one yet, we will create one by clicking **Create New**.

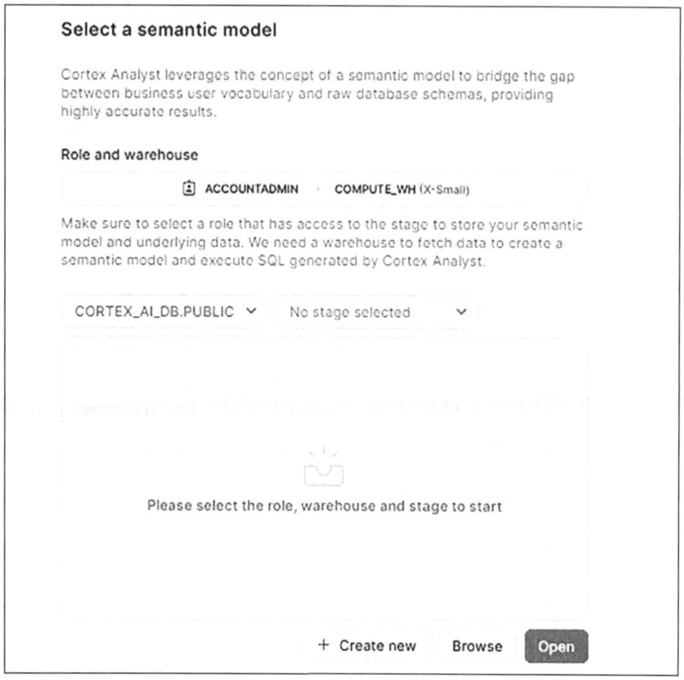

Figure 7.3: *Step 2 – Create a Semantic Model*

Step 3: Choose the stage (**`CORTEX_AI_STG`**), and provide details for the semantic model.

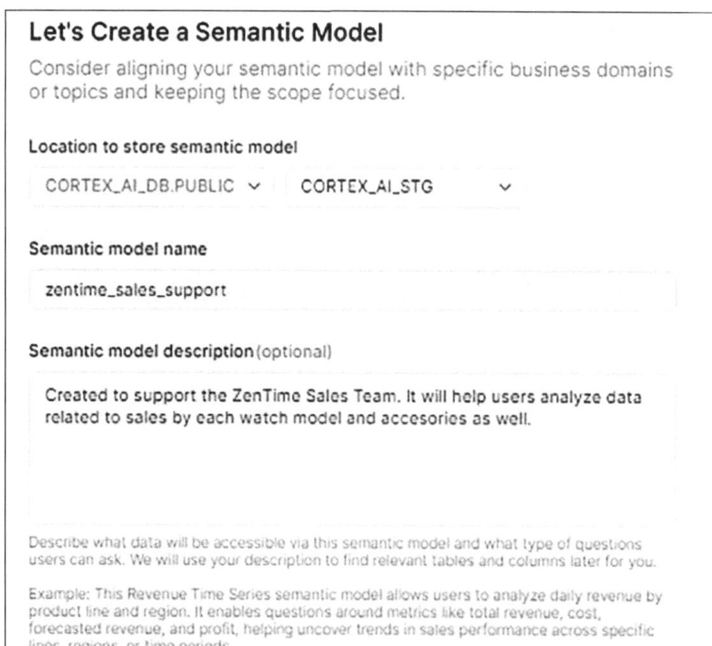

Figure 7.4: *Step 3 - Provide Details for the Model*

Step 4: Name the Model as **`zentime_sales_support.yaml`**.

Figure 7.5: *Step 4 -Name the Semantic Model*

Step 5: For now, skip the optional screen on **`Examples of User Questions`**.

Step 6: In the **`Select Data screen`** that follows, choose the three tables:

```
ZENTIME_PRODUCT_MASTER
ZENTIME_SMARTWATCH_SALES
ZENTIME_ACCESSORIES_SALES
```

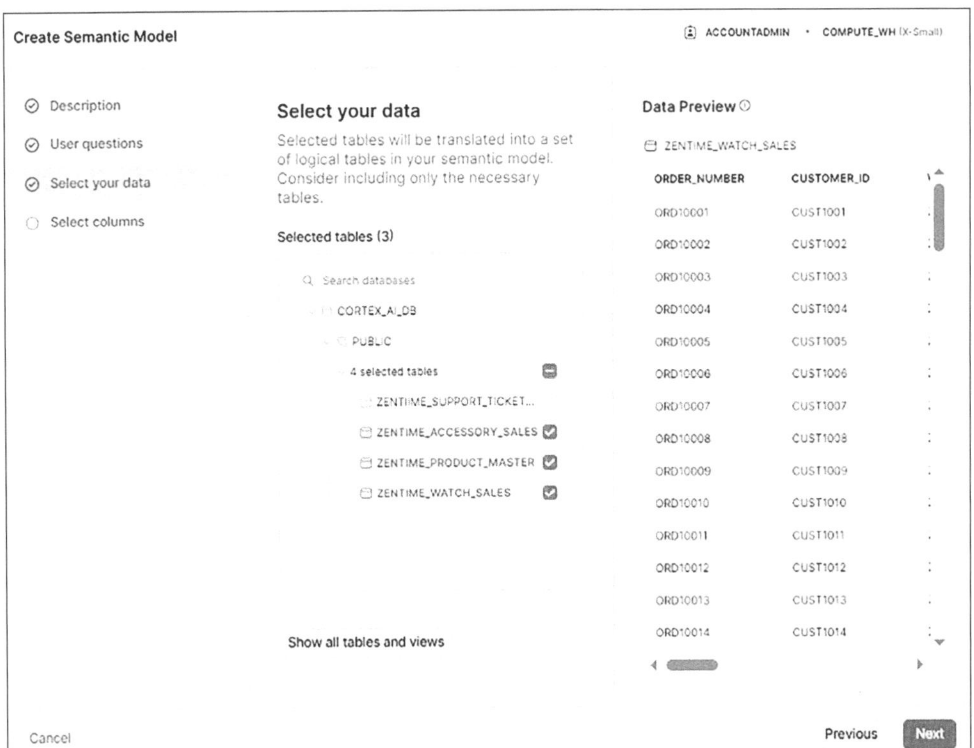

Figure 7.6: *Step 6 -Choose the Tables*

Step 7: In the **`Select Columns`** option, select the checkbox next to each of the three tables, to pick all the columns. Click **Done**.

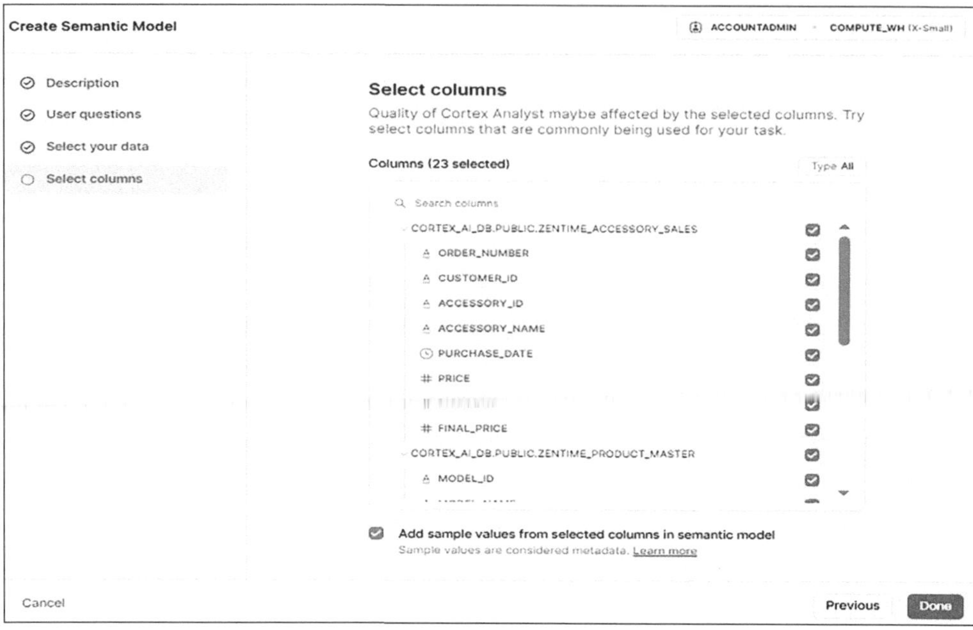

Figure 7.7: Step 7 – Select the Columns

Step 8: Let us ask a question, and get the response to ensure that the configuration is working correctly.

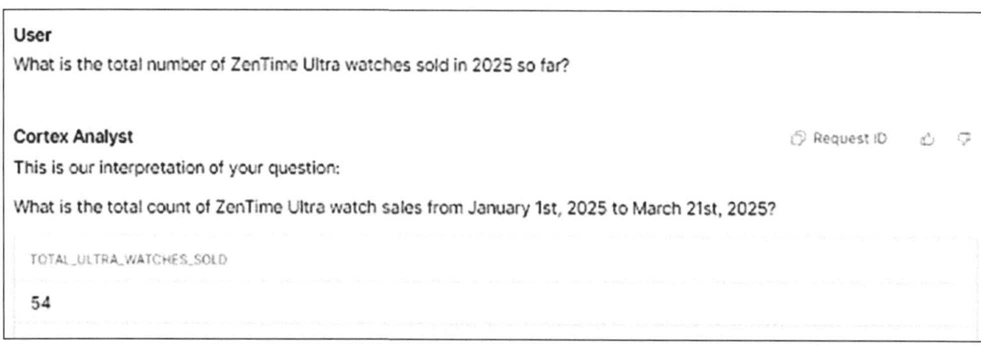

Figure 7.8: Step 8 - Ask a Question

As seen, Cortex Analyst has successfully interpreted the semantic model with the data by leveraging its advanced language models to transform natural language questions into precise SQL queries.

Step 9: Save it as a `Verified Query` by clicking `Add`.

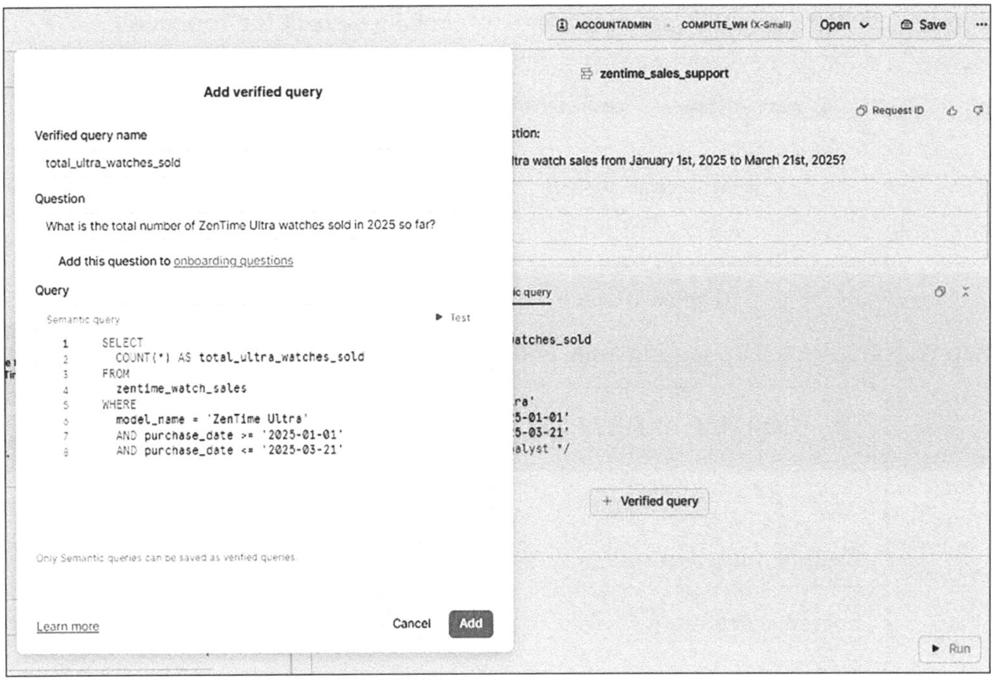

Figure 7.9: *Step 9- Save as Verified Query*

Verified queries in Cortex Analyst YAML files are example questions that have been tested to return the accurate answers. Their importance lies in guiding the model on what a correct, high-confidence answer looks like, ensuring a better end-user experience.

Step 10: Let us add one more query, and add it as a verified query.

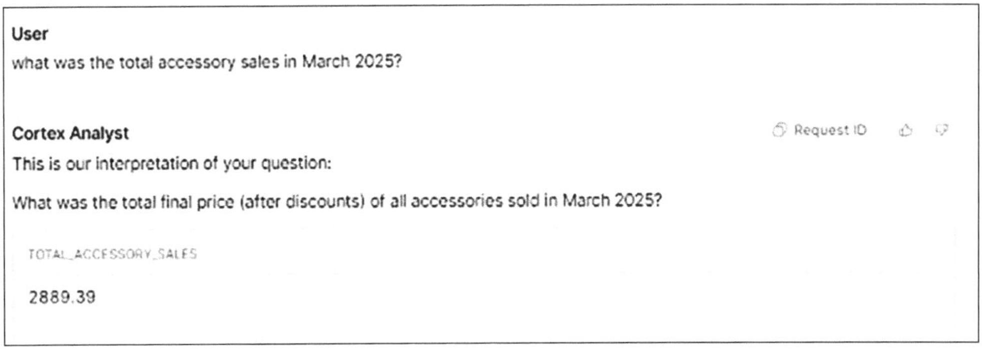

Figure 7.10: *Step 10- Ask and Add Another Query*

Step 11: Save the semantic model to stage by clicking **Save** at the top menu.

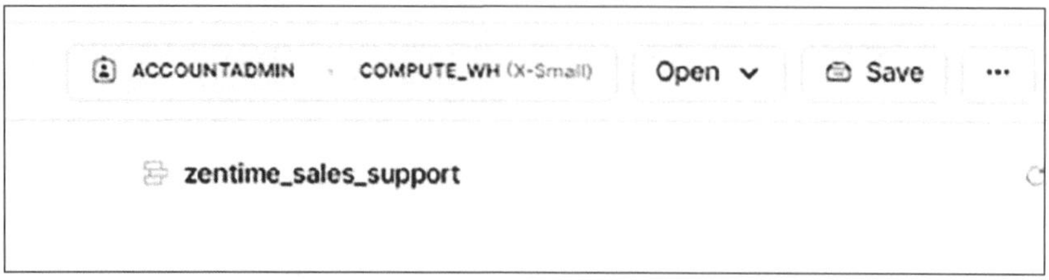

Figure 7.11: *Step 11 - Save the Model to Stage*

Step 12: Navigate to the staging area, and verify that the YAML file exists.

Figure 7.12: *Step 12 - Verify the Stage*

We successfully created and saved a YAML file, which we then utilized with Cortex Analyst, to answer questions in natural language. To access and query this file, anytime in future, users can navigate to the Snowflake AI/ML Studio, select the Cortex Analyst option, and then open the YAML file for further analysis and querying.

Building a Streamlit App

Now that the cortex analyst functionality was demonstrated successfully, ZenTime wanted to build a **`streamlit app`** with a chat interface, and provide access to the sales leadership to get feedback, and expand the context iteratively.

Hence, before we proceed, let us also try out making edits to the YAML file to make it more robust. So, let us add three additional synonyms to the **`zentime_sales_support.YAML`** file under the **`FINAL_PRICE`** column under both the sales and accessory table headers.

The synonyms added are **`paid_amount`**, **`sales_amount`**, and **`sold_for_amount`** (already added in the YAML file extract as shown in *Figure* 7.13).

These are added so that the model can interpret other similar references to the **`FINAL_PRICE`** column.

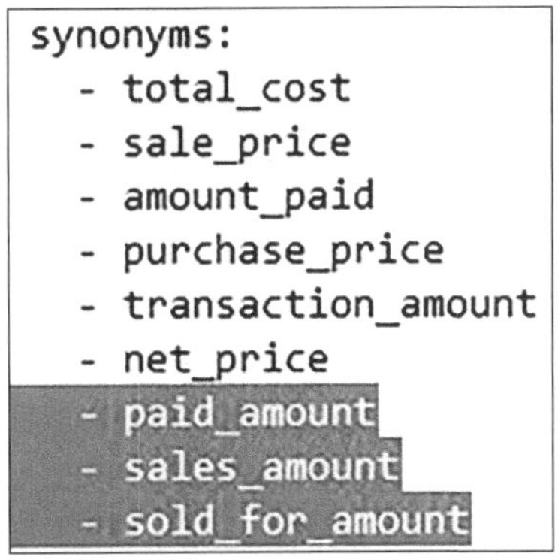

```
synonyms:
  - total_cost
  - sale_price
  - amount_paid
  - purchase_price
  - transaction_amount
  - net_price
  - paid_amount
  - sales_amount
  - sold_for_amount
```

Figure 7.13: *Adding Synonyms*

Let us now create the Streamlit application, and name it **`ZenTime_Sales_Bot_Cortex_Analyst`**.

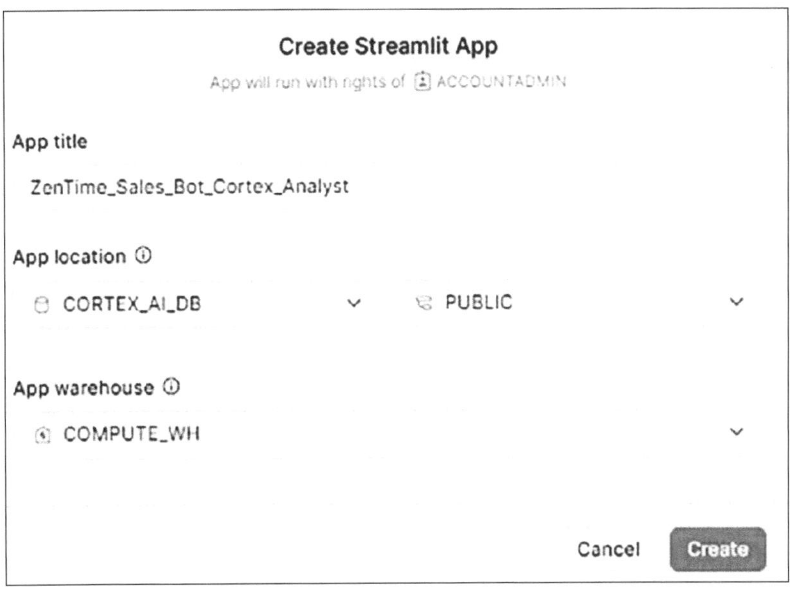

Figure 7.14: *Creating the Streamlit App*

The code for the app is in *ZenTime_Sales_Bot_Cortex_Analyst.py.*

Import the packages provided in the Package List.txt in the Streamlit app using the **`Packages`** > Find Packages option.

This Streamlit application showcases the capabilities of Snowflake Cortex Analyst through a chat branded as the ZenTime Sales Bot. Users can ask questions related to ZenTime's sales, and the app sends these prompts to the Cortex Analyst API using a semantic model (**`zentime_sales_support.yaml`**) hosted in a Snowflake stage.

Let us now start to interact with the application by asking our first question:

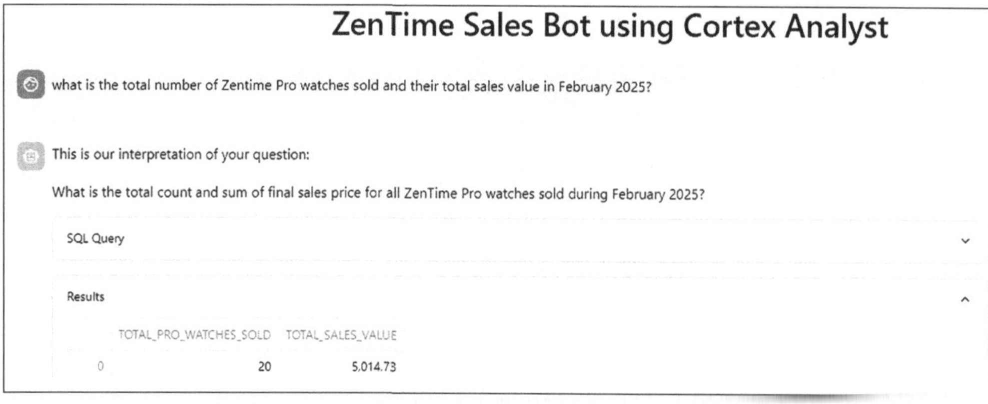

Figure 7.15: *A Question about Sale Price and Watches Sold*

Observing the above question closely, we can see that it involves multiple data transformations. Cortex Analyst interprets different components of the request: It understands "*total sales*" as a metric requiring summation of the sales column, "*number of watches sold*" as a derived metric that performs a count operation. Also, "**`February 2025`**" is used as a specific date filter and **`ZenTime Pro`** as a specific smartwatch model. Thus, the Cortex Analyst skillfully processes these different operations simultaneously, interpreting the natural language request, and converting it into the appropriate SQL transformations to deliver the requested results. Hence, by expanding the SQL Query option, we can look at the generated query.

SQL Query

```
WITH __zentime_watch_sales AS (
  SELECT
    model_name,
    purchase_date,
    final_price
  FROM cortex_ai_db.public.zentime_watch_sales
)
SELECT
  COUNT(*) AS total_pro_watches_sold,
  SUM(final_price) AS total_sales_value
FROM __zentime_watch_sales
WHERE
  model_name = 'ZenTime Pro'
  AND purchase_date >= '2025-02-01'
  AND purchase_date <= '2025-02-28'
 -- Generated by Cortex Analyst
;
```

Figure 7.16: *SQL Query Generated by Cortex Analyst*

Now, let us ask a question related to the distribution of data to emphasize Cortex Analyst's visual capabilities.

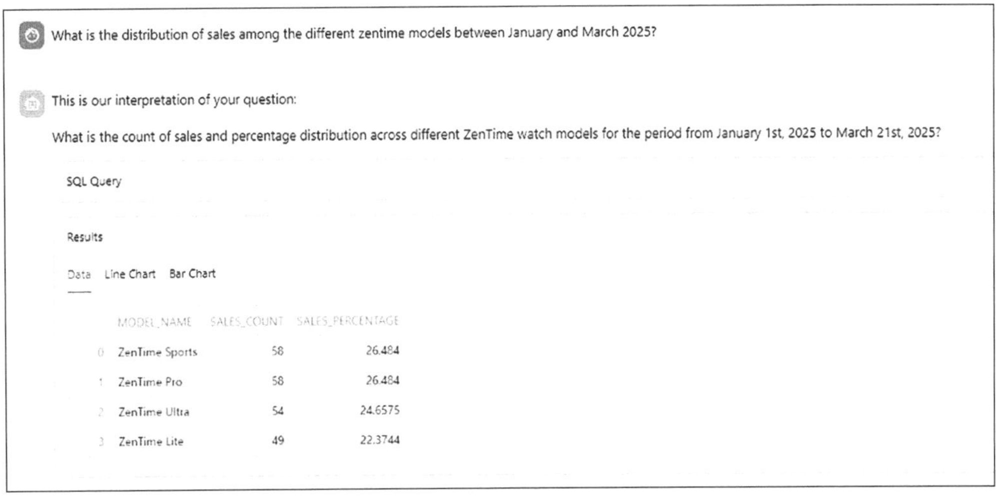

Figure 7.17: *A Question on Sales Distribution*

As we can see, Cortex Analyst understands that the question relates to data distribution, and shows the chart options in the output. So, let us look at the bar chart.

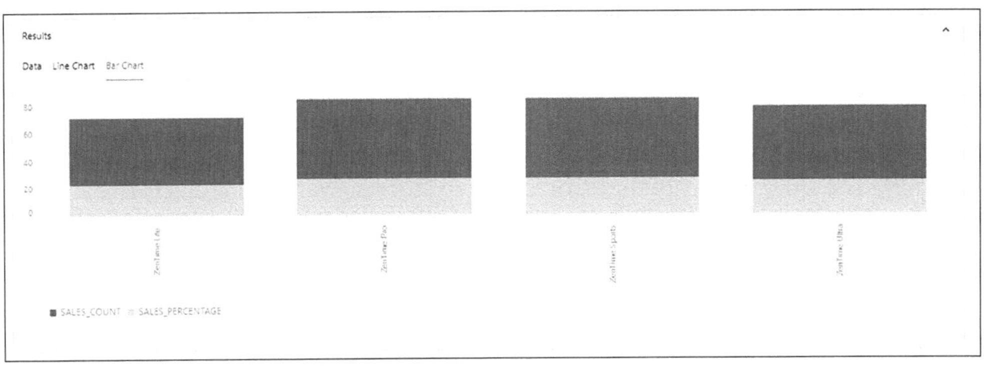

Figure 7.18: *Bar Chart Display*

Now, let us try a scenario where a user inadvertently enters a query with spelling errors.

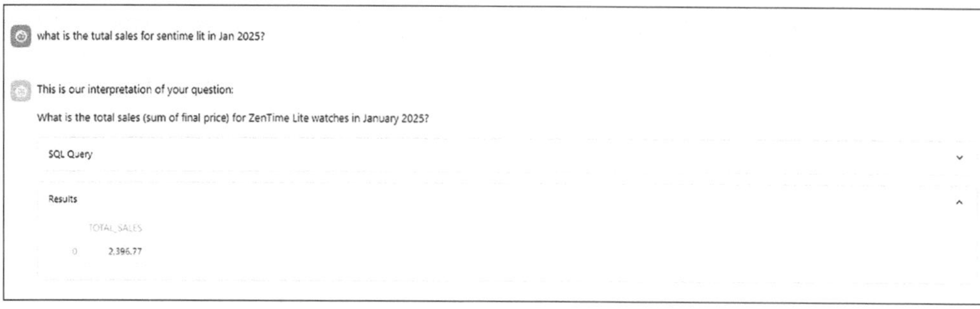

Figure 7.19: *A Question Containing Spelling Errors*

The word total is misspelled and even the model's name is incorrectly spelled (**`sentime lit`**, instead of **`ZenTime Lite`**).

Yet, the tool returned the correct results! So, let us look at the generated query.

SQL Query

```
WITH __zentime_watch_sales AS (
  SELECT
    model_name,
    purchase_date,
    final_price
  FROM cortex_ai_db.public.zentime_watch_sales
)
SELECT
  SUM(final_price) AS total_sales
FROM __zentime_watch_sales
WHERE
  model_name = 'ZenTime Lite' AND DATE_TRUNC('MONTH', purchase_date) = '2025-01-01'
 -- Generated by Cortex Analyst
;
```

Figure 7.20: *SQL Query Generated for the Question*

Examining the query reveals that Cortex Analyst intuitively recognized the intended references to "*total sales*" and "*ZenTime Lite*," demonstrating a robust ability to understand, and inherently correct user input.

Let us now look at the code in the streamlit application.

As seen in the code below, the function **`send_message()`** makes an API call to Snowflake's Cortex Analyst service by constructing a request body with the user's prompt structured as a message, and a reference to a semantic model file stored in Snowflake. It then uses the internal **`_snowflake.send_snow_api_request()`** method to send a POST request to the "**`/api/v2/cortex/analyst/message`**" endpoint. After receiving the response, the function either returns the parsed JSON content, if successful, or raises an exception with error details if the request fails, effectively acting as the bridge between the streamlit application, and Snowflake's natural language processing capabilities.

```
DATABASE = "CORTEX_AI_DB"
SCHEMA = "PUBLIC"
STAGE = "CORTEX_AI_STG"
FILE = "zentime_sales_support.yaml"


def send_message(prompt: str) -> dict:
    """Calls the REST API and returns the response."""
    request_body = {
        "messages": [
            {
                "role": "user",
                "content": [
                    {
                        "type": "text",
                        "text": prompt
                    }
                ]
            }
        ],
        "semantic_model_file": f"@{DATABASE}.{SCHEMA}.{STAGE}/{FILE}",
    }
    resp = _snowflake.send_snow_api_request(
        "POST",
        f"/api/v2/cortex/analyst/message",
        {},
        {},
        request_body,
        {},
        30000,
    )
    if resp["status"] < 400:
        return json.loads(resp["content"])
    else:
        raise Exception(
            f"Failed request with status {resp['status']}: {resp}"
        )
```

Figure 7.21: *An Extract from Streamlit Code*

The assistant responds with natural language answers, SQL queries, result sets, visualizations, and helpful suggestions. Now, when the SQL code is returned, it is executed on the active Snowflake session, and the results are displayed as tables or charts, as appropriate, ensuring an enhanced user experience.

The YAML file provides extensive configuration options to customize your experience. One notable feature is the "**`use_as_onboarding_question`**" parameter within the **`verified_queries`** section. By default, set to false, changing this to true causes your selected question to appear automatically when launching the Streamlit application. This is particularly useful for frequently asked questions like "*What was my total sales for this month so far?*", setting it as a verified query with the onboarding option enabled means it loads immediately upon accessing the application, allowing you to obtain instant results, including the generated SQL.

Another valuable configuration is the "**`custom_instructions`**" property. For instance, in the **`zentime_sales_support.yaml`** file, you will find this instruction: **`custom_instructions: "Display percentage metrics with % symbol and no decimal places"`**.

This formatting directive ensures that when you ask something like "*What percentage of the total watch sales in 2025 were ZenTime Ultra models?*", the response shows as "**`24%`**", rather than "**`0.24`**". This functionality, particularly, proves valuable when dealing with specialized formatting requirements, such as adding currency symbols appropriate to different regions, replacing null values with '**`N/A`**', applying bold formatting to highlight specific values, or properly formatting percentages as demonstrated here.

Cortex Analyst leverages these configuration options to significant effect by creating highly customized data interaction experiences. Analysts can pre-configure common queries for their sales teams, ensuring consistent formatting across all reports and dashboards. The custom instructions capability allows them to implement company-wide data standards, without requiring end users to remember specific formatting requests. For example, a Cortex Analyst might configure region-specific currency formatting, standardize how null values appear in reports, or ensure that all percentage-based KPIs display uniformly across the organization. This significantly improves the user experience by maintaining visual consistency, while reducing the technical burden on sales professionals who need quick access to properly formatted business intelligence.

The 3 R's of YAML Maintenance for Effective Analysis

It is key to note that the success of the analysis hinges on the quality of maintenance of the YAML file which is an iterative process. It involves identifying and resolving potential query errors by updating/editing the YAML file with accurate synonyms (as demonstrated in this use case), relationships, and so on. To ensure optimal performance, it is beneficial to adhere to the 3 **R**'s when managing the YAML file. Also, this helps to keep it **R**elevant, **R**ecent, and **R**obust. Let us elaborate on the context of this use case. Now that ZenTime has tested how this works, they can make the file more *Relevant* by adding tables and columns that are of interest to the sales team, also ensuring current and latest schema information (*Recency*) is maintained. By incorporating verified queries and maintaining a well-organized structure, they can create a *Robust* semantic model that effectively connects natural language concepts to their corresponding database entities, and successfully processes diverse user inquiries without errors. Thus, it might be a good idea to start with just what you need, and then enrich iteratively, as required.

Note that you could generate the semantic model in other ways too. For this use case, we used the approach within the Cortex Analyst option in the AI/ML Studio. You could also use the *semantic model generator* provided by Snowflake (https://github.com/Snowflake-Labs/semantic-model-generator). This is an open-source tool that automates creating the YAML-based semantic model. Rather than hand-coding a semantic model, data teams can launch the Streamlit app, and point it to the target table(s). The generator reads the table schema and metadata, auto-populating most of the model fields, such as dimensions, measures, and sample values based on the source data. Once the model is generated, the YAML file can be saved to a Snowflake stage, ready for Cortex Analyst applications to reference and translate the user questions into SQL. By simply pointing at a table, most components of the semantic model are populated automatically—eliminating repetitive manual work. A built-in interactive testing pane allows users to pose sample questions, view the generated SQL, save verified queries and iteratively refine the model before finalizing it.

Tools, such as the inbuilt Cortex Analyst option in Snowsight, and the Semantic Model Generator from Snowflake Labs significantly enhance efficiency, promote consistency across models, and enable organizations to scale semantic modeling efforts more easily, accelerating the deployment of Cortex Analyst applications with greater reliability. You could use these, or any other YAML file generation tool that you might be comfortable with. It is preferable to create the YAML file using one of these tools, and then edit as required, rather than create it from scratch, to avoid any errors in format and structure.

Overall, natural language querying with Cortex Analyst turns data analysis into a dialogue. It maps everyday language to SQL by using the semantic model as a bridge, executes queries, and translates results back into everyday language or easy-to-read output. This cycle greatly lowers the barrier to entry for data exploration. This represents a significant step towards democratizing analytics - letting more people in an organization ask questions and get insights, without needing to know the intricacies of data engineering. Hence, by combining conversational AI with the rigor of SQL on Snowflake's platform, Cortex Analyst delivers a powerful yet accessible analytic experience that was difficult to achieve at scale until now.

Unlocking Insights from Unstructured Data with Cortex Search

While Cortex Analyst deals with structured data queries, Cortex Search is the companion service in Snowflake Cortex AI that specializes in searching and extracting information from unstructured or text-heavy data. Cortex Search is described as an advanced hybrid search service that combines vector search (semantic similarity) with traditional keyword search. This means that it cannot only find exact text matches, but also understands the meaning and context. For example, finding relevant documents or passages, even if they do not contain the exact query terms, by using embeddings and AI models.

For instance, consider the word, "**refund**". Traditional keyword search would retrieve documents containing the exact term, "**refund**" in the content. Semantic search would retrieve documents about refunds, even if they do not contain the exact word - including content about Money back guarantees, Return policies, Reimbursement processes, Order cancellations, Purchase reversals, and so on. Semantic search understands the concept, rather than just matching the keyword. Cortex Search's distinctive strength lies in its ability to seamlessly blend traditional and semantic search methodologies into a unified experience.

Cortex Search leverages Retrieval-Augmented Generation (RAG), which we covered in Chapter 4, a powerful AI technique relevant context that is retrieved from a knowledge base, and then passed to a language model for answer generation. By using RAG, Cortex Search ensures that responses are both contextually grounded and based on enterprise-specific content, making the answers more accurate and verifiable. This is particularly useful in enterprise settings where factual consistency and traceability are critical.

In the Snowflake Cortex ecosystem, Cortex Search often powers use cases like document question-answering, semantic data discovery, and so on for applications that need information from text sources (such as PDFs, emails and logs). Cortex Search works by automatically chunking and vectorizing the text data that you register with it. You might point Cortex Search at a set of documents in a stage (for example, PDF reports or a table of text snippets). It will then break the documents into chunks (paragraphs or sections), create vector embeddings (numerical representations) for each chunk using an LLM-based model (Snowflake's Arctic models or others), and index them for fast similarity search. When a user asks a question or searches for information, Cortex Search can quickly find the most relevant chunks of text (in well under a second, even across large document sets). It also leverages keyword search in combination, which helps ensure that if exact matches exist, they are retrieved, and if not, the semantic matches via vectors are used. The **hybrid** approach maximizes both accuracy and completeness of the search results.

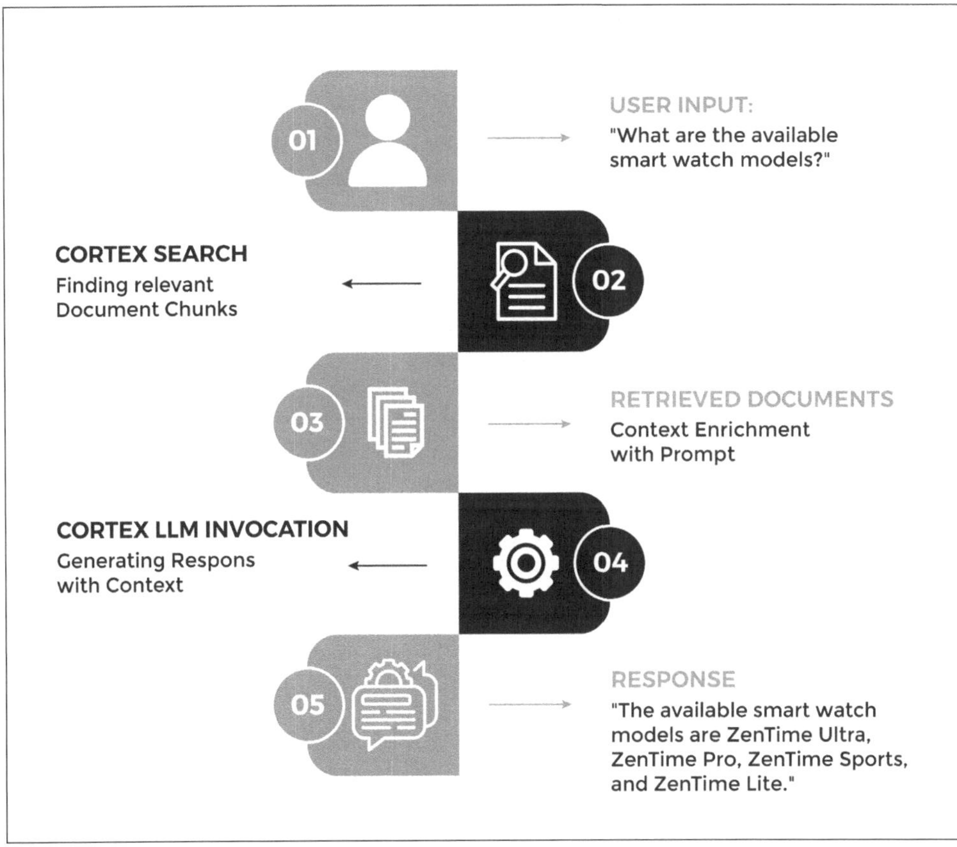

Figure 7.22: *Cortex Search*

Cortex Search also brings the concept of semantic or vector search to the fingertips of data teams who might not be familiar with AI models. Traditionally, implementing vector search would require setting up an embedding model, a vector database, and writing the code to query it. Snowflake Cortex Search abstracts all that you use SQL or a UI to load the data, and Snowflake handles the model inference as well as indexing behind the scenes. Queries to Cortex Search can be made through an API. It then returns the best matching pieces of text. This can be used directly (for example, to answer a question like "*find policy details regarding refunds*" from a set of policy documents), or indirectly to feed into a larger analysis.

Let us consider an example. The ZenTime team, having successfully implemented various generative AI use cases on Cortex, is looking to empower its customer support team with quick search capabilities, so that they can respond to customer queries swiftly.

They decide to build a cortex search agent. Now, let us go through the sequence of steps.

Step 1: Create a new staging area in `CORTEX_AI_DB` called `search_docs` to store the support guide.

```
USE CORTEX_AI_DB;
CREATE or REPLACE STAGE SEARCH_DOCS ENCRYPTION =
(TYPE = 'SNOWFLAKE_SSE') DIRECTORY = (ENABLE = true );
```

Step 2: The support guide (`ZenTime_Customer_Support_guide`) is the go to guide for the agents. The search service will leverage this document. Note that multiple documents can be utilized as well. For demonstration purposes, we will go with just this one comprehensive help guide. **Upload `ZenTime_Customer_Support_guide.pdf` to the newly created "`search_docs`" staging area.**

Step 3: List the documents in the `search_docs` staging area.

```
ls @search_docs;
```

It should return one row corresponding to the document we uploaded in Step 2.

Step 4: Break down the pdf contents, and store it as chunked sets of text.

The Snowflake UDF named `text_chunker` is created to process large text documents by breaking them into smaller, manageable chunks. A chunk is a small, meaningful section of text extracted from a larger file. The files are split into chunks, so that we can create vector embeddings for each part–making it easier to search, and retrieve relevant content accurately.

It uses LangChain's `RecursiveCharacterTextSplitter` to divide the input text into fragments (chunks) of 1512 characters (chunk size), each with 256 characters of overlap between the consecutive chunks. The chunk size and overlap can be tweaked as required. The function takes a string input (PDF text), and returns a table of text chunks, leveraging the Snowpark API and pandas for data handling. This chunking approach is commonly used in NLP and LLM applications to maintain the context, while processing the documents.

```
CREATE OR REPLACE FUNCTION text_chunker(pdf_text string)
returns table (chunk varchar)
language python
runtime_version = '3.9'
handler = 'text_chunker'
packages = ('snowflake-snowpark-python', 'langchain')
as
$$
from snowflake.snowpark.types import StringType, StructField, StructType
from langchain.text_splitter import RecursiveCharacterTextSplitter
import pandas as pd

class text_chunker:

    def process(self, pdf_text: str):

        text_splitter = RecursiveCharacterTextSplitter(
            chunk_size = 1512,
            chunk_overlap  = 256,
            length_function = len
        )

        chunks = text_splitter.split_text(pdf_text)
        df = pd.DataFrame(chunks, columns=['chunks'])

        yield from df.itertuples(index=False, name=None)
$$;
```

Figure 7.23: *Create Function to Chunk Text*

Step 5: Create a table to store the chunks.

```
CREATE OR REPLACE TABLE DOCS_CHUNKS_TABLE (
    RELATIVE_PATH VARCHAR(16777216),
    SIZE NUMBER(38,0),
    FILE_URL VARCHAR(16777216),
    SCOPED_FILE_URL VARCHAR(16777216),
    CHUNK VARCHAR(16777216),
    CATEGORY VARCHAR(16777216)
);
```

Figure 7.24: *Create DOCS_CHUNK_TABLE*

`RELATIVE_PATH`: It is the path to the file within the stage, without including the stage name itself. This is used to uniquely identify the file's location inside the stage, and help track where each chunk came from. In this example, it would just be the file name itself, as we do not have any subfolders within the stage to host the file.

- `SIZE`: Size of the document.
- `FILE_URL`: It is the original path to the file in the staging area (**`search_stage`**), used for reference.

- **SCOPED_FILE_URL**: It is a secure, temporary link that Snowflake uses to read and process the file during indexing for Cortex Search.
- **CHUNK**: As we already know, it is a section of text extracted from a larger file.
- **CATEGORY**: This Column is to allow future expansion of the search functionality to other areas such as Tech support, Billing, and so on, in addition to the Customer Support, who will be the first to leverage. This will hold the document category to enable filtering. We will populate this using the COMPLETE LLM function that we saw in Chapter 5.

Also, note that the Cortex Search service will inherently take care of embeddings, so it need not be created here.

Step 6: Populate the **doc_chunks_table**.

This code reads all the documents from the **@search_docs stage**, and uses the **PARSE_DOCUMENT** function as we saw in *Chapter* 5, to extract the readable text from the file in a structured way, using the **'LAYOUT'** mode which preserves the document's formatting. It then passes that text to **text_chunker** which breaks it into smaller, meaningful chunks.

```
INSERT INTO docs_chunks_table (relative_path, size, file_url,
                            scoped_file_url, chunk)

    SELECT relative_path,
            size,
            file_url,
            build_scoped_file_url(@search_docs, relative_path) as scoped_file_url,
            func.chunk as chunk
    FROM
        directory(@search_docs),
        TABLE(text_chunker (TO_VARCHAR(SNOWFLAKE.CORTEX.PARSE_DOCUMENT(@search_docs, relative_path, {'mode':
'LAYOUT'})))) as func;
```

Figure 7.25: *Insert into* DOCS_CHUNK_TABLE

Step 7: Determine the **CATEGORY** value.

This step creates a temporary table called **docs_categories** that assigns a short category (such as **Billing** or **Tech Support**) to each unique document in your **docs_chunks_table**. It does this by using prompt engineering with Snowflake's **CORTEX.COMPLETE** function, leveraging **snowflake_arctic** LLM which looks at the file name (from **relative_path**), and predicts what type of document it is based on the name. The result is a table with one row per document, showing the file path, and its predicted category which can be used later to filter or organize documents in Cortex Search.

```
CREATE OR REPLACE TEMPORARY TABLE docs_categories AS WITH unique_documents AS (
  SELECT DISTINCT relative_path  FROM docs_chunks_table
),
docs_category_cte AS (
  SELECT relative_path,
    TRIM(snowflake.cortex.COMPLETE (
      'snowflake-arctic',
      'Given the name of the file between <file> and </file> determine if it is Customer Support, Billing, Tech Support
etc.  Use max one or two words only. <file> ' || relative_path || '</file>'
    ), '\n') AS category
  FROM unique_documents
)
SELECT
  *
FROM
  docs_category_cte;
```

Figure 7.26: *Create Categories*

Step 8: Update the **CATEGORY** column in **doc_chunks** table.

Each chunk row in **docs_chunks_table** is updated by assigning it the predicted category from **docs_categories**, matching them using the file's **relative_path**. This way, every text chunk knows which category its source document belongs to.

```
UPDATE docs_chunks_table
  SET category = docs_categories.category
  FROM docs_categories
  WHERE  docs_chunks_table.relative_path = docs_categories.relative_path;
```

Figure 7.27: *Update Categories*

Step 9: Create the Cortex Search Service. This will further create the Cortex Search functionality to enable search over the chunk column from the **docs_chunks_table**. It will facilitate querying across all document categories, while maintaining their context.

```
CREATE or REPLACE CORTEX SEARCH SERVICE ZENTIME_CUSTOMER_SUPPORT_SERVICE
ON chunk
ATTRIBUTES category
warehouse = COMPUTE_WH
TARGET_LAG = '1 minute'
as (
    select chunk,
        relative_path,
        file_url,
        category
    from docs_chunks_table
);
```

Figure 7.28: *Create Cortex Search Service*

Step 10: Create a new Streamlit Application, and call it **Zentime Agent Support Bot Cortex Search**.

Import the packages provided in the Package List.txt in the streamlit app using the **Packages** > **Find Packages** option, before running the Streamlit application.

This Python file (**Zentime_Agent_Support_Bot_Cortex_Search.py**) creates a

Streamlit-based **ZenTime Support Assistant for Agents** that helps customer service representatives obtain answers to questions about ZenTime Smart Watches, from the support documents. When an agent asks a question, the system retrieves the most relevant document chunks based on semantic similarity (rather than just keyword matching), and then uses those chunks as a context for a large language model (**Llama 3.1-70B**) to generate accurate answers.

The workflow starts by initializing a Snowflake session, and configuring the Cortex Search service parameters. When a user inputs a question, the application retrieves similar document chunks using the **get_similar_chunks_search_service** function which can filter by category, if specified. These chunks are then incorporated into a prompt for the LLM, instructing it to answer questions based only on the provided context. The prompt engineering ensures that the assistant remains factual by explicitly telling it not to hallucinate, and to acknowledge when information is not available. It is then passed to an LLM (**llama3.1-70b**) for response generation leveraging the cortex complete function.

The interface provides a chat-like experience, and users can select specific document categories to narrow the search scope. The app also displays available documents at the top of the interface for transparency. The Cortex search driven approach combines the precision of Retrieval-Augmented Generation with the conversational capabilities of modern LLMs, providing ZenTime support agents with accurate and contextually relevant information to assist the customers.

Let us now ask a question. To assist with a customer query, the agent wants to know the available colors for the ZenTime Ultra model, and it correctly answers the question.

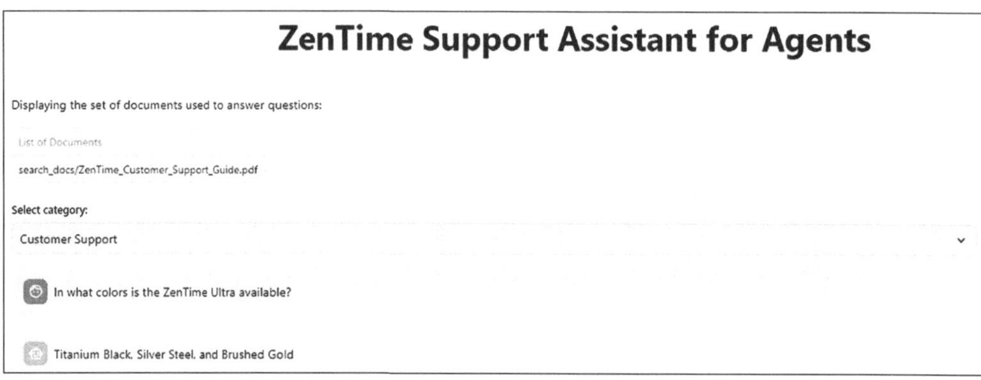

Figure 7.29: *Asking a Question from the Streamlit Application*

The answer can be found in the document where it says, "*Available in Titanium Black, Silver Steel, and Brushed Gold, the Ultra comes complete with a premium magnetic charging cable, quick start guide, and an extra silicon sport band in the box.*"

Let us now ask another question.

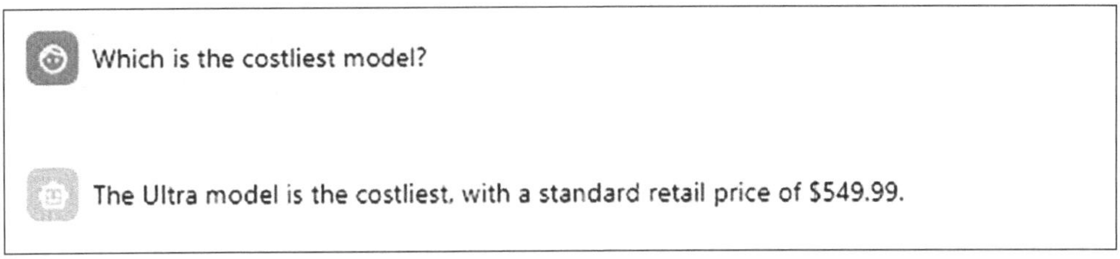

Figure 7.30: *Asking Another Question from the Streamlit Application*

The service scanned through all the ZenTime models, and retrieved the correct information. Notice that for this same question, it could give the answer, along with additional information like the price, and sometimes without it. That depends on the chosen model. Feel free to change the model from **`llama3.1-70b`** to any other, and experiment.

With the implementation of Snowflake's Cortex Search functionality, ZenTime support representatives now have 24/7 access to accurate, context-aware answers to assist customers effectively. The system's flexible architecture allows ZenTime to seamlessly expand its knowledge base by adding new categories, such as Billing, Technical Support, and so on, enhancing the scope and depth of customer assistance. This scalable approach ensures that as ZenTime's product line and service offerings grow, their support capabilities can evolve in parallel, maintaining consistent quality across all customer interactions. Additionally, please note that a Cortex Search Service can also be created through the AI/ML Studio using a no-code, step-by-step guided approach.

To summarize, Cortex Search is Snowflake's answer to making unstructured data accessible as structured data in analytics. By combining semantic vector search with classic search, it allows users to find information in a very natural way, as you can ask a question or describe what you are looking for, and it will find the content that matches, even if the phrasing differs.

Snowflake Cortex AI Agents: Orchestrating LLMs with Native Tools

Snowflake Cortex Agents are a fully managed framework for building "*agentic*" AI applications natively in the Snowflake Data Cloud. At a high level, a Cortex Agent can autonomously plan and execute multi-step data tasks by combining your enterprise data with powerful LLM reasoning. It integrates the structured data from Snowflake tables and the unstructured data (documents, text) using Snowflake's own tools, using an LLM to synthesize answers. In essence, Cortex Agents orchestrate across both structured and unstructured data sources (for example, Snowflake tables or

PDFs in stages), breaking down complex queries, retrieving relevant information, and generating answers for the user. Under the hood, the agent leverages Cortex Analyst for structured data (translating natural language into SQL) and Cortex Search for unstructured documents, alongside LLMs that analyze results and compose the final response. All this runs within Snowflake's secure environment, so that the data never leaves the platform.

Multi-Step Reasoning and Tool Orchestration

Unlike a simple question-answering bot, a Cortex Agent can perform multi-step reasoning and decision-making. Cortex Agents can break a request into sub-tasks for more precise results. It then routes each sub-task to the appropriate tool, such as for a structured data question, it will invoke Cortex Analyst (which maps business terms to SQL); for a document-related question, and will call Cortex Search to find the relevant text snippets. This dynamic tool selection is governed by Snowflake's security policies, ensuring that the agent only accesses the data the user is permitted to see.

Once the agent has a plan, it executes each step in sequence using the chosen tools and the LLM. Cortex Analyst might generate and run a SQL query to get the aggregated results from a table, while Cortex Search might vector-search a collection of documents for the relevant paragraphs. After each tool invocation, the agent enters a reflection phase where it evaluates the result returned, and decides whether it sufficiently answers the question, or if further action is needed. The LLM plays a key role here, acting as the agent's reasoning engine, such as it can interpret whether the data retrieved is adequate, or if the query needs refining. The agent may loop through **`planning`** > **`tool use`** > **`reflection`** multiple times, iterating or branching into additional steps, if necessary to gather all the required information. In our ZenTime example, the agent might first run a SQL query to find the recent orders, and then use the results to formulate a search for the issue raised.

After collecting all the pieces, the last step is response generation. The LLM composes a comprehensive answer, often incorporating citations or source references for transparency. The result is an assembled answer that addresses the user's complex query by blending data from SQL results, and documenting the text. Impressively, Cortex Agents handle this end-to-end without human intervention: they autonomously decide which actions to take in-order to fulfill the query, effectively chaining multiple LLM and Snowflake operations. Agents can even maintain context across turns in a conversation (multi-turn dialogue), enabling interactive analytics scenarios.

At the time of writing this book, Cortex Agents can leverage several powerful models for generating responses, including **`llama3.1-70b`**, **`llama3.3-70b`**, **`mistral-large2`**, and **`claude-3-5-sonnet`**. These models are specifically used for response generation, producing coherent, relevant, and human-like textual responses..

The two components that we created earlier for Zentime, the Cortex Agent that provides sales information and the Search, can be leveraged for an Agentic orchestration where the Cortex Agent routes sales queries to the analyst agent, and support related clarifications to the search agent. We have already created those agents in the previous topics, and will be reusing the same for the agent orchestration.

Now, we will create a new streamlit application (**`Zentime Cortex Agent.py`**) for the agent. Import the packages provided in the Package List.txt in the streamlit app using the **`Packages`** > **`Find Packages`** option, before running the streamlit application.

We create an AI-powered sales and support assistant for **Zentime**. As observed, it uses an agentic approach to intelligently respond to queries by leveraging two types of capabilities that we have seen in this chapter:

1. **Cortex Search**: It retrieves information from unstructured documents, specifically the **`zentime_customer_support_guide.pdf`**. This allows the search assistant (**`ZENTIME_CUSTOMER_SUPPORT_SERVICE`**) to extract natural language responses for customer support questions based on document context.
2. **Cortex Analyst**: This component interprets structured queries using a semantic YAML file (**`zentime_sales_support.yaml`**) that maps business concepts to the underlying Snowflake tables. It auto-generates SQL from the user input, and queries live data for questions related to sales, performance, or metrics.

The assistant then listens for user input through the chat interface. It sends the query to the Snowflake Cortex API (**`/api/v2/cortex/agent:run`**) with two tools enabled: **`cortex_search`** and the **`cortex_analyst_text_to_sql`**. Depending on the nature of the question, Cortex either searches the support document for answers, or Cortex Analyst generates SQL to query the sales data. An API call is made to the agent API endpoint (*"/api/v2/cortex/agent:run"*). The location of the semantic file is provided for the analyst agent, and the search service name is provided for the search agent.

```
CORTEX_SEARCH_SERVICES = "cortex_ai_db.public.ZENTIME_CUSTOMER_
SUPPORT_SERVICE"
SEMANTIC_MODELS = "@cortex_ai_db.public.cortex_analyst_stg/zen-
time_sales_support.yaml"
```

The function that invokes the api call leverages the **`llama3.3-70b`** LLM model, and defines the tools necessary for both the agents.

The response is processed in real-time, including extracting any SQL queries and citations from documents. Results are displayed in the chat, and if SQL is used, the output and the generated SQL query are both displayed.

```
def snowflake_api_call(query: str, limit: int = 10):

    payload = {
        "model": "llama3.3-70b",
        "messages": [
            {
                "role": "user",
                "content": [
                    {
                        "type": "text",
                        "text": query
                    }
                ]
            }
        ],
        "tools": [
            {
                "tool_spec": {
                    "type": "cortex_analyst_text_to_sql",
                    "name": "analyst1"
                }
            },
            {
                "tool_spec": {
                    "type": "cortex_search",
                    "name": "search1"
                }
            }
        ],
        "tool_resources": {
            "analyst1": {"semantic_model_file": SEMANTIC_MODELS},
            "search1": {
                "name": CORTEX_SEARCH_SERVICES,
                "max_results": limit,
                "id_column": "category"
            }
        }
    }
```

Figure 7.31: *Agent API Call*

Overall, this implementation showcases a multi-modal AI assistant that can answer both freeform support queries and data-driven analytical questions, making it a powerful unified interface for Zentime's customer support and business insights.

Now, when we ask a question regarding sales - "What was the top selling ZenTime model in 2025 ?", it is routed to the Analyst agent, and the answer is retrieved from the database, along with the SQL query.

Then for a subsequent question on return policy, you will notice that it is routed to cortex search.

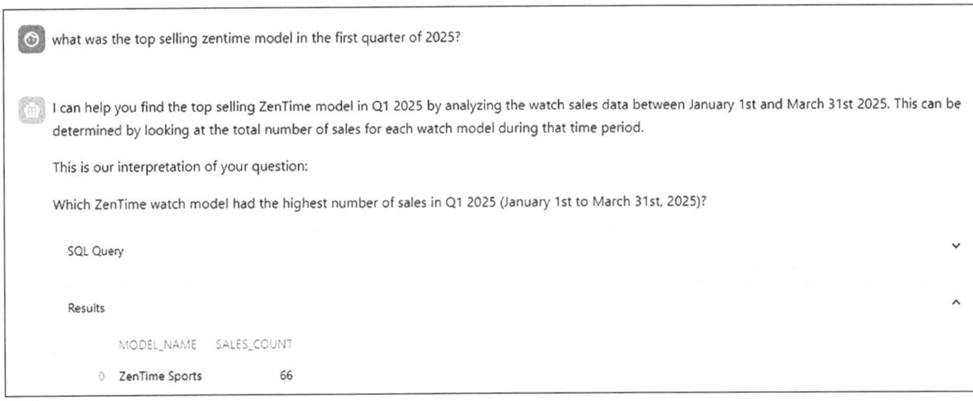

Figure 7.32: *Cortex Sales Analyst Agent Response*

We could expand the **SQL Query** tab, and retrieve the query.

```
WITH __zentime_watch_sales AS (
  SELECT
    model_name,
    purchase_date
  FROM cortex_ai_db.public.zentime_watch_sales
), model_sales AS (
  SELECT
    model_name,
    COUNT(*) AS sales_count
  FROM __zentime_watch_sales
  WHERE
    purchase_date >= '2025-01-01' AND purchase_date <= '2025-03-31'
  GROUP BY
    model_name
)
SELECT
  model_name,
  sales_count
FROM model_sales
ORDER BY
  sales_count DESC NULLS LAST
LIMIT 1
```

Figure 7.33: *The Generated SQL Query*

Let us ask a question that relates to the return policy (which is information contained in the document).

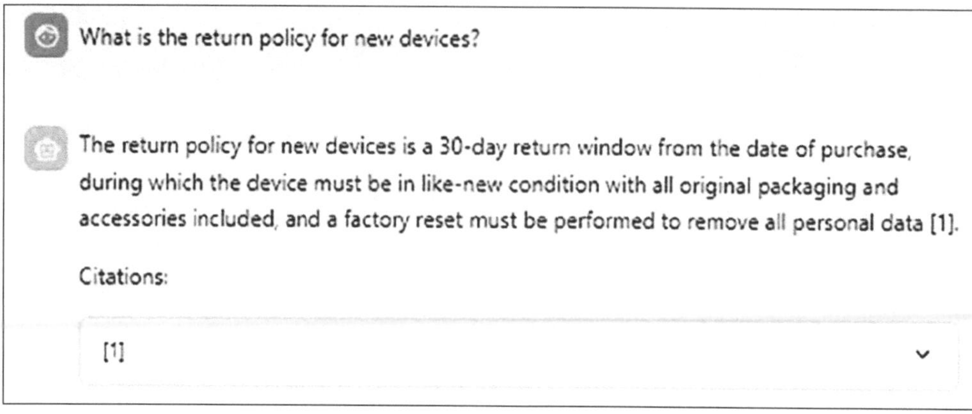

Figure 7.34: *Cortex Support Search Agent Response*

Under the hood, Cortex Agents detects when a user's query involves unstructured content, and intelligently routes the request to Cortex Search to fetch the relevant support data. Similarly, it identifies when the query pertains to structured data and seamlessly switches the context. By unifying Cortex Search and Cortex Analyst within a single conversational flow, Cortex Agents provide deeper, context-aware responses across diverse queries with Snowflake.

To summarize, Cortex Agents orchestrate queries across both unstructured (document) and structured (table/database) data. They parse the user request, plan tasks, and route it to the appropriate tool – **Cortex Search** for the unstructured data and **Cortex Analyst** for the structured data. After retrieving information from these tools, the agent evaluates the results and synthesizes a unified response back to the user. The process flow is as follows.

1. The user submits a query to the Cortex Agent.
2. The Cortex Agent processes the query, and chooses the right tool.
    a. If the query requires document-based (unstructured) data, the agent calls Cortex Search to retrieve the relevant information.
    b. If the query requires structured data (tables/databases), the agent calls Cortex Analyst to perform the needed SQL analysis.
3. The Cortex Agent then combines the outputs from Cortex Search and Cortex Analyst.
4. Finally, the agent synthesizes these insights and delivers a unified answer back to the User.

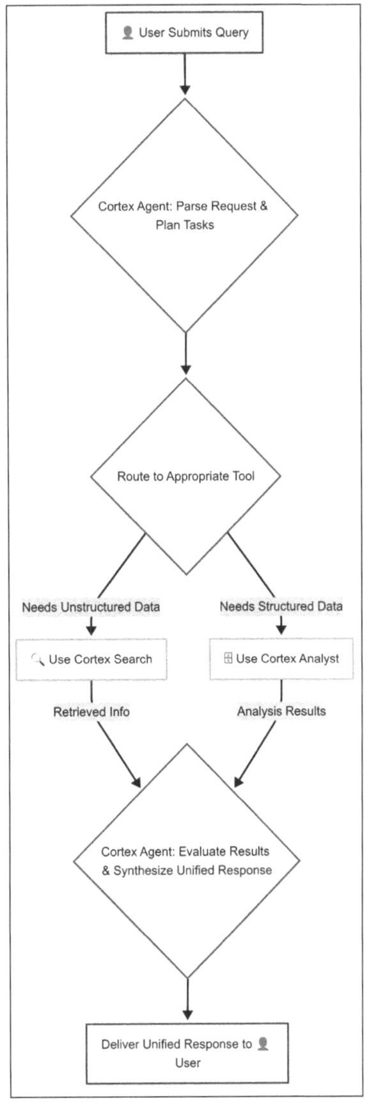

Figure 7.35: *Cortex Agent Process Flow*

This flow ensures that user queries are handled end-to-end: the agent uses the right tool for each data type, integrates the results, and generates a single coherent response grounded in Snowflake data.

In practice, Cortex AI agents could enable a wide range of business applications across industries. For instance, in customer support automation, an agent can automatically answer customer inquiries or assist support staff by drawing information from both a knowledge base (unstructured documents) and customer records (structured data), providing accurate, context-aware responses. In sales, a Cortex agent might analyze CRM data and communications to generate real-time sales insights – for example, summarizing pipeline status or identifying high-priority leads from both the database metrics and call transcripts. Similarly, in operations the agent could optimize workflows by correlating structured performance metrics with unstructured reports (like maintenance logs or emails) to pinpoint bottlenecks, and recommend improvements.

Other use cases span everything from financial reporting (from ledgers and reports) to marketing analytics, essentially wherever conversational data access can expedite decision-making. Looking ahead, these agents could become indispensable to the enterprise workforce as they integrate more deeply with the trusted data. They may serve as a foundational layer of enterprise intelligence—proactively uncovering insights, and enabling more autonomous, data-driven decision-making across the organization.

Thus, Cortex Agents represent a significant leap forward in enterprise AI integration, promising to revolutionize how organizations orchestrate complex, multi-step workflows across their data ecosystems. As these technologies continue to evolve, we can anticipate increasingly sophisticated agent capabilities that will enable deeper automation of knowledge work, alongside seamless integration with third-party agentic providers, creating a rich ecosystem where specialized AI agents can collaborate across platforms to deliver unprecedented business value and transformative data solutions.

Overview of Snowflake Copilot for SQL Assistance

As this chapter focuses on natural language processing capabilities, it is valuable to also discuss Snowflake Co-pilot briefly which provides AI-assisted functionality within the Snowflake ecosystem.

Snowflake Copilot is another innovative piece of the Snowflake AI capabilities. It is an AI-powered SQL assistant designed to help users (especially analysts and developers) to write, optimize, and understand SQL queries in Snowflake. Unlike Cortex Analyst, which is aimed at end users asking business questions, Copilot is geared toward those who are directly interacting with Snowflake via worksheets, notebooks, or IDEs. In essence, Copilot acts like a smart programming assistant (like GitHub Copilot or other code assistants, but focused on SQL and Snowflake tasks). It can take natural language prompts or questions, and produce SQL code, help troubleshoot errors, and explain Snowflake concepts, thus enhancing user productivity and decision-making by reducing the technical friction in working with data.

Snowflake Copilot runs on the same Cortex infrastructure - it is powered by an LLM that Snowflake fine-tuned and deployed securely within the Snowflake platform. This means two important things: Firstly, your data and metadata never leave Snowflake when Copilot is working (the model comes to the data, rather than sending your schema or queries out to an external service.). Secondly, Copilot respects Snowflake's governance – it knows who you are, and what data you have access to, and accordingly, it will tailor its assistance. For example, if you ask Copilot to query a table you do not have permissions for, it will not magically give you results for it. Similarly, its suggestions are based only on schemas you can see. This integration with Snowflake's security model ensures that Copilot can be used in enterprise settings, without exposing sensitive information, a critical requirement that influenced its design.

So how do users interact with Snowflake Copilot? Copilot is embedded in the Snowsight web interface (the Snowflake UI for running queries and building dashboards) as a side panel or chat interface. A user can click **`Ask Copilot`** in a worksheet or notebook which opens the Copilot chat. From there, you can type questions or commands in natural language. You could select the database and schema of your choice in the worksheet, and ask questions related to tables in that schema. For instance, you might ask: "*How do I calculate the year-over-year growth in* SQL?" and Copilot will understand that you are looking for a SQL pattern, and provide an example query or a snippet of SQL that uses window functions or self-joins to calculate year-over-year growth, perhaps, even tailoring it to the tables in your database, if you specify them.

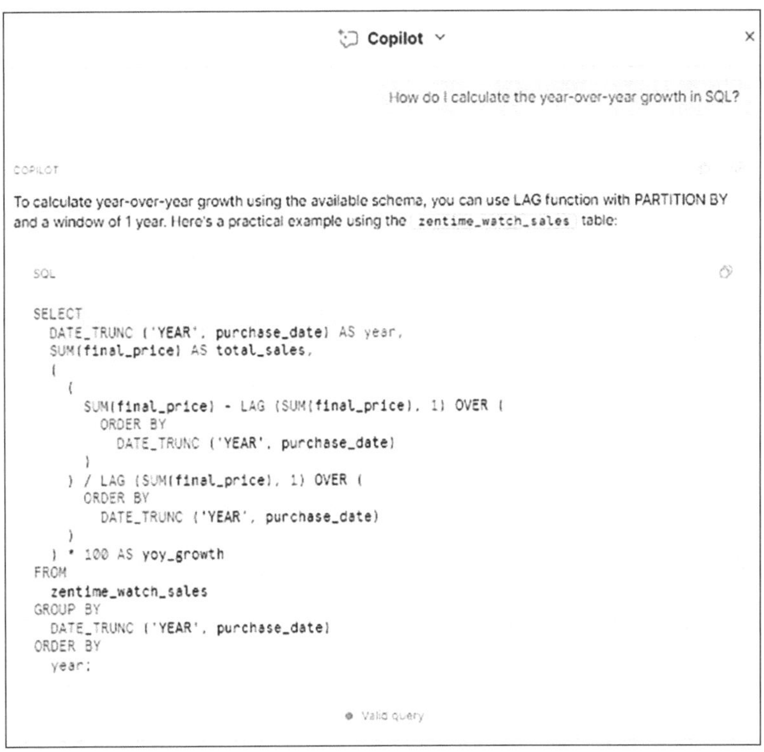

Figure 7.36: *Copilot – Help with SQL*

You could also directly request, "*write a query to provide the most sold smart watches in March* 2025," and Copilot will generate an SQL query for you (leveraging your schema's table and column names).

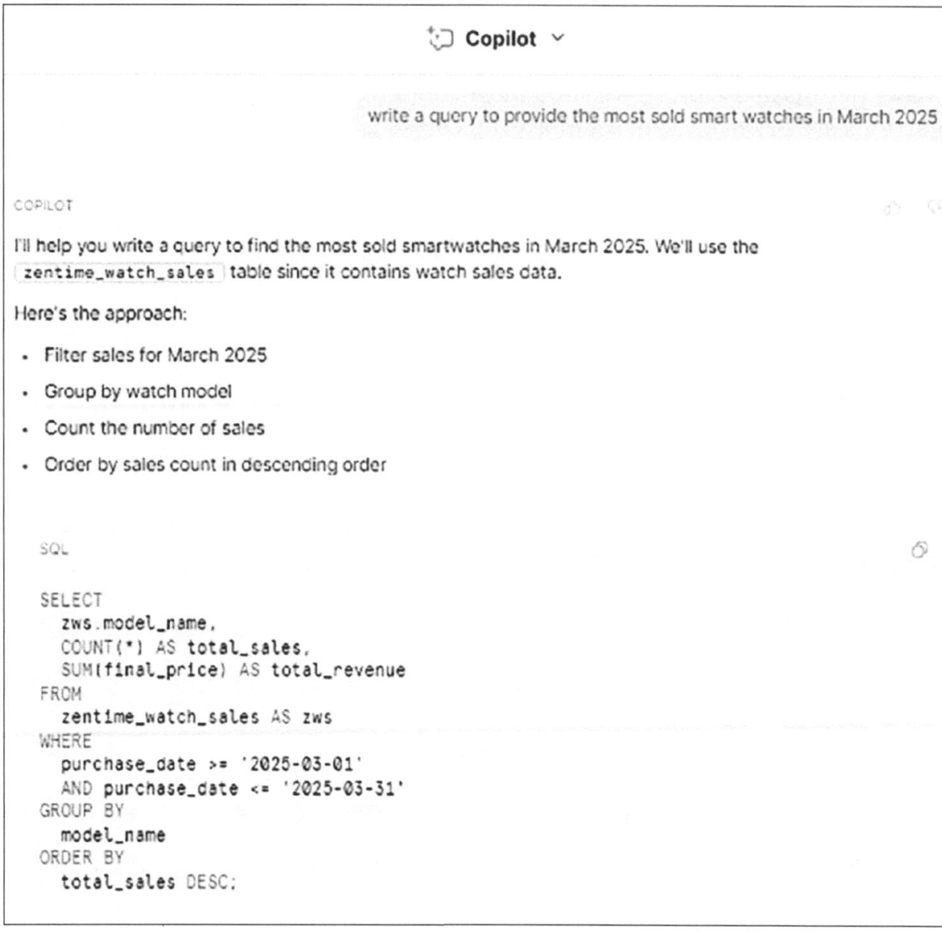

Figure 7.37: *Copilot - Help with Specific Query for Top- selling Model*

If the initial query is not exactly what you want, you can refine your request or ask Copilot to modify certain parts (for example, "*Now filter it to only include active customers*"). This iterative, conversational way of writing an SQL is much faster for many users than writing from scratch, especially for complex queries.

Another major use of Copilot is SQL optimization and troubleshooting. If you paste an SQL query into the Copilot interface and ask, "*How can I improve this query's performance?*" Copilot can analyze it, and suggest things like adding an appropriate filter, using a different join strategy, creating a clustering key, and so on, drawing on Snowflake best practices. Likewise, if you get an error from running a query, you can show the error to Copilot (or Copilot will notice it), and ask for help; it might explain the error (for example, a data type mismatch or a missing group by) and suggest a corrected query. This is immensely helpful for developers who are less familiar with Snowflake specifics or SQL nuances. Hence, it is like having a tutor or pair-programmer who specializes in Snowflake. In addition, Copilot can answer questions about Snowflake features and syntax. If someone asks, "*How do I create a secure view?*" or "*What's the syntax for the MERGE statement?*" Copilot will provide the explanation or a code. It basically serves as a context-aware documentation assistant. This means having an SQL expert is as good as a Snowflake manual at your side, 24/7, responding instantly. Note that you have the option to Export the chat as well.

Now, one could imagine a workflow where a data analyst uses Copilot to help build and validate the semantic YAML model (for Cortex Analyst) by asking Copilot things like how to structure a metric or write a particular SQL expression, and then deploys that model for business users to query via Cortex Analyst. They both leverage AI to lower the barrier: Copilot lowers the barrier for writing and understanding the code, and Cortex Analyst lowers the barrier for querying and interpreting data. From a decision-making perspective, Copilot can significantly speed up the work of data developers and analytics engineers (so they can build data products faster or do ad-hoc analysis more efficiently), and Cortex Analyst delivers insights directly to the decision-makers, without any intermediate steps. However, both ultimately help organizations to get more value out of the data by bringing AI assistance into the workflow. As part of the Cortex AI family, Copilot underscores Snowflake's strategy to embed AI deeply into its platform to assist users at all skill levels in working with the data.

Cortex Playground: A Quick Look

Beyond leveraging natural language for search, analysis, and conversational interactions through tools like Cortex Search, Analyst, Agents, and Copilot, there is also a growing need to experiment directly with AI and machine learning models to extend these insights further. Snowflake Cortex Playground (*currently in preview*) complements these capabilities by providing a simple yet powerful environment where both business users and technical teams can test AI models using natural language prompts leveraging their Snowflake data – without needing any deep machine learning expertise. Thus, it offers another step in the journey from querying insights to experimenting and personalizing AI-driven solutions.

Snowflake Cortex Playground is an interactive no-code environment within the Snowflake Data Cloud that makes it easy to experiment with AI and machine learning models using your existing Snowflake data. It is a part of Snowflake's Cortex AI & ML Studio, and provides a simple interface to try out various models – including advanced large language models – without writing complex code. With just a few clicks, users can connect a model to their Snowflake tables, and test completions directly on their business data. The Playground even lets you compare different model outputs side by side for the same input, helping you observe how each model performs, and decide which one fits your needs best. In short, Snowflake Cortex Playground serves as a convenient AI sandbox within Snowflake, allowing teams to quickly explore and validate AI ideas, before deploying them into production.

Users can choose from a list of models, enter a prompt and generate results. Everything happens securely inside Snowflake's environment, so that the data stays in place, while models come to the data.

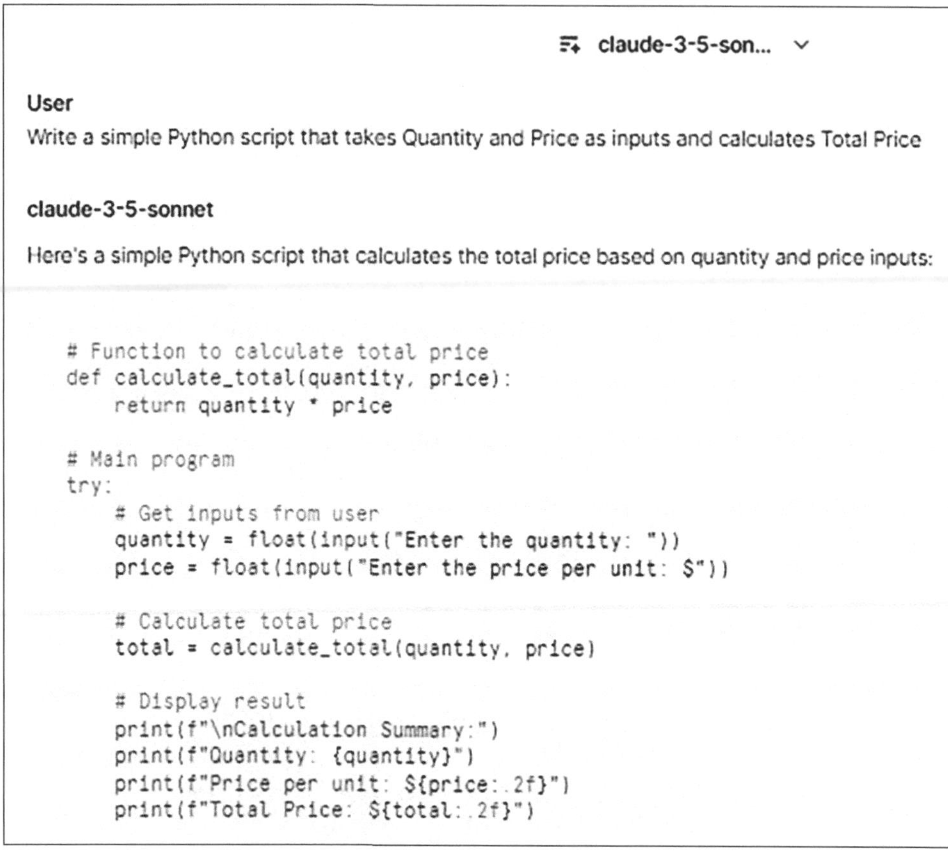

Figure 7.38: *Cortex Playground*

Developers can rapidly iterate on different models or settings via a fully managed service accessible through the Playground. The interface presents multiple result options, enabling users to choose the one that best fits their needs.

By making it easy to try multiple approaches, and test the model results, Snowflake Cortex Playground helps both business and technical users experiment, arriving at effective, tailored AI solutions more quickly and with less hassle. Additionally, by utilizing this and enabling easy experimentation upfront, teams can identify the optimal models and approaches early which can then be directly leveraged in their coding efforts. This significantly reduces the trial-and-error typically required during development, saving valuable time and effort, and accelerating the journey from insight to production deployment.

Conclusion

In this chapter, we explored how natural language can now be used as the interface between humans and data, dramatically lowering the barrier to insight. Cortex Analyst enables users to query structured data conversationally, with precision grounded in semantic models. Additionally, Cortex Search complements this by bringing unstructured content—like documents and emails—into the analytic fold, using semantic and vector search, powered by LLMs. Together, they allow organizations to surface knowledge that once lived in silos, making the enterprise data more accessible and usable than ever before. We also looked at Cortex Agents that orchestrate complex AI-powered workflows which combine reasoning, tool use, and LLM capabilities to automate sophisticated business processes within the data cloud. We also introduced Snowflake Copilot which supports data developers, analysts, and engineers by turning natural language into performant SQL, guiding query design, and accelerating development. Finally, we explored Cortex Playground, a no-code environment that allows quick and easy experimentation.

As these tools evolve, they do not just provide faster answers—they fundamentally reshape how teams interact with the data. By combining governed and secure access to information with the ease of conversational interfaces, Snowflake transforms natural language queries into actionable insights, enabling smarter and faster decisions across the enterprise.

In the next chapter, we extend this narrative further by diving into Document AI—where Snowflake's Cortex platform goes beyond question answering, and enters the domain of intelligent document understanding. From extracting structured information out of mountains of documents, Document AI promises to turn mountains of content from documents into usable intelligence. This next evolution builds upon what we have explored so far, pushing the boundaries of what is possible with language models and data-native AI.

CHAPTER 8
Unlocking Document Intelligence with Document AI

Introduction

In modern enterprises, a vast majority of data is unstructured – industry estimates suggest 80–90% of new enterprise data is unstructured. This includes documents like PDFs, scanned forms, images, emails, invoices, contracts, and more. Manually analyzing such documents is time-consuming and error-prone. Therefore, Document AI addresses this challenge by using artificial intelligence to "*read*" and comprehend documents, extracting valuable information locked in the unstructured text and images. In an enterprise context, Document AI enables organizations to parse and understand documents at scale, turning them into structured and actionable data within seconds.

This chapter explores how Snowflake Cortex's Document AI feature empowers intelligent document processing entirely within the Snowflake Data Cloud, helping businesses unlock insights from their unstructured documents into structured, actionable intelligence. Here, we will examine the core capabilities, implementation strategies, best practices, and real-world applications that enable organizations to extract maximum value from their document repositories.

Structure

In this chapter, we will cover the following topics:

- Introduction to Document AI
- Intelligent Document Processing with Document AI
- Implementing Document AI

- Best Practices
- Industry Use Cases

Introduction to Document AI

Document AI is an integrated suite of artificial intelligence capabilities designed specifically for document understanding and processing within the Snowflake Data Cloud platform. Unlike general-purpose AI solutions, Cortex Document AI is optimized for the unique challenges of document analysis, offering specialized functionality for extracting, understanding, and operationalizing document-based information. In essence, Document AI tools can automatically pull out structured data (such as names, dates, totals, addresses, and so on) from otherwise free-form text and layouts.

Snowflake's implementation of Document AI is a fully managed service as part of the Snowflake Cortex AI suite. It uses a Large Language Model (LLM) under the hood to achieve a deep understanding of documents, such as the "*Arctic-TILT*," a proprietary LLM, to extract data from documents. This means the model not only reads text, but also understands document structures (tables and form fields), and even content in graphical form such as logos, signatures, or checkboxes.

The model comes pre-trained on a wide variety of document types, enabling it to perform zero-shot extraction – finding relevant information from new document types, without any prior specific training. Additionally, Snowflake Document AI supports fine-tuning: For example, you can train the underlying model on your own documents to improve accuracy for your specific use case, with the fine-tuned model being private to your account. To summarize, Document AI is the technology that transforms the unstructured document content into structured data and insights, and Snowflake's Cortex Document AI offers this capability natively in the data platform. The subsequent chapters of this book will delve into this in greater detail.

Intelligent Document Processing with Document AI

Document AI in Snowflake Cortex provides a powerful solution for Intelligent Document Processing (IDP) – the end-to-end automated handling of documents. With Document AI, users can automatically perform tasks, such as *parsing*, *entity extraction*, *classification*, *summarization*, and even *semantic search* on document contents:

- **Parsing and OCR:** Document AI handles the low-level parsing of files, including OCR for scanned images. It can ingest various formats such as PDFs, images (PNG, JPEG, TIFF), Office documents (DOCX), emails (EML/HTML), text files, and so on, up to 125 pages or ~50 MB in size. The service will read the text from these documents (including printed or handwritten text via OCR), and interpret the layout (sections, tables, form fields). It also extracts the content from visual elements such as logos or signatures as needed, enabling a comprehensive parse of each document's contents.

- **Entity Extraction (Data Extraction):** A core capability of Document AI is extracting the specific fields or entities from the document. In Snowflake, when you create a Document AI model build, you define the "*data values*" you want to extract – each value is specified by a natural language question (for example, "*What is the Invoice Total amount?*" or "*What is the client's name on the contract?*"). The underlying LLM will locate the answer in the document, and return it along with a confidence score. This allows extraction of the structured data such as dates, totals, addresses, line items, and so on from the unstructured docs. The results come back in JSON format, with each value's answer and a confidence score. For instance, a Document AI model for invoices might return JSON with keys such as **`"Invoice_Num": "ABC120"`**, **`"Total": "565.55 USD"`**, each accompanied by a score indicating confidence . If an answer is not found, the model returns with high confidence that the field is absent (no value, only a score). This intelligent extraction works even on formats the model has not seen before (zero-shot) due to the broad training of the foundation model, and it can be further improved by fine-tuning with example documents.
- **Document Classification:** Beyond field extraction, Document AI can help classify documents by type or content. In fact, Snowflake Cortex Document AI can automatically classify and organize documents based on their content. For example, given a mixed set of documents, the AI could label which ones are invoices, which are contracts, which are receipts, and so on, if configured to do so. In Snowflake's Document AI workflow, classification can be achieved by building separate models for different document types, or by asking the model an identifying question (for example, "*Is this document an invoice, contract, or receipt?*") This classification ability helps to route documents to the appropriate processing pipeline, and apply the right extraction schema. It is especially useful in industries such as healthcare or finance where documents come in various forms, and need to be sorted (for example, identifying a patient intake form vs. a lab report).
- **Summarization:** Using the power of the LLM, Document AI can also produce summaries or narratives from a document's content. While the primary interface is geared toward Q&A style extraction, one can define a *value*, such as "*Summary*" with a question like "*Provide a brief summary of this document.*" The model will then generate a summary up to a certain length (Document AI answers are limited to ~512 tokens, or about 320 words). This is useful for quickly understanding lengthy documents – for example, summarizing a legal contract or a research report. Summarization leverages the same

comprehension capability of the model, and turns it into an abstracted overview of the document. In practice, Snowflake Cortex also offers general LLM functions that could be used to summarize the text extracted from Document AI, so that you have the flexibility in implementation. The key point is that Cortex's AI can deliver not just atomic data points, but also higher-level insights like summaries, when needed.

- **Semantic Search:** Document AI opens the door to semantic search on your documents. Once documents are processed, their text and extracted fields can be indexed or stored in Snowflake, enabling search through natural language queries. We could also leverage Cortex Search, a managed Retrieval Augmented Generation (RAG) service for semantic search over data which we covered in the previous chapter. In conjunction with Document AI, you could vectorize the textual content of documents (using Snowflake's text embedding models), and then query them semantically. For example, after processing a corpus of legal contracts, you could ask in plain English, "*Which contracts mention termination within 30 days?*" and find relevant documents. Cortex Search uses a combination of vector embeddings and ranking to retrieve relevant documents by meaning. This means the intelligence extracted by Document AI is not siloed instead, it becomes knowledge that can be queried. Business users can search documents by content, without writing complex SQL or doing keyword guessing. In short, the Document AI provides content understanding, and Cortex Search provides the ability to locate and utilize that content via semantic queries.

Behind the scenes, all these capabilities are delivered within Snowflake's platform. Because Document AI is built on Snowflake Cortex, all heavy processing occurs on Snowflake-managed infrastructure. The model is hosted securely within Snowflake. You do not need to export your data to external services – the documents and AI computations stay governed in your Snowflake environment. This tight integration of parsing, extraction, and search means you can build end-to-end document processing pipelines entirely in SQL and Snowflake tools, bringing document intelligence directly to your enterprise data cloud.

The recent release of a new version of the foundational Arctic-TILT model in Document AI delivers the following key enhancements:

- **Expanded language capabilities:** The system now processes documents, and handles queries in six additional languages - Spanish, French, German, Portuguese, Italian, and Polish.
- **Improved diacritic recognition:** The model accurately reads and extracts language-specific diacritical marks, such as Ñ.
- **Enhanced overall performance:** This includes that all the general quality improvements have been implemented across the model.

Implementing Document AI

ZenTime, our illustrative smartwatch manufacturer, having previously adopted and benefited from Cortex AI capabilities across various use cases, now intends to leverage Document AI for the purpose of transforming their PDF-formatted invoices into structured data, thereby enabling efficient querying and aggregation of information via SQL. This would streamline their operations, and enhance data accessibility.

Implementing Document AI in Snowflake involves a few key steps, and can be executed with SQL and Snowsight (Snowflake's web interface). Let us now cover this in detail for ZenTime's Intelligent Invoice Extraction use case as follows.

The initialization script is available in `Document_AI_Initialization_Steps.sql` (for Steps 1 through 10), and the script related to setting up and running predictions is in Document_AI_Predictions.sql (for Steps 24 through 31). The intermediate steps (Steps 11 through 23) are carried out within the Document AI interface in the AI & ML Studio on Snowsight.

Note: In Step 7, please replace `<YOUR USER ID>` with your logged in snowflake user name.

Step 1: Using `ACCOUNTADMIN` role to set up access.

Start by switching to the **`ACCOUNTADMIN`** role to ensure that you have the necessary privileges to set up roles, warehouses, databases, and grant access.

```
USE ROLE ACCOUNTADMIN;
```

Step 2: Create a custom role for Document AI.

This step creates a purpose-specific role for Document AI operations, and grants it the **`DOCUMENT_INTELLIGENCE_CREATOR`** role. This specialized Snowflake role provides the necessary privileges to create and manage Document AI processors, and run extraction operations.

```
CREATE ROLE DOC_AI_DEMO_ROLE;
GRANT DATABASE ROLE SNOWFLAKE.DOCUMENT_INTELLIGENCE_CREATOR TO
ROLE DOC_AI_DEMO_ROLE;
```

Step 3: Creating Dedicated Resources for Document AI Workloads.

Create a new database, schema, and warehouse to track Document AI usage. This separation simplifies the tracking of compute and storage costs. The dedicated warehouse, **`DOC_AI_DEMO_WH`** allocates compute resources specifically for Document AI processing, enabling better cost tracking, resource management, and performance optimization.

```
CREATE DATABASE DOC_AI_DEMO_DB;
CREATE SCHEMA DOC_AI_DEMO_DB.DOC_AI_DEMO_SCHEMA;
CREATE WAREHOUSE DOC_AI_DEMO_WH;
```

Step 4: Granting Document AI Role access to these resources.

This step grants the Document AI role access to the resources created in the previous step.

```
GRANT USAGE, OPERATE ON WAREHOUSE DOC_AI_DEMO_WH TO ROLE DOC_AI_
DEMO_ROLE;
GRANT USAGE ON DATABASE DOC_AI_DEMO_DB TO ROLE DOC_AI_DEMO_ROLE;
GRANT USAGE ON SCHEMA DOC_AI_DEMO_DB.DOC_AI_DEMO_SCHEMA TO ROLE
DOC_AI_DEMO_ROLE;
```

Step 5: Allow Document AI model Creation.

Grant the role or the ability to create Document AI models in the designated schema. We grant the role access to create "**`ML.DOCUMENT INTELLIGENCE`**" in the schema created. It allows you to create processors that can understand different document types like invoices or contracts, set up how information should be extracted, and manage your document processing workflows. This step grants the special permission needed to use Document AI in the respective schema, and enables the Document AI capabilities to be used within your environment.

```
GRANT CREATE SNOWFLAKE.ML.DOCUMENT_INTELLIGENCE ON SCHEMA DOC_AI_
DEMO_DB.DOC_AI_DEMO_SCHEMA TO ROLE DOC_AI_DEMO_ROLE;
```

Step 6: Granting Supporting Object Creation Privileges (Stage, Streams, and Tasks).

Document AI projects require supporting structures such as stages, tables, and automation components. The stage is needed to store documents, such as PDFs for processing, tables to store the structured results, stream to track changes or new files added to the stage, tasks to potentially automate processing (for example, scheduled predictions), and views to organize and present results from tables, if required.

We will grant these.

```
GRANT CREATE STAGE ON SCHEMA DOC_AI_DEMO_DB.DOC_AI_DEMO_SCHEMA TO
ROLE DOC_AI_DEMO_ROLE;
GRANT CREATE STREAM, CREATE TABLE, CREATE TASK, CREATE VIEW ON
SCHEMA DOC_AI_DEMO_DB.DOC_AI_DEMO_SCHEMA TO ROLE DOC_AI_DEMO_
ROLE;
GRANT EXECUTE TASK ON ACCOUNT TO ROLE DOC_AI_DEMO_ROLE;
```

Step 7: Grant the role to a user (in this example, it would be your user id, that is, the logged in snowflake user id), who will work on Document AI.

This ensures that they inherit the required privileges. This step assigns the Document

AI role to the current Snowflake user (Replace this with your snowflake login id), and grants them all the Document AI capabilities we have set up.

```
GRANT ROLE DOC_AI_DEMO_ROLE TO USER <YOUR USER ID>; --the logged in snowflake user
```

Step 8: Switching to the Document AI Role.

Now, we switch from the **ACCOUNTADMIN** role to the **DOC_AI_DEMO_ROLE**.

```
USE ROLE DOC_AI_DEMO_ROLE;
```

Step 9: Use the correct Database and Schema.

Explicitly set the context to the database and schema where Document AI operations will be performed. In the subsequent step, we will then create a new Stage in this document AI schema for storing the files.

```
USE database DOC_AI_DEMO_DB;
USE schema DOC_AI_DEMO_SCHEMA;
```

Step 10: Creating a Stage for Document Storage.

Once the Document AI model is published, we will be using it for predictions on the other documents. We need a stage to store such documents that are ready for predictions.

```
CREATE STAGE DOC_AI_DEMO_STAGE
  DIRECTORY = (ENABLE = TRUE) ENCRYPTION = (TYPE = 'SNOWFLAKE_
SSE');
```

Step 11: Now move to the Document AI User Interface.

Navigate to the Document AI option under AI and ML in the left menu.

Step 12: Switch the role to the Document AI role.

In the left menu, scroll all the way down, until you see your name displayed along with your current role. By default, it might be **ACCOUNTADMIN**, as seen in the following image. Change it to **DOC_AI_DEMO_ROLE** that we created earlier.

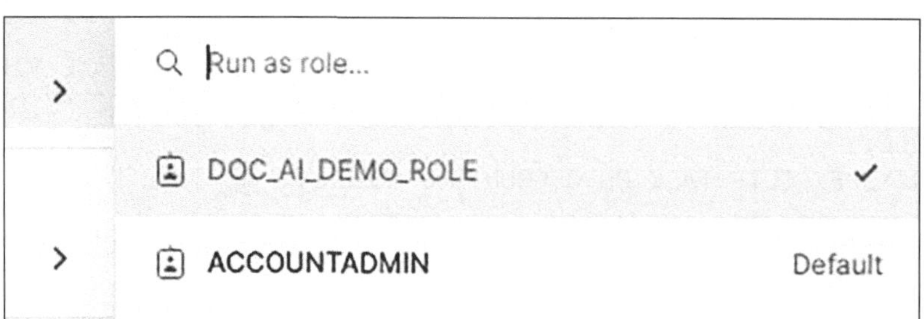

Figure 8.1: *Change to DOC_AI_DEMO_ROLE*

Step 13: Select Warehouse

Select the **`DOC_AI_DEMO_WH`** as the warehouse.

Figure 8.2: *Select Warehouse as DOC_AI_DEMO_WH*

Step 14: Create a new build for Invoice Processing

We will create a build to process ZenTime Invoices. Click `+ Build`. Let us call the build **`ZenTime_Invoices`**. Choose the **`DOC_AI_DEMO_DB`** and **`DOC_AI_DEMO_SCHEMA`** for the database and schema, respectively. You could add an optional description.

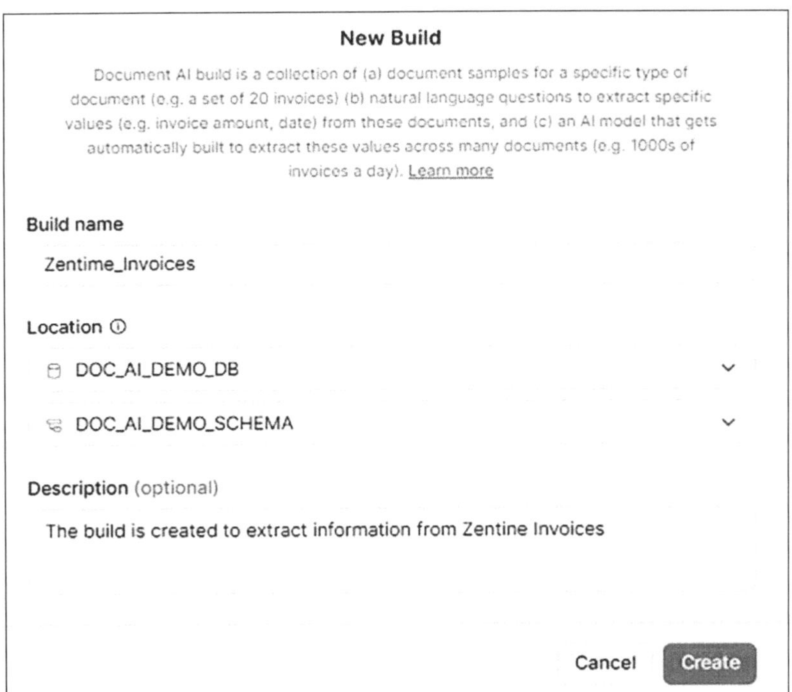

Figure 8.3: *Create a New Build for Invoices*

Step 15: Upload Invoice Documents for Processing.

We will upload three invoices for teaching the Document AI model. We will use the rest of the documents for predictions. Ensure that all the eight invoices have been downloaded to your local machine. From within the new build in the Document AI interface, browse and upload only the three invoices: **`Zentime_Invoice_1`**, **`Zentime_Invoice_2`**, and **`Zentime_Invoice_3`**. (The remaining five will be used later for predictions).

Click **`Upload Documents`**.

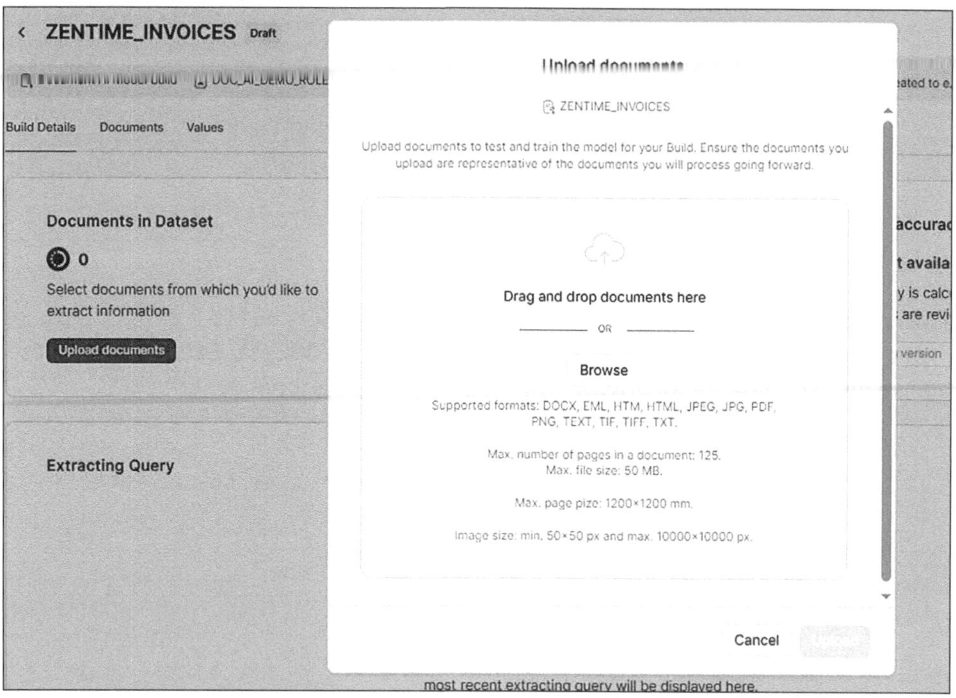

Figure 8.4: *Choose Invoice Documents for Upload*

Browse and choose the three files for upload.

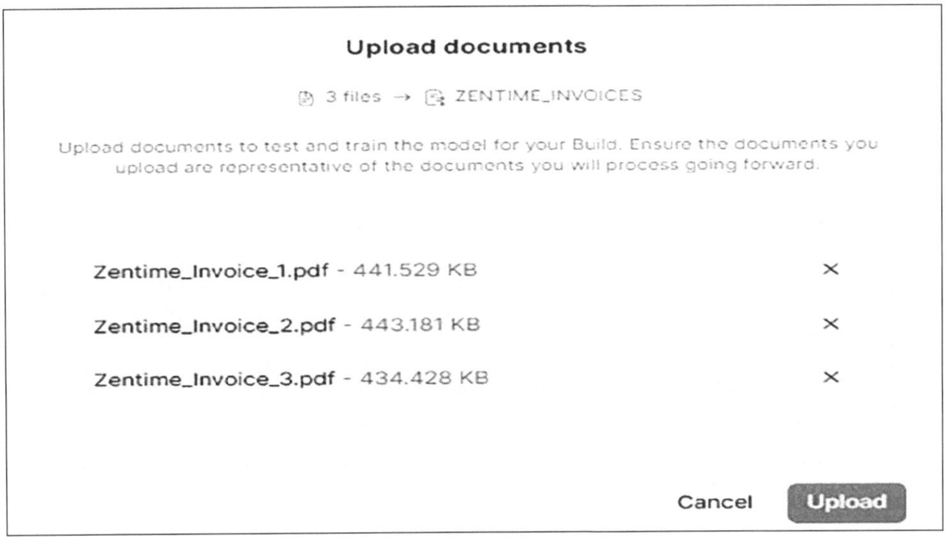

Figure 8.5: *Upload the Chosen Documents*

Click **`Upload`**.

(For this use case, we will use three documents for training. We will see that it provides results with maximum accuracy with just three documents. In real world scenarios, it is recommended to use at least twenty documents for training).

Step 16: Verify Upload.

After the three documents have been successfully uploaded, verify the same.

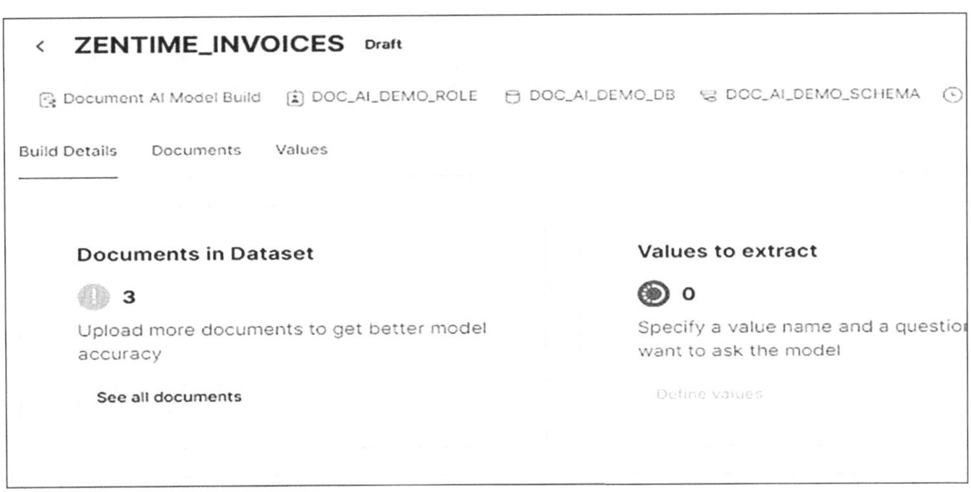

Figure 8.6: *Verify that the Documents are Uploaded*

Now click **See all Documents** to check the status. They will all be in **To Review** status.

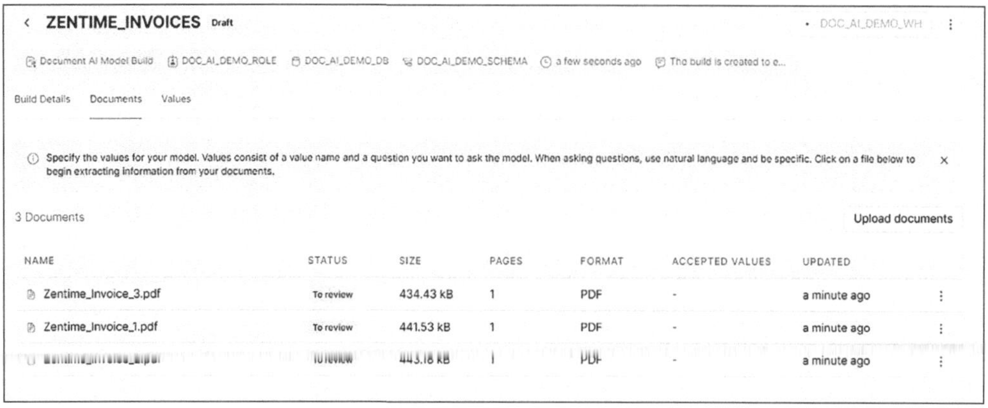

Figure 8.7: *Check the Status*

Step 17: Review the Uploaded Invoices.

Click any one of the invoices, and review.

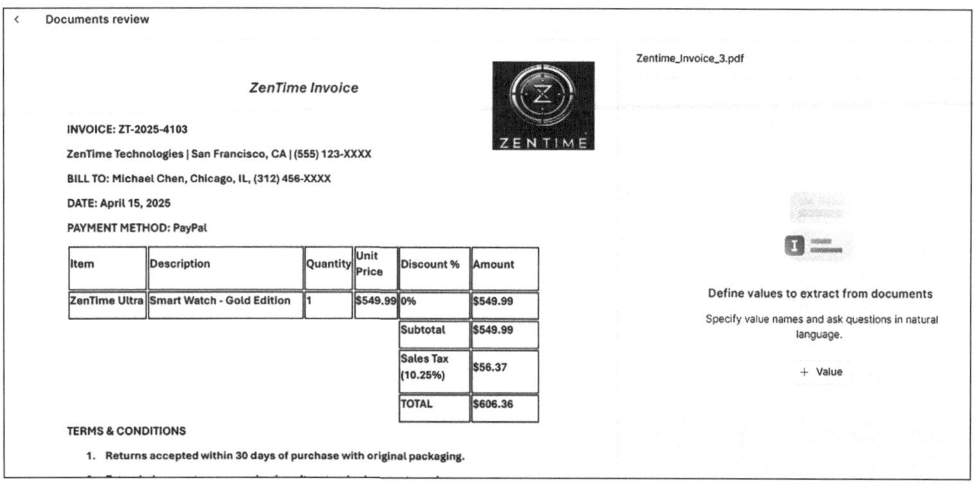

Figure 8.8: *Click on Any Document to Review*

Step 18: Define Values for Extraction.

We will go ahead, and define the values for extraction. ZenTime is interested in the invoice specifics such as ID and Date, along with the model that was sold, the total amount and the payment mode. This would help them with their initial SQL driven analysis and aggregations.

Click **Add Values**, and start adding them as shown in the following image. Notice that it auto-populates each value, once the field name and the question are entered. In fact, for the Item field, it concatenates the **Item** and **Description** which is what we wanted. Note that you could choose to override the generated answer, and add only the item name as well as force train the documents. But for our case, this is fine, and the way ZenTime wanted it, so that they can read the entire item name and description. together.

So, we will enter the following Value names and Questions.

```
InvoiceNumber    -    What is the invoice number?
InvoiceDate      -    What is the invoice date?
Item             -    What is the item?
InvoiceTotal     -    What is the invoice total?
```

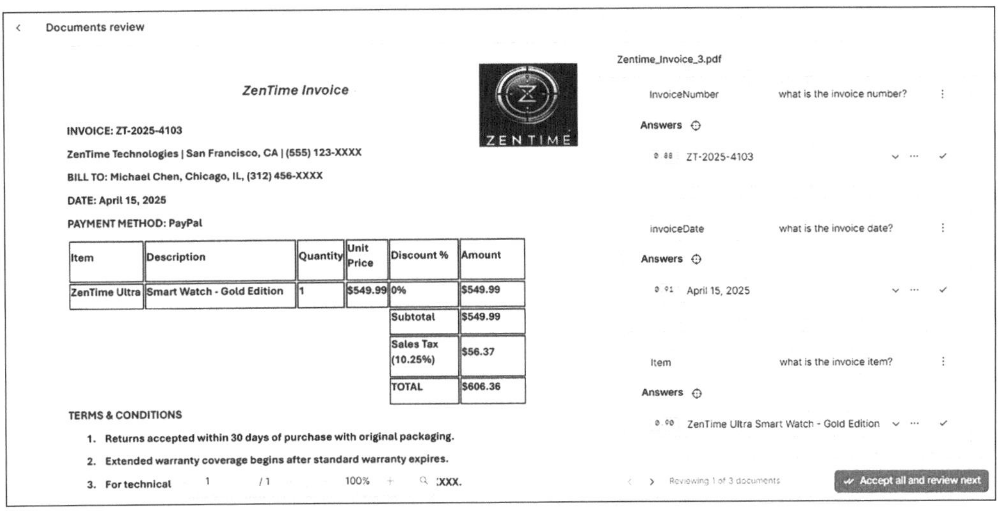

Figure 8.9: *Add Values*

Click **`Accept and review next`** to move to the next document.

Step 19: Review the Next Document.

Upon clicking **`Accept and review next`**, the next document is displayed for review. Note that the values are auto populated, based on the intelligence obtained from the processed first document. Verify that the values are correctly showing up, and click **`Accept and review next.`** Repeat this verification for the next document.

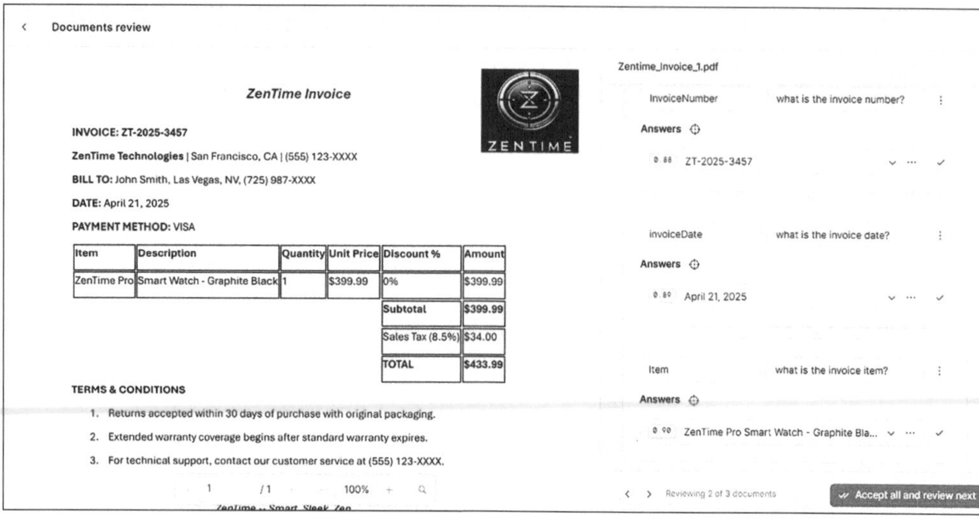

Figure 8.10: *Review and Accept Values for the Other Two Documents*

Step 20: Check the Status of the Documents.

The status of all the three documents in the **`ZENTIME_INVOICES BUILD`** should show **`Accepted`** as we have already processed and accepted each of the documents.

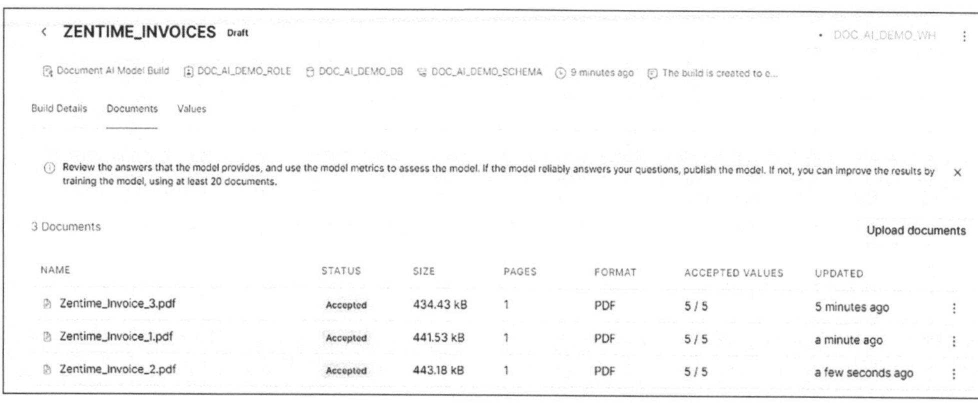

Figure 8.11: *Verify the Status of Documents*

Step 21: Train and Publish the Model.

Now that we have successfully processed and verified the build, we can publish this version. Note that explicit training (Train Model) is optional in our case (though recommended) as we accepted the values that were returned as generated by the model, without any manual overrides. Notice the model accuracy. (If we did perform any manual overrides while defining the values, we would need to train the model before publishing it so it learns the suggested patterns and remains highly accurate). Let us go ahead and publish the model version. Navigate to the **`ZENTIME_INVOICES`** build, and click **`Publish Version`**.

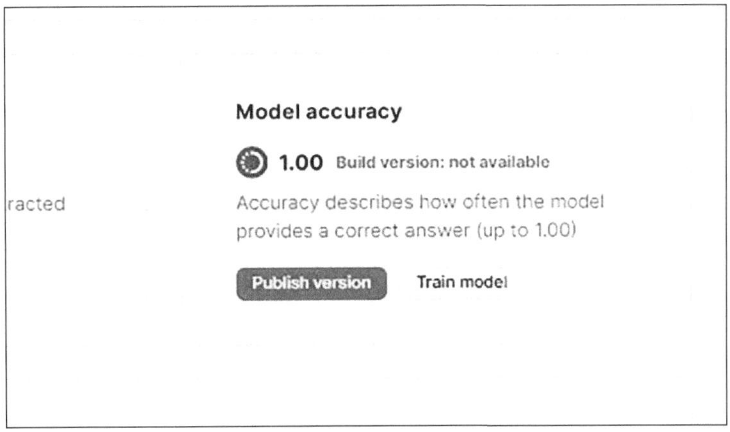

Figure 8.12: *Publish Version*

Step 22: Copy the Extraction Queries.

Notice that once the model version is successfully published, the extraction queries are displayed. These queries can be copied and stored for later use for predictions.

Figure 8.13: *Extraction Queries*

Step 23: Upload the other Invoices to Stage for Prediction.

Now that we have successfully published the model, we are ready to leverage the same for predictions. The remaining files need to be uploaded to the staging area, so that they can be leveraged for predictions. We will now upload the remaining five invoices.

Navigate to the staging area, `DOC_AI_DEMO_DB.DOC_AI_DEMO_SCHEMA.DOC_AI_DEMO_STAGE`

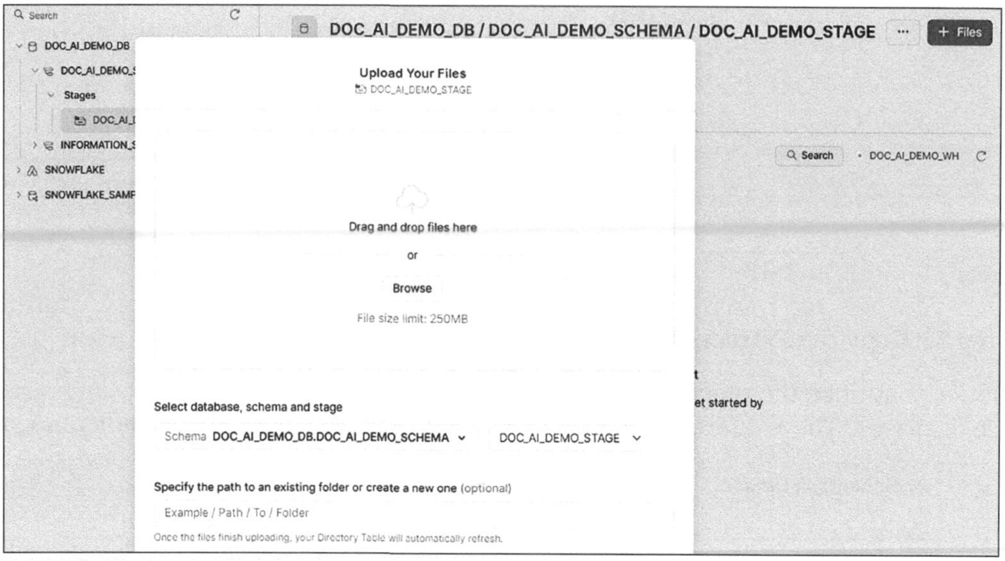

***Figure 8.14:** Navigate to DOC_AI_DEMO_STAGE*

Click **`+ Files`**. Upload the files: `Zentime_Invoice_4.pdf`, `Zentime_Invoice_5.pdf`, `Zentime_Invoice_6.pdf`, `Zentime_Invoice_7.pdf`, and `Zentime_Invoice_8.pdf`

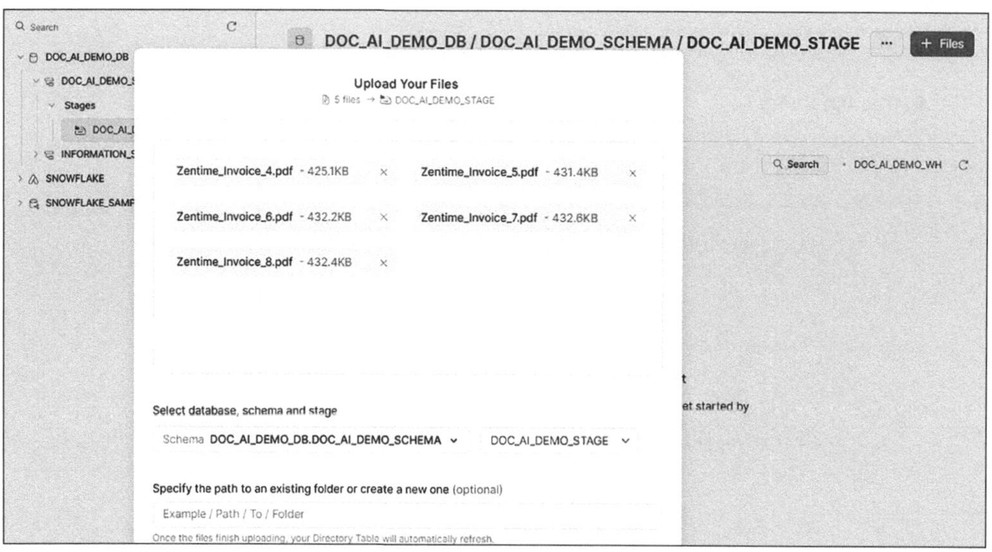

***Figure 8.15:** Upload the Files to Stage*

Click **Upload**. Verify that the files have been successfully uploaded.

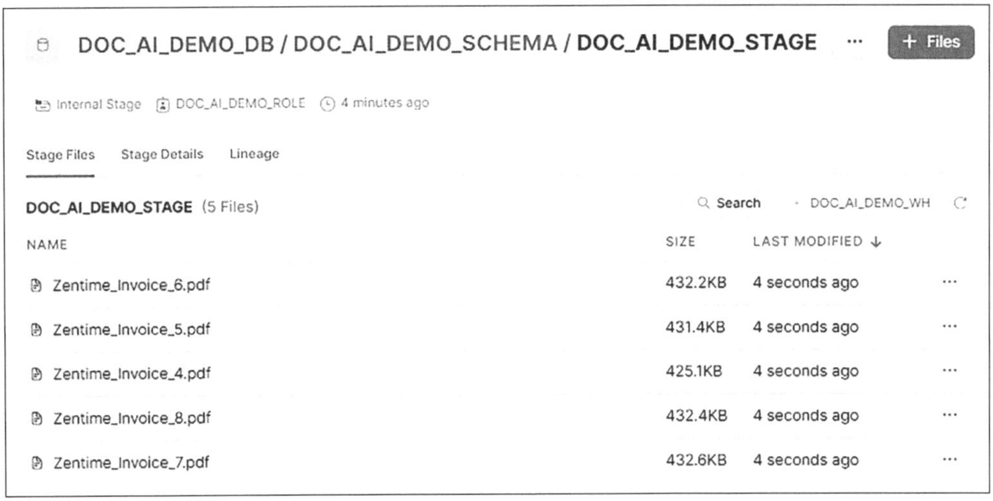

Figure 8.16: *Verify the Upload*

Step 24: Navigate to the Snow Sight SQL Interface, and set the Context.

We, now have the five new invoices uploaded to the stage and ready for predictions. We will next move to the Snowsight SQL interface for running the remainder of the steps, and executing predictions, starting with setting the context to use the appropriate warehouse, role, database, and schema. (Refer to **Document_AI_Prediction.sql** for executing the steps below.)

```
USE WAREHOUSE DOC_AI_DEMO_WH;
USE ROLE DOC_AI_DEMO_ROLE;
USE DATABASE DOC_AI_DEMO_DB;
USE SCHEMA DOC_AI_DEMO_SCHEMA;
```

Step 25: Creating a Stream on the Stage.

This step creates a stream on our document stage (**DOC_AI_DEMO_STAGE**). The stream tracks changes to the stage, such as when new documents are added, or the existing ones are modified. This helps to maintain a history of document uploads, and enables automated processing of the new or changed documents.

```
CREATE STREAM doc_ai_demo_stream ON STAGE DOC_AI_DEMO_STAGE;
```

Step 26: Refresh the Stage.

This step updates the stage's metadata to reflect any changes made to its contents, since the last refresh. This synchronizes the stage with its stream, ensuring that the stream has accurate information about the current state of your documents, before the processing begins.

```
ALTER STAGE DOC_AI_DEMO_STAGE REFRESH;
```

Step 27: Running Predictions on Documents using the Published Model.

We now process the documents in our stage using your published Document AI model (**ZENTIME_INVOICES**). The **GET_PRESIGNED_URL** function generates temporary access URLs for each document which the model uses to access and analyze the documents. (We could leverage the extraction queries that we copied in Step 22 for building this prediction query). Results are shown directly in the query output.

```
SELECT DOC_AI_DEMO_DB.DOC_AI_DEMO_SCHEMA.ZENTIME_INVOICES!
PREDICT(
GET_PRESIGNED_URL(@DOC_AI_DEMO_STAGE, RELATIVE_PATH), 1) as
ZenTime_Invoices_Model_Result
FROM DIRECTORY(@DOC_AI_DEMO_STAGE);
```

Step 28: Storing Prediction Results to a Table.

We will save the prediction results to a table.

```
CREATE OR REPLACE TABLE ZENTIME_INVOICE_MODEL_RESULTS AS
SELECT DOC_AI_DEMO_DB.DOC_AI_DEMO_SCHEMA.ZENTIME_INVOICES!
PREDICT(
GET_PRESIGNED_URL(@DOC_AI_DEMO_STAGE, RELATIVE_PATH), 1) as
Invoice_Model_Values
FROM DIRECTORY(@DOC_AI_DEMO_STAGE);
```

Step 29: Review the Raw Output from the Table.

We examine the raw output from the Document AI model. The results are then stored in a nested JSON structure that makes them comprehensive but difficult to work with directly in traditional database operations or reporting tools.

```
SELECT * FROM ZENTIME_INVOICE_MODEL_RESULTS;
```

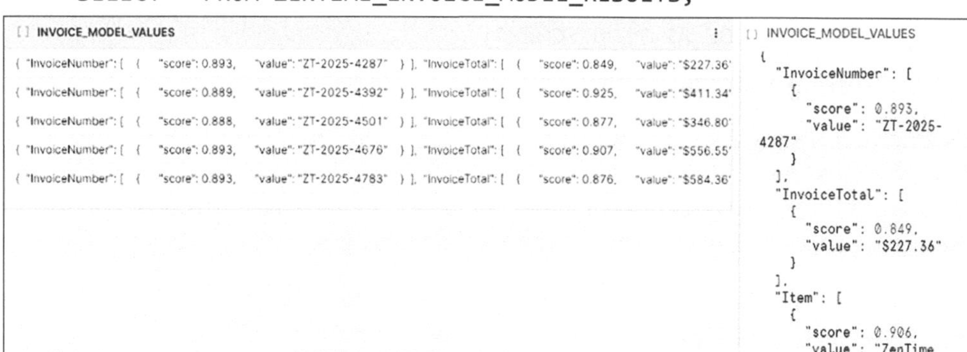

Figure 8.17: Review the Raw Output

Step 30: Normalize and Structure the Results.

To make the data usable for reporting, analytics, or further integration, normalize the model result. Each extracted field (invoice number, date, item, and so on) becomes its own column, making the data much easier to analyze, report on, and integrate with other business systems.

```
CREATE OR REPLACE TABLE ZENTIME_INVOICE_MODEL_RESULTS_NORMALIZED AS
SELECT
INVOICE_MODEL_VALUES:"InvoiceNumber"[0]:value::string AS INVOICE_
NUMBER,
INVOICE_MODEL_VALUES:"invoiceDate"[0]:value::string AS INVOICE_
DATE,
INVOICE_MODEL_VALUES:"Item"[0]:value::string AS ITEMS,
INVOICE_MODEL_VALUES:"PaymentMethod"[0]:value::string AS PAYMENT_
METHOD,
INVOICE_MODEL_VALUES:"InvoiceTotal"[0]:value::string AS TOTAL_
VALUE
FROM ZENTIME_INVOICE_MODEL_RESULTS;
```

Step 31: Verifying the Normalized Results.

Query the normalized table to verify that the extraction was successful, and the data is properly structured. You can now see all the extracted invoice information in a clean, tabular format with each field in its own column. This makes the data immediately usable for reporting, analytics, or integration with other business systems – completing the transformation from unstructured documents to structured and actionable data.

	INVOICE_NUMBER	INVOICE_DATE	ITEMS	PAYMENT_METHOD	TOTAL_VALUE
1	ZT-2025-4287	April 12, 2025	ZenTime Lite Smart Watch	AMEX	$227.36
2	ZT-2025-4392	April 10, 2025	ZenTime Pro Smart Watch	Discover	$411.34
3	ZT-2025-4501	April 7, 2025	ZenTime Sports Fitness Si	Apple Pay	$346.80
4	ZT-2025-4676	April 5, 2025	ZenTime Ultra Smart Watc	VISA	$556.55
5	ZT-2025-4783	April 2, 2025	ZenTime Ultra Limited Edi	Mastercard	$584.36

Figure 8.18: *Review the Final Normalized Output*

Implementation Summary

With the completion of these steps, ZenTime has successfully implemented Snowflake Cortex Document AI to transform their unstructured invoice documents into structured data for querying and reporting. The implementation journey began with proper setup of security roles and resources, continued through model training and deployment, and culminated in the automated extraction of key invoice information into well-organized tables.

ZenTime's invoices that were previously locked in PDF format are now available as structured data with clearly defined fields, such as invoice numbers, dates, line items, payment methods, and totals. This transformation unlocks significant business values, enabling advanced analytics, process automation, and system integration that was impossible with unstructured documents.

Here is a high-level flow of the process that we followed for this use case.

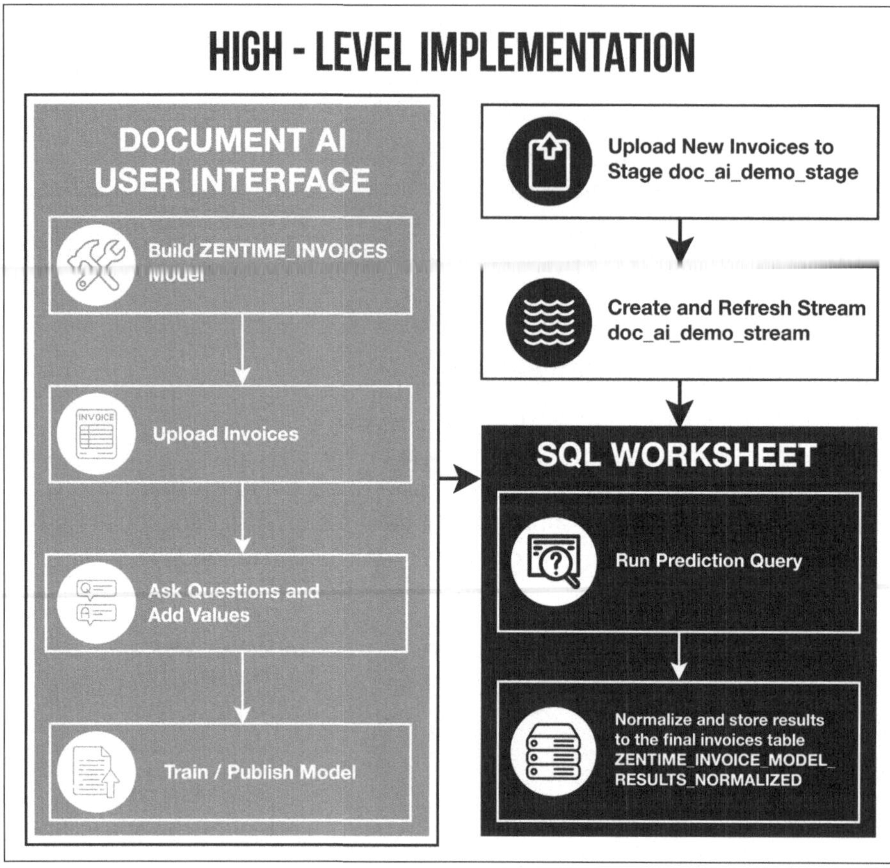

Figure 8.19: *Process Flow*

ZenTime can now build on their successful implementation by expanding the model's capabilities to extract the additional invoice fields as their business needs evolve. They may also fine-tune their current model using more examples for higher extraction accuracy. Automated pipelines can also be created to automate document processing.

Note that we could override some of the values, if required and train the model to learn from them before publishing. In our example, no overrides were necessary, as the model's responses to our queries were accurate and aligned perfectly with our requirements. As a result, an explicit training step was not needed and we could directly publish the model.

This Use case leveraging Cortex Document AI is a showcase of how structured intelligence from unstructured files can be achieved, without leaving the Snowflake platform. Organizations implementing Document AI on the Snowflake platform gain the unique advantage of processing documents where their data already resides, maintaining security, governance, and scalability throughout the document lifecycle. The combination of advanced AI capabilities with Snowflake's robust data platform enables a seamless flow from document ingestion to actionable insights.

As document volumes continue to grow exponentially, the traditional manual approaches to document processing become increasingly untenable. Document AI offers a scalable alternative that not only reduces costs, and accelerates workflows, but also enhances accuracy and enables entirely new analytical possibilities.

The future of intelligent document processing will see even more sophisticated capabilities emerge, with enhanced multimodal understanding, improved handling of complex document relationships, and deeper integration with business processes. Organizations that embrace Document AI today are positioning themselves to capitalize on these advancements, turning their document repositories from administrative burdens into strategic assets.

Thus, by implementing the approaches outlined in this chapter, you can begin your own journey toward document intelligence, unlocking the valuable information trapped in your organization's documents, and transforming it into a foundation for better decision-making, improved efficiency, and competitive advantage in an increasingly data-driven business landscape.

Best Practices

To ensure effective and accurate results when working with Document AI, it is important to follow a set of best practices. These guidelines help optimize model performance, improve extraction quality, and ensure the solution scales reliably across various document types and business scenarios. The following section outlines key considerations and recommendations to get the most out of your Document AI implementation.

- **Define Clear Document Understanding and Extraction Goals:** Begin your Document AI journey by thoroughly understanding your document types, and establishing specific extraction objectives. For optimal results, create dedicated models for each document category (separate models for invoices versus contracts, for instance). Identify the exact fields, you need to extract and formulate each as a precise, targeted question. When crafting these questions, incorporate the actual terminology found in your documents–using phrases such as "**`Invoice Number`**," "**`Total Due`**," or "**`Patient Name`**" that helps the model locate this information reliably. Specificity is crucial, so align your extraction questions with the document's language (ask "*What is the invoice due date?*" rather than a vague, "*When is it due?*"). This focused approach significantly improves extraction accuracy, and ensures you to capture exactly the information your business needs.

- **Collect Representative Document Samples:** For successful Document AI implementation, start with appropriate sample documents. Even with zero-shot extraction, testing the pre-trained model on a few examples helps to set expectations. When building your model, include diverse document samples that represent the variations you will encounter in production, such as different layouts, formats, and data values. If you plan to fine-tune the model, your training set becomes even more critical; include examples that highlight all potential field variations, including cases where information might be missing or formatted differently. Document quality matters significantly; ensure that your samples are clean and legible, as OCR confidence directly impacts extraction accuracy. The system provides an "`ocrScore`" to help identify problematic documents that might need preprocessing to enhance contrast or readability.
- **Refine Your Model through Iteration:** After initial document extraction, use the review interface to evaluate your model's performance. Correct any extraction errors, verify accurate results, and examine the overall accuracy metrics. If your model achieves high accuracy (90%+ on key fields), you might proceed directly to publishing. However, if you notice consistent issues—such as confusion between similar fields or missing information—utilize the "Train" option to fine-tune the model on your specific documents. This fine-tuning step is particularly valuable for documents containing industry-specific terminology or unique formatting. Before finalizing, test the fine-tuned model on fresh documents not included in your training set to ensure it handles new variations effectively. Publish your model only when you are confident in its performance. Remember that your Document AI implementation can evolve, that is, you can always update the model with additional document examples and retrain it as new document variations emerge in your business processes.
- **Optimize for Cost:** To optimize cost and performance, batch the documents using the FROM DIRECTORY method, instead of processing them, one by one. Use a sufficiently sized warehouse to enable parallel processing, and reduce wait times, for instance, larger warehouses support more concurrent model executions. Avoid scheduling tasks more frequently than needed, such as if documents are uploaded hourly, a one-minute interval might be excessive.
- **Implement Data Governance and Security:** Manage your extracted document data with appropriate governance controls, applying the same rigor, you would to any sensitive information. For documents containing PII or financial details, implement Snowflake's security features, including access controls, masking policies, and row access policies to protect the structured data. A salient advantage of Snowflake Document AI is that all processing occurs within Snowflake's secure environment—your document data never leaves

the platform which simplifies compliance requirements. Consider your encryption strategy: Documents in internal stages are automatically protected by Snowflake-managed keys, while external stages can leverage your cloud provider's encryption for additional security. Establish clear retention policies, that is if you do not need the original documents after extraction, consider purging them periodically to minimize risks, while retaining the structured results. When fine-tuning models, remember that the training data becomes a part of the model build to ensure that only authorized roles can create or access these resources, when working with sensitive documents.

- **Establish Maintenance and Monitoring Practices:** Develop a structured approach to maintain your Document AI implementation over time. Use Snowflake's Resource Monitor to track credit consumption by your AI warehouse, preventing unexpected costs, while ensuring sufficient resources for document processing. Plan for ongoing model evolution as your business needs change—you may need to extract additional fields or accommodate new document formats in the future. Snowflake supports multiple model versions, allowing you to create updated builds, while maintaining the existing pipelines. When ready to implement improvements, simply update your process to call the new model version. Maintain clear documentation of which model versions are actively used in your workflows, and deprecate outdated versions when they are no longer needed to keep your environment organized and efficient.

Industry Use Cases

Document AI represents a powerful technological advancement that can revolutionize how organizations manage the unstructured documents. By automatically converting these documents into structured, actionable data, this technology dramatically reduces manual processing, while increasing accuracy and operational efficiency. Organizations across mostly every sector stand to benefit from implementing Document AI solutions in their document-heavy workflows. We will list a few such applications here - each delivering considerable time and cost savings, while improving the data quality and accessibility.

- **Financial Services:** Accounts payable and finance teams deal with large volumes of invoices, receipts, and financial statements that come in as PDFs or scans. Document AI can automatically extract the key fields from invoices, such as vendor name, invoice number, date, line item details, total amounts, due date, and so on, and this can be fed to the finance systems for reconciliation. This dramatically speeds up a process that would otherwise require manual data entry. Over time, this builds a rich structured dataset of all invoice data that can be analyzed for spend patterns, cash flow forecasting, or audit compliance. Compliance and audit are also improved because the original documents and the extracted data are centrally stored and traceable. Financial institutions can also apply Document AI to loan application packages, that is extracting income and employment information from pay stubs, W-2s, tax returns, and so on, to automate loan underwriting decisions. This can shrink the loan processing time from days to minutes, giving institutions a competitive edge.

- **Healthcare:** Healthcare generates vast amounts of paperwork such as patient intake forms, physician notes, lab reports, insurance claims, prescriptions, and so on. Thus, Document AI can help providers and payers organize this data. For instance, a hospital network could use Document AI to extract patient demographics, diagnoses, and treatment codes from referral forms or faxed medical records, populating their Electronic Health Records (EHR) systems automatically. Similarly, insurance companies can process claim forms and supporting documents such as Document AI can read claim forms, pulling out policy numbers, patient info, procedure codes, and billed amounts, accelerating the claims adjudication process. One powerful use case is clinical data abstraction. Instead of a human manually reading through reports, an AI model can pull out the relevant medical terms and values. By freeing medical staff from paperwork, Document AI lets them focus more on patient care. It also aids in research, for example, once the unstructured clinical notes are structured, researchers can query and analyze the outcomes at scale. (Appropriate privacy safeguards, such as data masking, would need to be applied in such cases.)
- **Legal:** Legal departments and law firms contend with lengthy contracts and legal documents. Document AI can extract the key clauses or data points from contracts - such as parties involved, effective dates, renewal terms, payment terms, liability clauses, and so on. For example, a company's procurement department could upload all vendor contracts into Snowflake, and use Document AI to pull out renewal dates and termination notice periods. This makes it easy to know when contracts auto-renew or expire, enabling proactive vendor management. Another legal use case is e-discovery, such as during litigation, thousands of documents may need to be reviewed for relevance. Document AI coupled with Cortex Search allows lawyers to perform semantic search over document contents ("find documents mentioning environmental compliance in 2025") much faster than manual review. Summarization can also help here, for instance, a lawyer could get a quick summary of a 100-page contract to decide if it is relevant to a case. It is particularly advantageous, since sensitive documents (contracts, case files) do not leave the governed Snowflake environment.
- **Insurance:** Insurance companies rely on documents such as claim forms, police reports, medical reports, and property inspection documents, Automating these can expedite claims processing and policy underwriting. For instance, in an auto insurance claim, Document AI could extract information from the accident police report (date, location, vehicles involved, report narrative),

and from repair estimates. Adjusters then have the structured data to make decisions faster. In property insurance as well, when a homeowner submits a claim for damage, they often include inventories of lost items or contractor quotes, and then the AI could itemize and structure those automatically. On the underwriting side, consider life insurance applications: Applicants submit health questionnaires, doctor statements and lab results. The Document AI can read these, and pull out medical conditions or metrics needed for risk scoring. A real example: An insurance firm could use Snowflake to create a claims dashboard where every incoming claim is automatically logged with the key fields with a short summary of the incident. This reduces the time agents spend combing through attachments, and allows them to focus on higher-level decision-making or customer service. It also means faster payouts for customers, improving satisfaction.

- **Manufacturing and Supply Chain:** These industries deal with documents such as purchase orders, bills of lading, quality inspection forms, and equipment maintenance logs. Automating purchase order processing with Document AI (extracting PO number, items, quantities, prices, and so on) can streamline the supply chain operations by integrating directly into the ERP systems. Bills of lading and shipping documents can be parsed to track shipments, and feed data into logistics dashboards. In manufacturing, engineers might use Document AI to digitize maintenance records or inspection checklists that are filled out on paper, allowing for analysis of machine performance or defect rates. Quality control is another area as often defect reports or customer feedback forms are unstructured. So, AI can compile these into a database to identify the common issues.
- **Education:** In the education sector also, Document AI can streamline both academic and administrative operations. Universities and schools often deal with a large volume of unstructured documents, including student transcripts, application forms, recommendation letters, grade reports, and fee receipts. Document AI can extract the structured data from these sources, making it easier to store, search, and analyze. It can also be used to summarize long academic documents such as research papers and theses, aiding librarians, faculty, and researchers. Institutions can automate document validation during admissions, process bulk applications faster, and even perform compliance checks on accreditation documents. By turning scanned paperwork into usable data, Document AI not only saves time but also improves operational transparency, and student service efficiency.
- **Retail and E-Commerce:** Retailers and e-commerce companies manage a variety of unstructured documents, including product catalogs, purchase orders, supplier invoices, shipping manifests, and customer return forms. Document AI can automate the extraction of these key product details from vendor documents, reconcile invoice and order data, and process scanned

receipts and warranty cards from customers. In addition to back-office efficiency, Document AI can also enhance customer experience by structuring and categorizing user-submitted reviews or return reasons. It also aids supply chain visibility by parsing freight documents, and generating structured, real-time data for logistics dashboards.

- **Energy and Utilities:** In the energy and utilities sector, Document AI can streamline regulatory compliance, and operational reporting by extracting data from environmental audits, site inspection forms, maintenance logs, and scanned utility bills. Companies can automate the processing of handwritten field reports, and digitize decades' worth of infrastructure documentation. This structured data can then be used to analyze equipment reliability, monitor asset performance, and support predictive maintenance programs. Furthermore, energy providers can use Document AI to process customer onboarding forms, billing records, and rebate applications efficiently, while maintaining strict compliance with energy regulations.
- **Transportation and Aviation:** In the transportation and aviation sectors, Document AI can automate the processing of cargo manifests, maintenance logs, flight operation reports, passenger onboarding forms, and regulatory compliance documents. Airlines can digitize maintenance checklists to monitor aircraft readiness, and reduce manual inspection logging. Logistics teams can extract the structured data from shipping documents to improve routing and delivery accuracy. Thus, by converting complex, multi-format records into standardized formats, Document AI enhances operational reliability, safety tracking, and audit readiness across the transportation ecosystem.
- **Telecommunications:** Telecommunication providers manage a vast number of documents, including service agreements, installation records, customer support tickets, and compliance paperwork. Document AI can help extract the key details from customer contracts, streamline the provisioning process, and structure data from service logs or technical field reports. It enables faster issue resolution by classifying and summarizing the support documents, and accelerates internal operations, such as infrastructure audits and vendor invoice processing.
- **Media and Publishing:** In media and publishing, Document AI can be used to extract metadata from manuscripts, editorial notes, content submission forms, and licensing agreements. Publishers can automate the categorization of content, identify themes, and extract author credentials or copyright terms from submissions. For large content archives, Document AI can summarize and tag articles or research papers to support recommendation engines and semantic search. This helps to streamline editorial workflows, and improve content discovery for the end users.
- **Cross-Industry:** Virtually, every industry has back-office documents that

can be automated – HR forms (resumes, applications, performance reviews), financial statements, regulatory filings, emails and correspondence, and so on. For example, an HR department could use Document AI to parse resumes and extract candidates' education, skills, and years of experience, populating a recruiting database for easier search and filtering. Or a compliance team could feed in regulatory guidance documents and use Cortex to Q&A about the content (coupled with using general LLM capabilities beyond just extraction). Document AI can be used to automate the intake and processing of support tickets, application submissions, or signed forms—by extracting relevant data and labelling for easy access. This is especially useful for customer service, procurement, or HR teams managing high volumes of incoming communications, helping reduce response times, improve routing accuracy, and create structured data from semi-structured documents. The key idea is that Document AI serves as a versatile toolkit for transforming any document into a structured and information-rich data source. Organizations can find creative uses for it—for instance, from parsing energy meters in utility companies to reading research reports in investment firms to extracting key insights.

These use cases across industries highlight the transformative impact, such as faster processing, improved accuracy, newfound insights, and freed-up human talent to focus on higher-value tasks. Moreover, because Snowflake's Cortex leverages open and cutting-edge models, customers are tapping into world-class AI, with each document being processed. As this technology continues to evolve, we can expect even richer capabilities – from multilingual support to deeper semantic understanding, further bridging the gap between human knowledge locked in documents, and actionable data in our databases.

Conclusion

Snowflake Document AI represents a transformative approach to handling document-based information across the enterprise. As we have explored throughout this chapter, the ability to convert unstructured documents into structured ones, tabular knowledge unlocks significant business value that was previously inaccessible.

The journey to document intelligence begins with understanding your specific document needs, and establishing clear extraction goals. By following the best practices for document sampling, model iteration, security implementation, and ongoing maintenance, organizations can actually achieve remarkable improvements in document processing efficiency and accuracy.

We witnessed this impact firsthand through ZenTime's implementation example, where they successfully transformed their invoice processing from a manual, error-prone task to an automated, accurate workflow. By converting the essential invoice information into organized tables, ZenTime significantly improved their invoice processing speed, while also uncovering important insights that had been inaccessible within the PDF files, demonstrating the immediate business value of Document AI.

We also looked at the potential use cases for Document AI across various industries, offering inspiration for identifying opportunities within your own organization to leverage this powerful technology.

In the next chapter, we will explore how to implement Cortex with a focus on security, governance, and cost efficiency, highlighting the best practices to ensure safe, compliant, and cost-effective AI usage.

CHAPTER 9
Implementing Cortex with Security, Governance, and Cost Discipline

Introduction

Snowflake Cortex AI opens an exciting new chapter for enterprises by making advanced AI and machine learning capabilities natively available within the Snowflake Data Cloud. With Cortex, teams can easily build, deploy, and scale models using secure, governed, and performant infrastructure—all without moving the data outside the platform. This presents an incredible opportunity to accelerate innovation, while upholding the highest standards of trust, transparency, and efficiency.

As data scientists, engineers, and architects leverage Cortex AI to power a wide range of use cases—from predictive analytics and document understanding to generative AI and natural language interfaces—it becomes increasingly important to align these capabilities with enterprise-grade security, governance, and cost-optimization strategies.

As data scientists, engineers, and architects leverage Cortex AI to power a wide range of use cases—from predictive analytics and document understanding to generative AI and natural language interfaces—it becomes increasingly important to align these capabilities with enterprise-grade security, governance, and cost-optimization strategies. This chapter serves as your guide to implementing Cortex AI responsibly and effectively, within your Snowflake environment. Hence, in this chapter, you will learn how to:

- Secure your AI workloads

- Establish robust governance
- Optimize cost-efficiency

While this chapter provides a foundation and practical guidance on security and governance, the goal is not to adopt every feature, but to select and tailor those that best align with your specific business objectives and operational context. Also, it is crucial to recognize that these areas are ever-evolving–staying updated is essential to ensure ongoing effectiveness and compliance.

Structure

In this chapter, we will cover the following topics:

- Enterprise-Ready AI with Cortex
- Security Best Practices
- Governance Best Practices
- Cost Optimization Strategies
- AI Observability in Snowflake Cortex

Enterprise-Ready AI with Cortex

The rise of AI has transformed the way enterprises think about innovation, productivity, and customer experience. From predictive analytics to conversational agents and intelligent document processing, AI is no longer a futuristic capability–it is a strategic necessity. However, integrating AI into enterprise environments presents unique challenges. Most organizations must grapple with fragmented tools, complex data pipelines, compliance risks, and runaway costs. What is needed is not just powerful AI, but enterprise-ready AI–AI that is secure by design, governed at scale, and built with financial sustainability in mind. Snowflake Cortex stands out as an enterprise-ready AI platform that brings machine learning and generative AI capabilities directly to where the data lives–within the secure and governed environment of the Snowflake Data Cloud. This native integration eliminates traditional barriers to AI adoption, enabling faster time to value, without sacrificing control or escalating costs.

What truly differentiates Cortex is how it embodies the three critical pillars every enterprise demands - Security, Governance, and Cost Efficiency. These are not just checkboxes–they are foundational to building AI solutions that scale responsibly and sustainably. Successfully implementing Snowflake Cortex AI requires thoughtful integration of security, governance, and cost optimization practices. These three pillars work together to create a foundation for sustainable, trustworthy AI implementations that deliver business value, while managing risks and expenses. In the sections that follow, we will explore each of these pillars in detail, and show how Snowflake Cortex empowers organizations to deliver trusted, compliant, and financially sustainable AI solutions at scale.

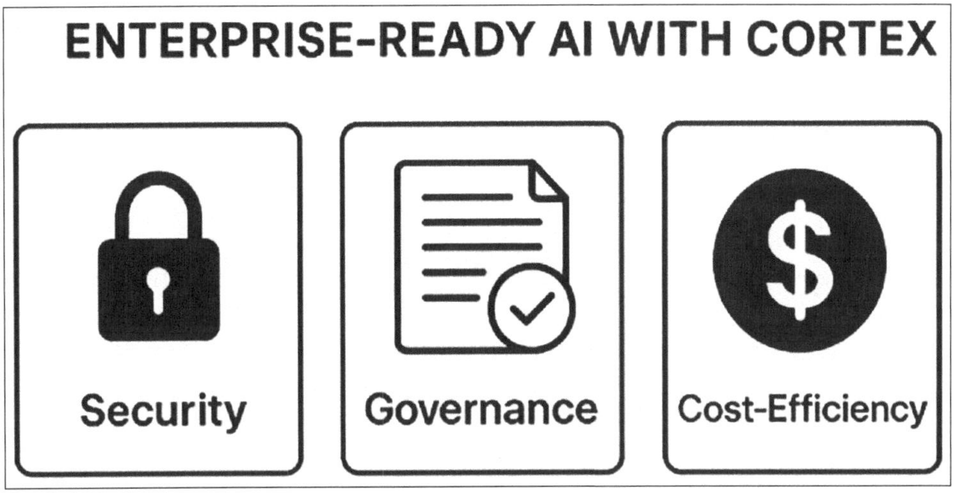

Figure 9.1: *The Three Pillars*

With best practices, you can confidently deliver AI solutions that are scalable, compliant, and cost-effective–ready to meet the needs of the modern, data-driven enterprises.

While this chapter provides fundamental strategies for governance, security, and cost optimization, Snowflake Cortex AI continues to evolve rapidly with exciting new capabilities. These enhancements will likely create additional opportunities to strengthen your implementation. Hence, by staying current and updated with Snowflake's latest developments, you will be well-positioned to leverage new features that further improve security controls, simplify governance processes, and increase cost efficiency. Also, the dynamic nature of Cortex AI promises ongoing improvements that will make these critical operational aspects even more effective and easier to implement.

Security Best Practices

Snowflake Cortex AI is built on Snowflake's secure data platform, inheriting robust security features by default. Nonetheless, you should implement additional safeguards and best practices for authentication, access control, encryption, and secure integrations. This section covers how to secure a Cortex AI deployment end-to-end.

Authentication and Authorization

Strong authentication and granular authorization are the first lines of defense.

Snowflake supports multiple authentication methods, and allows integration with enterprise identity systems:

- **Use Strong Authentication Methods:** Leverage Snowflake's support for key-pair (certificate) authentication, multi-factor authentication (MFA), OAuth tokens, or federated SSO (SAML/Okta), instead of basic passwords. For service accounts (for example, automated ML jobs), use key-pair authentication with periodic key rotation for security. OAuth with scoped access is recommended for external applications connecting to Snowflake.
- **Enforce SSO/MFA:** Enforce single sign-on through an Identity Provider for centralized control over user logins. Snowflake recently enabled new multi-factor authentication (MFA) methods for stronger account security. Users can now use hardware security keys (passkeys), fingerprint sensors, or authenticator apps as a second factor for login. Also, ensure that MFA is enabled for all interactive logins to mitigate credential theft.
- **Snowflake Roles for Authorization:** Snowflake uses Role-Based Access Control (RBAC) for all objects. Assign users to roles with the principle of least privilege. This ensures that each user or service has only the minimum permissions needed to perform its tasks, reducing security risks.
- **Separate Duties with Roles:** Design roles around job functions – for example, a `Cortex_DS` role for model developers and data scientists (permitted to run ML functions and view training data) versus a `Cortex_Admin` role for managing deployments and resources. The Snowflake's RBAC model allows role hierarchy (roles owning other roles) to simplify administration. Implement separation of duties so that no single role has unrestricted access (for example, one role publishes models, while the other approves them).
- **Regular Auditing of Accounts:** Periodically, review user access and role grants. Snowflake's `ACCOUNT_USAGE` views (for example, `GRANTS_TO_ROLES` view) can list who has which privileges. Remove or downgrade any excessive permissions (especially on sensitive data or management roles) to maintain compliance with the internal policies.
- **Programmable Access Tokens (PATs) for Service Authentication:** For programmatic access to Snowflake, especially in automated AI workflows – Programmable Access Tokens (PATs) offer a secure and scalable alternative to passwords. PATs are short-lived, random tokens that can be used by scripts, scheduled jobs, or machine learning pipelines to authenticate into Snowflake, without storing long-term credentials. They offer stronger security than static passwords by being randomly generated and having built-in / configurable expirations. They can be restricted by a network policy, authentication policy, and role, ensuring scoped and auditable access.
- **User-Based Access Control (UBAC):** UBAC is a recent significant advancement in Snowflake's security model, enabling access privileges to be granted directly

to individual users, instead of relying solely on roles. This approach enhances data protection by allowing fine-grained control over who can access the specific assets–such as Streamlit applications–especially when those assets are still in development or meant for a restricted audience. From a security perspective, UBAC reinforces identity-level accountability, and minimizes the risk of over-permissioning. Snowflake's `ACCESS_HISTORY` table complements this by recording exactly who accessed what, when, and how–providing essential activity trails and monitoring. This helps enforce traceability into actual usage, not just theoretical access.

- **Restricting Data Downloads via Snowsight UI for Enhanced Security:** By default, the Snowsight interface provides a download button that allows users to export query results as CSV files directly from the UI. This feature offers convenience for analysts and business users who need to work with data offline or in other tools. However, in sensitive environments, this capability can pose a security risk if not properly controlled. To strengthen data security and reduce the risk of unauthorized data movement, Snowflake provides the `DISABLE_UI_DOWNLOAD_BUTTON` parameter. When enabled (`ALTER ACCOUNT SET DISABLE_UI_DOWNLOAD_BUTTON = TRUE`), it disables the download option in the UI, allowing administrators to enforce tighter control over data access while still enabling users to query and analyze data within the platform. This control is especially valuable in regulated industries where data security, governance and compliance are top priorities.

By using strong authentication and carefully scoped roles, you ensure that only authorized identities can access Cortex AI features and the underlying data.

Securing Access to External Data Sources and APIs

AI projects using Snowflake Cortex often require external data integration. Therefore, secure the following connections properly:

- **External Data Sources:** When connecting Cortex to cloud storage such as S3 or Azure Blob, use Snowflake's External Stage with Storage Integration, instead of embedding credentials in the code. These integrations leverage Snowflake-managed IAM roles, eliminating the need to handle raw cloud keys, while granting minimal access permissions.
- **APIs and External Services:** Connect to the external APIs only through encrypted HTTPS channels from trusted endpoints. For sensitive operations, deploy API endpoints within your VPC, and implement PrivateLink to ensure that Snowflake can access them, without traversing the public internet, preventing man-in-the-middle attacks.

- **Credential Management:** Store authentication secrets in Snowflake's encrypted storage, or use Secrets Manager integration with Snowpark code. For external functions, utilize API integration objects to securely hold remote service authentication information, rather than hard-coding credentials in UDFs or queries.
- **Network Controls:** Implement Snowflake Network Policies to restrict outbound connections to approved hosts only. Configure DNS and firewall rules so that Snowflake can connect exclusively to whitelisted API endpoints, preventing misuse of external functions to call the arbitrary URLs.
- **Audit Requirements:** Maintain visibility by monitoring external data transfers through Query History logs. Review the data imported via features like Cortex Knowledge Extension to ensure that it comes from legitimate sources, and watch for patterns that might indicate unauthorized data movement.

Secure Model Deployment and API Management

- **In-Database Model Deployment:** Deploying Cortex models as user-defined functions (UDFs) or SQL functions integrates them into your Snowflake schema. (for example, the **`<model_name>!PREDICT`** syntax for Snowflake Document AI models). These become part of the Snowflake database schema. Ensure that only the appropriate roles have permission to execute these functions. For example, if you have a **`PREDICT_LOAN_DEFAULT`** function, you might only allow a *scoring* role to use it, and not the general analyst role. This prevents the misuse of models or overloading them with improper inputs.
- **API Access to Models:** When exposing models via Snowflake's REST API or external endpoints, implement secure token authentication for all calls. Consider deploying an API gateway to enforce rate limiting and IP filtering on the incoming requests. Never create open endpoints that bypass Snowflake's JWT or OAuth token requirements.
- **Cortex Analyst and Agents Security:** Natural language query features like Cortex Analyst must be embedded only in applications with proper authentication layers. Each request should map to a specific Snowflake role that restricts data access, ensuring that users can only retrieve information as per the allowed permissions when asking questions through AI assistants. This ensures a business user asking a question via an AI assistant cannot access data they are not allowed to see – the underlying Cortex will only return what that user's role permits. In general, it is important to determine whether any service operates using the role of its creator or the roles explicitly granted to it, as this distinction plays a key role in preventing unintended data exposure. Avoid using sensitive or compliance-regulated tables, especially those

protected by masking policies, with general-purpose AI services unless access is tightly scoped. Exercise caution with USAGE grants, as roles with access may potentially view the service's processed outputs. Regularly audit the roles used to create Cortex services, and if any have broad access to sensitive data, consider revoking their privileges or recreating the services under more restrictive roles. Misconfigurations can lead to users bypassing masking policies and accessing protected data without SELECT privileges, highlighting the importance of robust access control for secure deployments.

- **Secure Endpoints and Monitoring:** For custom model endpoints, implement TLS encryption and authentication, while monitoring for abuse patterns. Whenever possible, leverage Snowflake's native interfaces, rather than creating new microservices, reducing the attack surface by utilizing the platform's existing security controls.
- **Model Protection:** Some models themselves are sensitive intellectual property. Protect proprietary model assets by storing them in secure stages or tables. For sensitive intellectual property, use Snowflake's secure UDFs feature to hide implementation details from the end users, allowing them to run predictions without extracting model coefficients or prompts.
- **Cortex Guardrails for AI Responses:** Implement Cortex Guard for generative AI deployments to filter unsafe or unauthorized content in model outputs. This safety mechanism prevents accidental exposure of the sensitive data or toxic content by blocking or sanitizing problematic responses from the language models.

We looked at Guardrails in the chapter on LLM Functions. Here is the illustration again for reference.

```
from snowflake.cortex import Complete

def travel_guide_query(destination):
    messages = [
        {'role': 'system', 'content': '''You are a travel guide that provides helpful
        information about destinations in a friendly and safe manner.'''},
        {'role': 'user', 'content': f'''What are the top five must-see attractions
        in {destination}? Keep the descriptions for each attarction within 15 words'''}
    ]

    assign_params = {
        'guardrails': True,  # Ensures that the responses are safe
        'temperature': 0.7,  # Adjusts the creativity of the response
        'max_tokens': 200    # Limits the length of the response
    }

    response = Complete("llama3.1-405b", messages, options=assign_params)
    return response

# Example usage
print(travel_guide_query('Las Vegas'))
```

Figure 9.2: COMPLETE LLM *with Guardrails*

The result of the above execution is as follows. The Guardrails parameter adds a safety layer to filter and control the AI-generated content.

```
Las Vegas! Here are the top five must-see attractions in this vibrant city:
1. **The Strip**: Iconic stretch of elaborate displays, fountains, and grand casinos.
2. **High Roller Observation Wheel**: Panoramic views of the city from a 550-foot tall Ferris wheel.
3. **Fountains of Bellagio**: Stunning water show with over 1,200 fountains and 4,500 lights.
4. **Red Rock Canyon**: Breathtaking natural beauty with red rock formations and scenic hiking trails.
5. **The Mirage Volcano**: Large, erupting volcano outside The Mirage hotel, a classic Vegas landmark.
Stay safe, have fun, and enjoy the excitement of Las Vegas!
```

***Figure* 9.3:** *The LLM Output*

The Cortex AI Complete function includes a guardrails parameter that acts as a protective filter for the AI-generated content. When enabled, this feature automatically screens outputs to remove potentially harmful, inappropriate, or biased content before delivery. By setting guardrails=True, organizations ensure that their AI interactions maintain ethical standards and responsible practices across user-facing applications such as customer support, content generation, and recommendation systems. This built-in safety mechanism helps maintain appropriate boundaries, without requiring separate content moderation systems, particularly valuable when deploying AI capabilities in public-facing or sensitive contexts.

By layering these controls, model deployment in Cortex AI can be done in a zero-trust fashion, minimizing avenues for both data breach and misuse of the model. All model serving should happen through authenticated channels, and within Snowflake's secure environment, whenever possible.

Example

To get a practical view, let us consider an example where ZenTime, our fictional smartwatch manufacturer, wanted to enhance their products with personalized fitness recommendations based on users' activity patterns, without compromising with data privacy. They needed a secure way to process the sensitive biometric data, while delivering real-time insights into their customers' devices.

ZenTime implements their solution by deploying a Snowflake stored procedure that calls Cortex AI functions to analyze fitness patterns. This is exposed through a Snowflake external function that their mobile app accesses via a secured API gateway. The gateway requires device-specific authentication tokens, and restricts access to the verified ZenTime devices. The function operates under a limited "**`fitness_insights`**" role that can only access the required activity data, no other personal information. All interactions are logged in Snowflake's query history, creating a complete audit trail, while delivering personalized workout recommendations directly to users' watches.

To ensure secure and compliant access to the sensitive data, ZenTime could implement

Role-Based Access Controls (RBAC) across their Snowflake environment. By assigning permissions based on specific user roles—such as data scientists, analysts, and business stakeholders—they could enforce the principle of least privilege, ensuring that users can only access the data relevant to their responsibilities. This could not only reduce the risk of data exposure, but also streamline development workflows by eliminating unnecessary access bottlenecks. Role-specific access could also help them maintain auditable access trails, and align with internal compliance policies as well as the external regulatory requirements. When a limited set of stakeholders is needed to preview an internal dashboard, User-Based Access Control (UBAC) could be leveraged, granting access to the Streamlit dashboard to this restricted audience, simplifying collaboration, while reducing unnecessary exposure. They could also strengthen access security by requiring engineers and data scientists to authenticate using passkeys or authenticator apps when accessing Cortex AI resources, adding an extra layer of protection against unauthorized access. This would ensure that only trusted personnel can run or deploy AI models, supporting both security and compliance needs.

Additionally, Zentime could consider incorporating Programmable Access Tokens (PATs) to enable secure and role-specific access for their AI workloads. By assigning unique PATs to different services—like data ingestion pipelines or model training jobs—they can enforce the least-privilege access, and automate token rotation. The administrators also disabled the Download button in Snowsight using the **`DISABLE_UI_DOWNLOAD_BUTTON`** parameter in production. This ensured that only authorized applications could access and process customer data, helping the company meet stringent data privacy regulations and prevent unauthorized exports. These practices help Zentime maintain a robust security posture, while scaling their AI operations efficiently.

Governance Best Practices

Governance in AI/ML projects ensures that data and models are managed in a transparent, compliant, and accountable manner. Snowflake Cortex AI leverages Snowflake's native governance capabilities, while adding specialized controls for AI workflows. This section explores essential governance practices for maintaining oversight of your AI pipelines.

Data Lineage and Transparency

Establishing clear data lineage is fundamental to AI governance, such as:

- **End-to-End Lineage Tracking**: Maintain comprehensive records of the data used in training and inference. Use Snowflake's **`OBJECT_DEPENDENCIES`** and Information Schema to document dependencies between objects. Whenever you create training datasets (example, via a **SELECT** into a training table), document or tag them with source references, ensuring that you can trace model input data back to raw sources which is crucial for debugging and compliance.

- **Query and Access Logging**: Leverage Snowflake's automatic query logging to create the audit trails of all model interactions.

  A few key such objects are:

  ```
  QUERY_HISTORY
  ACCESS_HISTORY
  CORTEX_FUNCTIONS_USAGE_HISTORY
  CORTEX_FUNCTIONS_QUERY_USAGE_HISTORY
  ```

  These logs provide evidence of who ran what operations, when, and on which data—essential for troubleshooting and compliance verification. For instance, if a model output is questioned, or you need to gather more details related to the LLM function that was executed, you can find the exact query which produced it, and thereby see which data and parameters were used. It is also a good practice to run Cortex functions on data stored in tables, instead of free flow text within the Cortex LLM functions, for better tracking.

  Now, let us look at a couple of these views of relevance to Cortex.

CORTEX_FUNCTIONS_USAGE_HISTORY

The **SNOWFLAKE.ACCOUNT_USAGE.CORTEX_FUNCTIONS_USAGE_HISTORY** view provides a comprehensive tracking of all Cortex AI function executions across your Snowflake account. It captures detailed metrics on function calls, including user information, execution timestamps, resource consumption, and token usage for Cortex AI operations such as language model completions, document processing, and classification tasks.

Organizations leverage this view to implement robust governance frameworks by establishing usage patterns, attributing costs to specific teams or projects, and ensuring compliance with the internal policies. Security teams can identify unusual access patterns, while finance departments can analyze credit consumption trends to optimize budgeting through request batching or parameter adjustments.

```
SELECT * FROM SNOWFLAKE.ACCOUNT_USAGE.CORTEX_FUNCTIONS_USAGE_
HISTORY;
```

START_TIME	END_TIME	FUNCTION_NAME	MODEL_NAME	TOKEN_CRED
2025-03-26 00:00:00.000 -0700	2025-03-26 01:00:00.000 -07	SUMMARIZE		0.000130800
2025-03-26 00:00:00.000 -0700	2025-03-26 01:00:00.000 -07	COMPLETE	llama3.1-8b	0.000091200
2025-03-26 00:00:00.000 -0700	2025-03-26 01:00:00.000 -07	EMBED_TEXT	snowflake-arctic-eml	0.000000800
2025-03-26 00:00:00.000 -0700	2025-03-26 01:00:00.000 -07	COMPLETE	llama3.1-405b	0.001917000
2025-03-26 00:00:00.000 -0700	2025-03-26 01:00:00.000 -07	CORTEX_GUARD		0.000525500
2025-03-26 00:00:00.000 -0700	2025-03-26 01:00:00.000 -07	COMPLETE	claude-3-5-sonnet	0.003827550
2025-03-26 00:00:00.000 -0700	2025-03-26 01:00:00.000 -07	EMBED_TEXT	snowflake-arctic-eml	0.000000480
2025-03-26 00:00:00.000 -0700	2025-03-26 01:00:00.000 -07	EXTRACT_ANSWER		0.000011440
2025-03-26 00:00:00.000 -0700	2025-03-26 01:00:00.000 -07	TRANSLATE		0.000412500
2025-03-26 00:00:00.000 -0700	2025-03-26 01:00:00.000 -07	SENTIMENT		0.000002880

Figure 9.4: *Cortex_Functions_Usage_History*

CORTEX_FUNCTIONS_QUERY_USAGE_HISTORY

This view is a part of Snowflake's **ACCOUNT_USAGE** schema, and provides granular, query-level insights into how Cortex AI functions are used across your Snowflake account.

While **CORTEX_FUNCTIONS_USAGE_HISTORY** gives you aggregated daily summaries, this view dives deeper—offering per-query level details for each invocation of a Cortex function.

This level of detail proves invaluable for organizations implementing strict governance frameworks or detailed cost allocation models, as it enables precise attribution of AI resource consumption to specific workloads, users, or business initiatives. Security and compliance teams can examine the exact nature of each AI request, while data engineers can troubleshoot performance issues by analyzing query patterns that lead to inefficiencies or errors. By incorporating this data into monitoring dashboards, organizations gain the actionable intelligence needed to optimize both the technical implementation, and financial aspects of their Cortex AI deployments.

```
SELECT * FROM SNOWFLAKE.ACCOUNT_USAGE.CORTEX_FUNCTIONS_QUERY_
USAGE_HISTORY;
```

QUERY_ID	WAREHOUSE_	MODEL_	FUNCTION_NAI	TOKENS	TOKEN_CREDI
01bb42ca-0004-caeb-0000-00066d6f3	4	mistral-7b	COMPLETE	681	0.000081720
01bb42d8-0004-ccc2-0000-00066d6f6	4		CLASSIFY_TEXT	207	0.000287730
01bb42da-0004-ccc2-0000-00066d6f6	4		EXTRACT_ANSWER	115	0.000009200
01bb42da-0004-ccc2-0000-00066d6f6	4		SENTIMENT	18	0.000001440
01bb42da-0004-ccc2-0000-00066d6f6	4		SENTIMENT	18	0.000001440
01bb42dc-0004-ccc2-0000-00066d6f6	4		SUMMARIZE	1068	0.000106800
01bb42dc-0004-ccc2-0000-00066d6f6	4		TRANSLATE	78	0.000117000
01bb42dc-0004-ccc2-0000-00066d6f6	4	mistral-7b	COMPLETE	226	0.000027120
01bb42dc-0004-ccc2-0000-00066d6f6	4		TRANSLATE	197	0.000295500
01bb42d8-0004-ccc2-0000-00066d6f6	4		CLASSIFY_TEXT	382	0.000530980

Figure 9.5: *Cortex_Functions_Query_Usage_History*

To summarize - If you are looking to analyze individual Cortex AI function calls, such as tracing with specific query used as how many tokens, incurred what cost, or failed due to an error, then **`CORTEX_FUNCTIONS_QUERY_USAGE_HISTORY`** is the ideal view. It provides granular, per-query visibility into function usage, making it suitable for debugging, cost attribution, and user-level audits. On the other hand, if your focus is on understanding the overall daily usage trends—such as how many times a function was used per role or user, or how many total tokens were consumed per day—then **`CORTEX_FUNCTIONS_USAGE_HISTORY`** offers a summarized, high-level perspective. Both views complement each other: one delivers operational details, and the other offers aggregated insight for cost tracking and governance.

- **Transparent Workflows**: Build ML pipelines using Snowflake Tasks and Streams to make processes inspectable. By centralizing operations within Snowflake (using SQL and Python stored procedures), you reduce the shadow processes, and improve visibility for governance tools.
- **Lineage in AI Functions:** Note that some Cortex features like Cortex Search indexes or vector stores are Snowflake objects that inherently contain references to the source data. For example, a Cortex Search service might be built over a table or view - Snowflake knows that, and you can list the base table. Similarly, if using PREDICT on Document AI, the model training dataset is within Snowflake. Document these linkages so that if a model's output is wrong, you can identify if the source data was stale or altered. Diligent lineage capture fosters stakeholder trust by demonstrating that AI systems use appropriate data in responsible ways.

Model Lifecycle Management

Governing the model lifecycle requires structured approaches to versioning and change control:

- **Model Versioning**: Implement systematic versioning through naming conventions (for example, `churn_model_v2`) or path structures (`@ml_stage/models/churn/2.0/model.pkl`). Maintain a model registry table with comprehensive metadata, including version numbers, descriptions, training datasets, and performance metrics. This is particularly relevant in the Snowpark ML context.
- **Approval Workflows**: Treat model deployments such as code releases with formal approval processes. Enforce role separation (for example, only `CORTEX_ADMIN` can promote models to production), and consider integrating with CI/CD pipelines for automated testing and deployment.
- **Testing and Validation:** As part of approval, have a validation step in Snowflake. For example, compare the new model's predictions vs the old model on a recent sample of data stored in Snowflake. This can be done via a stored procedure that runs both models, and stores results for comparison. By doing this in Snowflake, you leverage the same data and environment as production, increasing fidelity. Only promote the model, if it meets performance or bias criteria in this test.
- **Deployment and Rollback Strategies**: Design deployments with easy rollback capabilities. Consider shadow deployments where new models run alongside the existing ones with limited traffic until proven stable. Document clear rollback procedures to quickly address issues, utilizing Snowflake's Time Travel capabilities, when needed.
- **Access Control on Models:** Combine versioning with RBAC, that is, only allow the production inference role to use the production model version. If someone tries to use a not-yet-approved model function, they should not have privileges. As noted earlier, the model-level RBAC features can enforce this by controlling which roles can execute a given model or function.
- **Monitoring Model Performance:** Compare the current inference metrics against the original training data to identify shifts. In this context, we will look at AI observability in detail towards the end of this chapter.
- **Storing Predictions and Setting Thresholds**: Store predictions and outcomes to periodically calculate accuracy metrics within Snowflake. Set thresholds for acceptable performance, and then create alerts for deviations.

Thus, by instituting such best practices, you create an environment where models can be updated confidently and securely.

Metadata Management

Comprehensive metadata management supports both governance and operational efficiency:

- **Data Cataloguing**: Utilize Snowflake's Horizon Catalog or third-party tools to maintain descriptions, ownership information, and classification tags for all data assets and AI components. This helps to answer, "*What does this model do? What data was it trained on?*" quickly. Cortex AI powers the Horizon Data Catalog to automate discovery and tagging. It can scan and classify data assets which could include identifying which tables feed into the ML pipelines. Utilize these features to reduce the manual documentation effort.
- **Model Metadata**: Record detailed information for each model version, including the training data, hyperparameters, authors, and applicable usage domains–either in a dedicated model registry table or attached directly to model objects, when supported.
- **Business Glossary**: Maintain standardized definitions of features and metrics to ensure consistent interpretation across departments and use cases – a glossary of key features and metrics used in your AI projects (for example, definition of "**`attrition_rate`**" or "**`cust_risk_score`**"). This is part of governance to ensure that everyone interprets model inputs/outputs consistently. If using a catalog, link these glossary terms to Snowflake columns or model outputs. Cortex AI solutions often involve data across departments, so agreed definitions are critical.
- **Classification and Tagging**: Apply tags to identify the sensitive data, experimental models, and production assets. Use these tags to enforce security policies, and improve discoverability. Take advantage of Snowflake's governance tools, including Data Classification (for sensitive data identification), and Object Tagging (for classification). Label all the sensitive or important objects. For example, tag datasets with "**`PII`**" or "**`Model Training Data`**." Tag models with "**`experimental`**" vs. "**`production`**." These tags can be used to enforce policies - Snowflake can prevent copying a tagged "**`PII`**" dataset to a non-compliant environment via governance rules. For instance, we could create a TAG for Personally Identifiable Information (PII) and apply that to specific columns such as Email, Phone, and so on.
- **Generate Automated Metadata Descriptions:** Snowflake provides a feature that enables the generation of descriptions for tables and columns, which plays a critical role in establishing effective data governance. Leveraging Large Language Models (LLMs) within Cortex, Snowflake can analyze the metadata of database objects to produce meaningful and context-aware descriptions. These auto-generated descriptions serve as a valuable resource

for both business users and developers by enhancing data understanding and accessibility.

Users can generate these descriptions directly in Snowsight using the "**Generate with Cortex**" option. Furthermore, the generated content can be manually edited and enriched with additional context as needed. This capability is available at both the table and column levels, offering a scalable and intelligent approach to metadata documentation.

To generate descriptions using Cortex, begin by navigating to the desired object–either a table or a view–for which you want to create metadata descriptions. Once located, open the **Table Details** or **View Details** in a new tab. Click **Generate with Cortex** to initiate the automated description process. After the description is generated, you can review and make any necessary edits to ensure accuracy and clarity. Finally, click **Save** to store the description.

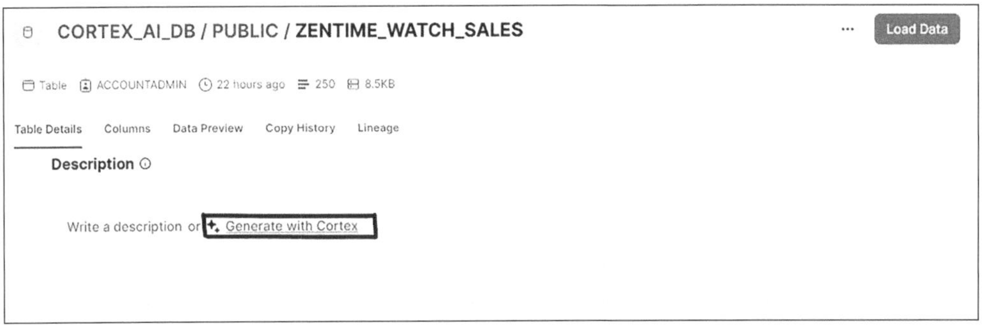

Figure 9.6: *Generate Description with Cortex*

The table description generated by Cortex is provided as follows:

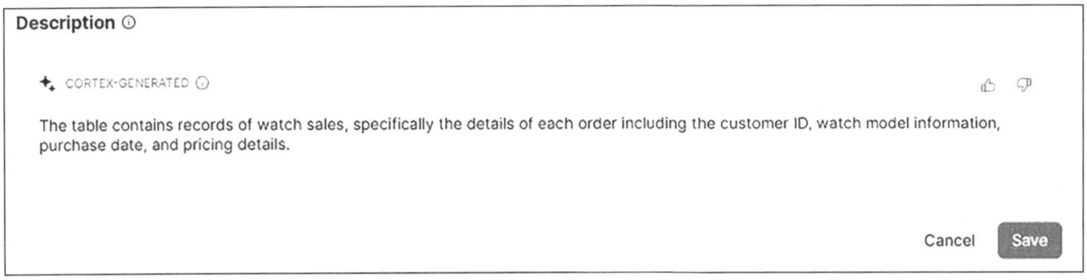

Figure 9.7: *Cortex Generated Description*

A similar method can be used to generate and manage descriptions at the individual column level as well. To do this, navigate to the **Columns** tab, located next to the **Table Details** tab. Here, you can then either generate descriptions individually using the **Generate with Cortex** option next to each column, or generate them for all columns at once by selecting the Generate Descriptions option at the top (next to the Search option). In both cases, within the pop-up that appears, you have the option to **`Generate column descriptions using sample values`**, which enhances accuracy by leveraging the context of actual values in the columns. Then click **`Generate`**. It is important to then review the generated descriptions in the subsequent step, and edit, if required as well as save. Once saved, these descriptions become available in the Comments column, when you run a **`Describe`** command on the table (Example: **`DESCRIBE TABLE CORTEX_AI_DB.PUBLIC.ZENTIME_WATCH_SALES;`**), providing valuable information for both business users and developers. (Try adding column level descriptions, and describe the table to view them).

Generating automated table and column descriptions with Cortex helps streamline data cataloguing by quickly creating clear, consistent metadata, making it easier for users to discover, understand, and trust the data, without manual effort. It enhances data governance, and boosts searchability across the catalog.

- **Monitoring Metadata Changes:** Just as we monitor data, monitor metadata changes. Regularly export your metadata (tags, descriptions, and so on), and keep a versioned copy. This way, you can detect any accidental or malicious changes to the catalog (for example, an object losing its sensitive classification tag).

By treating metadata with the same care as the data itself, you create a transparent environment where AI assets are properly documented, easily discovered, and effectively governed throughout their lifecycle.

Let us look at an implementation example of how ZenTime, our fictional smart watch manufacturer, could leverage these governance principles discussed above.

Example

In continuation of our illustrative example, let us consider how ZenTime, our hypothetical smart watch manufacturer, implemented a comprehensive governance framework for their sleep analysis AI feature. They established end-to-end lineage tracking by creating a dedicated registry table documenting all data sources, transformations, and model versions used in their sleep score algorithm. Each model version carries metadata, including training datasets, performance metrics, and approval signatures from both the data science lead and medical advisor.

Their governance process requires any new sleep model version to undergo a structured approval workflow, such as: First validation on historical data, then a staged rollout starting with employee devices before wider release. This is enforced through Snowflake role separation where only the **`ZENTIME_AI_ADMIN`** role can promote models to production. They maintain a rollback capability through a model router function that can instantly revert to the previous stable version, if anomalies are detected.

To enhance their metadata management, ZenTime implemented Snowflake's object tagging system extensively throughout their AI pipeline. They created standardized tags such as "**SLEEP_DATA**", "**HEALTH_METRICS**", and "**BIOMETRIC_INPUT**" to classify the data assets, while model objects carry tags indicating their status ("**EXPERIMENTAL**", "**VALIDATION**", "**PRODUCTION**") and sensitivity level. These tags are then integrated with access controls so that only authorized roles can interact with the production models or sensitive biometric data. ZenTime's data governance team created automated processes that scan for untagged objects in their AI pipeline, and enforce tagging standards. This comprehensive tagging strategy allows them to quickly identify all components involved in their sleep analysis feature, simplify impact analysis when making changes, and demonstrate to auditors that sensitive health data is properly classified and protected throughout the AI workflow.

In addition to these strategies, ZenTime could also leverage Cortex-generated descriptions at both the table and column levels to enhance data governance and improve the metadata clarity. By using the "**Generate with Cortex**" feature in Snowsight, they could auto-document their health insights datasets and models, enabling faster onboarding for new developers and analysts. This will also help the Zentime to automate metadata creation, making data cataloguing faster, more accurate, and improving overall data discovery and usability. Additionally, this metadata enrichment could significantly accelerate their ability to understand data structures and relationships, helping them to create better-structured YAML files for use with Cortex Analyst. This will also assist in streamlining prompt construction, and improving the accuracy and relevance of AI-driven insights.

Effective governance of Snowflake Cortex AI implementations requires a strategic combination of technical controls, organizational processes, and continuous monitoring. By establishing comprehensive data lineage tracking, implementing structured model lifecycle management, and maintaining robust metadata practices, organizations can build trustworthy AI systems that deliver value, while minimizing risks. Snowflake's native governance capabilities provide a solid foundation for Cortex AI governance, offering detailed audit logs, fine-grained access controls, and rich metadata tools. As AI capabilities continue to evolve, organizations should regularly review and update their governance frameworks to address the emerging risks, incorporate new Snowflake features, and align with evolving regulatory requirements. With this disciplined approach, Cortex AI can become a trusted, transparent, and compliant cornerstone of your data strategy.

Cost Optimization Strategies

Running AI/ML workloads can be resource-intensive, so cost optimization is essential to ensure that your Snowflake Cortex AI projects are economically sustainable. Snowflake's usage-based model (credits for compute, storage, and specialized services) offers many levers to control costs. In this section, we cover strategies for efficient resource allocation, managing compute across environments, tracking usage, optimizing model retraining and inference, and leveraging Snowflake features such as auto-suspend and scheduling to minimize waste.

Efficient Resource Allocation and Warehouse Sizing

Choosing the right size and type of compute resources (virtual warehouses) for your AI tasks has a major impact on cost:

- **Warehouse Sizing Best Practices:** Start with the smallest warehouse that can handle your workload, and scale up only if needed. Using different warehouses for different workloads is the best practice. For example, a small or medium warehouse for lightweight scoring queries, and a larger warehouse for heavy feature engineering or training queries. If you are unsure, begin with a smaller size and monitor performance, scaling up gradually, until SLAs are met.
- **Use Multi-Cluster for Concurrency, Not Oversizing:** If your use case involves sporadic bursts of many simultaneous queries (for example, many users calling a prediction at once), consider a multi-cluster warehouse, instead of a single huge warehouse. A multi-cluster warehouse can automatically start additional clusters to handle the concurrent load, and shut them down when idle. This can be more cost-efficient than running one giant warehouse at full size all the time. For example, 2 clusters of Medium may serve concurrent users better than one X-Large, and when concurrency is low, you might only have 1 cluster running.
- **Token-Based Services:** Snowflake Cortex includes certain AI functions that are billed by usage (tokens or documents). For instance, Cortex LLM functions use a token-based pricing model – you pay based on characters processed. Similarly, Document AI uses Snowflake-managed compute that scales per use. In those cases, optimize by trimming the input size (for example, do not feed extremely long text if not needed, use the `COUNT_TOKENS` helper to check the length).
- **Avoid Warehouse Over-Provisioning:** It is common to overestimate and use a larger warehouse "`just in case`," but that often leads to underutilization and wasted credits. Monitor your warehouse load via the `LOAD_HISTORY` or query history. If you see that the average queue wait times are near zero, and CPU utilization is low, you likely can step down a size. Also, prefer scaling out (multi-cluster) for concurrency, instead of scaling up beyond what is needed for single-query performance. Many ML tasks are more data-parallel, benefiting from multiple clusters for parallel queries, rather than one big node.
- **Auto-Suspend Warehouses:** Always enable auto-suspend on warehouses, with a short timeout for `dev/test` and moderate for prod. Auto-suspend means a warehouse will shut down after X seconds of inactivity, saving you from paying, when no queries are running.

(In this context, Snowflake recently introduced its **Generation 2 Warehouse**, designed to deliver significantly enhanced performance and scalability. With faster query execution, intelligent workload management, and improved concurrency handling, Gen 2 Warehouses are optimized for demanding analytics and AI workloads. This could be particularly beneficial when running complex operations such as model inference, data transformation, or real-time analytics. For more details refer to https://docs.snowflake.com/en/user-guide/warehouses-gen2).

To summarize, tie your warehouse sizing to actual workload needs, and continually re-evaluate. It is better to start small and adjust upward than to start large, and waste credits. Snowflake's elastic compute makes it easy to resize on the fly (even automatically via multi-cluster), so take advantage of that flexibility to optimize the cost.

Managing Compute Usage Across Development, Testing, and Production

Different environments (**`dev`**, **`test`**, **`prod`**) have different usage patterns, and isolating them can both control cost and improve governance.

- **Separate Warehouses per Environment:** Do not run development experiments on the production warehouse. Give each environment its own warehouse (or set of warehouses), possibly in separate Snowflake resource monitors (to cap their usage). For example, allocate a small warehouse for development where data scientists can test queries freely. This prevents expensive dev queries from accidentally impacting production workloads or incurring huge costs. Similarly, a dedicated ETL warehouse, ML training warehouse, and inference warehouse can compartmentalize costs, and allow more granular budgeting.
- **Use Roles to Control Environment Access:** Combine RBAC and warehouses to enforce environment separation. A role **`dev_data_scientist`** might only have **`USAGE`** on the dev warehouse and on a dev schema, whereas **`prod_data_scientist`** can use the prod inference warehouse. By limiting who can even use the production compute, you avoid scenarios such as someone running a massive training job on the prod warehouse over prod data by mistake.
- **Promotion of Code:** A good practice is that the same individual does not manually run things in production; instead, they promote code or models from dev to prod. In Snowflake, this could mean your ML pipelines are encapsulated in stored procedures or tasks. Developers test those in dev (on smaller data or cloned data), and when ready, an automated process (with appropriate prod role) deploys them to production. This way, interactive use of prod is minimized – production jobs run in a controlled, repeatable way. This also reduces unexpected ad-hoc resource usage in prod.
- **Align Warehouse Sizes with Environment Needs:** Development and testing

typically need smaller warehouses (since they deal with samples or shorter runs), and they can tolerate a bit more latency. Production might need larger or multi-cluster warehouses for performance. Also, production workloads might justify a higher-cost edition of Snowflake (for security), whereas dev can be on a lower tier if in a separate account. Some organizations even use separate Snowflake accounts for dev/test vs. prod to hard-enforce isolation, but that can add complexity in syncing the data. Alternatively, use separate *databases* for dev and prod in one account, with strict role separation and cost monitoring per warehouse.

- **Scheduling Windows:** Manage when certain tasks run. For example, heavy model training or batch scoring should ideally happen during off-peak hours for cost efficiency. Use Snowflake Tasks with cron schedules to run nightly or weekend jobs. This not only organizes work, but also ensures that, say, the expensive training job is not accidentally run multiple times a day.
- **Cost Chargeback and Monitoring per Environment:** To incentivize responsible usage, track cost per environment. Snowflake's **`WAREHOUSE_METERING_HISTORY`** or usage views can show credits by warehouse. Tag warehouses or use naming conventions (for example, "**`DEV_`**" vs "**`PROD_`**") to easily aggregate. If you show the dev team how much their playground cost this month, they may be more mindful next time and clean up unused tables, and so on. Some companies set notional budgets - for example, dev has X credits per month - and use a resource monitor to enforce it (by suspending or alerting when the budget nears exhaustion).

In essence, isolate and tailor resources for each stage of the life cycle. This prevents the uncontrolled usage in dev from impacting the reliability and cost of prod, and vice versa. It also allows more accurate cost attribution–you know exactly how much you spend on experimentation versus production inference which helps in ROI analysis of your AI projects.

Tracking Resource Consumption and Cost Observability

Visibility into where and how credits are consumed is vital for optimization. Snowflake provides a rich set of usage data that you should exploit:

- **Snowflake Account Usage Data:** Snowflake's built-in views (in the **`SNOWFLAKE.ACCOUNT_USAGE`** schema) give detailed information on credit consumption. The key ones include:
  - **`QUERY_HISTORY`:** Each query with columns for **`EXECUTION_TIME`**, **`CREDITS_USED`**, and so on.
  - **`WAREHOUSE_METERING_HISTORY`:** Credits used by each warehouse per hour

  - **`DATABASE_STORAGE_USAGE_HISTORY`:** Your storage usage over time.
  - **`FUNCTION_USAGE`:** Usage of objects such as UDFs or external functions which can attribute cost of serverless tasks. Using these, you can build a Cost Dashboard that breaks down credits by workload, by user, by project, and so on. For example, track how many credits were spent on Cortex LLM functions this week (these might appear as function usage entries or as part of warehouse usage depending on implementation).
- **Snowflake Cost Management Interface:** Snowflake has been introducing easier cost management UIs. Ensure that your team monitors those for anomalies. The interface provides particularly useful cost insights.

***Figure 9.8**: Cost Management*

- **Resource Monitors**: Snowflake's Resource Monitors not only enforce quotas, but also provide a way to track consumption relative to a limit.

  For example, if you set a monthly 1000 credit limit on the **`ML Training`** warehouses, the resource monitor can alert at 80% or suspend at 100%. Use these as guardrails to catch runaway costs (like if someone accidentally triggers an hourly retraining that was meant to be daily, the monitor will cap the impact).

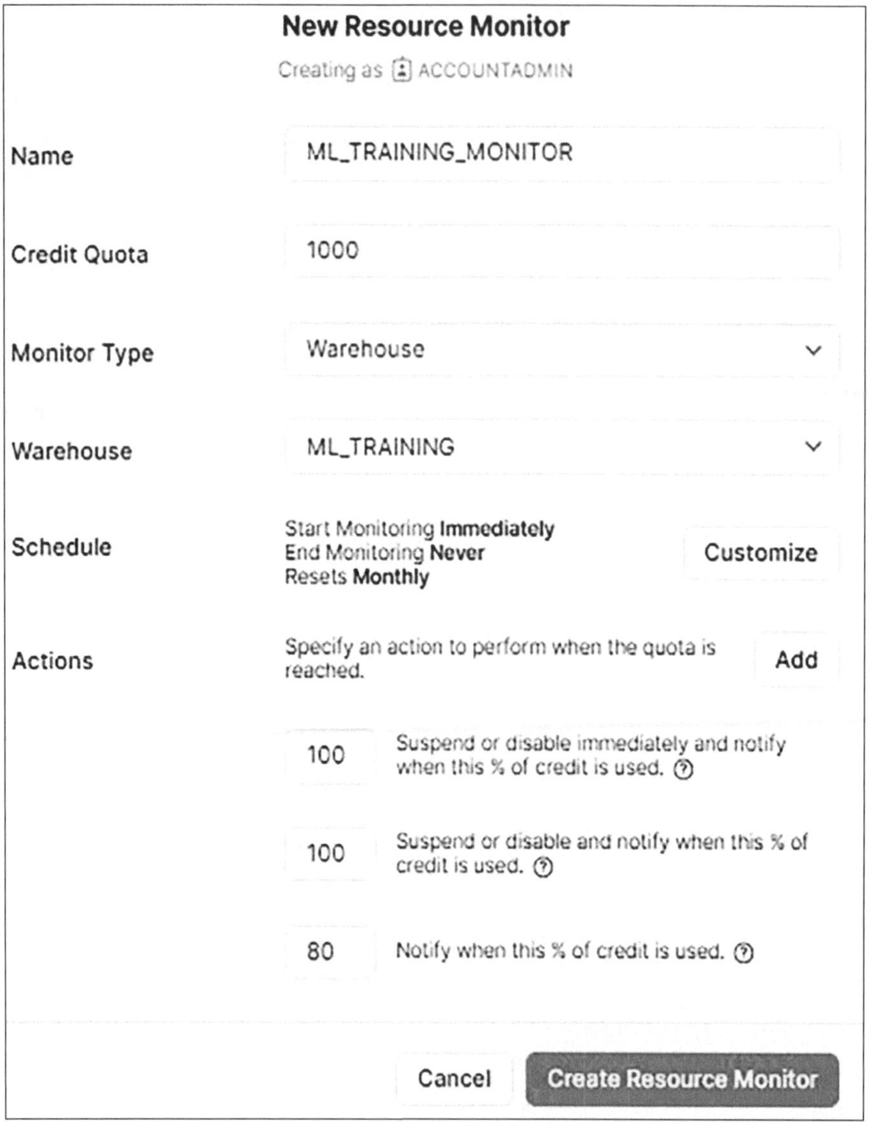

Figure 9.9: *Resource Monitor*

- **Detailed Query Profiling:** For expensive operations, dive into the Query Profile (available in UI or via SQL). Perhaps, a certain feature engineering query is scanning a huge dataset due to not using pruning. Understanding the cost drivers at the query level (for example, large data scans, repeated calls to an external function) helps optimize code which directly translates to cost savings. The Query History option (**`Monitoring`** > **`Query History`**) provides this profiling functionality. Further drill-down on the chosen query to look at specifics.

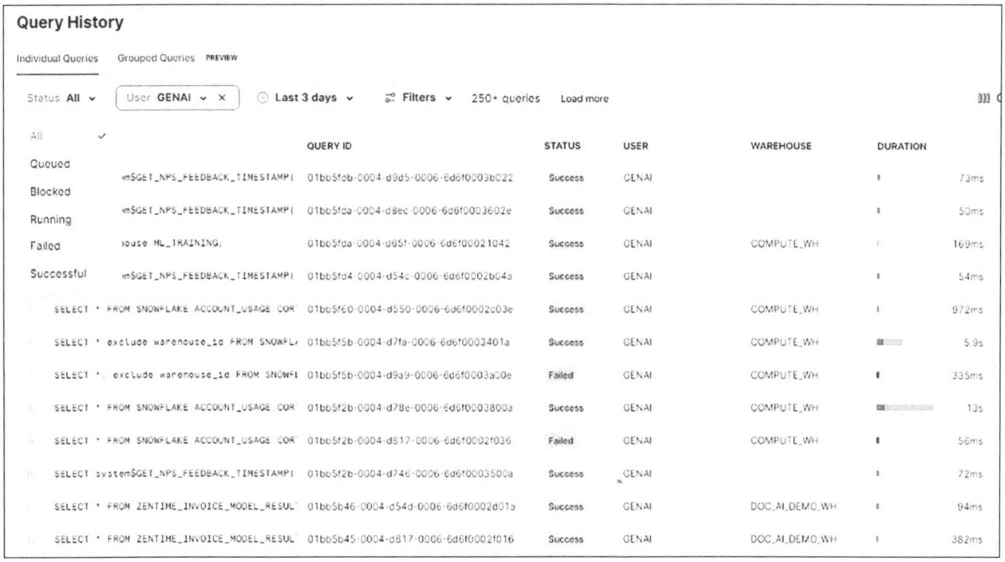

Query History

Individual Queries | Grouped Queries PREVIEW

Status All ⌄ | User GENAI ⌄ × | Last 3 days ⌄ | Filters ⌄ | 250+ queries | Load more

All ✓ / Queued / Blocked / Running / Failed / Successful

	QUERY ID	STATUS	USER	WAREHOUSE	DURATION
m$GET_NPS_FEEDBACK_TIMESTAMP(	01bb5fdb-0004-d9d5-0006-6d6f0003b022	Success	GENAI		73ms
m$GET_NPS_FEEDBACK_TIMESTAMP(	01bb5fda-0004-d8ec-0006-6d6f0003602e	Success	GENAI		50ms
iouse ML_TRAINING;	01bb5fda-0004-d65f-0006-6d6f00021042	Success	GENAI	COMPUTE_WH	169ms
m$GET_NPS_FEEDBACK_TIMESTAMP(	01bb5fd4-0004-d54c-0006-6d6f0002b04a	Success	GENAI		54ms
SELECT * FROM SNOWFLAKE.ACCOUNT_USAGE.COR	01bb5f60-0004-d550-0006-6d6f0002c03e	Success	GENAI	COMPUTE_WH	972ms
SELECT * exclude warehouse_id FROM SNOWFL	01bb5f5b-0004-d7fa-0006-6d6f0003401a	Success	GENAI	COMPUTE_WH	5.9s
SELECT *, exclude warehouse_id FROM SNOWFL	01bb5f5b-0004-d9a9-0006-6d6f0003a00e	Failed	GENAI	COMPUTE_WH	335ms
SELECT * FROM SNOWFLAKE.ACCOUNT_USAGE.COR	01bb5f2b-0004-d78e-0006-6d6f0003800a	Success	GENAI	COMPUTE_WH	13s
SELECT * FROM SNOWFLAKE.ACCOUNT_USAGE.COR	01bb5f2b-0004-d817-0006-6d6f0002f036	Failed	GENAI	COMPUTE_WH	56ms
SELECT system$GET_NPS_FEEDBACK_TIMESTAMP(	01bb5f2b-0004-d746-0006-6d6f0003500a	Success	GENAI		72ms
SELECT * FROM ZENTIME_INVOICE_MODEL_RESUL	01bb5b46-0004-d54d-0006-6d6f0002d01a	Success	GENAI	DOC_AI_DEMO_WH	94ms
SELECT * FROM ZENTIME_INVOICE_MODEL_RESUL	01bb5b45-0004-d817-0006-6d6f0002f016	Success	GENAI	DOC_AI_DEMO_WH	382ms

Figure 9.10: *Query History*

- **Effectively Leverage the Metering views:** Snowflake provides two key metering views to track Cortex AI usage: **`METERING_DAILY_HISTORY`** offers a daily summary of credit consumption by service type, while **`METERING_HISTORY`** delivers a more granular, time-based breakdown–typically hourly–for deeper analysis. Both are essential for monitoring, optimizing, and attributing AI-related spend over time.

  `SNOWFLAKE.ACCOUNT_USAGE.METERING_DAILY_HISTORY:`

  This view provides a daily breakdown of credit usage across various Snowflake services, and when filtered for **`SERVICE_TYPE = 'AI_SERVICES'`**, it specifically highlights credit consumption related to Snowflake's AI capabilities–such as Cortex LLM functions, Document AI, and other machine learning features. By querying this view with the AI service filter, you can track how many credits are being consumed each day by AI-related workloads, making it a valuable tool for monitoring the cost impact of generative AI, model inference, summarization, and other intelligent services within Snowflake.

```
SELECT *
FROM  SNOWFLAKE.ACCOUNT_USAGE.METERING_DAILY_HISTORY
WHERE SERVICE_TYPE ='AI_SERVICES';
```

SERVICE_TY	USAGE_DA	CREDITS_USED_COMPU	CREDITS_USED_CLOUD_SERVIC	CREDITS_USI	CREDITS_ADJUSTMENT_CLOUD_SERVIC
AI_SERVICES	2025-03-26	0.016389160	0.000000000	0.016389160	0.0000000000
AI_SERVICES	2025-03-28	0.068343334	0.000000000	0.068343334	0.0000000000

Figure 9.11: *Metering Daily History*

  `SNOWFLAKE.ACCOUNT_USAGE.METERING_HISTORY:`

This view provides a detailed, time-based record of credit usage across Snowflake services, offering more granularity than the **METERING_DAILY_HISTORY** view.

Instead of summarizing usage by day, this view breaks down consumption into smaller time windows—often hourly or by session—allowing you to closely analyze when and where credits are being used. It offers a fine-grained breakdown of Cortex AI-related credit consumption over brief time intervals—typically hourly. This allows teams to go beyond daily summaries and zoom in on when specific AI services were actively consuming resources, helping to trace cost spikes, monitor workloads, and fine-tune usage.

When **SERVICE_TYPE = 'AI_SERVICES'**, the entries in this view reflect credit usage for operations involving Cortex LLM functions, Document AI, search indexes, and other generative or predictive AI features built into Snowflake. By analyzing **START_TIME, END_TIME**, and **CREDITS_USED**, you can determine exactly which hours or time windows incurred the highest AI-related compute costs. This is especially useful in environments with automated agents, natural language interfaces, or high-volume LLM use—where usage may fluctuate throughout the day.

For example, if you notice an unexpected spike in AI costs on a given day, querying **METERING_HISTORY** with a filter for **SERVICE_TYPE = 'AI_SERVICES'** will allow you to pinpoint the exact time, and correlate that usage with known workloads, user activity, or scheduled tasks.

This query below provides an hourly breakdown of Cortex AI credit usage, showing when the most credits were consumed by AI services such as LLM functions or Document AI. It helps identify peak usage periods for **AI_SERVICES** by grouping credit consumption by hour and ordering from highest to lowest usage.

```
SELECT
    START_TIME::TIMESTAMP AS EXECUTION_START_TIME,
    SUM(CREDITS_USED) CONSUMED_CREDITS,
    SERVICE_TYPE
FROM
    SNOWFLAKE.ACCOUNT_USAGE.METERING_HISTORY
WHERE SERVICE_TYPE='AI_SERVICES'
GROUP BY
    EXECUTION_START_TIME, SERVICE_TYPE
ORDER BY
    CONSUMED_CREDITS DESC;
```

STARTING_HOUR	TOTAL_CREDITS_CONSUMED	SERVICE_TYPE
2025-03-28 01:00:00.000	0.068343334	AI_SERVICES
2025-03-26 00:00:00.000	0.016389160	AI_SERVICES

Figure 9.12: *Metering History*

In short, this view gives you real-time, time-series level observability for Cortex AI services–ideal for detailed cost attribution, performance tuning, and identifying optimization opportunities in Snowflake's AI-driven workloads.

- **Iterate and Optimize:** If you notice the dev warehouse sits idle most of the time but occasionally spikes, and does not auto-suspend quick enough, shorten its auto-suspend or ask developers to start/stop as needed. If a particular nightly job always uses 30% of a Medium warehouse for 2 hours, perhaps run it on a Small warehouse for 3 hours instead (cheaper if it still finishes within any time requirements). Continuous tuning is part of the cost governance discipline.
- **Detect Cost Anomalies:** Snowflake's cost anomaly detection feature (in preview) leverages historical usage data to automatically identify days when consumption significantly deviates from expected patterns. It distinguishes between account-level and organization-level anomalies, providing tools to investigate root causes, such as pinpointing specific accounts, warehouses, or queries responsible for unexpected cost fluctuations. It allows you to programmatically identify and investigate anomalies at various levels – Organization, Account, Warehouse, and Query. For further information, refer to: https://docs.snowflake.com/en/user-guide/cost-anomalies. By proactively alerting users to these anomalies, you could enable timely interventions to address inefficiencies and optimize spending. It can be accessed both programmatically as well as through Snowsight. Integrating this feature helps investigate root causes, take corrective action, reducing unexpected costs and improving overall spend efficiency as part of a broader cost-optimization strategy.

Transparency in resource consumption is empowering – when teams see where the credits go, they often find creative ways to reduce waste. Snowflake's pay-as-you-go nature rewards efficiency, so investing time in monitoring usually pays for itself.

Model Cost Optimization

ML-specific cost considerations include how often to retrain models (which can be expensive) and how to serve inferences efficiently:

- **Function Optimization:** Use optimized functions and avoid unnecessary calls. Snowflake Cortex provides specialized functions such as **`TRY_COMPLETE`** to handle errors cheaply, for example, using **`TRY_COMPLETE`** instead of **`COMPLETE`** can save re-running queries that error out, by catching exceptions and returning **`NULL`**. Also, use the smallest suitable Cortex model function (for instance, if **`SUMMARIZE`** by default uses a comparatively big model but you only need a quick summary, consider if a smaller model or truncating input yields acceptable results). As the Cortex model catalog includes large, medium, small models, choose the smallest model that best meets your requirements to save both tokens and compute time.

- **Caching and Reuse:** Cache results of expensive model inference when possible. If the same input is scored repeatedly, store the result in a lookup table. For example, if you classify customer feedback text, store the classification in a table so you do not re-run the LLM on the same comment next time. Snowflake's result set caching might help for identical queries, but explicit caching in tables gives you more control (especially if queries vary but input repeats) and you could include the logic to run incrementally.
- **Optimize Data Access in Pipelines:** Ensure your model pipelines are not scanning more data than needed. If you have a very wide table but the model needs only 5 columns, create a slim view or table for model use to reduce I/O. Less data processed means less cost.
- **Review Inference Rates:** Sometimes, models are called more often than necessary. For example, an upstream system might be calling for a prediction every minute for the same entity where hourly would suffice. By aligning inference frequency with business needs, you can cut down calls (and thus cost). This is more of an application architecture point but important – do not waste Snowflake compute on unused predictions.
- **Cost-Aware Model Selection:** During model development, consider cost as a factor. A more complex model might give slightly higher accuracy but could be much more expensive to run (especially true with deep learning vs simpler models). If that accuracy gain is marginal, a simpler model could drastically cut inference costs (faster queries, less resource usage). With Cortex AI offering everything from small models to giant LLMs, you have options. Perhaps use a smaller generative model for most queries and only fall back to a large model for particularly challenging cases – a two-tier approach that optimizes cost.

By instituting policies on how often to retrain and being mindful of inference patterns, you ensure that you are not doing "extra work" that users do not benefit from. Every CPU cycle or token processed should ideally produce value. Policies and reviews (like quarterly examining if you retrain schedule or model choice is still appropriate) will keep costs aligned with business value.

Let us look at an implementation example for the cost optimization principles discussed above.

Example

As an example, let us suggest, as an illustrative case study, how ZenTime could implement a comprehensive cost optimization strategy for their Cortex AI-powered health insights feature. They could begin by right-sizing their warehouses across environments–using X-Small warehouses for development work where data scientists test new algorithms on sample datasets, Medium warehouses for their nightly batch scoring processes, and a Multi-Cluster Small warehouse for handling real-time inference during peak usage hours.

To control development costs, ZenTime could create separate warehouses for each environment with appropriate auto-suspend settings (2 minutes for development, 5 minutes for production) and implement resource monitors that alert at 80% of the monthly budget allocation. They could establish a robust cost attribution system by tagging all AI-related warehouses and tracking usage through custom dashboards built on Snowflake's **`METERING_HISTORY`** and **`CORTEX_FUNCTIONS_USAGE_HISTORY`** views. Zentime could schedule routine tasks that leverage Snowflake's **`ANOMALY_INSIGHTS`** class to monitor and track usage anomalies across accounts, warehouses, queries, and hourly consumption, ensuring timely detection and resolution of unexpected cost spikes.

For their sleep analysis model, ZenTime could optimize token usage by implementing a tiered approach–using a lightweight model for standard sleep pattern analysis while only invoking the more expensive, comprehensive model when anomalous patterns are detected. They could also develop a caching mechanism that stores recent inference results for frequently accessed data, reducing redundant processing. By scheduling their intensive model retraining jobs to run during weekend off-hours and implementing drift-based retraining (only retraining when performance metrics indicate actual drift), they could reduce their model maintenance costs while maintaining the same quality of insights. A dedicated view was created with only the columns needed for the model, ensuring data processing remains efficient, focused, and cost-effective.

By strategically combining resource right-sizing, LLM cost optimization, metadata governance, and secure access practices, ZenTime could effectively scale their AI initiatives while maintaining transparency, operational discipline, and strong alignment with business goals.

AI Observability in Snowflake Cortex

Snowflake recently introduced AI Observability as a preview feature within its Cortex platform, marking a significant advancement in how organizations can monitor, evaluate, and optimize their AI applications. AI Observability is designed to integrate seamlessly with the broader Snowflake ecosystem, leveraging the platform's existing data governance, security, and scalability features. This comprehensive capability enables data teams to gain unprecedented visibility into AI model behavior, performance, and data quality across the entire lifecycle.

AI observability is the practice of monitoring and understanding AI model behavior, performance, and outcomes in detail – it "shines a light into the black box" of AI models to improve their reliability, security, and transparency. In the context of Snowflake Cortex AI, observability tools help data scientists and architects ensure that generative AI applications (like those built with Snowflake's Cortex LLM functions, Agents, and Search) produce relevant, correct, and trustworthy outputs before and after deployment. This high-level overview covers the core observability concepts (such as answer relevance, context relevance, correctness and groundedness), all within the Snowflake ecosystem.

Observability: Core Concepts

In retrieval-augmented generation (RAG) applications – a common design for enterprise AI apps – Snowflake Cortex AI emphasizes a "RAG *triad*" of quality metrics: context relevance, groundedness, answer relevance, correctness and coherence. These metrics provide localized evaluations of each stage of a RAG pipeline so developers can pinpoint the root cause of poor performance (for example, whether an issue stems from bad retrieval or from the generative model's response). An LLM-as-judge technique is used, where an AI model evaluates the quality of responses based on the query and context. This allows systematic evaluation even when ground-truth answers are unavailable.

Each of the triad components addresses a different aspect of answer quality in Snowflake Cortex AI:

- **Context Relevance:** Measures whether the retrieved context (for example, documents or data fetched by Cortex Search) is relevant to the user's query. Low context relevance indicates a retrieval problem – the system is not fetching the right data to answer the question. An LLM-based evaluator compares the user query with the retrieved context to score how well they match
- **Groundedness:** Measures whether the AI's answer is *grounded in the provided context*, i.e., fully supported by the retrieved data. This addresses the risk of hallucination. A response with high groundedness should contain only information that can be found or verified in the supplied context. The implementation even uses chain-of-thought reasoning in the LLM judge to assess groundedness
- **Answer Relevance:** Measures if the AI's response actually answers the user's query and stays on topic. Importantly, this is judged without requiring a known correct answer – it is about relevance, not exact correctness. A high answer relevance score means the model's response addresses the question asked (even if it might not be factually perfect), whereas a low score might indicate the answer is off-base or incomplete in relation to the query.

- **Correctness:** Correctness refers to whether the AI's output is factually accurate – regardless of whether it appears plausible. In Snowflake Cortex AI observability, this goes a step beyond groundedness. While groundedness checks whether an answer can be verified from the retrieved context, correctness considers whether the answer is objectively right, even if that specific fact was not in the context. This becomes particularly relevant in use cases where models might need to draw from general knowledge or when human evaluation is used to establish ground-truth answers. In practice, Snowflake users can test correctness by comparing AI-generated responses with known correct answers (when available) or by using LLM-as-a-judge mechanisms to score factual accuracy across different runs.

  For example, if a RAG application is answering questions about corporate policy documents, correctness would measure whether the AI response accurately reflects the policy – even if the exact sentence it is based on is not quoted word-for-word from the document.

- **Coherence:** Coherence assesses how logically consistent and well-structured the response is. In other words, does the answer flow naturally, follow a clear train of thought, and avoid contradictions? Even if a response is correct and grounded, it might still be hard to understand or confusing. That is where coherence comes in. Snowflake Cortex AI observability frameworks (especially when using TruLens or Cortex's evaluation tools) can leverage LLM-based coherence scoring to evaluate whether the answer is easy to read, logically arranged, and complete. Coherence is especially important in customer-facing applications, documentation summarization, or anything where human readability matters.

Snowflake Cortex AI Observability helps ensure that generative AI outputs are not only accurate but also contextually appropriate and traceable to source data. For example, a low context relevance score can flag issues in the data retrieval step (perhaps, the wrong documents are being fetched), while a low groundedness score highlights that the model's answer contains information not supported by the retrieved data. These insights let developers quickly zero in on whether to adjust the retrieval (for example, refine Cortex Search queries or indexes) or the generation (for example, choose a different LLM or prompt) to improve overall answer quality. In summary, metrics like answer relevance, context relevance, and groundedness form the core of AI observability in Cortex AI by quantifying answer quality and trustworthiness. They directly contribute to making AI applications more transparent and reliable, since each answer can be judged on how well it used available data and satisfied the user's question.

Beyond evaluating answer quality, AI observability in Snowflake Cortex encompasses ongoing metrics tracking and monitoring practices to maintain model performance in production. Snowflake's observability framework allows developers to log detailed traces of each AI application run – capturing every step from the input prompt and retrieval queries to the LLM's final response. By tracing each step (using standards such as OpenTelemetry for instrumentation, integrated via the TruLens SDK), teams can debug issues at a granular level. For instance, if an answer is incorrect or slow, the trace can reveal whether the bottleneck was in the retrieval call, the model inference, or elsewhere. This level of visibility accelerates root-cause analysis and helps maintain optimal performance and accuracy.

Let us look at an example. For demonstration purposes, we will use two simple synthesized PDF documents related to the Airline domain. One related to passenger experience and another on ticketing policies. We will build a cortex search service and then implement AI observability on top of it to examine key metrics.

The stage **`airline_stg`** needs to be created first and the PDFs uploaded. (Create Objects and Load **`Data.sql`**). The queries and the respective ground truth responses are loaded to the table **`CORTEX_AI_DB.OBSERVABILITY_SCHEMA.airline_queries_answers`** from the csv file. The notebook **`Airline-ai-observability.ipynb`** demonstrates how to implement AI observability for an airline search service using Snowflake Cortex and TruLens. The notebook begins by listing and verifying the airline-related PDF documents that were uploaded to the Snowflake stage. It then parses the documents using Cortex's **`PARSE_DOCUMENT LLM`** function and then chunking the text into smaller segments for efficient retrieval. The **`SPLIT_TEXT_RECURSIVE_CHARACTER`** function divides text into smaller segments through a recursive process, optimizing content for text embedding or search indexing applications. It produces an array of text chunks derived from the original content based on specified parameters. This function is particularly useful when preparing text data for natural language processing tasks that require standardized text chunk sizes. The code then creates a search service using these chunks with vector embeddings from the Snowflake Arctic embedding model. This is followed by a class CortexSearchRetriever that connects to a Snowflake Cortex Search Service and retrieves search results based on a query. The search results are retrieved as a list of chunks.

The core focus is on building a Retrieval-Augmented Generation (RAG) system with integrated instrumentation for monitoring and evaluation. Using TruLens-OpenTelemetry for tracing, the code configures each component of the RAG pipeline (retrieval, generation, and the overall query process) with specific span types and attributes. This enables comprehensive observability of the system's performance. The **`airline_queries_answers`** table loaded earlier, is basically a set of test queries to evaluate the RAG system. The answers available in this table are compared with the LLM's responses to gauge performance by computing various metrics that we discussed earlier.

Cortex leverages OpenTelemetry to enable observability by capturing Spans, which represent discrete units of work within the system. These spans can include details about the retriever, Large Language Model (LLM) invocations, key metadata, token usage, cost metrics, and more. All this information is structured and stored using the observability schema, which holds both spans and metrics for analysis.

A Python class named RAG is used to orchestrate the retrieval and generation logic. This class is initialized with a retriever and provides three core methods:

1. **`retrieve_context`** – Uses the retriever to gather relevant context.
2. **`generate_completion`** – Calls the LLM using the COMPLETE function to generate a response based on the context and question.
3. **`query`** – Combines the above methods to handle end-to-end request processing.

Each of these methods is decorated with an instrument decorator. This decorator enriches the methods with observability metadata, including SpanType and SpanAttributes. The SpanType identifies the nature of the operation (for example, retrieval or generation), while SpanAttributes describe the inputs and outputs of the method. These spans help define the data points for evaluation—for instance, a context relevance metric would evaluate attributes from the retrieval span.

The complete function from Snowflake Cortex is called with a query and a defined prompt template. This template, which can be customized, instructs the LLM to act as an airline assistant and respond based on the provided context. The function sends this prompt, along with any necessary arguments, to the LLM. The query method then orchestrates the full flow by invoking the retrieval and generation methods sequentially. This serves as the entry point to the RAG workflow and is the method typically called by the end user.

Following this, the application is registered using TrueApp, which allows for tracking experiments and storing metadata such as the application's name and version. We integrate this using a Truelens connector. Tracing data and evaluation results are stored in a dedicated database and schema configured specifically for observability.

To run evaluations, we instantiate TrueApp with the desired application name and version. We then execute batch experiments—called runs—against a consistent dataset. This batch evaluation enables us to compare model performance over time and measure any improvements. Once the run is initiated, it processes each query in the batch, after which we can view all the associated metrics, which we explained at the beginning of this section (such as context relevance, answer relevance, groundedness and so on,) that were captured during the process.

These evaluation metrics are powered by a modern approach known as "`LLM-as-a-Judge`". In this method, a large language model is given the original question, the generated answer, and a set of grading criteria. Based on these inputs, the LLM can objectively assign a score to the response, allowing for automated, scalable evaluation without manual intervention.

The notebook demonstrates how to register the application, configure experiment runs using test queries, and compute various evaluation metrics such as coherence, relevance, and correctness. Once these evaluations are complete, we can navigate to the AI/ML Evaluation section and open the corresponding experiment run we created earlier. There, we will find detailed performance results for each query, providing insights into the RAG system's effectiveness and areas for improvement. By diving into lower-scoring outputs, we can identify specific areas where the application underperforms. For instance, if a query has a low context relevance score, it likely means the retriever failed to locate sufficient or appropriate information for the LLM to answer accurately. This often occurs when the underlying knowledge base is outdated or lacks the required content. In such scenarios, improving the performance might simply involve updating the RAG pipeline with more current or enriched documents, ensuring the retriever has access to fresher and more relevant data. This feedback loop between evaluation and iteration is central to refining and maintaining high-performing AI applications.

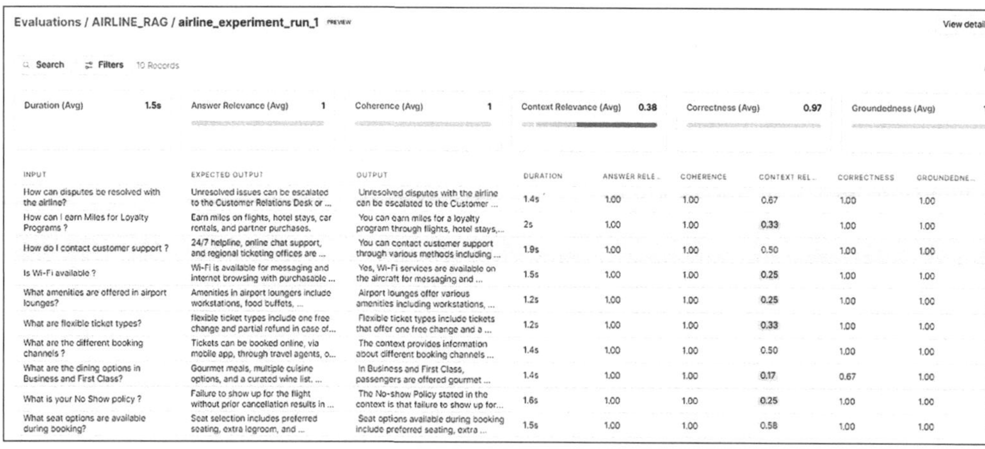

Figure 9.13: *AI Observability Evaluation*

Subsequently, you could choose to modify prompts as needed and tailor them for better response quality. The interface also provides functionality to compare different models, allowing you to analyze which one excelled in specific metrics and use these insights to guide further customization efforts.

Additionally, to automate the handling of newly added documents, you could consider implementing streams and tasks that automatically process and chunk incoming data. These can be scheduled to run at defined intervals, ensuring new content is ingested and prepared consistently without manual intervention.

In the Zentime scenario, they could monitor how effectively an AI model summarizes smartwatch sensor data or answers user queries, identify potential errors or hallucinations, and ensure outputs remain accurate and aligned with expectations before deploying to production.

In summary, AI observability in Snowflake Cortex AI is a vital component for building dependable, enterprise-grade AI applications on the Snowflake Data Cloud. By monitoring answer relevance, context relevance, groundedness, and other key metrics, organizations can ensure their AI remains relevant, accurate, and grounded in truth. Robust evaluation and tracing practices help catch issues early - whether it is a hallucinated answer or a slow response - and enable continuous improvement of AI models.

Conclusion

Secure all points of entry, govern all data, and model processes, and then optimize the costs. Security measures ensure that your AI assets and sensitive data remain protected from threats, while robust governance frameworks provide transparency, accountability, and compliance throughout the AI lifecycle. Cost optimization strategies enable you to maximize the value of your Cortex AI investment by eliminating waste, and aligning resource consumption with business priorities.

As demonstrated through our ZenTime examples, organizations can successfully balance these considerations by implementing role-based access controls, establishing clear model development and deployment processes, maintaining comprehensive audit trails, and continuously monitoring resource utilization. The most successful implementations treat these areas not as separate concerns, but as interconnected aspects of a unified approach to AI operations.

Snowflake's platform provides the technical foundations through built-in security features, extensive auditing capabilities, and flexible consumption models. By establishing appropriate controls, processes, and monitoring from the outset, you can create a Cortex AI environment that is secure, well-governed, and cost-effective–allowing you to focus on extracting valuable insights and building transformative AI capabilities for your business. By investing in observability today and in the future, data scientists and architects can confidently deploy AI models in production within Snowflake, knowing they have the tools to monitor, troubleshoot, and trust those models, every step of the way.

As Cortex AI continues to evolve with new features and capabilities, so also should your approach to managing these critical aspects of your implementation. The organizations that maintain this balance will be best positioned to capture the tremendous opportunities that Snowflake Cortex AI offers, while effectively managing the associated responsibilities.

In the next chapter, we will dive into real-world, industry-specific use cases of Cortex across sectors–from healthcare to finance, unlocking powerful AI-driven outcomes tailored to each domain.

CHAPTER 10
Industry Use Cases and Case Studies

Introduction

Generative AI is no longer a futuristic trend–it is a present-day enabler of business transformation across industries. From summarizing documents, and analyzing sentiment to generating code, answering questions, and interpreting structured data, Large Language Models (LLMs) are driving new levels of productivity and insight. Platforms such as Snowflake Cortex bring these capabilities natively into the data cloud, making them governed, secure, and instantly scalable across enterprise use cases.

Throughout this book, we have explored the foundational features of Snowflake Cortex AI, as well as their application in practical workflows, such as data enrichment, classification, sentiment prediction, summarization, document processing, and natural language querying, and so on. These examples highlighted how generative AI can be applied directly inside Snowflake to enhance business agility, and reduce operational overhead.

In this chapter, we will now shift our focus to a broader view–examining use cases across multiple industries, and observe how Cortex AI delivers measurable value. We will also walk through real-world examples and implementations leveraging generative AI in industry-specific contexts. Importantly, these demonstrations will utilize synthesized datasets with limited volumes, as our primary intent is to highlight Cortex's powerful capabilities and practical implementation. While Snowflake's industry-leading platform excels at seamlessly processing petabytes of data with unparalleled performance and scalability, the emphasis here is on demonstrating the functional capabilities and business value of Cortex AI solutions, rather than processing capacity.

The potential of Cortex AI is truly immense, and what is presented here only scratches the surface of possibilities across these industries. These examples offer a glimpse of what is achievable, providing conceptual understanding that organizations can expand upon, and adapt to their specific challenges. As Cortex AI continues to evolve, anticipate even more sophisticated applications emerging across these sectors and beyond, transforming how businesses leverage their data for competitive advantage. As the use cases in this chapter unfold, take the opportunity to experiment with the other models supported by Snowflake Cortex, that align with the respective scenarios and capabilities. Modifying prompts, incorporating custom datasets, and exploring different model types can help deepen understanding and build practical proficiency in applying AI to real-world problems.

Structure

In this chapter, we will cover the following topics:

- Process to Upload the Data to Tables and Stages
- Realty Sector: AI-Driven Review Analysis for Realtors
- Healthcare: AI-Powered Hospital Search Assistant Bot Using Cortex Search
- IT Security: From Prompt to Python: LLM-Driven Code Generation
- Insurance: Deriving Sentiment from Customer Reviews
- Finance: AI-Assisted Customer Risk Assessment
- Information Technology: Summarization and Insight Generation from Tables
- Telecom: Customer Attrition Prediction and Reasoning
- Education: Student Performance Analysis
- Retail Sales: QA Bot for a Home Appliance's Retailer using Cortex Analyst
- Customer Service: Predicting Call Center Employee Churn
- Food and Hospitality: AI-powered Menu Intelligence
- Consumer Electronics: Aspect-Based Sentiment Decoding of Customer Emails
- Airlines: Translating and Summarizing Multilingual Call Transcripts
- Media and Publishing: Enhancing Content Promotions
- Cortex AI for Social Media Analytics
- From Data to Decisions: Visualizing Cortex AI with Streamlit
- Manufacturing Case Study: AI-Powered Quality Control
- Snowflake Cortex: Expanding the Frontiers of Data and AI

Process to Upload Data to Tables and Stages

Most of the use cases would involve loading files to either a table or to a staging area. The following are the steps for reference:

Procedure to Load the Table from the File

1. Sign in to Snowsight.
2. Download the provided `csv` file from the folder.
3. In Snowsight, from the menu on the left, **`Select Data`** > **`Add Data`**.
4. Choose **`Load data into a Table`**.
5. Browse and choose the **`.csv`** file.
6. Choose **`CORTEX_AI_DB.PUBLIC`**, as the schema (or any other schema, as specified in the use case), and then choose **`create a new table`**
7. Provide the name of the new table to be the same as the file name. Click **`Next`**.
8. In the left menu, expand **`view options`** under the File Format.
9. Ensure that the Header option is set to **`First Line contains Header`**.
10. Click **`Load`**.

Procedure to Upload the Files to the Stage

1. Sign in to Snowsight.
2. Select Data from the left-side navigation menu.
3. Select your database, **`CORTEX_AI_DB`** (or as specified in the use case).
4. Select your schema - "**`PUBLIC`**".
5. Select Stages, and then select the appropriate stage (**`CORTEX_AI_STG`**, or as specified in the use case).
6. From the top right, Select the **`+ Files`** button.
7. Drag and drop the file(s) into the UI or browse to choose file(s).
8. Select upload to upload your file(s).

Realty Sector: AI-Driven Review Analysis for Realtors

In the real estate industry, customer and prospect reviews offer valuable insights into agent performance, service quality, and overall experience of buying or renting a property. However, manually sifting through, and interpreting thousands of textual reviews is time-consuming and subjective. To address this, a real estate company can leverage Snowflake Cortex's LLM capabilities to automatically summarize and categorize reviews, using structured and reproducible AI logic.

The core of this use case is built around a table, named `` `Realtor_Customer_Reviews` `` which stores customer feedback. Using Snowflake Cortex and Streamlit, reviews are processed using two specialized prompt templates. The first prompt ('**prompt_category**') instructs the LLM to assign a review to a strictly controlled list of categories, such as Agent Support, Services, Property Related, Process Related or Pricing. Each review is limited to exactly one category to ensure clarity in analysis and reporting.

The second prompt (`` `prompt_summary` ``) is designed to produce a concise summary of each review, limited to twelve words or fewer, so that the essence of the reviews is captured. This enables business users to quickly scan the highlights of customer sentiment, without reading full-text entries.

When a user clicks '**Summarize & Categorize**' in the Streamlit app, Snowflake executes a SQL command using the `` `llama3-8b` `` model. The query reads from the `` `Realtor_Customer_Reviews` `` table, and writes the processed results to a new table, `` `Realtor_Customer_Results` ``. For demonstration purposes, this table is created on the fly, and contains two columns–`` `SUMMARY` `` and `` `REVIEW_CATEGORY` ``–that are directly usable in dashboards or reports. In a production setup, this can be an incrementally loaded table, rather than being created at the run-time.

The business relevance of this solution is substantial. Real estate professionals gain near-instant visibility into what their customers are praising or complaining about. Management teams can detect patterns by category–such as consistent issues in responsiveness or standout performance in communication–enabling faster action and better service. Moreover, by summarizing reviews and constraining them into business-friendly categories, the organization builds a foundation for sentiment analysis, trend tracking, and operational improvement over time.

This use case illustrates how Snowflake Cortex, paired with well-engineered prompts and a clean Streamlit interface, can transform unstructured text into structured insight. Hence, this is a prime example of how generative AI can bridge the gap between customer voice and business decision-making in real estate.

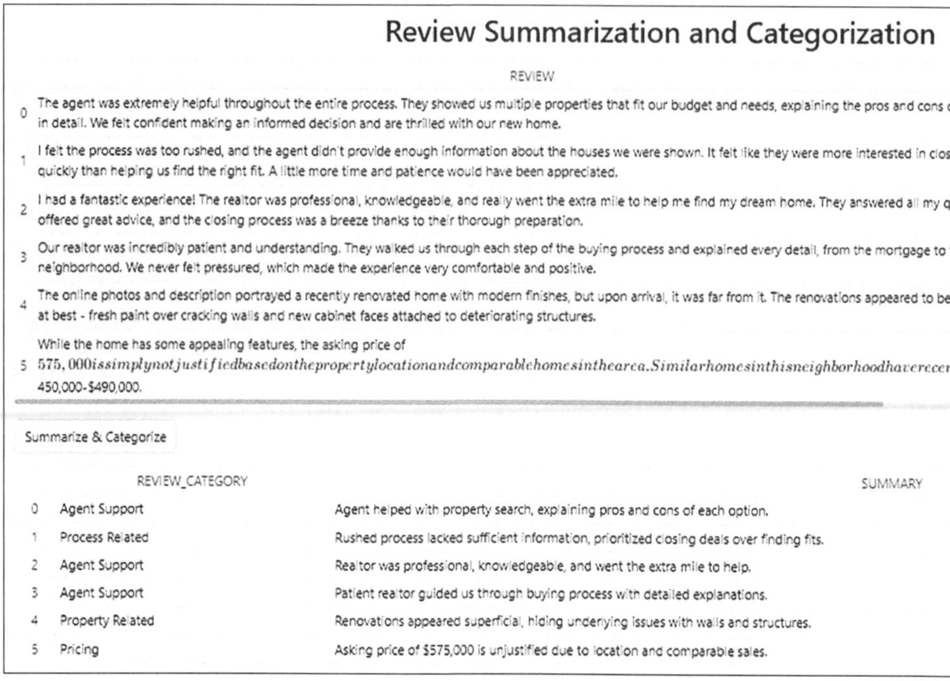

Figure 10.1: *Realtor Reviews - Summarization & Categorization*

Steps

Folder: Realty - Review Summarization and Categorization

1. Load data from **`Realtor_Customer_Reviews.csv`** to **`CORTEX_AI_DB.PUBLIC.REALTOR_CUSTOMER_REVIEWS`**.
2. Create a new Streamlit application in **`CORTEX_AI_DB`** called Realtors Review Analysis.
3. Copy the contents from Realtors Review Analysis.py, and paste it into the Streamlit application.
4. Import the packages from the Package List.txt into Streamlit, using the **`Packages`** > **`Find Packages`** box.
5. Now, run the Application.

Healthcare: AI-Powered Hospital Search Assistant Bot Using Cortex Search

Hospitals manage an enormous volume of operational documents across departments, such as billing, claims processing, and safety guidelines. These documents often contain critical, yet hard-to-navigate information related to procedures, claims, billing, and incident protocols. The proposed use case leverages Snowflake Cortex Search to build a conversational, AI-powered document question-answering system that enables hospital staff to interact with this knowledge through natural language–quickly, securely, and accurately.

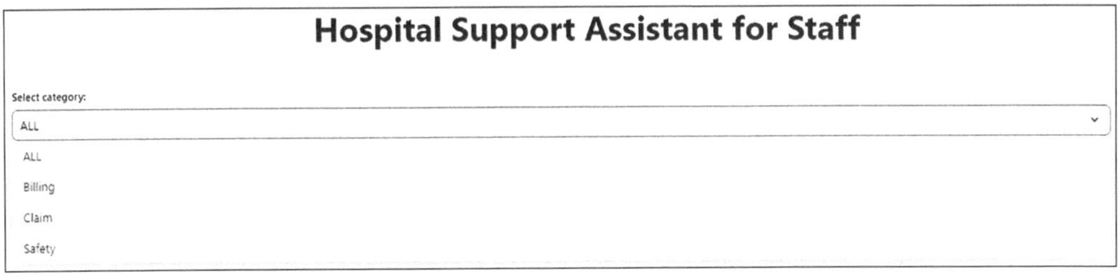

Figure 10.2: *Hospital Support Assistant - Category Selection*

The system allows the staff to choose from one of the three supported categories: Billing, Claims, or Safety. Once a category is selected, the user can enter a free-form natural language question. The application built using Streamlit, filters document chunks by category using Cortex Search's native filter capability. These documents, which have been previously uploaded to Snowflake stages, are preprocessed into semantically meaningful chunks, and stored in a structured format. When a user submits a query, Cortex Search retrieves the most relevant document segments using vector and keyword-based semantic search. These results are used as the context for Snowflake's LLM, which then generates a grounded, context-aware response.

This process mirrors the architecture and methodology described in *Chapter 7, Natural Language Queries to Actionable Insights*, where we provided a detailed walkthrough and explored how hybrid search capabilities–combining semantic vector similarity with structured filters–enable enterprise-ready document intelligence. As in that chapter, this implementation benefits from Cortex Search's ability to isolate high-relevance text fragments quickly and securely, directly within the Snowflake platform. The indexed chunks, category-based filtering, and prompt engineering strategies discussed in *Chapter* 7 are fully applied here, ensuring consistency and reliability in implementation. The cortex search service called **`HEALTHCARE_SEARCH_SERVICE`** is created in **`CORTEX_AI_DB.HOSP_SEARCH`**.

At the heart of this system is a carefully engineered prompt that ensures the model answers only using content explicitly present in the retrieved chunks. This avoids hallucination, and promotes factual accuracy. Snowflake's **`Complete()`** function is used to call the LLM directly within the Snowflake environment, maintaining data governance and security throughout the workflow. The response is concise and traceable, and optionally, the application may display links to or references from the original documents used in generating the answer – supporting audit and verification.

The benefits of this system are significant: Hospital teams save valuable time, otherwise spent manually reviewing complex documentation or waiting on subject matter experts to respond to queries. The staff can also make decisions faster and with greater confidence, improving both operational efficiency and compliance. In the long term, this also supports knowledge retention across the organization, and reduces administrative overhead.

Here is a screenshot of a question for the Billing Category.

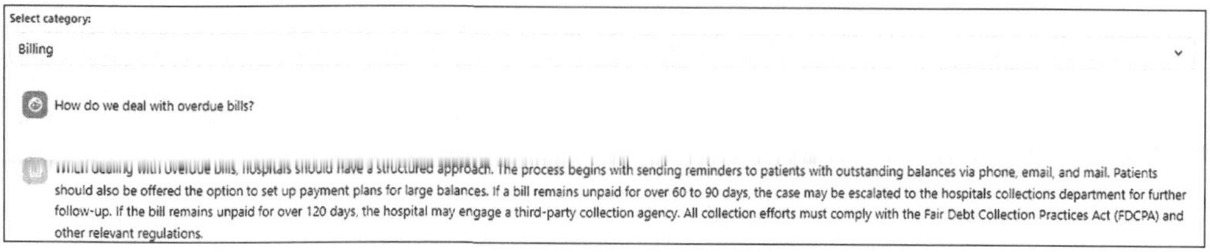

Figure 10.3: *Billing Category Question*

This solution can be expanded further to include more categories and additional documents, within the categories as well. By applying Cortex AI in this way, hospitals can unlock meaningful insights from their existing documentation, and empower their teams with real-time, accurate information, using nothing more than a well-phrased question.

Steps

Folder Name: Hospital Search Assistant Bot

1. From the Script folder, run the **`Create_Schema_and_Stage.sql`** to create the **`HOSP_SEARCH`** schema and "**`docs`**" stage.
2. After executing the previous step, load the three documents from the Documents folder – Billing, Claims and Safety to the "**`docs`**" stage.
3. From the Script folder, run each individual step in the **`Create_HealthCare_Search_Service.sql`**.
4. Create a new Streamlit application called "**`Hospital Document Search Assistant`**" in **`CORTEX_AI_DB`** and schema **`HOSP_SEARCH`** (Remember to choose the schema as well).
5. Import the packages from the Package List.txt into Streamlit, using the **`Packages`** > **`Find Packages`** box.
6. Copy the contents from the Hospital Document Search **`Assistant.py`** into this Streamlit application.

7. Run the **`Application`** > **`Select Category`** >**`Ask to ask a question`** pertaining to the respective document.

IT Security: From Prompt to Python: LLM-Driven Code Generation

The ability to translate natural language instructions into working code represents a major leap in productivity. This use case highlights how Snowflake Cortex's LLM capabilities can be leveraged to convert the user intent–expressed in plain English–into executable Python logic for a real-world application: detecting suspicious login behavior.

Security and operations teams often define rules, such as 'flag users with more than 3 failed login attempts in a day' to catch anomalies or prevent unauthorized access. These rules are typically handed over to engineers to implement as part of data pipelines or alerting systems. This back-and-forth can delay the response time, create silos, and introduce room for misinterpretation. With Snowflake Cortex, this process can be automated using`**LLM_COMPLETE ()**` to generate the Python code directly from these rule descriptions.

In this scenario, the failed login data is stored in a Snowflake table named `**user_logins**`, while a configurable threshold is stored in a separate `**login_threshold_config**` table. A prompt is constructed and passed to an LLM (we leverage snowflake-arctic which is especially suited for SQL and code generation), requesting it to generate a code that identifies users exceeding the threshold. The results are written to a table that is created, if it does not exist. The resulting Python logic can be reviewed, customized, or deployed as part of a Snowpark or Streamlit-based workflow.

```
SELECT
  SNOWFLAKE.CORTEX.COMPLETE(
    'snowflake-arctic',
    'Write Python code that reads failed login data from a Snowflake table called `user_logins`, which has columns:
user_id, date, and failed_logins. Also read a threshold value from another table called `login_threshold_config`, which
contains a single column `threshold`. Generate a query or logic that identifies users who had more than the threshold
number of failed login attempts in a single day. write to a table called suspicious_users with columns: user_id, date,
total_failed_logins, and a flag `is_suspicious` (True if failed_logins > threshold). Create this table if it is not already
there.Provide the required package installations as well'
  ) AS generated_code:
```

Figure 10.4: *Prompt for Code Generation*

The key advantage of this use case is the ability to empower business or security analysts to generate a logic, without needing to write the code themselves. By entering their intent in natural language, they enable Cortex to return optimized, readable Python that aligns with the internal data structures and policies. This not only saves the engineering time, but also accelerates the iteration and testing of rules.

Beyond login detection, this pattern can be extended to generate code for data quality checks, fraud scoring logic, operational alerts, or even ETL scripts–making it a foundational approach for intent-driven development. The entire process remains within Snowflake, preserving data governance and security, while dramatically increasing agility. This example demonstrates how Snowflake Cortex can bridge the gap between idea and implementation, turning natural language prompts into operational Python code in seconds.

Once generated, the Python code can be exported into Snowpark for scheduled execution, integrated with Streamlit for interactive analysis, wrapped in a UDF for real-time scoring, or versioned and deployed as part of a secure CI/CD pipeline. This becomes the foundation of a fully automated, explainable, and adaptable operational intelligence layer—transforming natural language into production-ready value.

Steps

Folder: IT Security - Code Generation

1. Run the SQL commands in **`code-generation.sql`**, and verify the results.
2. Tweak the prompt, or Change the model as necessary, and examine the results.

Insurance: Deriving Sentiment from Customer Reviews

In the Insurance industry, understanding customer sentiment plays a critical role in shaping product offerings, improving service delivery, and proactively addressing customer dissatisfaction. This use case demonstrates how an insurance company can leverage Snowflake Cortex to predict the sentiment directly from customer review data, and visualize the outcome using a Streamlit dashboard.

The process begins with customer feedback stored in the `INSURANCE_CUSTOMER_REVIEWS` table where each row includes a `REVIEW_TEXT` column. A Streamlit app reads these reviews and uses the `SNOWFLAKE.CORTEX.SENTIMENT()` function to generate a numerical sentiment score for each review. These scores range from -1 to 1, indicating negative to positive sentiment, respectively. The results are written to a new table named `INSURANCE_CUSTOMER_SENTIMENT` for downstream use and persistent analysis.

To convert the sentiment score into a clear label, the following logic is applied within the application:

- If the score is greater than 0.5, the sentiment is classified as **`'POSITIVE'`**.
- If the score is less than -0.5, it is labeled as **`'NEGATIVE'`**.
- All other scores are categorized as **`'NEUTRAL'`**.

(These cut-off points are not fixed – they can be adjusted based on how strict or flexible, we want the sentiment classification to be.)

This labeled sentiment data is then visualized in a bar chart, providing business users with a high-level view of the overall sentiment distribution. The chart is then embedded within the Streamlit interface, making it easy to track trends, detect spikes in negative sentiment, or measure the impact of recent policy or service changes.

The business impact of this solution is substantial. Insurance companies can quickly identify unhappy customers, monitor satisfaction trends, and assess how recent events or product changes are being perceived. This insight allows teams to take proactive measures in customer support, product refinement, and strategic communication–ultimately driving loyalty and retention. By integrating Snowflake Cortex's sentiment capabilities with a live dashboard, the company builds a real-time feedback loop that transforms the raw reviews into actionable intelligence.

REVIEW	SCORE	SENTIMENT
I have been with this insurance company for several years now, and overall, my experience has been satisfactory. However, the claim process could be smoother. The customer service team was polite, but it took too long to get my claim approved. I appreciate the comprehensive policy coverage, though.	0.351415	NEUTRAL
I recently had to file a claim after an accident, and I was pleasantly surprised by how easy the process was. The customer service team was responsive and kept me updated throughout. I'm happy with the service, and I will recommend them to my friends.	0.861728	POSITIVE
This company offers decent coverage options, but the premium rates are too high compared to other providers. I also had a poor experience with their customer service. It took several calls to get a response, which is unacceptable.	-0.430714	NEUTRAL
My policy renewal process was seamless. The representative I spoke to was very knowledgeable and explained the policy details clearly. I appreciate the transparency and professionalism of the team.	0.865433	POSITIVE

Figure 10.5: *Sentiment Prediction*

The following image visualizes the distribution of sentiments:

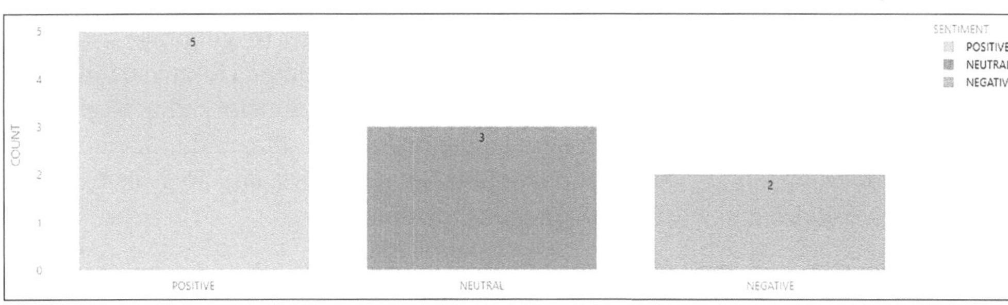

Figure 10.6: *Sentiment Distribution*

Steps

Folder Name: Insurance - Customer Sentiment Analysis

1. From the **`Dataset`** folder, Import data from **`INSURANCE_CUSTOMER_REVIEWS.csv`** to **`CORTEX_AI_DB.PUBLIC. INSURANCE_CUSTOMER_REVIEWS`**.
2. Create a new Streamlit application in **`CORTEX_AI_DB`** called Sentiment Analysis.

3. From the Script folder, copy the contents from Sentiment Analysis.py, and paste it into the Streamlit application.
4. Import the packages from the Package List.txt into Streamlit using the **`Packages`** > **`Find Packages`** box.
5. Run the Application.

Finance: Cortex AI-Powered Customer Risk Assessment

In the financial industry, accurately identifying high-risk customers is essential for informed decision-making around lending, underwriting, and risk mitigation. This case demonstrates how Snowflake Cortex can be used in a hybrid architecture–combining traditional machine learning with large language models–to classify and explain financial risk in a transparent and explainable way.

The architecture involves a two-step process: First, a Snowflake-native ML classifier is used to assign a binary '**`risk_flag`**' (either **`'High'`** or **`'Low'`**) to each customer profile. Then, for customers flagged as '**`High Risk`**', Snowflake Cortex's LLM (specifically `**llama3-70b**`) is used to generate human-readable explanations for why the customer is considered risky. This hybrid approach brings together the speed and precision of ML with the contextual reasoning of LLMs, enabling teams to make confident decisions, and communicate the rationale clearly.

For customers flagged as "**`high risk`**," we use Cortex LLM to generate a detailed, natural language explanation. The prompt includes the customer's financial indicators, and asks the model to justify why the customer might be considered a '**`high risk`**'. This explanation layer is critical for compliance, internal audits, and enhancing trust in AI-driven decisions. It also helps underwriters, loan officers, and analysts to quickly grasp the key risk drivers, without digging into raw numbers.

The reasoning step uses the **`LLM_COMPLETE`** function and a structured prompt includes all relevant financial fields such as annual income, credit score, loan amount, and so on. This further instructs the LLM to return the top 2 significant reasons for classifying the customer as 'high risk'.

Here is an example of the instruction passed to the model:

*"You are provided with a dataset containing financial risk predictions. Analyze the attributes and provide the **top 3 significant reasons** why this customer is considered a **high financial risk**. Clearly mention the column names used in your reasoning based on the list of columns below. **List of Columns:***

The business benefits of this approach is substantial, such as: Risk professionals no longer rely on opaque model outputs but gain immediate access to contextual explanations aligned with their decision-making framework. Auditors, compliance teams, and customer-facing staff, all can benefit from the clarity and interpretability offered by this hybrid solution. Readers are also encouraged to experiment with other models, such as `mistral-7b` and `snowflake-arctic`, to compare the effectiveness and tone of generated reasoning across use cases. Please note that based on the needs of the organization, this use case can be further streamlined by introducing a model registry and versioning the prediction model by leveraging the versioned model for reasoning, using LLMs. Here is a sample from the display for one of the rows.

```
The top 3 significant reasons why this customer is considered a high financial
risk are:

1. **High Debt-to-Income Ratio**: The customer's debt-to-income ratio is
63.9%, indicating that a significant portion of their income is dedicated to
debt repayment. This suggests that they may struggle to manage their debt
obligations, increasing their financial risk. (Column: DEBT_TO_INCOME_RATIO)
2. **Low Credit Score**: The customer's credit score is 527, which is
considered low. A low credit score can indicate a history of missed payments,
high credit utilization, or other credit-related issues, making it more
challenging for the customer to secure credit or loans at favorable interest
rates. (Column: CREDIT_SCORE)
3. **High Number of Late Payments**: The customer has made 6 late
payments in the last year, which can negatively impact their credit score and
increase their financial risk. This suggests that the customer may struggle to
manage their finances and make timely payments. (Column:
LATE_PAYMENTS_LAST_YEAR)
```

Figure 10.7: *Financial Risk Analysis*

Steps

Folder Name: Financial Risk Analytics

1. From the Dataset folder, import the data from **`Financial_Risk.csv`** to **`CORTEX_AI_DB.PUBLIC.FINANCIAL_RISK`**.
2. From the Scripts folder, review and execute each command in **`Financial Risk Analysis_ML_Classifier.sql`**. Then, ensure that the commands have completed successfully.
3. Create a new Streamlit application in **`CORTEX_AI_DB`** called Financial Risk Analysis.
4. Copy the contents from Financial Risk Analysis.py, and paste it into the Streamlit application.
5. Import the packages from the Package List.txt into Streamlit, using the **`Packages`** > **`Find Packages`** box.
6. Run the Application.

Information Technology: Summarization and Insight Generation from Tables

Understanding the structure and trends within a table is one of the most crucial steps in any data analysis or application development process. This use case enables this analysis to be fully automated, using Large Language Models (LLMs), turning the tabular data into richly explained narratives that highlight data distributions, trends, and anomalies.

It focuses on leveraging the `` `SNOWFLAKE.CORTEX.COMPLETE()` `` function, powered by the `` `llama3-70b` `` model, to analyze any chosen table, and generate comprehensive summaries. The database, schema and table information are then accessed from the **`INFORMATION_SCHEMA`** in Snowflake. The model is guided by a well-engineered prompt to identify the key fields, their distributions, outliers, anomalies, and other patterns. Users are encouraged to experiment with other models such as `` `mistral-7b` ``, `` `snowflake-arctic` ``, or others, available in Cortex AI to determine what works best for their domain.

The solution is delivered via a Streamlit interface that allows users to:

- Select the Database, Schema, and Table interactively.
- Preview the data in real time before analysis.
- Click **`Generate Summary`** to invoke the LLM for insight generation.

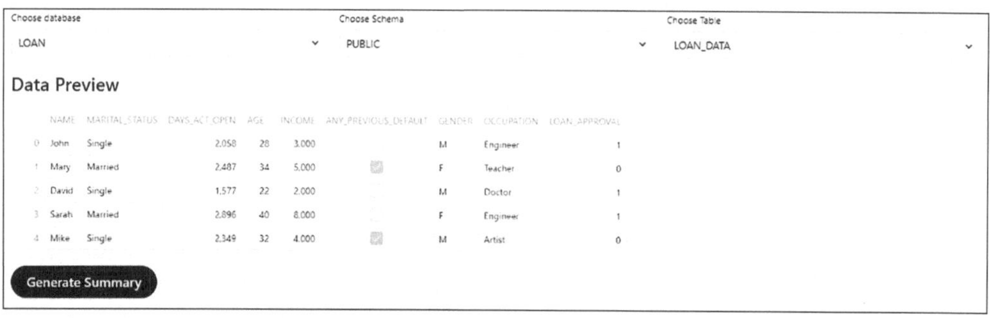

Figure 10.8: *Table Explainer Interface*

Once the user clicks '**`Generate Summary`**', the application sends the selected table's data to the **`COMPLETE`** function, along with the custom prompt. The result is a detailed narrative that includes:

- A holistic summary of the dataset.
- Highlights on key columns and their distributions.
- Identification of outliers or anomalies.
- Additional noteworthy patterns or correlations.

This solution dramatically reduces the time required to understand the complex datasets. It is particularly valuable for both developers who need to validate and explore datasets quickly, and business users who need an insight, without writing any SQL. The LLM not only generates an instant data profile, but also provides depth and reasoning that traditional dashboards or profiling tools cannot match.

Steps

Folder Name: Table Explainer

1. Create a new Streamlit application in `CORTEX_AI_DB`, and call it Table Explainer.
2. Copy the contents from the `Table Explainer.py` to this new Streamlit application.
3. Import the packages from the Package List.txt into Streamlit, using the `Packages` > `Find Packages` box.
4. Run the application, and choose a table to generate the summary.

Telecom: Customer Attrition Prediction and Reasoning

Customer attrition in the telecommunications sector represents a significant business challenge with direct consequences on revenue and market share. The cost of acquiring a new customer can be five times higher than retaining an existing one which is why minimizing the churn has become a strategic priority for telecom operators, globally. Effective churn management requires not only identifying the customers at risk, but also understanding the reasons behind their dissatisfaction. This helps to prioritize at-risk customers, personalize outreach, and reduce the overall churn, using predictive and generative AI working together.

This use case leverages a powerful hybrid AI approach, using Snowflake Cortex. We use Snowflake's native machine learning capabilities to build a classification model that predicts, whether a customer is likely to churn (`` `churn_flag` ``). The model ingests features, such as tenure, contract type, number of support calls, recent complaints, streaming usage, and service quality indicators. These predictors are well-established churn drivers in the telecom domain, and yield high predictive performance.

To complement this prediction with interpretability, we use Snowflake Cortex LLM's `` `LLM_COMPLETE ()` `` function to generate natural language explanations, leveraging the `claude-3-5-sonnet` LLM. (Feel free to explore and test with additional models as well.) For each customer flagged as high risk (`` `churn_flag = 'Yes'` ``), a structured profile is converted into a prompt that includes behavioral, usage, and service issue data.

The LLM then returns a concise explanation of why the customer might churn. This allows support and retention teams to proactively address concerns, and personalize retention offers.

The prompt starts off as follows:

*"You are provided with a dataset containing telecom customer churn predictions. Analyze the attributes and provide the **top 2 reasons** why this customer is likely to **churn**. Clearly mention the column names used in your reasoning based on the list of columns below.*

***Columns : List of Column Names**"*

This hybrid approach significantly enhances operational decision-making. While the ML model ensures accurate and scalable churn prediction, the LLM ensures that these predictions are understandable by business teams. This is particularly important in customer-facing industries where human judgment still plays a pivotal role in intervention. By building this workflow entirely within Snowflake, organizations benefit from centralized governance, data security, and seamless deployment.

The significance of this use case lies in its direct business impact. Reducing churn by even a small percentage can lead to millions in saved revenue, annually. The combination of predictive and generative AI within Snowflake empowers telecom companies to move from reactive to proactive customer management, enhancing both satisfaction and profitability. Like in the Financial Risk Analysis use case, organizations can further choose to enhance this use case by introducing a model registry, and versioning the prediction model as well as leveraging the versioned model for reasoning, using LLMs.

	CUSTOMER_ID	PRED_CLASS	SUMMARY
0	60,015	"Churn"	1. High customer dissatisfaction indicated by 5 support calls in the last 3 months (SUPPORT_CALLS_LAST_3_MONTHS) combined with 3 complaints (NUM_COMPLAINTS_LAST_6_MONTHS) and a recent billing dispute (RECENT_ISSUE_SUMMARY) 2. Month-to-month contract (CONTRACT_TYPE) with relatively high monthly charges of $91.11 (MONTHLY_CHARGES) makes it easier for the customer to switch providers without long-term commitment penalties
1	60,061	"No-Churn"	
2	60,000	"Churn"	
3	60,041	"Churn"	1. High number of service issues: The customer experienced 3 service downtimes in the last 30 days (SERVICE_DOWNTIME_LAST_30_[
4	60,074	"No-Churn"	Not likely to Churn

Figure 10.9: *Telecom Churn Analysis*

Steps

Folder Name: Telecom Churn Analytics

1. From the Dataset folder, import the data from **`Telecom_Churn.csv`** to **`CORTEX_AI_DB.PUBLIC.TELECOM_CHURN`**.
2. From the Script folder, review and execute each command in **`Telecom_Churn_Analysis_ML_Classifier.sql`** to ensure that the commands have completed successfully.

3. Create a new Streamlit application in CORTEX_AI_DB called Telecom Churn Analysis.
4. Copy the contents from Telecom Churn Analysis.py, and paste it into the Streamlit application.
5. Import the packages from the Package List.txt into Streamlit, using the **`Packages`** > **`Find Packages`** box.
6. Run the Application.

Education: Student Performance Analysis

In the education sector, personalized feedback and performance analytics are critical in improving learning outcomes. This highlights how Snowflake Cortex can be applied to automate the evaluation of student assessments, and generate rich, AI-driven insights that go beyond scores.

The system begins with a master answer key stored in the `` `MASTER_ANSWER_KEY` `` table, containing correct answers for five core subjects: Mathematics, Physics, Chemistry, Technology, and General Aptitude. Student answers are then uploaded as CSV files into a Snowflake staging area, and are loaded into a central `` `STUDENT_ANSWERS` `` table via the Streamlit application.

Thus, Streamlit Interface provides a simple and intuitive way for users to:

- Load all available answer sheets into Snowflake with a single click.
- Select a student from a dropdown.
- Calculate Marks and Generate Performance Feedback option to evaluate the student.

Once selected, the student's responses are compared with the master answer key. The application then calculates the total marks and percentage, and displays a table showing the question, correct answer, selected option, and a binary mark. The result also indicates whether the student has passed or failed based on a 40% threshold.

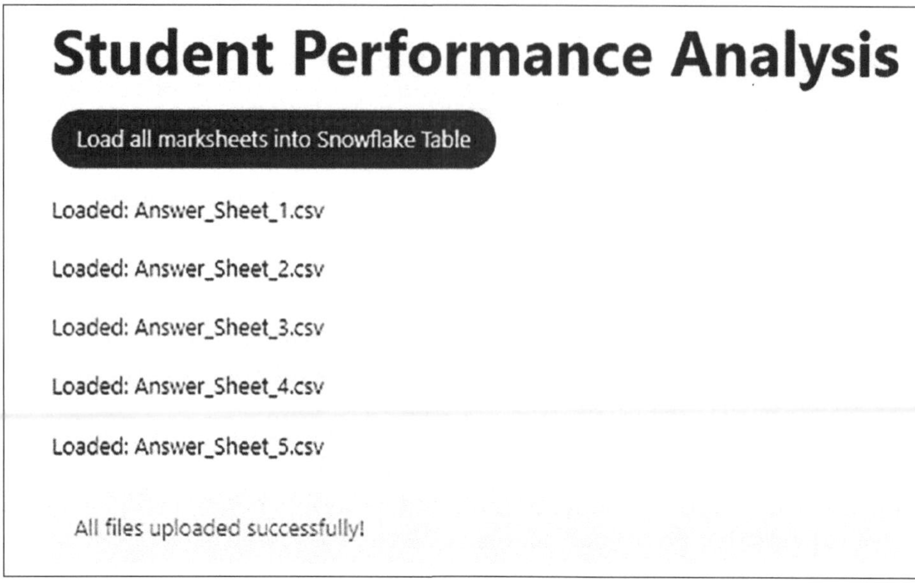

Figure 10.10: *Load Student Answer Sheets*

Once the answer sheets are loaded, the user can click **`Calculate Marks and Generate Performance Feedback`** to retrieve the results.

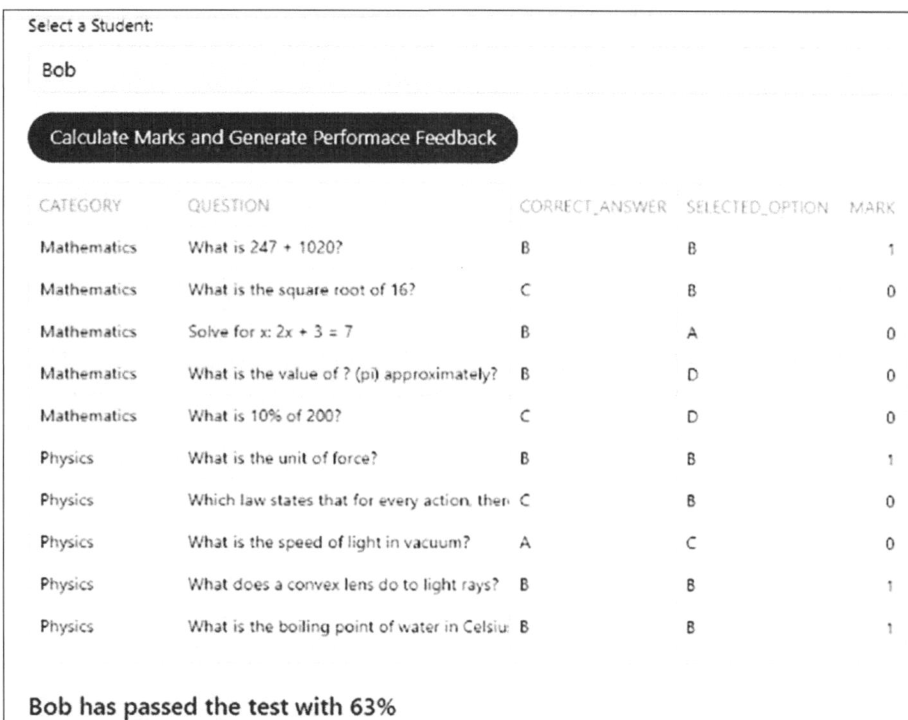

Figure 10.11: *Student Selection and Marks Display*

Bob has passed the test with 63%

Here's your AI-driven feedback report based on the quiz performance:

Strengths The student demonstrates exceptional performance in Literature, showing consistent understanding and mastery of the subject by scoring perfectly. The student also shows strong competency in General Aptitude, achieving full marks in this category.

Areas for Improvement The student shows significant challenges in Mathematics, scoring only 1 out of 5 questions correctly. Chemistry performance needs substantial improvement as the student was unable to answer any questions correctly. Physics performance is inconsistent with only 3 correct answers out of 5, indicating gaps in understanding of key concepts. While Technology shows good results, maintaining consistency across all STEM subjects would be beneficial for overall academic growth.

Personalized Study Recommendations I recommend implementing a structured study plan focusing primarily on strengthening the STEM subjects, particularly Mathematics and Chemistry. For Mathematics, start with fundamental concepts and gradually progress to complex topics, using practice problems and interactive learning tools. For Chemistry, consider using visual aids, molecular models, and laboratory experiments to better understand chemical concepts and reactions. Allocate at least 2 hours daily for these subjects, with emphasis on problem-solving and practical applications. Maintain a study journal to track progress and identify specific areas of difficulty. Consider seeking additional support through tutoring or study groups, particularly for Mathematics and Chemistry. While maintaining strong performance in Literature and General Aptitude, redirect more study time to weaker subjects. Regular self-assessment and practice tests would help monitor improvement in these areas.

Figure 10.12: *AI Generated Feedback*

`Claude-3-5-sonnet` LLM is leveraged to analyze the students' responses in-depth. The application passes the response table to Cortex, along with a prompt instructing the model to:

- Highlight the student's strengths (only if performance in a subject is above a certain threshold).
- Describe areas for improvement in a narrative format.
- Provide a personalized study plan, based on the student's actual performance.

The output is an AI-generated performance feedback report tailored to each individual. This empowers teachers, parents, and students with deeper understanding, beyond the raw scores.

The significance of this use-case lies in its ability to merge the structured data (student responses) with the contextual power of LLMs to generate meaningful educational feedback. It provides educators with a scalable tool for personalized learning recommendations, while students receive actionable insights that they can act on immediately.

This approach not only streamlines student evaluation, but also introduces a new standard in automated educational feedback–one that is data-informed, adaptive, and deeply personalized. The solution can be further refined by experimenting with different models and prompt variations to enhance its effectiveness.

Steps

Folder Name: Student Performance Analysis

1. From the Script folder, review and execute each command in Student Performance Analysis.sql to ensure that the commands have completed successfully.
2. After executing the previous step, go to the Dataset folder and import the data from **`Master_Answer_Key.csv`** to **`CORTEX_AI_DB.PUBLIC. MASTER_ANSWER_KEY`**.

3. Load all the five answer sheets from the folder "**Load Answer Sheets to STUDENT_STG**" to the staging area - **STUDENT_STG**.
4. Create a new Streamlit application in **CORTEX_AI_DB** called Student Performance Analysis.
5. Copy the contents from Student Performance Analysis.py, and paste it into the Streamlit application.
6. Search and import the packages from the Package List.txt into Streamlit, using the **Packages** > **Find Packages** box.
7. Run the Application.

Retail Sales: QA Bot for a Home Appliances Retailer using Cortex Analyst

Retail organizations generate massive amounts of transactional data from daily sales across various store locations. Store leaders and regional executives are often tasked with making quick decisions based on this sales performance data which can involve analyzing metrics, such as best-selling products, profitability trends, salesperson productivity, and promotion outcomes. This data is often stored in structured formats, but querying and analyzing it typically requires technical knowledge or dependence on central analytics teams.

The use case leverages Snowflake Cortex Analyst to build a conversational, AI-powered sales question-answering system that enables store leaders and business users to interact with the sales data using natural language–quickly, securely, and accurately.

Users are empowered to ask free-form natural language questions related to sales transactions, store performance, product bundles, and profitability. The application uses Cortex Analyst's semantic understanding and built-in tabular reasoning capabilities to interpret the question, and generate relevant SQL queries against a structured retail sales dataset. This dataset is defined by a metadata YAML file named **Retail_Sales.yaml** and saved in the Snowflake staging area **cortex_ai_stg**.

The Cortex Analyst agent then reads this YAML schema which describes fields such as **Invoice_ID**, **Product_Name**, **Store_Location**, **Quantity**, **Unit_Price**, **Promotion_Applied**, **Retail_Price_After_Discount**, **Cost_Price**, **Gross_Margin**, and **Total_Profit**. When a user submits a query, Cortex dynamically translates the request into SQL, executes it against the governed data table in Snowflake, and provides a grounded, context-aware response. This allows store managers to get instant answers to business-critical questions, without needing to understand SQL or BI tools.

This process mirrors the architecture and methodology described in *Chapter 7, Natural Language Queries to Actionable Insights*, leveraging Cortex Analyst. The use of YAML metadata, and Cortex's ability to interpret business queries ensures consistent and high-fidelity outputs. All processing happens within the Snowflake platform, maintaining enterprise-grade security and governance.

This system is especially useful for store managers, regional heads, and retail executives who need to monitor performance across multiple locations. It also enables them to identify top-performing products, evaluate the effectiveness of promotions, assess sales team contributions, and optimize delivery vs. pickup operations—all in real time.

The benefits of this approach are substantial: It significantly reduces the time spent in analyzing reports, empowers non-technical users with immediate insights, and enables proactive business decisions. It drives operational efficiency, and ensures alignment with sales targets and KPIs.

This implementation can also be expanded to include other datasets, such as inventory levels, customer feedback, or loyalty programs, further enhancing its analytical reach. Thus, by applying Cortex AI in this way, retailers can unlock valuable insights from their structured datasets, and empower decision-makers at every level of the organization—using nothing more than a natural language question.

Steps

Folder Name: Retail Sales

1. From the Dataset folder, import the data from **`Retail_Sales.csv`** to **`CORTEX_AI_DB.PUBLIC. RETAIL_SALES`**.
2. Then load the YAML file **`sales.yaml`** to **`CORTEX_AI_DB.PUBLIC.CORTEX_AI_STG`**.
3. Create a new Streamlit application in **`CORTEX_AI_DB`** called Retail Sales Assistant.
4. From the Scripts folder, copy the contents from Sales Assistant Bot.py, and paste it into the new Streamlit application.
5. Search and import the packages from the Package List.txt into Streamlit using the **`Packages`** > **`Find Packages`** box.
6. Run the Application.

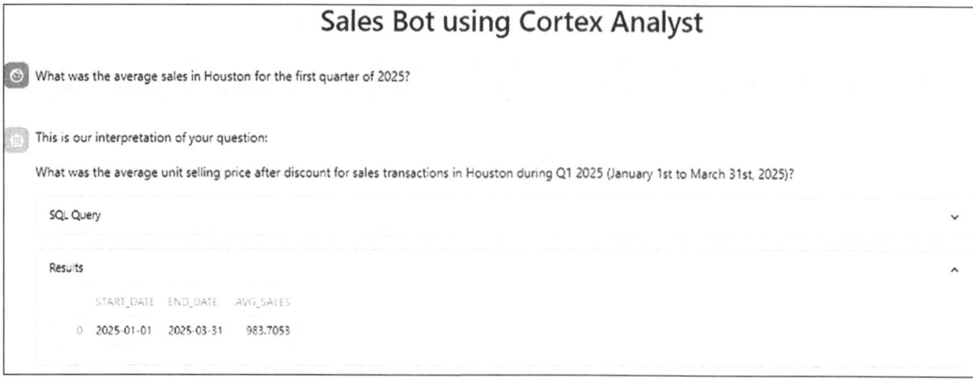

Figure 10.13: *Retail Sales Bot*

Customer Service: Predicting Call Center Employee Churn

In the call center industry, employee retention is a critical driver of operational efficiency, customer satisfaction, and cost control. High churn rates—often exceeding 30% annually—lead to increased recruitment and training costs, service disruptions, and declining morale among the remaining staff. To address this challenge, organizations must adopt predictive strategies that not only identify churn risks early, but also provide clarity and confidence in those predictions.

This use case demonstrates how Snowflake Cortex's native machine learning capabilities can be harnessed to accurately forecast employee churn in a call center environment. The model is then trained on a curated set of structured features, such as tenure, absenteeism rate, shift type, quality scores, customer satisfaction ratings, manager changes, warnings issued, salary levels, and promotion history. These features provide a comprehensive view of employee engagement, performance, and job satisfaction.

Thus, by using Cortex's classification model, each employee is scored with a churn likelihood. The binary target variable Churn indicates whether the employee is likely to leave (1) or stay (0). With an optimized dataset of 200 records and logically driven labels, the model achieves a high degree of predictive accuracy, exceeding 82%, making it a reliable foundation for proactive HR interventions.

Once deployed, this model can be used to run periodic churn predictions across the employee base. HR managers and team leads can query the model within Snowflake, and identify employees with high churn probability, allowing them to design personalized retention strategies—such as role adjustments, recognition programs, or targeted coaching—before the employee disengages fully.

Snowflake Cortex also ensures that these insights are explainable. Feature importance metrics reveal the key drivers influencing churn predictions, helping the HR teams understand which aspects–such as low satisfaction scores or frequent manager changes–are most correlated with attrition. This transparency not only builds trust in the model, but also informs strategic workforce planning.

The ability to forecast churn with precision, explain the contributing factors, and take timely action, represents a significant advancement in employee lifecycle management for call centers. Furthermore, running this workflow entirely within Snowflake maintains data security, supports compliance, and ensures scalability across distributed teams. As call centers continue to adopt AI to improve internal operations, solutions such as Snowflake Cortex offer a practical and responsible path to smarter workforce retention.

As seen in the image, the predicted churn class of 0 or 1 is displayed, along with the respective probability.

SALARY_HIKE_PERCENTAGE	INCENTIVE_PAYOUT_LAST_QUARTER	TRAVEL_ALLOWANCE	PRED_CLASS	PROBABILITY
17	433	Yes	"0"	0.999
19	214	Yes	"0"	0.906
14	538	Yes	"1"	0.751
11	697	No	"0"	0.998
5	819	No	"0"	0.991
5	169	No	"0"	0.998
0	238	Yes	"1"	0.983
4	587	Yes	"0"	1
15	452	No	"0"	0.958

Figure 10.14: *Call Center Employee Churn*

Steps

Folder Name: Customer Service

1. From the Dataset folder, import the data from **`CALL_CENTER_EMPLOYEE_CHURN.csv`** to **`CORTEX_AI_DB.PUBLIC. CALL_CENTER_EMPLOYEE_CHURN`**.
2. From the **`Scripts`** folder, review and execute each command in **`Call Center Employee Churn ML_Classifier.sql`** to ensure that the commands have completed successfully.
3. Create a new Streamlit application in **`CORTEX_AI_DB`** called Call Center Churn Prediction.

4. Copy the contents from **`Call Center Churn Prediction.py`**, and paste it into the Streamlit application.
5. Import the packages from the **`Package List.txt`** into Streamlit, using the **`Packages`** > **`Find Packages`** box.
6. Run the Application.

Food and Hospitality: AI-Powered Menu Intelligence

Snowflake recently announced preview access to multimodal support in Cortex AI **`COMPLETE`**, allowing users to analyze and process images together with text using advanced vision AI models–all accessible through the standard SQL commands. This integration eliminates the need for complex external systems or API connections, as images can be processed directly from Snowflake or external storage locations. This use case will leverage the same.

Restaurants, food delivery platforms, and hospitality providers often manage expansive and evolving menus consisting of both proprietary and vendor-supplied food items. Consistent classification of these menu items–by meal type, cuisine, dietary preference, and food category–is essential for maintaining structured digital catalogs, enhancing searchability, enabling dietary filters, and improving customer engagement. However, manual tagging of food images is resource-intensive, prone to inconsistencies, and does not scale well across the distributed operations.

This case demonstrates an automated approach using Snowflake Cortex's **`COMPLETE`** function, integrated within a Streamlit dashboard, to intelligently classify food images, and generate the descriptive metadata. Upon uploading the food images, the system utilizes Large Language Models (LLMs) to extract the relevant attributes, including Meal Type (for example, Breakfast, Lunch, Dinner), Cuisine (for example, American, Indian, Chinese, Italian), Type (Vegetarian or Non-Vegetarian), and Food Category (for example, Main Course, Appetizer, Dessert). The system also produces a concise, engaging description suitable for menu presentation, enhancing visual merchandising and digital experience.

Figure 10.15: *Menu Item Classification*

"**`pixtral-large`**" is leveraged as the underlying large language model. This app begins by allowing users to load and classify the menu item images stored in a Snowflake stage, (**`@MULTIMODAL_DEMO_STG`**). When the user clicks the "**`Load and Classify Menu Item Images from Stage`**" the application executes a Snowflake SQL query that uses the **`CORTEX.COMPLETE`** function to classify each image based on a carefully crafted prompt. This prompt instructs the model to extract the **`item name`**, **`meal type`**, **`cuisine`**, **`type`** (vegetarian or non-vegetarian), and a brief restaurant-styled description. The results are then stored in the **`MENU_ITEM_IMAGES_CLASSIFIED`** table.

Users can now select a specific image from the dropdown list. The selected image is fetched directly from the Snowflake stage, and the corresponding classification result is retrieved from the table. Both the image and its classified metadata are then displayed one below the other in the Streamlit interface. All classification results are securely processed within the Snowflake Data Cloud, ensuring centralized governance, auditability, and integration with the existing data pipelines.

Figure 10.16: *Menu Image Classification and Labelling*

This setup enables menu managers, chefs, or digital experience teams to visually explore, generate and validate AI-generated food item classifications – streamlining menu enrichment and digital cataloging directly, within the Snowflake ecosystem. Thus, by replacing manual menu curation with AI-driven insights, this solution improves operational efficiency and reduces time to market for menu updates across platforms, ultimately contributing to better customer satisfaction and operational agility.

Steps

Folder Name: Food and Hospitality

1. Create a new stage - **`CORTEX_AI_DB.PUBLIC.MULTIMODAL_DEMO_STG`** (Run **`Create Stage.sql`** in the **`Script`** folder).
2. Load all the image files from the **`Dataset`** folder to **`CORTEX_AI_DB.PUBLIC.MULTIMODAL_DEMO_STG`**.

3. Create a new Streamlit application in **`CORTEX_AI_DB`** called Menu Item Classification.
4. Copy the contents from **`Menu Item Classification.py`**, and paste it into a Streamlit application.
5. Import the packages from the **`Package List.txt`** into Streamlit using the **`Packages`** > **`Find Packages`** box.
6. Run the Application, and choose a menu item.

Consumer Electronics: Aspect-Based Sentiment Decoding of Customer Emails

Zentime, our illustrative smart watch brand, receives a high volume of customer emails every month–ranging from support queries and technical complaints to product feedback and brand praise. Traditionally, sentiment analysis on this unstructured text would generate a single overall score for each message. While helpful, this approach often oversimplifies the customer's experience by assigning a general tone–positive, negative, or neutral–without revealing which specific aspects of the interaction are driving that sentiment. However, the new **`ENTITY_SENTIMENT`** function in Snowflake Cortex AI changes that. It enables detailed, aspect-based sentiment analysis by not only examining the message content, but also allowing teams to define entities (such as "**`Brand`**", "**`Product`**", "**`Service`**", "**`Design`**", and so on), returning sentiment scores for each of them individually, along with an overall sentiment. This makes it a powerful tool that can disseminate various sentiments embedded in a single message as well as isolate them based on specific aspects, rather than collapsing everything into a single, blended sentiment score.

This nuanced breakdown is especially useful for businesses such as Zentime that deal with multifaceted customer feedback. For instance, a customer may be impressed by the aesthetics and build quality of the Zentime Ultra Smart watch, yet frustrated by poor customer service and unresolved technical issues. A traditional sentiment model might average these out as neutral or mixed, providing no clear signal on what is working and what needs attention. In contrast, **`ENTITY_SENTIMENT`** will highlight *positive sentiment* for the "**`Brand`**" and "**`Design`**" entities, while showing *negative sentiment* for "**`Product`**" and "**`Service`**"–giving internal teams a precise view of the praise and pain points, within the same message.

In one such example (corresponding to the first row in the dataset), say a customer wrote by saying that they loved the design and reputation of the Zentime Ultra but had been experiencing technical issues and difficulty getting help from customer support. Let us look at the email.

Date: April 16, 2025
Subject: Zentime Ultra – Brand I trust, but product has been disappointing

Dear Zentime Support Team,

I've always been a fan of **Zentime** and really admire how your brand continues to lead with innovation and style. The design language, attention to detail, and overall brand experience have always stood out to me. It's clear that Zentime cares about building something more than just another gadget — and that's what keeps me loyal.

Unfortunately, my experience with the **Zentime Ultra Smart Watch** has not lived up to the high standards I've come to associate with your brand. The device frequently lags, and core features like the heart rate monitor and push notifications are unreliable at best. I've attempted both restarts and a full factory reset, but the issues persist. As someone who values both function and form, this has been genuinely disappointing.

To add to the frustration, I've had difficulty reaching your support team. I submitted a help request through your website over a week ago and haven't received any follow-up. I also attempted to use the support chat in the app, but it disconnected multiple times before I could get help.

I continue to believe in the **Zentime brand**, but I'm currently losing confidence in the **product experience**. I hope this can be resolved soon, as I'd really like to see the Ultra deliver on its full potential.

Best regards,
Taylor Morgan

Figure 10.17: *Customer Email for Aspect-based Sentiment Analysis*

After loading the email contents to a table, we analyze this with the **`ENTITY_SENTIMENT`** function:

```
SELECT *,
  SNOWFLAKE.CORTEX.ENTITY_SENTIMENT(
    email_content,
    ['overall', 'Brand', 'Product', 'Service', 'Design']
  ) AS entity_sentiment_output
FROM CORTEX_AI_DB.PUBLIC.CUST_EMAILS;
```

As mentioned, we look at customer sentiments from the perspectives of the "**`Brand`**", "**`Product`**", "**`Service`**" and "**`Design`**", as well as an overall sentiment to better understand both granular and general perceptions.

```
{
  "categories": [
    {
      "name": "overall",
      "sentiment": "mixed"
    },
    {
      "name": "Brand",
      "sentiment": "positive"
    },
    {
      "name": "Design",
      "sentiment": "positive"
    },
    {
      "name": "Product",
      "sentiment": "negative"
    },
    {
      "name": "Service",
      "sentiment": "negative"
    }
  ]
}
```


Figure 10.18: *Entity Sentiments*

When analyzed through the **`ENTITY_SENTIMENT`**, Snowflake Cortex returned a mixed overall sentiment for the first row, but clearly surfaced a positive sentiment for "**`Brand`**" and "**`Design`**", while flagging a negative sentiment for "**`Product`**" and "**`Service`**". These predictions align well with the sentiments expressed by the customer. This level of granularity makes it easier for product teams to focus on technical bugs, while the support department can prioritize follow-ups–without missing the bigger picture of ongoing customer appreciation for the brand and design language.

Now, let us look at the second email where the customer reports a positive opinion about the brand, product, and design, and also has an overall positive experience, but has concern regarding the support, which they would like to be addressed.

> **Date:** April 25, 2025
> **Subject:** Zentime Ultra experience – fantastic product, minor support lag
>
> Dear Zentime Support Team,
>
> I wanted to take a moment to share some feedback on my experience with the Zentime Ultra Smart Watch, which I've been using for a few weeks now. First of all, I'm thoroughly impressed. The product works flawlessly — the performance is smooth, the health tracking features are accurate, and the integration with my devices has been seamless. It's quickly become an essential part of my daily routine.
>
> The design of the watch is absolutely beautiful. It has a clean, modern look and feels premium on the wrist. I've already had multiple people ask what I'm wearing, and I'm proud to say it's Zentime. You've clearly put a lot of thought into how it looks and feels.
>
> As for the brand itself, I've come to really appreciate what Zentime represents — thoughtful innovation paired with elegant design. You've definitely won me over, and I'll be keeping an eye on your future releases.
>
> The only hiccup I encountered was with customer service. I submitted a query about syncing with a third-party fitness app, and unfortunately didn't get a reply for several days. I eventually resolved it on my own, but the delayed response was a bit disappointing given how excellent everything else has been.
>
> Overall, I'm really pleased with the product and the brand experience. This small support issue aside, you've built something that truly stands out. Keep up the great work!
>
> Best regards,
> Emily Chen

Figure 10.19: *Another Customer Email for Aspect-based Sentiment Analysis*

As we can see in this example, the **`ENTITY_SENTIMENT`** output accurately captures the customer's experience by highlighting a positive sentiment toward the brand, product, and design, while clearly flagging a negative sentiment for service due to a delayed support response–resulting in an overall positive impression that acknowledges the praise, without overlooking the service concern.

```
{
  "categories": [
    {
      "name": "overall",
      "sentiment": "positive"
    },
    {
      "name": "Brand",
      "sentiment": "positive"
    },
    {
      "name": "Design",
      "sentiment": "positive"
    },
    {
      "name": "Product",
      "sentiment": "positive"
    },
    {
      "name": "Service",
      "sentiment": "negative"
    }
  ]
}
```

Figure 10.20: *Entity Sentiments for the Second Email*

Following these predictions, we will create a table, named **`cust_entity_Sentiment`** that transforms the **`ENTITY_SENTIMENT`** output stored in the JSON format into structured, column-wise sentiment data. It flattens each sentiment category from the JSON, and then pivots them into individual columns such as **`brand_sentiment`**, **`product_sentiment`**, and so on, while retaining the original id and **`email_content`** for each record. This allows for easier querying, analysis, and visualization of aspect-based sentiment insights at the row level.

In this case, we have leveraged two such examples to illustrate how aspect-level sentiment can reveal both customer appreciation and dissatisfaction, within the same message. Now, imagine the impact of running this analysis on hundreds or thousands of customer support emails across a month. By doing so, Zentime can build a comprehensive, data-driven understanding of how customers feel about each area of the business–identifying trends, surfacing recurring complaints, measuring the success of product updates, and prioritizing improvements with precision.

By deploying this capability, Zentime can now automatically generate rich, structured feedback from unstructured communications. This not only enables better root-cause analysis and prioritization across departments, but also allows for the creation of sentiment dashboards that track trends by specific entities over time, detect emerging issues, and measure the effectiveness of improvements over time. In short, Cortex's **`ENTITY_SENTIMENT`** brings clarity to the chaos of customer communication–turning qualitative aspect level feedback into concrete, actionable insights.

(As of April 15th, 2025, the **ENTITY_SENTIMENT** *function is available in preview in Snowflake)*

Steps

Folder Name: Consumer Electronics

1. The **cust_emails.csv** contains two sample emails. From the Dataset folder, load data from **cust_emails.csv** to the table **CORTEX_AI_DB.PUBLIC. CUST_EMAILS**.
2. Run each individual query from **Entity Sentiment.sql**, and verify the results.

Airlines: Translating and Summarizing Multilingual Call Transcripts

Consider a leading airline that serves passengers across a diverse set of international routes–including French-speaking, Spanish-speaking, and German-speaking regions. With this global footprint comes a multilingual challenge, that is customer support teams regularly receive calls in various languages, making it difficult for English-speaking supervisors and leadership to fully understand the voice of the customer, and act upon it.

To address this challenge, the airline could leverage Snowflake Cortex's Translate and Summarize functions to process the call transcripts efficiently. Each incoming call transcript–whether in French, Spanish, or German or other supported language–can be ingested into Snowflake, and then automatically translated to English using the Cortex Translate function. Following that, the Cortex Summarize function condenses these translated transcripts into concise and meaningful summaries that capture the essence of the conversation, such as: What the customer needed, how the agent responded, and what was the action taken.

Hence, what makes this especially powerful is the simplicity and elegance of execution–the entire pipeline can be executed using just a few lines of SQL within Snowflake.

```
SELECT *,
  SNOWFLAKE.CORTEX.TRANSLATE (CALL_TRANSCRIPT,'','en')
TRANSLATED_TRANSCRIPT,
  SNOWFLAKE.CORTEX.SUMMARIZE(TRANSLATED_TRANSCRIPT) TRANSCRIPT_
SUMMARY
  FROM AIRLINE_CALL_TRANSCRIPTS;
```

Note that we are not specifying the source language in the query, and Cortex inherently detects the same. This allows teams to handle multilingual data seamlessly, without complex pre-processing.

LANGUAGE_	CALL_TRANSCRIPT	TRANSLATED_TRANSCRIPT	TRANSCRIPT_SUMMARY
de	Kunde: Ich möchte meinen Flug auf morgen umbuchen. Age	Customer: I would like to rebook my flight for tomorrow. Age	Customer requests to rebook a flight for the next day, and
de	Kunde: Mein Gepäck ist beschädigt angekommen. Was kanı	Customer: My luggage arrived damaged. What can I do? Ag	Customer reported damaged luggage, agent will help with
de	Kunde: Ich habe spezielle Ernährungsbedürfnisse. Kann ich	Customer: I have special dietary needs. Can I request a spe	Customer requests special menu due to dietary needs. Ag
es	Cliente: Hola, necesito cambiar el asiento de mi vuelo a clas	Customer: Hi, I need to change my seat to business class if	Customer requested to change seat to business class with
es	Cliente: Perdí mi conexión en Madrid y necesito que me rep	Customer: I lost my connection in Madrid and need to resch	Customer lost connection in Madrid and needs to reschec
es	Cliente: ¿Puedo llevar una maleta adicional sin costo? Agen	Customer: Can I bring an extra suitcase at no cost? Agent: E	Customer asked about bringing an extra suitcase for free,
fr	Client : Bonjour, j'ai réservé un vol pour Paris mais je n'ai pas	Client: Hello, I booked a flight to Paris but I haven't received	Client reported missing flight confirmation email with book

Figure 10.21: *Translated and Summarized Transcripts*

This approach enables leadership and customer support leads to gain quick and actionable insights into customer interactions. With access to clear-cut summaries, they can identify common concerns, monitor satisfaction trends, and make faster decisions. And if they want to dive deeper into a particular case, they can easily review the translated full transcript, ensuring that there are no language barriers to understanding or action.

Additionally, this entire process can be fully automated using Snowflake Tasks. By scheduling SQL scripts that continuously translate and summarize new call transcripts, the airline can maintain a real-time stream of insights, without any manual intervention. All processing remains secure and governed within the Snowflake platform, making the solution not only powerful and scalable—but also seamlessly operational. To take it one step further, the airline can build a Streamlit app directly within Snowflake to give stakeholders a visual interface to browse summaries, filter by language, agent, or sentiment, and click through to view the full translated transcripts. This allows customer support managers, QA teams, and executives to explore customer interactions through an intuitive dashboard—unlocking the full potential of AI-powered insights, without ever leaving the data environment.

Steps

Folder Name: Airline Call Transcripts

1. From the **`Dataset`** folder, import the data from **`airine_call_transcripts.csv`** to **`CORTEX_AI_DB.PUBLIC. AIRLINE_CALL_TRANSCRIPTS`**.

2. From the **`Scripts`** folder, review and execute the commands in **`airline_translated_call_transcripts.sql`**, and verify the results.

Media and Publishing: Enhancing Content Promotions

Before diving into the use case, let us first explore the newly introduced Boost and Decay features in Cortex Search.

Cortex Search Services allow you to boost or lower the ranking of specific results using numeric or timestamp metadata respectively. This is particularly useful when fields, such as popularity metrics or recency indicators can enhance relevance scoring dynamically at the query time.

You can define two types of ranking signals when submitting a query:

- **Numeric Boost** increases the ranking of results based on higher numeric values like engagement metrics. (Number of - **`clicks`**, **`likes`**, **`comments`**, **`retweets`**, and so on.)
- **Time Decay** favors recently updated content by reducing the influence of older timestamps over time (**`last_modified_timestamp`**, **`last_reviewed_timestamp`**, **`last_accessed`**, and so on.)

Now that we have an understanding of this feature, let us proceed with the use case to see it in action. Consider a media and publishing house that specializes in technical and educational content. With an extensive catalog covering programming, AI, Python, Java and Data Science, the organization faces an ongoing challenge: How to decide which books should be featured on the homepage, included in digital campaigns, or recommended to readers. Traditionally, these decisions might rely on bestseller charts or manual editorial picks–but as topics like "AI" evolve rapidly, this static approach could fall short of capturing what is both timely and relevant.

To improve this process, the publishing house could adopt a metadata-driven scoring framework–one that uses a combination of reader engagement and content freshness to guide promotional decisions. This approach would allow the team to go beyond simple keyword matching or sales metrics, and instead prioritize content that is actively resonating with the audience, and recently updated.

Let us consider a scenario where the publishing team wants to spotlight books relevant to the "AI" ecosystem. As part of the setup, all books from the catalog are loaded along with their latest like and review counts, ensuring that both the content and engagement signals are available for intelligent scoring. They filter their catalog for books, whose descriptions reference AI or related tools. This initial filter might include titles, such as "**`AI for Beginners`**," "**`Applied AI for Developers`**," and so on.

To prioritize which of these should be featured, the team applies a two-tiered scoring system:

1. **Engagement-Based Boosting**: First, they look at user engagement–specifically, how many likes and reviews each book has received on their platform. They assign a weight of "*1 to likes and 2 to reviews*", recognizing that reviews often indicate deeper interaction and readership. For instance, a book with 600 likes and 100 reviews would earn a higher engagement score than one with 800 likes, but only a handful of reviews. This method ensures that books which have not only been read, but also actively discussed are given priority.

2. **Recency Weighting via Time Decay**: Next, they factor in the last modified timestamp of each book's content—particularly important for tech topics that evolve quickly. By applying, perhaps a 200-hour time decay threshold (little over a week), they give a higher weightage to books that were recently updated in the past week with new frameworks, examples, or chapters. Books updated more than 200 hours ago start to see their influence taper off in the scoring system. This means, for example, a book like "*Python Deep Learning Guide*," despite having high engagement, might be deprioritized if it has not been updated in weeks—whereas "*AI for Beginners*," updated just days ago, gets a meaningful lift in its overall score. This helps the publishing company stay more current, and do more "*point-in-time*" promotions, rather than letting promotion strategies become outdated.

Through this combined approach, the publishing team can make data-informed promotional decisions. Books that are both popular and up-to-date can be surfaced first, ensuring that what they feature aligns with both reader interest and content relevancy. Rather than relying on static bestseller lists, they use this dynamic metadata framework to continuously refresh their curated selections.

Further, the team can keep the data regularly refreshed, and build a Streamlit app with a free-text submission form where users can enter keywords (for example, "**`AI`**", "**`Python`**"), and submit them to execute a Cortex Search-driven Boost query on the book description that retrieves top results based on factors such as reviews or likes. Similarly, another free-text input can allow users to specify a time delay in hours, which when submitted, triggers a Cortex Search query leveraging Decay logic, prioritizing the recently updated books. This setup not only makes the application interactive and user-driven, but also provides readily actionable insights to help streamline and optimize content strategy effectively.

Ultimately, this approach helps the publishing house deliver more relevant and timely recommendations to readers—especially for a domain like AI, where new tools and techniques emerge frequently. It also supports better author visibility, more meaningful promotions, and a stronger connection with a technically savvy audience.

Steps

Folder Name: Media and Publishing

1. Import data from **`TECH_BOOKS_CATALG.csv`** in the dataset folder

2. **`CORTEX_AI_DB.PUBLIC.TECH_BOOKS_CATALOG`**.

3. Review and execute the SQL commands in "**`Search - Boost and Time Decay.sql`**". The SQL file executes both Boost and Time Decay specific analysis explained above. There is also a comparison query that compares the results before and after boosting.

4. Create a new Streamlit application in **CORTEX_AI_DB**, called the Boost and Decay.py.
5. Copy the contents from Boost and Decay.py, and paste it into a Streamlit application.
6. Import the packages from the Package List.txt into Streamlit, using the **Packages** > **Find Packages** box.
7. Run the Application.

Cortex AI for Social Media Analytics

Social media platforms are a goldmine of customer insights, public sentiment, and market trends. However, extracting actionable intelligence from this vast and unstructured data can be challenging. With the advent of Snowflake Cortex AI, organizations can now efficiently analyze social media data using powerful, in-database Large Language Models (LLMs) and AI functions. This document explores how Snowflake Cortex AI can be used for social media analytics, highlighting the key use cases, benefits, architecture, and implementation strategies.

We have seen all of Cortex LLM functions, such as **SENTIMENT**, **CLASSIFY_TEXT**, **SUMMARIZE**, and **COMPLETE** with detailed examples. Social media analytics presents a compelling use case that brings all these capabilities together to drive real-time, actionable insights. By leveraging these functions in tandem, organizations can not only analyze, but also respond to social signals in a meaningful and scalable way.

Snowflake Cortex AI brings the power of generative AI and machine learning directly into the Snowflake Data Cloud. This eliminates the need for complex data movement, and enables near real-time analysis within a governed and scalable environment. Social media analytics benefits immensely from these capabilities because data is often unstructured (text, images, and so on), and insights must be timely and relevant, as well as large volumes of data must be processed quickly. Cortex simplifies AI adoption by offering pre-built LLM functions such as sentiment analysis, text summarization, classification, and text generation that can be applied directly via SQL.

One of the most common applications is sentiment analysis. With the **SENTIMENT()** function, brands can instantly evaluate customer sentiment from tweets, comments, reviews, and posts. This allows marketing and customer service teams to track brand perception over time, identify crises before they escalate, and segment feedback by tone. For instance, a simple SQL query can return sentiment scores for every social media post, allowing real-time monitoring of customer emotions.

Text classification is another powerful capability. The **CLASSIFY_TEXT()** function categorizes the unstructured text into predefined categories, such as **Praise**, **Complaint**, **Inquiry**, or **Feedback**. This enables auto-tagging of comments for workflow routing, and helps in identifying frequently mentioned product issues. Analysts can then build dashboards that reflect the volume and type of customer interactions across various platforms. For example, an analyst could define categories (for example, "**`Product Quality`**", "**`Pricing Concern`**", "**`Feature Request`**", "**`Customer Service`**"), and use Cortex to classify each social media mention. This quickly tells which topics are most frequent. If "**`Pricing Concern`**" appears in many mentions, it flags a potential issue to address.

Summarization plays another critical role, when dealing with lengthy comment threads, campaign reviews, or influencer content. The **`SUMMARIZE()`** function helps condense these into key insights, making it easier for decision-makers to digest large volumes of feedback. Grouped by user, topic, or campaign, these summaries can serve as valuable inputs to marketing strategies and performance evaluations. For instance, summarizing all ZenTime smartwatch social media comments about a specific model during a week might reveal that many customers are talking about "*battery life and screen size*" - indicating those are hot topics.

For customer engagement teams, response generation through the **`COMPLETE()`** function provides a practical solution for AI-assisted replies. By passing a prompt like "**`Respond politely to [comment]`**," teams can generate context-aware and brand-aligned responses to incoming social media messages. This dramatically reduces the response time, and ensures consistency in communication. The tone of such responses can also be customized, so that it connects better with the audience.

From a competitive intelligence standpoint, Snowflake Cortex AI transforms social media competitor analysis by enabling organizations to process vast amounts of unstructured competitive data directly within their data warehouse. Using functions like **`SENTIMENT()`** to compare brand perception across competitors, **`CLASSIFY_TEXT()`** to categorize competitor mentions by topic, and **`SUMMARIZE()`** to distill the key themes in competitor conversations; businesses can track shifts in competitor positioning. They can also identify features receiving positive mentions in competing products, measure audience reactions to competitor campaigns, and detect emerging threats or opportunities. This comprehensive view allows for data-driven competitive strategy, without requiring a specialized ML expertise or complex data movement, as all analysis happens within the secure Snowflake environment using familiar SQL commands that can be easily integrated into the existing business intelligence dashboards. Further, the sentiment for each post can be computed directly in the data warehouse, allowing easy aggregation (for example, "*percentage of positive mentions per day*") and visualization. Businesses can set up alerts on sentiment trends, and proactively address a negative feedback to improve customer experience.

Advanced analytics can also be used to extract brand names, people, products, or places from posts. This helps in identifying who or what customers are talking about. Additionally, by combining hashtag usage with sentiment analysis, organizations can identify trending topics, campaign buzz, and even viral moments in their social media landscape. Using these tools, trend analysis becomes much easier. Analysts can identify emerging trends on social media early – whether it is a new feature that customers love, a complaint that's gaining traction, or a viral hashtag relevant to the business. Snowflake Cortex speeds up this process by handling the heavy NLP computations within the Snowflake. As a result, businesses can quickly get a pulse on conversation topics, and adapt their strategies (product, marketing, and PR), according to the insights.

The architecture for implementing Snowflake Cortex in social media analytics involves several stages. First, data ingestion is handled using tools such as Snowpipe, third-party APIs, or ETL platforms to bring in data from Twitter, Facebook, Instagram, or Reddit. Then, data preparation involves cleaning and normalizing the text by removing emojis, links, and other noise. Once the data is ready, the Snowflake Cortex AI functions are applied through SQL queries, and the results are stored in analytic tables. Finally, visualization tools like Streamlit, Power BI, and so on, can be used to present real-time dashboards for sentiment tracking, complaint categorization, influencer analysis, and so on.

There are numerous benefits of using Snowflake Cortex AI for social media analytics. Since all processing happens within the Snowflake platform, there is no need to move data outside for analysis, ensuring security and performance. In fact, SQL-native functions make AI accessible to analysts, without requiring machine learning expertise. Cortex is also highly scalable, capable of handling millions of rows effortlessly, and offers governance features like role-based access control to maintain data compliance.

Metrics that can be tracked using this setup include net sentiment score over time, volume of posts by classification, summaries of product feedback, top emerging hashtags, and AI-generated responses awaiting approval. These metrics provide a comprehensive view of how customers are interacting with the brand online.

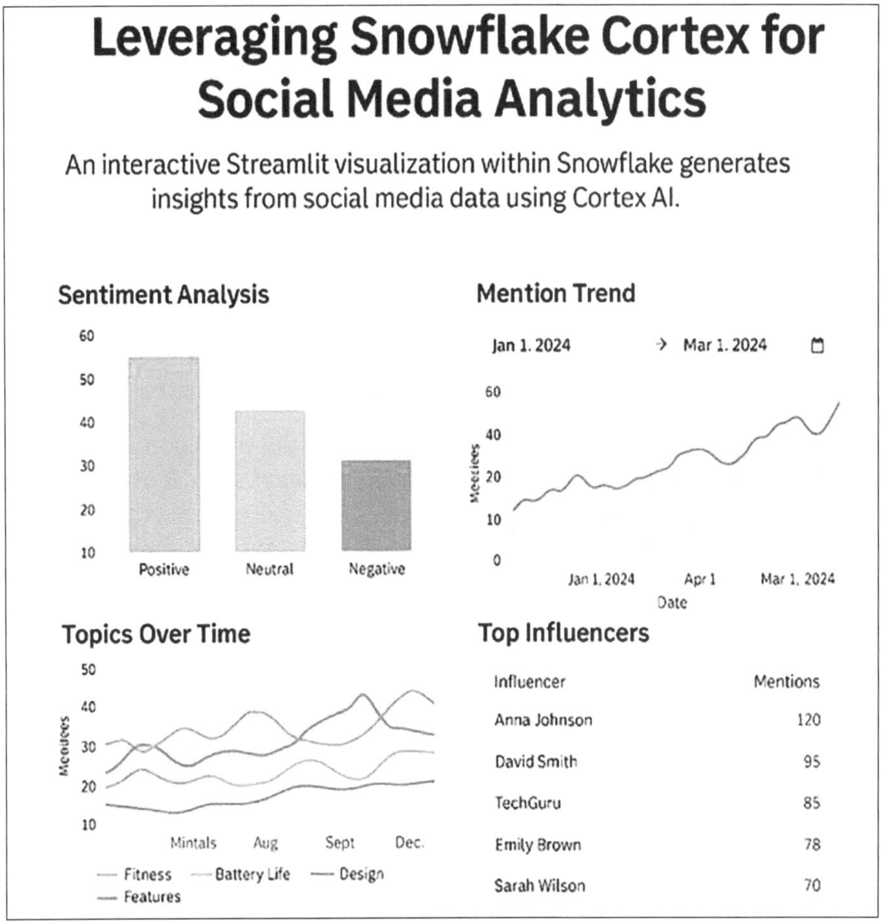

Figure 10.22: *A Representative Image - Cortex for Social Media Analytics*

Advanced use cases include Voice of Customer analysis by combining the product reviews with the social media data for early crisis detection through negative sentiment spikes, influencer-brand voice alignment checks, and auto-generated summaries of campaign performance. All of these add strategic value to marketing, PR, and customer success teams.

Therefore, to further sharpen insights, brands can leverage Snowflake Cortex Search with boosts and decays to dynamically rank and prioritize the social media content. By applying numeric boosts to engagement signals—such as likes, shares, or comments—and applying time decays to deprioritize older posts, teams can actually ensure that the most recent and highly relevant conversations float to the top of their dashboards and analysis pipelines. This makes it easier to track live sentiment shifts, emerging trends, and immediate feedback.

Let us hypothesize how Zentime, our fictional smartwatch company, that aims to stay competitive by deeply understanding what their customers are saying online, could formulate a social media analytics strategy. As their user base expands, so does the volume of content generated about their products on platforms such as Twitter, Instagram, and Reddit. Without a scalable way to analyze this feedback, valuable insights could easily get lost in the noise.

To address this challenge, Zentime could adopt Snowflake Cortex as a strategic solution for social media analytics. They could build an automated data pipeline that ingests daily social media mentions directly into Snowflake. Once stored, these posts could be processed using Cortex's **`SENTIMENT`** function to assign sentiment scores, offering a live dashboard of public opinion. If a firmware update sparked negative reactions about battery performance, a drop in sentiment could alert the product team to investigate and respond quickly, possibly issuing a fix before the issue escalates.

Zentime could also use the **`CLASSIFY_TEXT`** function to tag the incoming feedback into themes, such as "**`Performance Issues`**," "**`Feature Requests`**," or "**`Customer Support`**." This classification would allow the company to track which topics are gaining traction, and prioritize resources accordingly. For instance, if mentions related to "Design Aesthetics" suddenly surge with positive sentiment, that could validate recent improvements to product styling.

Influencer tracking might also become part of their Cortex-powered analytics suite. By combining engagement metrics with sentiment analysis, Zentime could identify which voices are shaping public perception. If a tech influencer's positive review led to a spike in engagement, the team might analyze that post using the **`SUMMARIZE`** function to distil the key points resonating with their audience. These insights could then be repurposed into the marketing copy or used to inform future design decisions.

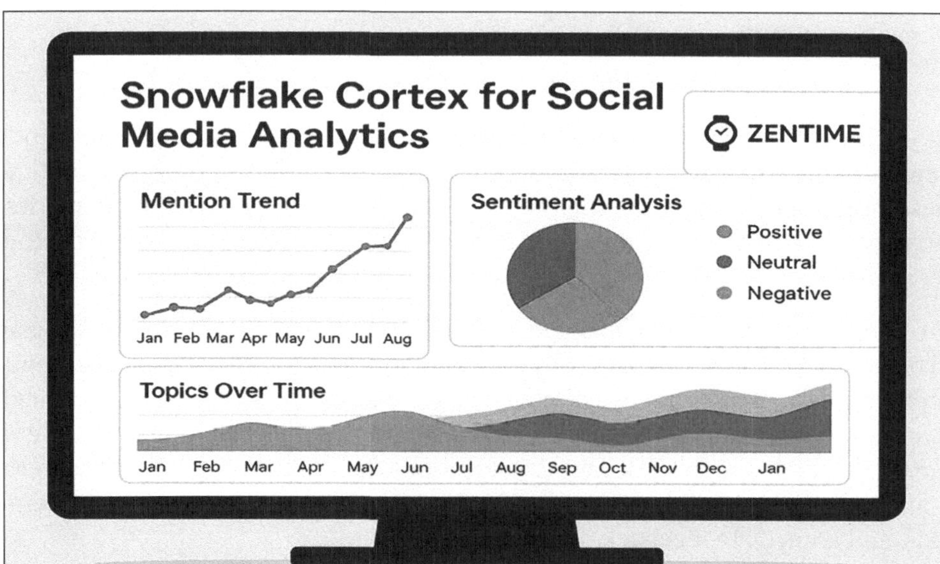

Figure 10.23: *Zentime Dashboard Illustrative Image*

They could leverage Snowflake Cortex Search Boost and Decays for intelligent ranking. For example, they could monitor posts mentioning keywords such as "**`battery`**," "**`sleep tracking`**," or "**`fitness sync`**." Posts with high interaction would also be boosted to reflect their impact, while a 48-hour time decay threshold could help the team focus on what is currently resonating. This would enable Zentime's marketing and product teams to detect praise or complaints faster, amplify timely customer stories, push impactful stories to gain more traction, and even auto-prioritize influencer content–ensuring they stay close to their audience, and act on fresh, high-value insights.

Furthermore, with Streamlit-enabled intuitive visualizations, the team can easily generate and interact with a wide variety of plots, such as time series plots to monitor follower growth over time, bar charts to compare engagement metrics, pie charts to visualize audience demographics, heatmaps to identify peak activity periods, and word clouds to highlight trending topics as well as commonly used keywords. These visual tools significantly enhance the team's ability to derive actionable insights from the social media data.

By leveraging Snowflake Cortex, Zentime would have the ability to move from reactive responses to proactive engagement. They could detect emerging issues, monitor the effectiveness of product changes, and amplify feedback loops with real-time insights. Rather than relying on fragmented tools and delayed reports, the entire social media analytics lifecycle would remain integrated, timely, and actionable within Snowflake.

In conclusion, Snowflake Cortex AI empowers organizations to unlock real-time, AI-driven insights from social media with minimal effort. By using Cortex's in-database LLM capabilities, companies can enhance their brand monitoring, customer engagement, and marketing strategies in a scalable and secure manner. Whether it is summarizing a thousand tweets or classifying live Instagram comments, Cortex provides a powerful toolkit for next-generation social media analytics. With the foundational pieces in place, they can build powerful social listening dashboards, driving timely insights and better business outcomes.

From Data to Decisions: Visualizing Cortex AI with Streamlit

You have just run a sentiment analysis across 10,000 customer reviews–Cortex function executed in seconds. But now what? A table full of scores and summaries will not tell the story to your leadership team–or your frontline managers. This is where visualizing Cortex AI output becomes more than just a nice-to-have. It becomes essential.

Throughout this book, we have seen and leveraged many examples of Streamlit within Snowflake to visualize our results–ranging from sentiment analysis and review classifications to displaying predictions and interacting with chatbots. Each example reinforces how the seamless integration between Cortex AI and Streamlit enables fast, secure, and insightful analytics experiences. The ability to build rich front-end components, display real-time Cortex outputs, and maintain full governance over sensitive data has transformed how AI is consumed and trusted within organizations.

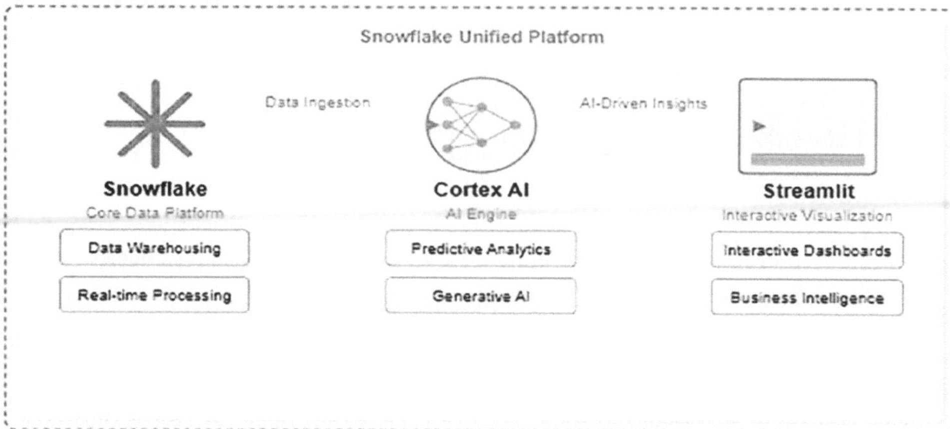

Figure 10.24: *Data > AI > Visualization*

As organizations increasingly rely on AI for faster as well as smarter outcomes, the importance of intuitive, real-time, and explainable dashboards cannot be overstated. Snowflake Cortex brings powerful AI capabilities directly into the data warehouse, offering prebuilt, no-code functions such as **`SNOWFLAKE.CORTEX.SUMMARIZE`**, **`SNOWFLAKE.CORTEX.CLASSIFY_TEXT`**, and **`SNOWFLAKE.CORTEX.SENTIMENT`**. These functions enable users to analyze the text, predict future trends, classify content, and extract meaning from documents–all within a governed, secure, and performant environment. However, the real value of these functions is best realized when their outputs are visualized meaningfully.

Dashboards powered by Cortex AI make abstract predictions tangible and accessible. They allow business users and stakeholders to explore model outputs, without needing to understand the underlying ML mechanics. For example, sentiment and summarization outputs can be transformed into customer experience dashboards that convert large volumes of feedback into concise summaries and emotional trends. Classification results can be shown as interactive charts grouped by risk or urgency, supporting use cases such as fraud detection, support prioritization, or contract intelligence. Forecasting models, when visualized with overlays and confidence bands, make future trend predictions more digestible for use in sales, supply chain, or finance teams.

One of the most compelling advancements in the Snowflake ecosystem is the native integration of Streamlit in Snowflake. This allows developers to create and deploy interactive dashboards directly within the Snowflake environment–without data ever leaving the platform. This zero-ETL approach significantly reduces latency, and improves security and compliance. By combining Snowpark for Python and Streamlit, developers can trigger Cortex AI functions, store outputs in views or materialized tables, and visualize those insights using custom interactive components–all in a unified workflow. These apps can be embedded into the existing portals or shared securely with stakeholders, making AI outputs not only operational, but also collaborative.

Within Streamlit, developers can build highly customized UI elements to surface AI insights. Think AI-generated summaries displayed beside customer feedback, drop-downs to filter classification results, sliders to adjust forecast horizons, or even buttons to regenerate sentiment analysis based on new inputs. It empowers users to explore AI insights in a hands-on, contextualized manner. Additionally, Snowflake's governance layer ensures that every interaction within the dashboard respects access controls, data masking policies, and role-based permissions–making these dashboards enterprise-ready from day one.

Visual patterns matter greatly when working with AI insights. Confidence heatmaps can help communicate model certainty. Sentiment timelines show emotional fluctuations over time. Forecasts come alive when accompanied by anomalies and variance ranges. With Document AI outputs, dashboards can also visualize structured data extracted from unstructured files–such as invoice fields, contract terms, or handwritten notes–bridging the gap between documents and the data.

Industry use cases reinforce this value. Retailers can use dashboards to visualize product review sentiment at scale. Healthcare providers could track patient risk flags based on classified clinical notes. Finance teams can spot anomalies in spend behavior and revenue patterns. In each case, Streamlit-powered dashboards within Snowflake deliver not just numbers but narratives–AI-powered stories that are clear, timely, and actionable.

Thus, as organizations continue to adopt Cortex AI, the ability to visualize those insights directly where the data lives–with Streamlit embedded in Snowflake–is a game-changer. It shortens the time from insight to impact, empowers non-technical users, and enables explainable AI in operational workflows. The next evolution involves generative dashboards, where users can ask natural language questions, and get dynamic, AI-generated charts and insights through Cortex Analyst, further blending the power of LLMs with the simplicity of visual storytelling.

While Streamlit is a powerful and native option for visualizing Cortex AI outputs within the Snowflake ecosystem, Snowflake's seamless integration capabilities make it easy to connect to leading Business Intelligence (BI) tools, such as Tableau, Power BI, Looker, ThoughtSpot, and so on. These tools can consume Cortex-generated data–including predictions, summaries, classifications, and sentiment scores–from Snowflake tables in real time, enabling rich dashboards that combine AI insights with operational and business metrics.

This flexibility empowers data and business teams to embed generative AI insights directly into their existing workflows and reporting ecosystems. For example, customer sentiment classified by Cortex can be visualized alongside NPS scores in Tableau, or AI-generated churn explanations can be added to Power BI customer retention dashboards. These visual layers help democratize AI outputs and drive action across all business units, without requiring users to interact with LLMs directly.

As we saw in the context of our social media analytics case study - To bring these insights to life, Zentime took advantage of Streamlit in Snowflake. By using Streamlit, Zentime's data science team built visual tools that display real-time sentiment scores, trending topics, and influencer activity without moving data outside the secure boundaries of Snowflake. For instance, the Streamlit dashboard could feature a line chart showing sentiment trends over time for each product model, heatmaps of the most discussed features, and pie charts categorizing feedback themes. Additionally, filters could enable business users to filter data by geography, influencer handle, or date range—all within a simple, intuitive interface. This seamless integration ensures that decision-makers across marketing, product, and customer experience teams can explore insights and act on them quickly, backed by governed and up-to-date data.

Thus, Cortex AI combined with Streamlit in Snowflake represents a new era of AI-powered business intelligence—one where machine learning models are no longer hidden in notebooks, but instead come to life in dashboards that think, respond, and evolve with your data. By making AI insights visual, interactive, and secure—and through the many examples we have explored throughout this book—organizations can confidently democratize data science, foster trust, and turn insights into smarter decisions at scale.

Manufacturing Case Study: AI-powered Quality Control

To demonstrate the use case, let us explore a simulated scenario from a typical manufacturing environment. Visual quality inspection is a vital process in the manufacturing sector, for detecting defects in components such as gears, bearings, and pipes. Let us imagine a manufacturer of industrial components who needs to inspect part images daily—gears, bearings, and pipes, for defects like cracks, rust, or other irregularities. This setting represents a common challenge in industrial quality assurance, where early detection of faults is essential to maintaining product standards and operational efficiency. The company relied on manual visual inspection, which was time-consuming, inconsistent, and difficult to scale. Traditional approaches such as manual checks or isolated AI models could be error-prone and often disconnected from enterprise data systems.

Figure 10.25: *Parts Manufacturing - Illustrative Image*

Snowflake's powerful combination of the FILE data type (*currently in preview*) and Cortex LLM functions provides a transformative alternative: enabling scalable, secure, and AI-powered inspection workflows directly within the Snowflake Data Cloud. The manufacturer decides to leverage these capabilities to make this process seamless.

Figure 10.26 *Representative image of Defective and Non-Defective Parts*

Business Challenges

- Manual inspection of parts created operational delays and introduced human error.
- Vision systems deployed locally lacked centralized governance and auditability.
- Image data was siloed, making it difficult to correlate quality insights with other operational data.
- Scaling a uniform AI solution across the board was cumbersome and cost-prohibitive due to infrastructure and integration complexity.

The Snowflake Cortex Solution

Faced with such challenges, the company pursues a centralized, scalable, and governed solution. By leveraging Snowflake Cortex LLM with the FILE data type, the organization would be able to automate defect detection, streamline operations, and unify inspection data, all within the secure boundaries of their existing Snowflake platform. This use case also serves as an opportunity to explore the newly released FILE data type (*now available as a preview feature*), and understand how it can transform the way unstructured data, like images, is seamlessly handled within the platform.

Let us walk through the high-level steps first and then expand the use case further.

Folder Name: Manufacturing

1. **Stage Creation:** As we know, to work with unstructured data in Snowflake, it must first be uploaded to an internal or external stage, from which it can then be accessed and processed by Snowflake functions. The process begins by creating a stage (`PARTS_STAGE`) for storing parts images.

2. **Upload Images:** Now upload all the images in the Dataset folder to this stage from Snowsight

3. **Query the Stage:** Once images are uploaded to this stage, they can be queried.

   ```
   SELECT * FROM DIRECTORY(@PARTS_STAGE);
   ```

   This would return a row for each of the Parts Images that were uploaded to stage.

4. **Understanding the TO_FILE Function:** Now let us examine the **`TO_FILE`** function. This is a file function that constructs a value of type `FILE`, allowing you to work with unstructured data like images. You can generate a `FILE` object using the **`TO_FILE`** by providing a scoped file URL, a stage with a file path, or a metadata object. We will leverage the **`FILE_URL`** here. Using Snowflake's **`DIRECTORY()`** function and the **`TO_FILE()`** system function, each image was programmatically converted into a FILE object:

   ```
   SELECT TO_FILE(FILE_URL) FROM DIRECTORY (@PARTS_STAGE);
   ```

Now look closely at any specific row returned by this statement.

```
TO_FILE(FILE_URL)

{
  "CONTENT_TYPE": "image/jpeg",
  "ETAG": "921e2ece46705b1b7fc4c6caac9d875f",
  "LAST_MODIFIED": "Mon, 12 May 2025 05:03:39 GMT",
  "RELATIVE_PATH": "Part1.JPG",
  "SIZE": 10363,
  "STAGE": "@CORTEX_AI_DB.PUBLIC.PARTS_STAGE"
}
```

Figure 10.27 *Sample row with the To_File Function on FILE_URL*

Notice that it returns very useful information such as the type of file (**CONTENT_TYPE**), along with other metadata such as last modified timestamp, size of the file, and so on. (Also note that the **TRY_TO_FILE** function could also be used instead of **TO_FILE**. **TRY_TO_FILE** returns null if the URL is invalid, access to the stage is denied, or the required file metadata is missing, instead of erroring out in such scenarios).

5. **Create Tables:** We will now create the **PARTS_TABLE** table with this unstructured column by leveraging the file data type. We will also store the Relative_Path so we have the file name and the last modified date, so we keep track of extraction dates. Also, create tables for storing the results - **PARTS_STATUS_CLASSIFICATION** table (final part defect classification results) and the **PARTS_FOR_ESCALATION** table (to store details of parts that need further escalation).

6. **Populate PARTS Table:** Insert data to this table by selecting the relative path, last modified timestamp, and a `FILE` object–created using the **TO_FILE(FILE_URL)** function, from files in the **PARTS_STAGE** directory.

7. **Classify Parts and Detect Defects:** We can now leverage the **COMPLETE()** function to process all images in batch, classifying the part, detecting if it is defective, and summarizing the defect. This is loaded to the **PARTS_STATUS_CLASSIFICATION** table.

```
INSERT INTO PARTS_STATUS_CLASSIFICATION (SELECT FILE_NAME,
EXTRACTION_DTTM,SNOWFLAKE.CORTEX.COMPLETE('Claude-3-5-sonnet',
'Classify the part name in one or two words.Ignore any defect
present in the part and just name it.',PARTS_IMAGE ) AS part_
type,
SNOWFLAKE.CORTEX.COMPLETE('Claude-3-5-sonnet', 'In exactly one
word mention if the part is Good or Defective',PARTS_IMAGE ) AS
part_status,
CASE WHEN part_status='Defective' THEN
SNOWFLAKE.CORTEX.COMPLETE('Claude-3-5-sonnet', 'In ten words or
less summarize the defect', PARTS_IMAGE) ELSE 'No Defect' END De-
```

```
fect_Summary
FROM parts_table P
WHERE NOT EXISTS (SELECT 1 FROM PARTS_STATUS_CLASSIFICATION PS
WHERE PS.FILE_NAME  = P.FILE_NAME));
```

This query uses Snowflake Cortex with the Claude 3.5 Sonnet model to analyze images in the **`parts_table`**. It performs the following:

- Classifies the part name in one or two words **(`part_type`)**
- Determines part condition as either "Good" or "Defective" **(`part_status`)**
- Summarizes the defect in 10 words or less *only if* the part is defective (**`Defect_Summary`**)

The **`NOT EXISTS`** clause ensures that only new or unprocessed files are considered to avoid redundant analysis.

Note that the prompts can be engineered to be more specific and relatable as required, based on further experimentation. Each row containing the image of parts is examined and the query returns the part name, along with the status of whether or not it is defective, along with a summary of the defect.

FILE_NAME	EXTRACTION_DTTM	PART_TYPE	PART_STATUS	DEFECT_SUMMARY
Part4.JPG	2025-05-14 02:45:26.000 -0700	Metal Pipe	Defective	Cracked metal pipe showing significant structural damage.
Part1.JPG	2025-05-11 22:03:39.000 -0700	Spur Gear	Good	No Defect
Part2.JPG	2025-05-11 22:03:39.000 -0700	Spur Gear	Defective	Metal gear has visible crack through center.
Part5.JPG	2025-05-11 22:03:39.000 -0700	Ball Bearing	Good	No Defect
Part6.JPG	2025-05-11 22:03:39.000 -0700	Ball Bearing	Defective	Cracked outer race of ball bearing.
Part7.JPG	2025-05-11 22:03:39.000 -0700	Spur Gear	Good	No Defect
Part8.JPG	2025-05-11 22:03:39.000 -0700	Spur Gear	Defective	Rusty metal gear with visible crack through center.
Part3.JPG	2025-05-14 02:50:16.000 -0700	Metal Pipe	Good	No Defect
Part10.JPG	2025-05-14 05:02:44.000 -0700	Flat Washer	Good	No Defect

Figure 10.28: *Defect details using Cortex* COMPLETE

The use case demonstrated how Snowflake can seamlessly handle unstructured image data, transform it into structured insights using LLMs, and automate a traditionally manual process with governed, scalable infrastructure.

Further, to feed the images to Snowflake, the manufacturer could leverage a combination of SnowSQL CLI, Python and Snowpipe API to ingest the images to an internal stage via scheduled jobs or could even upload images to a cloud storage location (such as AWS S3, Azure Blob, or GCS) and create an external stage in Snowflake (and use the `TO_FILE` just like they would with an internal stage as shown in this demonstration).

Going further, to make this solution production-ready and support ongoing operations, the manufacturer could consider implementing CDC (Change Data Capture) logic to process only newly added or modified files in the stage. For example, using the **`METADATA$FILENAME`** and **`METADATA$LAST_MODIFIED`** fields, they can maintain a reference table (for example, a table called **`"PROCESSED_FILES"`**) of already-processed files. A simple left join against this reference will help identify and process only the new or updated files. This ensures inserting only fresh rows, thereby avoiding redundant re-processing / duplication, enhancing performance, and keeps the solution cost efficient.

On top of this, the manufacturer could also choose to build a Streamlit app within Snowflake that serves as a simple, visual front end for quality analysis teams, making the solution not only powerful and cost-effective, but also user-friendly and well-governed. This would also allow a mechanism for human reviewers to approve, reclassify, or escalate. Leveraging Streamlit charts, the manufacturer could show defect trends, parts that are frequently defective, defect rates, and so on. Further by adding batch id or lot information/ supplier information, they could also get trends by specific batches and suppliers. The insights could potentially be powerful and actionable.

To Summarize the data flow:

- Images are generated by devices on the shop floor or inspection line.
- A scheduled lightweight Python script uploads them these images every hour to a Snowflake internal stage (Or to an external stage from a cloud storage)
- The staged image files are listed using **`DIRECTORY(@stage name)`** and converted via `TO_FILE()` function and stored in a Snowflake table.
- The images are analyzed using Snowflake Cortex's `COMPLETE()` function, calling a vision-capable LLM to identify part types, defect status, and a brief defect summary.
- To ensure only new or modified files were processed, the team could add a Change Data Capture (CDC) layer using either the file metadata or a dedicated logic for maintaining load / extraction dates and use it for processing new records. This ensures efficient and incremental processing while avoiding duplication.
- A Streamlit UI provides visual oversight and actionable insights. The UI comes with an **Escalate Part** option with every row, which when clicked, writes to an Escalation table for supervisors to approve or act upon, according to defined processes. This UI could additionally include plots that enhance the applicability and potential of this use case. For example, if supplier data is available, that can be another attribute and could provide useful visual insights. This unified UI view helps bridge the gap between AI automation and human oversight all within Snowflake's governed framework.

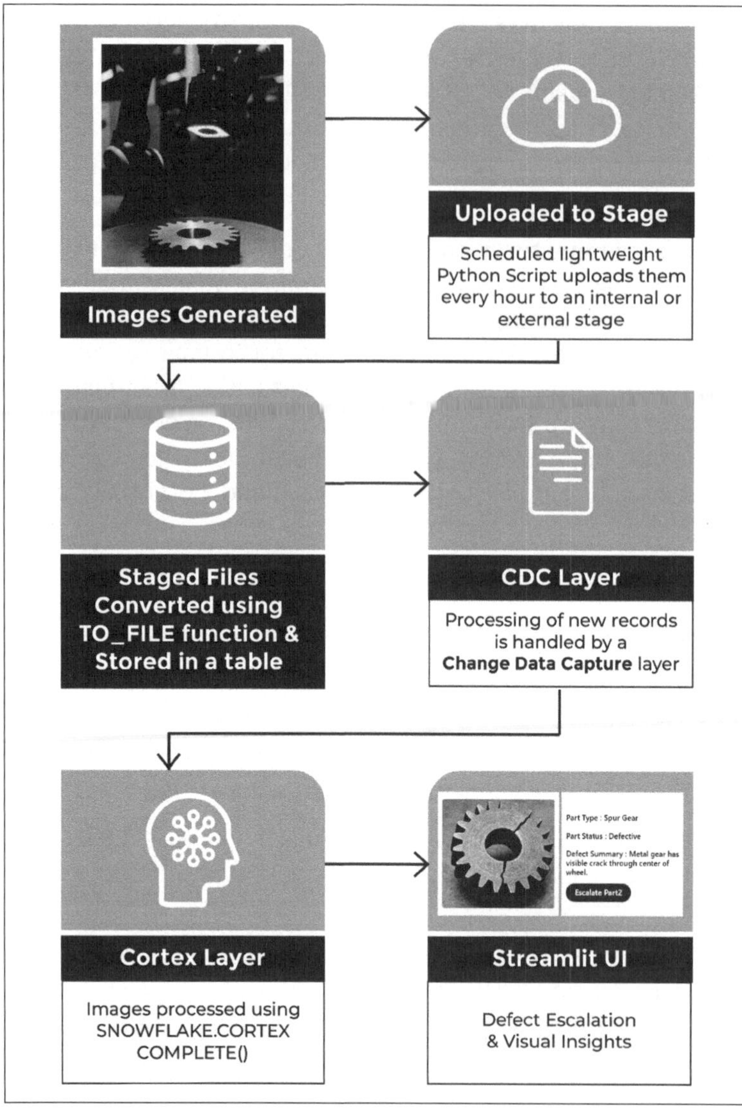

Figure 10.29: *High-Level Process Flow*

Steps:

As discussed, the implementation could be further enhanced and customized by incorporating script-driven image extraction criteria along with the CDC logic outlined in the preceding section. The Streamlit application can also be expanded by adding approval workflows, reclassification options, and visualizations such as extraction date-specific defect trends or supplier/batch-wise patterns—depending on the availability and relevance of such data. (*While these enhancements are not covered in the book, they are presented here as food for thought—ideas that readers may consider exploring according to their requirements. They reflect specialized customization possibilities that extend beyond the scope of this book but offer valuable direction for readers looking to scale or specialize the solution).*

The steps for demonstrating the **TO_FILE** function for processing the images and visualizing them are as follows. These steps would serve as a good starting point for further improvisation.

Folder Name: Manufacturing

1. Go to the Dataset folder and import data all the image files to this newly created stage **(PARTS_STAGE**)
2. Review and execute each command in **Classify Parts and Defects.sql**. Ensure that the commands have completed successfully. Verify and examine results.
3. Create a new Streamlit application in **CORTEX_AI_DB** called **Quality Control**
4. Copy the contents from **Quality Control.py** and paste it into this Streamlit application
5. Search and import the packages from the **Package List.txt** into Streamlit using the **Packages -> Find Package**s box
6. Run the Application

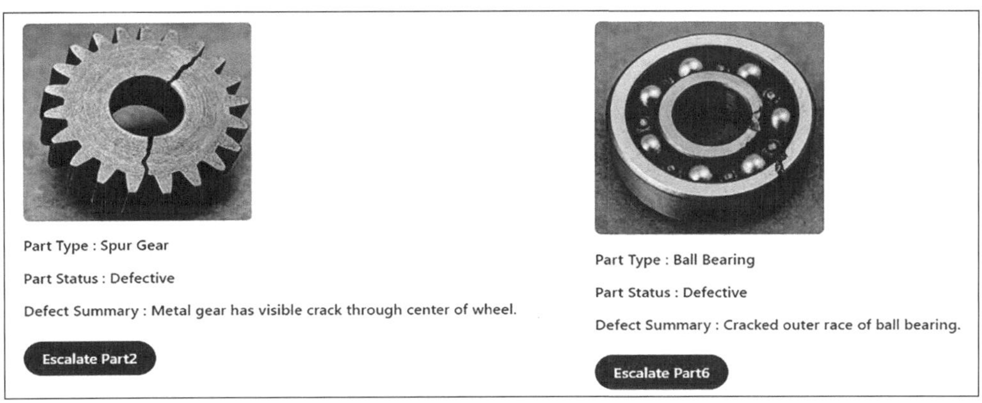

***Figure 10.30:** Streamlit Application Screenshot*

Note that, as image data scales, cost optimization is crucial to maintaining a solution that is both scalable and cost-efficient. With the powerful combination of Snowflake's FILE data type, Cortex LLM functions, incremental CDC logic, and Streamlit-based user interfaces, the manufacturer could now automate visual inspections with accuracy, scale, and transparency. This solution not only reduces inspection time and improves defect detection but is also user-friendly and actionable. It would thus simplify the visual inspection workflow, allowing for quicker and more reliable defect identification, while also strengthening data governance by consolidating image files and AI-generated insights within Snowflake for improved transparency and oversight.

Snowflake Cortex: Expanding the Frontiers of Data and AI

Our journey through cross-industry use cases reveals how Snowflake Cortex is more than just a platform – it is the living pulse of AI innovation within the Snowflake Data Cloud. Today, it empowers organizations with an extraordinary suite of native AI capabilities: RAG, Fine-Tuning, Cortex Search, Analyst, AI Agents, native LLM functions, multimodal intelligence, Document AI, robust AI observability, and more - all seamlessly woven into the data they trust.

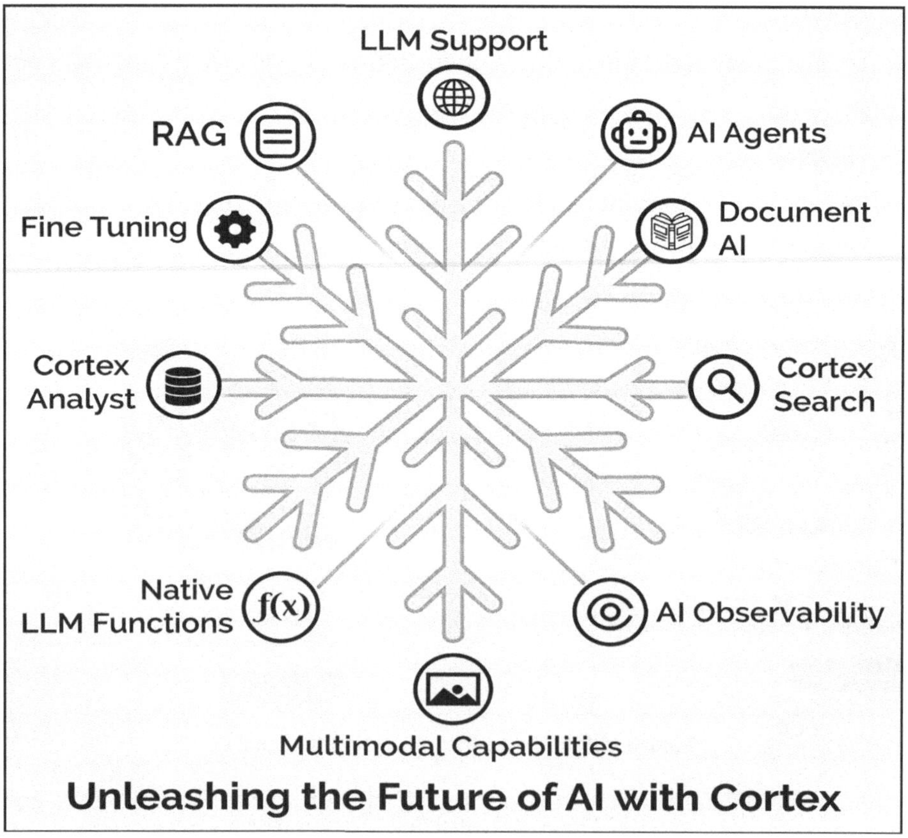

Figure 10.31: *Unleashing the Future of AI with Cortex*

What makes Cortex truly stand out is how rapidly it continues to evolve, delivering new capabilities at an impressive pace - continually expanding and innovating alongside the needs of tomorrow. Every new capability, every new branch, represents another step toward a future where data and intelligence seamlessly converge. As we have seen, Cortex supports an ever-expanding portfolio of LLMs, with new models being adopted swiftly as they emerge. Features and enhancements are introduced frequently, consistently expanding what Cortex can deliver. By democratizing AI, Cortex empowers users across skill levels–from data scientists to business analysts–to build, explore, and deploy powerful and intelligent solutions, without needing a deep ML expertise.

Its growing portfolio of LLMs and native capabilities reflects a commitment to meeting the future head-on, equipping enterprises to act on data faster and smarter. Adopting Cortex means entering a dynamic, ever-expanding ecosystem–one that learns, adapts, and scales with your ambitions. By embracing Cortex, enterprises are not just adopting a tool - they are stepping into a living ecosystem of possibility – one that grows more insightful, customer-centric, and powerful with every passing day.

Conclusion

To sum up, the transformative power of Snowflake Cortex becomes vividly clear when viewed through the lens of real-world industry use cases. Across sectors as diverse as healthcare, real estate, finance, insurance, telecom, education, retail, customer service, hospitality, media and publishing, IT security and manufacturing, Cortex enables organizations to move beyond experimentation and deliver AI solutions that are truly operational, impactful, and scalable.

Each use case in this chapter highlights a key strength of Cortex–whether it is enabling realtors to better understand customer sentiment, helping hospitals guide patients through intelligent search assistants, empowering IT teams to generate Python code on the fly using natural language prompts or supporting manufacturers in automating visual inspections. From predicting employee churn in customer service centers to deriving insights from structured and unstructured data, Cortex demonstrates flexibility and enterprise-readiness in a wide array of contexts.

What ties all these examples together is Cortex's ability to bring AI directly to where the data lives, within the governed and secure Snowflake platform. Organizations no longer need to cobble together disjointed tools or move sensitive data outside of trusted environments to unlock AI value. As we look ahead, the use cases for Cortex AI will only continue to grow. Its native integration, ease of use, AI democratization and enterprise-grade reliability make it an indispensable tool for forward-thinking organizations, ready to lead in the age of AI.

In the next chapter, we will wrap up with a conclusion that covers the key takeaways, emerging trends, next steps, and final thoughts on leading AI transformation in your organization.

CHAPTER 11
Conclusion and Next Steps

Introduction

Throughout this book, the transformative power of Snowflake Cortex AI in reshaping the modern data landscape has been a central theme. By enabling organizations to natively integrate advanced artificial intelligence and machine learning capabilities directly within the Snowflake Data Cloud, Cortex eliminates the traditional barriers between data storage, processing, and intelligent analytics. This unification allows teams across functions–from data science to business operations–to build, scale, and operationalize AI solutions more efficiently and securely.

To bring these innovations to life, we followed the journey of Zentime, a fictional smartwatch manufacturer navigating real-world challenges and opportunities. Through ZenTime's story, we explored how Cortex AI supports a wide range of use cases. We also explored how generative AI capabilities in Cortex enable critical business priorities, from personalized marketing to intelligent customer service and multimodal analysis that blends structured data with images and documents. Each chapter highlighted how even the most complex AI-driven workflows can now be achieved using simple SQL, within a governed and scalable data platform.

As we conclude, it is time to reflect and consolidate the most valuable insights and practical takeaways from this journey–lessons that can inspire and guide real-world AI transformation across industries.

Structure

In this chapter, we will cover the following topics:

- Summary and Key Takeaways
- Future Trends
- Next Steps

- Final Thoughts: Leading the AI Transformation
- Brief Note on Key AI/ML Innovations from Summit 2025

Summary and Key Takeaways

The journey through Snowflake Cortex AI has been a deep exploration into the convergence of artificial intelligence and modern data platforms. At the heart of this transformation lies the evolving role of AI in enterprise ecosystems—not just as a tool for data scientists, but as a foundational capability woven into the core of business processes. Throughout this book, we have unpacked the progression from traditional machine learning to the revolutionary potential of generative AI, and how this shift is democratizing intelligence across industries.

We began by understanding the broader AI landscape—how machine learning, deep learning, NLP, and computer vision have transitioned from academic topics to powerful enterprise applications. These technologies are now redefining how organizations make decisions, interact with customers, and optimize operations. But it is generative AI, underpinned by architectures, such as transformers and powered by LLMs, that marks a turning point. It enables machines to not only interpret data, but also generate new content, simulate reasoning, and engage with human-like fluency. The rise of generative AI is not just a technical milestone—it is a strategic imperative for businesses aiming to stay ahead.

In this evolving AI-first world, Snowflake stands out not just as a data warehouse, but as a unified data and AI platform. In fact, Snowflake Cortex AI brings the intelligence layer directly into the Data Cloud, empowering users to build, deploy, and operationalize AI, without moving data out of their governed and secure environment. With Cortex, the barriers that traditionally existed between data engineering, ML development, and business intelligence are dissolving. Teams can now collaborate on the same platform, leveraging native ML and LLM capabilities that are scalable, intuitive, and performant.

One of the most powerful enablers of this shift is the suite of built-in machine learning functions offered by Snowflake. These functions—ranging from classification and forecasting to anomaly detection and automated insights—allow organizations to embed AI into their workflows using simple SQL-like syntax. This accessibility means data analysts can perform tasks that once required specialized ML knowledge, driving a more inclusive and agile AI adoption. By removing the complexity of model training and infrastructure management, Cortex shifts the focus from technical configuration to business impact.

We then explored the foundational role of large language models in shaping modern AI systems. LLMs are now at the center of enterprise innovation, powering use cases from document summarization and translation to chat-based interfaces and semantic search. Through Retrieval-Augmented Generation (RAG) and prompt engineering, we demonstrated how these models can be tailored to deliver grounded, domain-specific responses. Embedding search, vector databases, and contextual retrieval are no longer advanced features–they are prerequisites for building intelligent systems that understand not only language, but also the meaning.

Figure 11.1: *Summary and Key Takeaways*

This integration is further enhanced by the availability of prebuilt LLM functions within Snowflake Cortex. Organizations can instantly leverage functions, such as `COMPLETE`, `SENTIMENT`, `SUMMARIZE`, and `TRANSLATE` to unlock natural language understanding at scale. These are not experimental features–they are production-grade tools built for reliability, performance, and control. They allow teams to deliver AI features, without the overhead of managing GPUs, ML pipelines, or external APIs, all while staying within the governance boundaries of the Snowflake platform.

Yet, no model fits all scenarios out of the box. Fine-Tuning emerged as a critical capability that allows organizations to infuse their models with domain-specific expertise, tone, and intent. Through Cortex Fine-Tuning, users can customize LLMs using their own datasets, ensuring that the model outputs reflect brand voice, compliance requirements, or specialized terminology. The process is seamless, secure, and efficient—enabling hyper-personalized experiences in customer support, content generation, or decision intelligence. Organizations can enhance cost efficiency by training smaller, task-specific models using the output of larger foundation models. This teacher-student approach—where a large model generates high-quality labeled data that is then used to train a lightweight model—enables faster inference, lower compute costs, and easier deployment while still retaining domain relevance and accuracy.

We also explored how natural language interfaces are making data truly self-serve. With Cortex Analyst, business users can query data conversationally, transforming natural questions into meaningful and actionable answers. Similarly, Cortex Search enables semantic exploration of the unstructured content, such as PDFs, contracts, and reports, uncovering insights previously locked away in documents. Together, these capabilities represent a fundamental shift, that is, no longer does understanding data require SQL proficiency or scripting expertise—just curiosity and a question! We also explored Cortex Agents which represent a new era in AI orchestration, where multiple models and functions can be coordinated to perform complex tasks based on natural language inputs. By combining intent detection, retrieval, and function chaining, Cortex AI Agents serve as intelligent intermediaries between the users and the data, automating decision-making workflows and delivering contextualized outputs. Backed by the powerful Large Language Models (LLMs), a Cortex agent can interpret natural language queries and plan multi-step data retrieval strategies. It uses tool orchestration to dynamically choose the right tools for each subtask. For structured data, the agent employs a Cortex Analyst guided by a semantic model of the database to translate natural language into accurate SQL queries. For unstructured data such as documents or logs, it invokes Cortex Search to perform semantic retrieval using text embeddings and hybrid (semantic + keyword) search techniques.

Moving on, we looked at how Document AI pushes the boundaries of intelligent automation by allowing enterprises to extract structured insights from the unstructured, messy document formats. From invoices and claims to customer emails and feedback forms, organizations can now deploy intelligent document processing workflows that are accurate, scalable, and natively integrated into the AI Data Cloud. Combined with Snowflake's governance and security framework, this ensures that every document processed is not just a data point—but a trusted, explainable, and traceable source of insight.

And while the technical capabilities of Cortex are impressive, they would be incomplete without the enterprise readiness that Snowflake brings. Across the board, we emphasized the importance of data governance, security, cost control, and AI observability. In Cortex, AI does not come at the cost of compliance. With built-in role-based access, fine-grained permissions, cost monitoring, and transparent usage metrics, organizations can now scale AI with confidence, knowing that they remain secure and accountable.

What truly brings the narrative together is the wide array of real-world use cases and industry applications we explored. Through case studies in retail, healthcare, real estate, finance, telecom, education, and more, we saw how Cortex AI is not just a toolkit–it is a catalyst for business transformation. We also looked at the more recently introduced features, such as the **ENTITY_SENTIMENT** function, Multimodal capabilities, and Boost and Decay controls in Cortex Search, the FILE data type – each demonstrated through real-world use cases to highlight their impact, from understanding the aspect level sentiment, to fine-tuning search relevance based on factors like recency and popularity, to enabling image-driven text classification and generation.

Throughout the book, the fictional company, Zentime, introduced as a storytelling anchor, helped humanize these applications–showing how one company's journey through Cortex could mirror the aspirations and challenges faced by many.

In reflecting on the entire journey, one key truth stands out: The convergence of data and AI is not a luxury–it is a necessity in today's world. Snowflake, through its Cortex AI offering, has positioned itself as a strategic platform for this convergence. By bringing AI, LLMs, prompt orchestration, vector search, fine-tuning, document intelligence, and natural language interfaces into a single governed platform, Snowflake Cortex AI enables organizations to move faster, act smarter, and unlock the full potential of their data.

Future Trends

Thus, Snowflake Cortex AI is evolving at a rapid pace, positioning itself at the forefront of enterprise AI innovation. The focus is on bringing AI to the data (rather than moving data to AI) in a secure, scalable way, with fully managed LLM integrations, enhanced governance features, and tools that make AI accessible across the enterprise. In this section, we examine the key emerging features and directions for Cortex AI, and how they align with the broader industry trends.

One clear trend is the *expanding support for Large Language Models (LLMs)* within Snowflake Cortex. Snowflake initially launched Cortex with access to leading models from providers, such as Anthropic, Meta (Llama), Google, Mistral, and even its own Snowflake Arctic model. Looking forward, Snowflake is continually adding to this roster of models. A recent partnership with Microsoft now enables OpenAI's models (including GPT-4) to be used natively in Snowflake's secure environment. This integration–delivered via Azure OpenAI Service–gives enterprises seamless access to some of the most popular LLMs directly within Cortex AI, simplifying deployment and enhancing data security for AI use cases.

Meta's Llama 4 Large Language Models are also now available in Snowflake Cortex AI. It now provides secure access to Meta's Llama 4 Maverick and Llama 4 Scout models within its protected environment. Meta claims that Llama 4 Scout stands as a premier model in its category, globally, featuring an exceptional context window capability of up to 10 million tokens. According to Meta, these advanced models undergo training with extensive collections of unlabeled text, image, and video data, enabling them to deliver sophisticated and immersive user experiences.

More recently, Snowflake Cortex integrated Claude Opus 4 and Claude Sonnet 4 models on the very same day they were released by Anthropic. This swift integration ensures that Snowflake users have immediate access to the latest advancements in generative AI within their data platform. Claude Opus 4 is tailored for complex tasks that require deep reasoning, code generation, and problem-solving, while Claude Sonnet 4 offers a balanced approach, delivering both speed and thoughtful responses for applications that demand a blend of efficiency and accuracy. Snowflake's ability to rapidly integrate cutting-edge models like these highlights its commitment to delivering state-of-the-art AI capabilities to its users–and we can expect more such timely integrations of new and advanced LLMs in the future.

In practice, this means developers and data scientists can choose from a diverse range of models (open-source and proprietary), without a complex external infrastructure.

We can also expect future enhancements in the Cortex Fine-Tuning area, such as additionally supported models, support for larger model sizes, and more efficient fine-tuning versatility, while Snowflake handles the heavy lifting of hosting and serving those models.

Industry-wide, there is a growing emphasis on AI ethics, fairness, and transparency - especially as AI moves from experimentation into core business processes. The Snowflake Cortex approach is to extend Snowflake's robust data governance to AI models and outputs. Snowflake has features, such as Snowflake Cortex Guard (which we explored in *Chapter* 5, *LLM Functions in Cortex*), an AI "content firewall" that filters and flags unsafe or toxic outputs from LLMs. By leveraging an LLM itself to perform these safety checks, Cortex Guard helps enterprises deploy generative AI responsibly - blocking hateful or confidential information from ever reaching the end-users. Responsible AI is a growing industry mandate, and guardrails will be increasingly standard as organizations seek to comply with the ethical guidelines and regulations. Anticipate Snowflake to continue enhancing these safeguards, possibly adding bias detection, explainability reports, and compliance auditing for AI. In fact, as we saw in Chapter - 9, the integration with open-source observability tools, such as TruLens already enables tracking of model performance, coherence, groundedness, and correctness in real-time within Snowflake Cortex. This kind of AI observability gives teams visibility into how models are behaving on production data – a trend, we will see that intensify as models become central to decision-making. Future updates may deepen these capabilities.

Snowflake is also folding AI governance into its broader platform governance frameworks. Snowflake Horizon, for example, is the unified governance layer covering compliance, security, privacy, and access controls across data *and* AI assets. Combined with features, such as Snowflake Trail (detailed audit logging) and the new Polaris Catalog for comprehensive data cataloging, the platform is gearing up to meet the stringent governance needs of AI-driven workloads. These investments underscore an important future trend: *enterprise AI platforms must not only be powerful, but also trustworthy and accountable*. Thus, we can expect Snowflake to keep strengthening its AI governance capabilities.

A major theme in Cortex's evolution is making AI accessible to a wider range of users in the enterprise. Snowflake recognizes that success with AI is not just about data scientists coding models – it is also about business analysts, domain experts, and executives being able to interact with AI-driven insights. Analyst, Copilot, Studio, and Search – share a common goal, that is, make AI in Snowflake easy to use and enterprise-ready. They cater to different personas (business users, data engineers, developers, and so on), reflecting that the future of AI is a team sport. We will likely see continued improvements in usability, such as even more natural conversations with data, more pre-trained solutions, and deeper integration with third-party business applications.

AI Agents are emerging as the cornerstone of enterprise AI strategy, and Snowflake Cortex is well equipped, continually evolving and adding new capabilities to support this shift. The agentic paradigm—where autonomous or semi-autonomous agents plan, reason, retrieve, and act—represents a significant leap forward in AI's usability and sophistication. They enable agentic AI applications—essentially, AI that can chain together reasoning and actions to fulfill a user's intent. Instead of a single prompt and response, an agent can iteratively plan, call multiple Cortex functions or queries, and arrive at a result (for example, interpreting a high-level request, such as "*Analyze our sales and draft a summary report*"). This concept is akin to how emerging "AutoGPT"-style agents work, but are applied to the enterprise data cloud.

Notably, Cortex Agents (which we explored in *Chapter 7, Natural Language Queries to Actionable Insights*), can integrate with popular enterprise software and communication channels, such as Microsoft 365 Copilot, Slack and Microsoft Teams, bringing these AI capabilities directly into the tools employees use daily. By orchestrating Snowflake's LLM functions, SQL queries, and possibly external APIs, Cortex Agents can automate complex workflows that previously required human intervention or custom code. A recent advancement allows the development of an MCP Server for Cortex Agents, enabling seamless integration of Cortex Agent capabilities as native tools within chat clients. This breakthrough bridges the gap in LLMs that traditionally lack external agent orchestration, allowing agents to interact directly with Cortex workflows and test connections with tools such as Claude Desktop. In the next few years, we can imagine Cortex Agents becoming even more versatile.

Snowflake's secure environment and governance could play a big role in taming these autonomous agents for enterprise use, for example, ensuring an agent only accesses data it is permitted to, and logging its actions (which ties back to observability). Research in autonomous AI (such as improved planning algorithms and tool integration for LLMs), is moving quickly, and will also likely influence product features in Cortex. Looking forward, Cortex AI would potentially expand its support for even more agentic frameworks, potentially integrating with emerging ecosystems. There is already reference material in Snowflake Quickstarts (quickstarts.snowflake.com) for building workflows with agentic frameworks, such as "*smolgents*" from Hugging Face. Therefore, Cortex is positioning itself to be the backbone for operationalizing AI agents at scale, securely and reliably.

At a broader level, the world is moving toward AI-infused autonomy across the enterprise. The future is not just AI-powered–it is agent-augmented. And with Cortex AI at the center of this transformation, Snowflake is enabling businesses to stay ahead–integrating intelligence not just at the edge, but at the core of how organizations operate and innovate.

Snowflake Cortex's roadmap is strongly aligned with a key industry movement, such as the convergence of data platforms and AI platforms. Increasingly, cloud data warehouses such as Snowflake have transformed into cloud-native AI platforms, offering end-to-end support for data storage, processing, model training, inference, and application development in one place. This trend is driven by the necessity of keeping the data and computation close for efficiency and governance.

Another significant trend is multi-modal AI which we touched on earlier with Cortex Search. Multi-modal AI refers to AI systems that can process and combine different data types - text, images, audio, structured data, and so on. Companies can now unlock a new dimension of intelligence by combining structured and unstructured data–including images, documents, and natural language–within a single, governed platform. Previously, analyzing unstructured assets such as images or handwritten forms required external tools and complex data pipelines. Now, with simple SQL and Cortex's **`COMPLETE`** function, data scientists, analysts, and business users can tap into the power of large language and vision models directly within the Snowflake environment. This innovation bridges the gap between traditional metrics and rich, perceptual data–bringing AI-powered image and document analysis into everyday analytics and decision-making.

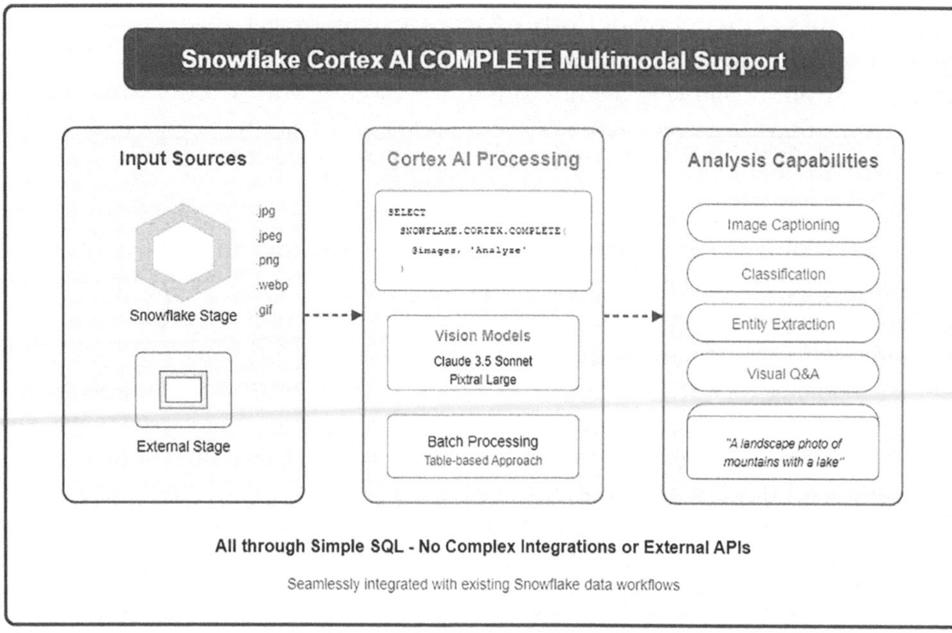

Figure 11.2: *Cortex Multimodal Support*

The enterprise implication of this capability is huge: Many business problems span multiple data modalities (think of a customer support scenario involving voice transcripts, chat logs, and relational customer data, all at once). Empowering users to seamlessly analyze and process images alongside text using advanced vision AI models—directly through simple SQL commands and without the need for complex integrations or external APIs—is a game changer. The new capabilities incorporate advanced vision models, including Claude 3.5 Sonnet and Pixtral Large, offering comprehensive visual analysis features, such as image comparison, captioning, classification, entity extraction, and visual question answering. Users can perform flexible image analysis with intuitive SQL syntax for both single and multiple images, supporting common formats (`.jpg`, `.jpeg`, `.png`, `.webp`, `.gif`), while also benefiting from efficient batch image processing that seamlessly integrates with the existing data workflows through table-based approaches. By having multi-modal AI "*under one roof*," Snowflake can eliminate the need for separate, siloed AI tools (no more exporting images to a vision AI service - you can do it in place). This unification simplifies architecture, and ensures consistent governance across all data types. It is a trend very much in line with enterprise desires to consolidate platforms and reduce data movement. At this time, only text and images are supported; video and audio formats are not yet supported.

For example, marketing teams can correlate ad performance data with visual elements, such as color palettes or the presence of human faces in creatives, uncovering new insights into what drives user engagement and conversion across segments. Retailers can analyze product photo attributes, such as brightness, framing, or presentation–and link them to transaction histories to understand which visual styles influence purchase behavior. In manufacturing, image-based quality inspections can be connected to production data, flagging visual defects that lead to downstream failures or returns. Healthcare organizations can extract metadata from imaging systems, and correlate it with patient demographics or treatment outcomes to support clinical decisions. Food delivery platforms benefit by automating image descriptions of menu items, and associating them with customer ratings or reorder behavior, streamlining both content creation and performance tracking.

Even document-heavy domains such as finance and insurance are transformed: teams can extract structured insights from scanned tax forms, handwritten signatures, or lengthy financial statements–accelerating processes, such as loan approvals and compliance checks. By enabling SQL-driven analysis that combines visual and textual intelligence, Snowflake Cortex's multimodal capabilities empower businesses to gain deeper, more context-rich insights–reducing time-to-value, improving personalization, and enhancing every data-driven experience.

Another interesting frontier is the tight integration of Cortex AI with enterprise communication platforms, such as Microsoft Teams, Slack, and Co-Pilot. These integrations signal a powerful shift: AI is no longer confined to dashboards or SQL queries–it is becoming a seamless layer within tools where employees already spend their time. Imagine team members conversing naturally in Teams or Slack, and invoking Cortex AI directly to ask questions, such as: "*What were our top-performing campaigns last quarter?*" or "*Summarize this meeting transcript, and highlight the key decisions*", and get instant answers powered by Snowflake's native LLMs and Cortex Agents–delivered in the context of where the work is happening. As a matter of fact, Cortex LLM functions and Cortex Agents can be triggered behind the scenes, pulling insights from Snowflake, summarizing content, and delivering answers in real time–right within the chat thread.

Similarly, Microsoft Co-Pilot integrations bring Cortex's power to knowledge workers by enabling them to interact with structured and unstructured data conversationally, while using productivity tools such as Excel, Outlook, or Word. With native connectors and streamlined authentication, Snowflake ensures secure, governed, and context-aware interactions between business users and enterprise data.

This convergence between AI and communication tools opens use cases, such as:AI-driven task automation triggered by conversations.

- Meeting summarization and action item extraction.
- Real-time document intelligence within collaborative environments.
- Proactive insights and alerts surfaced in Teams or Slack based on data anomalies.

- Knowledge retrieval using Cortex RAG pipelines for enterprise chatbots.

This trend represents a broader move toward ambient intelligence–AI that is always present, contextually aware, and proactive. Thus, by embedding Cortex AI into daily workflows and communication interfaces, organizations reduce the time to decisions dramatically, democratizing AI access across roles and departments.

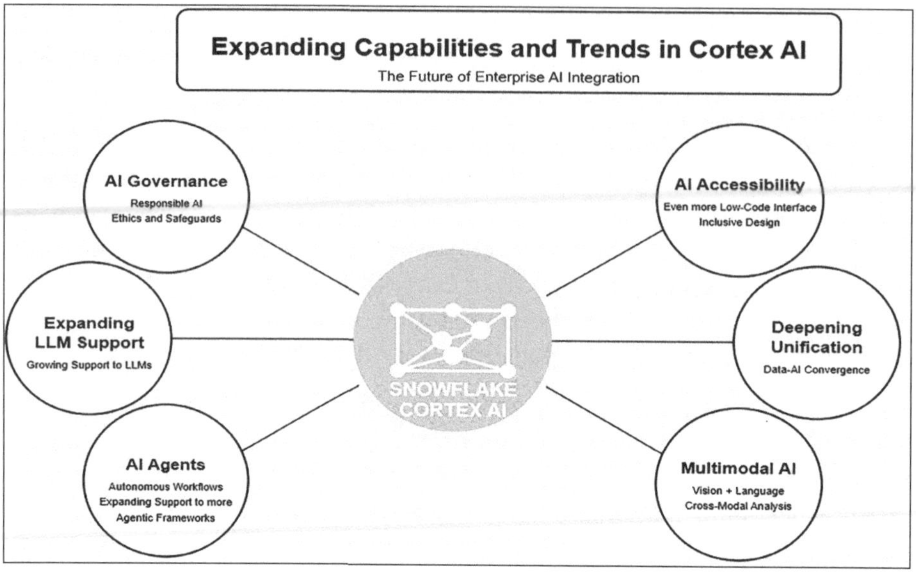

Figure 11.3: *Evolving and Emerging Trends*

As we look ahead, the trajectory of Snowflake Cortex AI reveals a future that is not just more intelligent–but more integrated, conversational, and embedded in everyday business tools. Snowflake is evolving rapidly from a data cloud to an intelligent action platform, and Cortex AI sits at the center of this transformation. As enterprises embrace this shift, Snowflake Cortex will continue expanding its capabilities to support multi-modal interactions, personalized agents, and autonomous workflows–all while keeping data secure, governed, and in one place.

To summarize, the future of Snowflake Cortex AI is one of continuity and expansion. It will continue the trajectory of bringing cutting-edge AI capabilities into the comfortable, controlled environment of the Snowflake Data Cloud. Moreover, recent integrations, such as with Microsoft Azure OpenAI and other model providers give unprecedented choice of AI models. Innovations in LLM support, from fine-tuning to agentic orchestration, will allow companies to solve new classes of problems with AI. Enhanced governance, security, and observability will remain a linchpin - ensuring all this power is wielded responsibly and transparently. And overarching it all is a drive to democratize AI, making it more accessible across roles and skill levels through expanded modalities, intuitive no-code interfaces, and seamless embedding into everyday business workflows.

Next Steps

As we conclude our journey through Snowflake Cortex AI, it is clear that this field is dynamic and continually evolving. The chapters of this book have equipped you with a deep understanding of Cortex's capabilities. However, mastering enterprise AI is a lifelong learning process. In this section, we offer guidance on expanding your skills beyond this book, and provide resources to help you stay at the forefront. Whether you are a data scientist building models, an architect designing solutions, or a technology executive shaping strategy, there are tailored paths to continue your development. We also share some closing reflections on how you can leverage what you have learned to lead AI transformation in your organization. Staying current in AI and data science requires ongoing education. Fortunately, there is a wealth of high-quality resources and communities available. Here are a few recommended avenues to continue learning:

- **Official Snowflake Training and Certification**: Snowflake offers comprehensive education programs through Snowflake learning (https://learn.snowflake.com/) and SnowPro certifications (https://learn.snowflake.com/en/certifications/). These programs now encompass AI/Data Cloud skills, and can validate your expertise in Cortex AI's latest features. For example, pursuing the *SnowPro Core or Advanced certifications* will deepen your knowledge of Snowflake's platform, including integrating AI/ML into data pipelines. More recently, Snowflake introduced the SnowPro Associate: A Platform Certification, or an entry-level credential designed to validate foundational skills in the Snowflake AI Data Cloud. This certification assesses knowledge in areas, such as data management, AI/ML integration, and the use of Snowflake Cortex LLM functions. Snowflake's Hands-On Labs and Essentials Workshops are also excellent for practical experience. These interactive labs often cover new features such as LLM functions or Snowpark ML, helping you apply concepts in a guided environment.
- **Online Courses and MOOCs:** Several online courses focus specifically on Snowflake and AI/ML. A highly recommended starting point is the "*Introduction to Generative AI with Snowflake*" course on Coursera, created in partnership with Snowflake. This course walks through implementing common AI use cases on Snowflake - from summarization and sentiment analysis to fine-tuning a foundation model - making it ideal for data scientists and ML engineers looking to apply their skills to the Snowflake Cortex environment. Snowflake has also launched an AI Data Cloud Academy (https://www.snowflake.com/data-cloud-academy-generative-ai-llm/), with on-demand courses (for example, Generative AI and LLM) that provide hands-on tutorials in using Cortex functions.
- **Technical Communities and Forums:** Engaging with the community can significantly accelerate your learning. The Snowflake Community forums

(community.snowflake.com) are a great place to ask questions, share best practices, and learn from fellow practitioners. Here, you will find discussions on topics, such as optimizing queries, troubleshooting fine-tuning jobs, and architecture tips. Snowflake's blogs are also valuable for staying updated on new features, and how they are implemented in real scenarios. Outside of Snowflake-specific channels, consider joining the broader data science communities. Platforms such as Kaggle (for practical data science challenges), or Stack Overflow (for quick technical Q&A), can expose you to a wider range of problems and solutions. There are many impactful Snowflake conferences – attending events, such as Snowflake Summit, Snowflake data for breakfast events will not only keep you informed on announcements, but also allow you to network with peers who are solving similar problems. Snowflake Summit is a premier event that showcases the latest innovations shaping the future of data, AI, and applications. Be sure to stay tuned for key announcements and updates from the summit on not just Cortex AI, but all things Snowflake. Local Snowflake communities across many cities organize frequent Snowflake meetups. Such meetups are a great place to share knowledge and exchange ideas. There are numerous webinars on niche topics that Snowflake frequently hosts. Be sure to sign up!

- **Focus on Governance and Cost:** As organizations scale their AI initiatives on Snowflake, two core focus areas emerge as vital to long-term success - effective governance and strategic cost management. Stay updated on Snowflake's governance features. Likewise, master the tools for monitoring usage and optimizing cost in Snowflake – for AI workloads, this might include understanding the Provisioned ones. Consider developing internal guidelines for AI solution design in your company that cover these aspects (security review checklists for using Cortex, cost estimation models, and so on). This will position you as a leader in creating enterprise standards for AI that ensure success and compliance.
- **Snowflake's Generative AI Labs and Tutorials:** Use Snowflake's official QuickStart guides (`quickstarts.snowflake.com`), and sample notebooks (many are available in Snowflake's documentation or Quick starts site) to practice building models with your own data. For example, try implementing custom chatbots using Cortex Search and LLM functions, or experiment with the fine-tuning QuickStart to train a model on a sample dataset. These guided exercises reinforce the skills from this book, and often introduce pro tips (such as performance tuning or cost optimization for ML workloads).
- **Advanced AI Courses and Books:** Beyond Snowflake-specific content, consider broadening your machine learning, MLOps expertise, and Agentic AI frameworks, through specializations and courses. These concepts refine your understanding of how LLMs and other models work under the hood. Additionally, books, such as "*Designing Machine Learning Systems*" or "AI

Engineering," both authored by Chip Nguyen, can provide an insight into designing robust ML pipelines - knowledge you can apply when orchestrating complex workflows.

- **Honing Cloud and Data Engineering Skills:** Enterprise AI often requires working with data at scale. Gaining familiarity with cloud data engineering will complement your Snowflake skills. While Snowflake allows you to do most work in-platform, knowing how to integrate with AWS S3, Azure data lakes, or GCP services (for data ingest or additional ML tasks), can be invaluable. Similarly, it is valuable to gain familiarity with external data processing frameworks for scenarios where large-scale preprocessing is required outside of Snowflake. As many companies use a mix of tools, being versatile will enhance your ability to deliver end-to-end solutions.
- **Community Contribution and Projects:** A great way to deepen expertise is to apply Snowflake Cortex to real-world projects. If your organization has internal projects, volunteer to lead a proof-of-concept using Cortex AI for a new use case (perhaps, an idea sparked from the case studies in *Chapter 10, Industry Use Cases and Case Studies*). Alternatively, contribute to open-source or public examples - Snowflake's developer relations team often welcomes community contributions to their sample repositories. You could, for instance, share a project on GitHub demonstrating how to use Cortex for image analysis or how to integrate Cortex with a Streamlit app (as discussed in the use cases). Teaching others through blog posts or lightning talks at meetups will also reinforce your mastery, and connect you with the community of Snowflake AI enthusiasts.

Final Thoughts: Leading the AI Transformation

Throughout this book, we have traversed the landscape of Snowflake Cortex AI - from fundamental concepts to hands-on implementation and enterprise integration. The journey does not end here; in many ways, it is just the beginning. Armed with practical knowledge and a vision of future trends, you are well-prepared to be a change agent for AI in your organization. Recall how, in the opening chapters, we discussed the transformative potential of AI and the promise of technologies, such as generative AI. Now, having delved into *how* to realize that potential with Snowflake's platform, it is time to turn our knowledge into action.

As organizations embrace the next phase of AI adoption, it is imperative to approach this journey with clarity, intention, and a commitment to responsible innovation. The following closing reflections serve as a strategic foundation for those leading enterprise AI transformation–guiding actions, shaping culture, and ensuring long-term impact. Together, they provide a framework for navigating complexity and driving meaningful progress in the age of AI, as you navigate through the exciting AI transformation journey.

Figure 11.4: *Leading the AI Transformation*

- **Embrace a Mindset of Innovation:** The field of AI, especially in the enterprise data cloud context, is in a phase of explosive innovation. New models, features, and best practices will continue to emerge. Approach these changes with curiosity and openness. Encourage your teams to experiment with new Cortex features (for instance, trying out Cortex Agents or new multimodal functions as they become available) – small prototypes can lead to big breakthroughs. An innovative mindset also means not fearing failure: some AI experiments will falter, but each offers learning that brings you closer to success.
- **Balance Vision with Pragmatism:** As a leader or practitioner, you now understand the art of the possible with Snowflake Cortex AI. It is equally important to ground that in your organization's reality. Identify use cases where

AI can truly move the needle – perhaps it is improving customer experience with a chatbot, optimizing the supply chain with better forecasts, or enhancing decision-making with real-time insights. Focus on delivering a few impactful wins using the techniques learned (maybe revisiting the industry case studies from *Chapter 10, Industry Use Cases and Case Studies* for inspiration). Each success will build momentum and justify further investment in AI. At the same time, keep an eye on the long-term vision: architect your solutions in a way that they can scale and adapt, and keep evangelizing the broader possibilities to stakeholders. You are the bridge between what AI can do *in theory* and what it achieves *in practice* for your business.

- **Champion Data Culture and Ethics:** Technical prowess alone will not guarantee effective AI transformation. It also requires a culture that values data-driven decision-making and ethical technology use. Be an advocate for data literacy in your team – share some of what you have learned in this book with colleagues beyond the tech group, so they understand the "*why*" behind AI initiatives. Simultaneously, uphold the highest standards of responsibility. Use the governance tools in Cortex, implement Cortex Guard for safety, and ensure transparency with users of AI systems. This will build trust, an invaluable asset as AI becomes more user-facing. In the long run, organizations that marry innovation with ethics will earn greater loyalty from customers and approval from regulators.
- **Knowledge Sharing:** Staying connected and sharing knowledge with the broader Snowflake community is key to continuous learning and innovation. Snowflake offers a wide range of events, both virtual and in-person, with many cities hosting regular Snowflake meetups. Attending these events as often as possible keeps you up to date with the latest innovations, while also providing invaluable opportunities to connect with fellow Snowflake practitioners and expand your professional network. Hearing how a peer implemented, say, an AI-powered supply chain optimization using Snowflake Cortex can spark ideas and cautionary lessons for your own projects. The Snowflake Squad (https://www.snowflake.com/en/snowflake-squad/) is an official recognition program that celebrates active contributors to the Snowflake community. It highlights individuals who share knowledge through forums, social media, blogs, events, and more, offering them exclusive perks such as badges, private forums, and insider access. It is a way to recognize and empower advocates who help grow the Snowflake ecosystem. The Snowflake Data Superheroes program (https://www.snowflake.com/en/data-superheroes/), includes many experienced architects who share their implementations and tips – reading their blogs or attending their webinars can be extremely useful.
- **Lifelong Learning and Adaptability:** Perhaps the most important takeaway is that learning never stops. By staying engaged with the resources and communities mentioned, you will keep your skills sharp and be ready to adapt

as the AI landscape shifts. Today's cutting-edge (such as the integration of sophisticated Multimodal capabilities or the advent of autonomous agents) could become standard tomorrow, and new frontiers (quantum machine learning? more generalized AI agents?) will arise. Adopting a lifelong learning habit ensures you remain not just relevant but at the vanguard of these developments.

Brief Note on Key AI/ML Innovations from Summit 2025

Building on our discussion about lifelong learning and adaptability as a key takeaway, let us take a moment to highlight some of the standout AI/ML features unveiled at the recent Summit 2025, which took place June 2–5 in San Francisco. At the heart of these announcements is a clear theme: democratizing AI across the enterprise by making advanced capabilities accessible to everyone—from developers to business users. As seen earlier in the book, features like AI Observability and agents are part of this evolving landscape. These announcements offer a glimpse of these innovations, while more detailed documentation, practical examples, and real-world usage patterns will continue to emerge rapidly. Here is a high-level summary.

(For more details and specifics on these AI capability announcements and more, please refer to https://www.snowflake.com/en/blog/agentic-ai-ready-enterprise-data/).

Snowflake introduced Snowflake Intelligence (public preview soon), a natural language interface that lets business users query structured and unstructured data without SQL (More information: https://www.snowflake.com/en/blog/intelligence-snowflake-summit-2025). It enables natural language conversations, secure access to structured and unstructured data, and the generation of accurate insights, just like reasoning through questions with a trusted colleague. Agents can be configured to act on insights by sending notifications, updating records in other systems, or triggering workflows.

Complementing this, Cortex Agents, along with tools such as Cortex Analyst and Cortex Search, which we have explored earlier in the book, enable developers to build reliable, production-ready AI applications that reason across structured and unstructured data, using LLMs, SQL, and semantic search to orchestrate workflows. These are supported by the Model Context Protocol (MCP) Server (private preview soon) to standardize agent integration across data systems. With built-in Deep Research Agents, users can go beyond simple queries to analyze data and understand key trends. For example, an operations lead might ask, "Why have delivery times increased in the Northeast this month compared to last month?" Snowflake Intelligence synthesizes logistics data, customer feedback, and regional reports to deliver a clear, actionable answer—on the spot.

With Snowflake Cortex Knowledge Extensions (generally available soon on the Snowflake Marketplace), organizations can enrich proprietary data with trusted external sources such as Stack Overflow and Associated Press and more, driving deeper insights and better decisions–while ensuring enterprise-grade security and governance.

With Cortex AISQL (public preview), teams can now analyze multimodal data–such as documents and images–within SQL. A Quickstarts reference is already available. Do try it out! (https://quickstarts.snowflake.com/guide/getting-started-with-cortex-aisql/index.html#0). This includes upgraded Document AI with schema-aware table extraction in 28 languages and improved retrieval through Cortex Search.

Cortex Search features APIs and an admin UI (both generally available), while custom vector embeddings and Quality Evaluation Studio are in public preview. Automatic Semantic model generation (private preview) and Charts (public preview) offer faster, visual insights, and Snowpark Container Services are generally available on AWS and Azure (coming soon to GCP).

As we have seen briefly in Chapter 9, to support scalable, trustworthy GenAI, Snowflake released AI Observability (generally available) for evaluating LLM performance using trace logs and scoring. Access to top models such as GPT-4.1, Claude Opus 4, and Mistral is now generally available, with provisioned throughput (GA on AWS and Azure) ensuring consistent inference. The new AI Governance Gateway (private preview) enables access control, usage tracking, and responsible content filtering.

On the ML front, the Data Science Agent (private preview) brings agentic AI to predictive modeling, generating full ML pipelines from natural language prompts. Distributed training APIs and ML Jobs (generally available soon) support scalable model development from any IDE. Experiment tracking (private preview), model registry, and feature serving via Snowpark Container Services (GA) ensure smooth deployment, including Hugging Face integration (private preview). ML Observability (generally available) rounds out the lifecycle with monitoring and alerts.

These advancements showcase Snowflake's commitment to delivering AI that's intuitive, powerful, and secure–ready for enterprise scale. This closing snapshot of the book reinforces the importance of staying engaged with ongoing advancements. As previously noted, keeping pace with events like these–and embracing a mindset of lifelong learning–will be key to unlocking the full potential of modern, enterprise-ready AI. And as this truly exciting list of features continues to evolve, be sure to look out for hands-on examples, early use cases, and opportunities to apply them or experiment in your own work as they become available–because those who explore first, lead first!

Conclusion

The advent of Snowflake Cortex AI represents a significant step in making AI integral to the enterprise data experience - bringing powerful models to where the data lives, under robust governance. You have learned how to harness this power, and you have glimpsed what is on the horizon. It is an exciting time to be in the field of data and AI, and each of you, as readers and practitioners, could shape that future in your own organizations. The ultimate success of any technology lies in the human ingenuity that guides it. I hope you feel inspired to apply the insights gained, continue exploring, and lead with creativity and confidence. The AI journey is a long one, but with the right skills and mindset, you are poised to navigate it, and drive meaningful transformation.

As we close this book, consider how your own organization can embrace this vision. AI is no longer the domain of the few–it is the opportunity of the many. Snowflake Cortex has emerged as a full-fledged AI platform within the data cloud, firmly aligned with the broader trajectory of enterprise AI. With the tools, frameworks, and guidance explored here, you are now equipped to begin or accelerate your AI journey with Snowflake Cortex. The frontier of AI and data is vast, and with Snowflake Cortex, that frontier is yours to shape. Thank you for being a part of this exploration. Wishing you the best as you continue your journey into the ever-evolving world of enterprise AI with Snowflake Cortex and beyond – looking forward to seeing the innovations and impact you create!

Index

A

C

P

R

S

T

V